BROOKLANDS BOOKS

PORSCHE 356

Gold Portfolio

1953 - 1965

Compiled by
R.M.Clarke

ISBN 1 85520 2344

Brooklands Books Ltd.
PO Box 146, Cobham, KT11 1LG
Surrey, England

Printed in Hong Kong

BROOKLANDS BOOKS

BROOKLANDS ROAD TEST SERIES

Abarth Gold Portfolio 1950-1971
AC Ace & Aceca 1953-1983
Alfa Romeo Giulietta Gold Portfolio 1954-1965
Alfa Romeo Giulia Berlinas 1962-1976
Alfa Romeo Giulia Coupés 1963-1976
Alfa Romeo Giulia Coupés Gold P. 1963-1976
Alfa Romeo Spider 1966-1990
Alfa Romeo Spider Gold Portfolio 1966-1991
Alfa Romeo Alfasud 1972-1984
Alfa Romeo Alfetta Coupés & Saloons Gold Portfolio 1974-1987
Alfa Romeo Alfetta GTV6 1980-1987
Allard Gold Portfolio 1937-1959
Alvis Gold Portfolio 1919-1967
American Motors Muscle Cars 1966-1970
Armstrong Siddeley Gold Portfolio 1945-1960
Aston Martin Gold Portfolio 1972-1985
Austin Seven 1922-1982
Austin A30 & A35 1951-1962
Austin Healey 100 & 100/6 Gold P. 1952-1959
Austin Healey 3000 Gold Portfolio 1959-1967
Austin Healey Sprite 1958 1971
BMW Six Cyl. Coupés 1969-1975
BMW 1600 Collection No.1 1966-1981
BMW 2002 Gold Portfolio1968-1976
BMW 316, 318, 320 (4 cyl.) Gold P. 1975-1990
BMW 320, 323, 325 (6 cyl.) Gold P .1977-1990
BMW 5 Series Gold Portfolio1981-1987
BMW M Series Performance Portfolio1976-1993
Bristol Cars Gold Portfolio 1946-1992
Buick Automobiles 1947-1960
Buick Muscle Cars 1965-1970
Cadillac Automobiles 1949-1959
Cadillac Automobiles 1960-1969
Chevrolet 1955-1957
Chevrolet Impala & SS 1958-1971
Chevrolet Corvair 1959-1969
Chevy El Camino & SS 1959-1987
Chevy II Nova & SS 1962-1973
Chevelle & SS Muscle Portfolio 1964-1972
Chevrolet Muscle Cars 1966-1971
Chevy Blazer 1969-1981
Chevrolet Corvette Gold Portfolio 1953-1962
Chevrolet Corvette Sting Ray Gold P. 1963-1967
Chevrolet Corvette Gold Portfolio 1968-1977
High Performance Corvettes 1983-1989
Camaro Muscle Portfolio 1967-1973
Chevrolet Camaro Z28 & SS 1966-1973
Chevrolet Camaro & Z28 1973-1981
High Performance Camaros 1982-1988
Chrysler 300 Gold Portfolio 1955-1970
Chrysler Valiant 1960-1962
Citroen Traction Avant Gold Portfolio 1934-1957
Citroen 2CV 1948-1988
Citroen DS & ID 1955-1975
Citroen SM 1970-1975
Cobras & Replicas 1962-1983
Shelby Cobra Gold Portfolio 1962-1969
Cobras & Cobra Replicas Gold P. 1962-1989
Cunningham Automobiles 1951-1955
Daimler SP250 Sports & V-8 250 Saloon Gold Portfolio 1959-1969
Datsun Roadsters 1962-1971
Datsun 240Z 1970-1973
Datsun 280Z & ZX 1975-1983
De Tomaso Collection No. 1 1962-1981
Dodge Charger 1966-1974
Dodge Muscle Cars 1967-1970
Dodge Viper on the Road
Excalibur Collection No. 1 1952-1981
Facel Vega 1954-1964
Ferrari Cars 1946-1956
Ferrari Collection No. 1 1960-1970
Ferrari Dino 1965-1974
Ferrari Dino 308 1974-1979
Ferrari 308 & Mondial 1980-1984
Motor & T&CC Ferrari 1966-1976
Motor & T&CC Ferrari 1976-1984
Fiat Pininfarina 124 & 2000 Spider 1968-1985
Fiat-Bertone X1/9 1973-1988
Ford Consul, Zephyr, Zodiac Mk.I & II 1950-1962
Ford Zephyr, Zodiac, Executive, Mk.III & Mk.IV 1962-1971
Ford Cortina 1600E & GT 1967-1970
High Performance Capris Gold P. 1969-1987
Capri Muscle Portfolio 1974-1987
High Performance Fiestas 1979-1991
High Performance Escorts Mk.I 1968-1974
High Performance Escorts Mk.II 1975-1980
High Performance Escorts 1980-1985
High Performance Escorts 1985-1990
High Performance Sierras & Merkurs Gold Portfolio 1983-1990
Ford Automobiles 1949-1959
Ford Fairlane 1955-1970
Ford Ranchero 1957-1959
Thunderbird 1955-1957
Thunderbird 1958-1963
Thunderbird 1964-1976
Ford Falcon 1960-1970
Ford GT40 Gold Portfolio 1964-1987
Ford Bronco 1966-1977
Ford Bronco 1978-1988
Holden 1948-1962
Honda CRX 1983-1987
Hudson & Railton 1936-1940
Jaguar and SS Gold Portfolio 1931-1951
Jaguar XK120, 140, 150 Gold P. 1948-1960
Jaguar Mk.VII, VIII, IX, X, 420 Gold P.1950-1970
Jaguar 1957-1961
Jaguar Mk.2 1959-1969
Jaguar Cars 1961-1964
Jaguar E-Type Gold Portfolio 1961-1971
Jaguar E-Type V-12 1971-1975
Jaguar XJ12, XJ5.3, V12 Gold P. 1972-1990
Jaguar XJ6 Series II 1973-1979
Jaguar XJ6 Series III 1979-1986
Jaguar XJS Gold Portfolio 1975-1990
Jeep CJ5 & CJ6 1960-1976
Jeep CJ5 & CJ7 1976-1986
Jensen Cars 1946-1967
Jensen Cars 1967-1979
Jensen Interceptor Gold Portfolio 1966-1986
Jensen Healey 1972-1976
Lagonda Gold Portfolio 1919-1964
Lamborghini Cars 1964-1970
Lamborghini Countach & Urraco 1974-1980
Lamborghini Countach & Jalpa 1980-1985
Lancia Fulvia Gold Portfolio 1963-1976
Lancia Stratos 1972-1985
Land Rover Series I 1948-1958
Land Rover Series II & IIa 1958-1971
Land Rover Series III 1971-1985
Land Rover 90 & 110 1983-1989
Land Rover Discovery 1989-1994
Lincoln Gold Portfolio 1949-1960
Lincoln Continental 1961-1969
Lincoln Continental 1969-1976
Lotus & Caterham Seven Gold P. 1957-1989
Lotus Elite 1957-1964
Lotus Elite & Eclat 1974-1982
Lotus Elan & SE Gold Portfolio 1962-1974
Lotus Elan Collection No. 2 1963-1972
Lotus Cortina Gold Portfolio 1963-1970
Lotus Europa Gold Portfolio 1966-1975
Lotus Turbo Esprit 1980-1986
Motor & T&CC on Lotus 1979-1983
Marcos Cars 1960-1988
Maserati 1965-1970
Maserati 1970-1975
Mazda RX-7 Collection No. 1 1978-1981
Mercedes Benz Cars 1949-1954
Mercedes Benz Competition Cars 1950-1957
Mercedes Benz Cars 1954-1957
Mercedes Benz Cars 1957-1961
Mercedes 190 & 300 SL 1954-1963
Mercedes 230/250/280SL 1963-1971
Mercedes Benz SLs & SLCs Gold P. 1971-1989
Mercedes S & 600 1965-1972
Mercedes S Class 1972-1979
Mercury Muscle Cars 1966-1971
Metropolitan 1954-1962
MG Gold Portfolio 1929-1939
MG TC 1945-1949
MG TD 1949-1953
MG TF 1953-1955
MG Cars 1959-1962
MGA & Twin Cam Gold Portfolio 1955-1962
MG Midget 1961-1980
MGB Roadsters 1962-1980
MGB MGC & V8 Gold Portfolio 1962-1980
MGB GT 1965-1980
Mini Cooper Gold Portfolio 1961-1971
Mini Muscle Cars 1961-1979
Mini Moke 1964-1989
Mopar Muscle Cars 1964-1967
Morgan Three-Wheeler Gold Portfolio 1910-1952
Morgan Plus 4 & Four 4 Gold P. 1936-1967
Morgan Cars 1960-1970
Morgan Cars Gold Portfolio 1968-1989
Morris Minor Collection No. 1 1948-1980
Shelby Mustang Muscle Portfolio 1965-1970
Mustang Muscle Cars 1967-1971
High Performance Mustang IIs 1974-1978
High Performance Mustangs 1982-1988
Oldsmobile Automobiles 1955-1963
Oldsmobile Cutlass & 4-4-2 1964-1972
Oldsmobile Muscle Cars 1964-1971
Oldsmobile Toronado 1966-1978
Opel GT 1968-1973
Packard Gold Portfolio 1946-1958
Pantera Gold Portfolio 1970-1989
Panther Gold Portfolio 1972-1990
Plymouth Barracuda 1964-1974
Plymouth Muscle Cars 1966-1971
Pontiac Tempest & GTO 1961-1965
Pontiac Muscle Cars 1966-1972
Pontiac Firebird & Trans-Am 1973-1981
High Performance Firebirds 1982-1988
Pontiac Fiero 1984-1988
Porsche 356 Gold Portfolio 1952-1965
Porsche Cars in the 60's
Porsche Cars 1960-1964
Porsche Cars 1964-1968
Porsche Cars 1968-1972
Porsche Cars 1972-1975
Porsche 911 1965-1969
Porsche 911 1970-1972
Porsche 911 1973-1977
Porsche 911 Carrera 1973-1977
Porsche 911 Turbo 1975-1984
Porsche 911 SC 1978-1983
Porsche 914 Collection No. 1 1969-1983
Porsche 914 Gold Portfolio 1969-1976
Porsche 924 Gold Portfolio 1975-1988
Porsche 928 1977-1989
Porsche 944 Gold P. 1981-1991
Range Rover Gold Portfolio 1970-1992
Reliant Scimitar 1964-1986
Riley Gold Portfolio 1924-1939
Riley 1.5 & 2.5 Litre Gold Portfolio 1945-1955
Rolls Royce Silver Cloud & Bentley 'S' Series Gold Portfolio 1955-1965
Rolls Royce Silver Shadow 1965-1981
Rover P4 1949-1959
Rover P4 1955-1964
Rover 3 & 3.5 Litre Gold Portfolio 1958-1973
Rover 2000 & 2200 1963-1977
Rover 3500 1968-1977
Rover 3500 & Vitesse 1976-1986
Saab Sonett Collection No.1 1966-1974
Saab Turbo 1976-1983
Studebaker Gold Portfolio 1947-1966
Studebaker Hawks & Larks 1956-1963
Avanti 1962-1990
Sunbeam Tiger & Alpine Gold P. 1959-1967
Toyota MR2 1984-1988
Toyota Land Cruiser 1956-1984
Triumph TR2 & TR3 1952-1960
Triumph TR4, TR5, TR250 1961-1968
Triumph TR6 Gold Portfolio 1969-1976
Triumph TR7 & TR8 1975-1982
Triumph Herald 1959-1971
Triumph Vitesse 1962-1971
Triumph Spitfire Gold Portfolio 1962-1980
Triumph 2000, 2.5, 2500 1963-1977
Triumph GT6 1966-1974
Triumph Stag 1970-1980
TVR Gold Portfolio 1959-1990
VW Beetle Gold Portfolio1935-1967
VW Beetle Gold Portfolio1968-1991
VW Beetle Collection No.1 1970-1982
VW Karmann Ghia 1955-1982
VW Bus, Camper, Van 1954-1967
VW Bus, Camper, Van 1968-1979
VW Bus, Camper, Van 1979-1989
VW Scirocco 1974-1981
VW Golf GTI 1976-1986
Volvo PV444 & PV544 1945-1965
Volvo Amazon-120 Gold Portfolio 1956-1970
Volvo 1800 Gold Portfolio 1960-1973

BROOKLANDS ROAD & TRACK SERIES

Road & Track on Alfa Romeo 1949-1963
Road & Track on Alfa Romeo 1964-1970
Road & Track on Alfa Romeo 1971-1976
Road & Track on Alfa Romeo 1977-1989
Road & Track on Aston Martin 1962-1990
Road & Track on Auburn Cord and Duesenburg 1952-1984
Road & Track on Audi & Auto Union 1952-1980
Road & Track on Audi & Auto Union 1980-1986
Road & Track on Austin Healey 1953-1970
Road & Track on BMW Cars 1966-1974
Road & Track on BMW Cars 1975-1978
Road & Track on BMW Cars 1979-1983
Road & Track on Cobra, Shelby & Ford GT40 1962-1992
Road & Track on Corvette 1953-1967
Road & Track on Corvette 1968-1982
Road & Track on Corvette 1982-1986
Road & Track on Corvette 1986-1990
Road & Track on Datsun Z 1970-1983
Road & Track on Ferrari 1975-1981
Road & Track on Ferrari 1981-1984
Road & Track on Ferrari 1984-1988
Road & Track on Fiat Sports Cars 1968-1987
Road & Track on Jaguar 1950-1960
Road & Track on Jaguar 1961-1968
Road & Track on Jaguar 1968-1974
Road & Track on Jaguar 1974-1982
Road & Track on Jaguar 1983-1989
Road & Track on Lamborghini 1964-1985
Road & Track on Lotus 1972-1981
Road & Track on Maserati 1952-1974
Road & Track on Maserati 1975-1983
R& T on Mazda RX7 & MX5 Miata 1986-1991
Road & Track on Mercedes 1952-1962
Road & Track on Mercedes 1963-1970
Road & Track on Mercedes 1971-1979
Road & Track on Mercedes 1980-1987
Road & Track on MG Sports Cars 1949-1961
Road & Track on MG Sports Cars 1962-1980
Road & Track on Mustang 1964-1977
R&T on Nissan 300-ZX & Turbo 1984-1989
Road & Track on Peugeot 1955-1986
Road & Track on Pontiac 1960-1983
Road & Track on Porsche 1951-1967
Road & Track on Porsche 1968-1971
Road & Track on Porsche 1972-1975
Road & Track on Porsche 1975-1978
Road & Track on Porsche 1979-1982
Road & Track on Porsche 1982-1985
Road & Track on Porsche 1985-1988
R&T on Rolls Royce & Bentley 1950-1965
R&Ton Rolls Royce & Bentley 1966-1984
Road & Track on Saab 1972-1992
R&T on Toyota Sports & GT Cars 1966-1984
R&T on Triumph Sports Cars 1953-1967
R&T on Triumph Sports Cars 1967-1974
R&T on Triumph Sports Cars 1974-1982
Road & Track on Volkswagen 1951-1968
Road & Track on Volkswagen 1968-1978
Road & Track on Volkswagen 1978-1985
Road & Track on Volvo 1957-1974
Road & Track on Volvo 1975-1985
Road & Track - Henry Manney at Large and Abroad

BROOKLANDS CAR AND DRIVER SERIES

Car and Driver on BMW 1955-1977
Car and Driver on BMW 1977-1985
Car and Driver on Cobra, Shelby & Ford GT40 1963-1984
Car and Driver on Corvette 1956-1967
Car and Driver on Corvette 1968-1977
Car and Driver on Corvette 1978-1982
Car and Driver on Corvette 1983-1988
Cand D on Datsun Z 1600 & 2000 1966-1984
Car and Driver on Ferrari 1955-1962
Car and Driver on Ferrari 1963-1975
Car and Driver on Ferrari 1976-1983
Car and Driver on Mopar 1956-1967
Car and Driver on Mopar 1968-1975
Car and Driver on Mustang 1964-1972
Car and Driver on Pontiac 1961-1975
Car and Driver on Porsche 1955-1962
Car and Driver on Porsche 1963-1970
Car and Driver on Porsche 1970-1976
Car and Driver on Porsche 1977-1981
Car and Driver on Porsche 1982-1986
Car and Driver on Saab 1956-1985
Car and Driver on Volvo 1955-1986

BROOKLANDS PRACTICAL CLASSICS SERIES

PC on Austin A40 Restoration
PC on Land Rover Restoration
PC on Metalworking in Restoration
PC on Midget/Sprite Restoration
PC on Mini Cooper Restoration
PC on MGB Restoration
PC on Morris Minor Restoration
PC on Sunbeam Rapier Restoration
PC on Triumph Herald/Vitesse
PC on Spitfire Restoration
PC on Beetle Restoration
PC on 1930s Car Restoration

BROOKLANDS HOT ROD 'MUSCLECAR & HI-PO ENGINES' SERIES

Chevy 265 & 283
Chevy 302 & 327
Chevy 348 & 409
Chevy 350 & 400
Chevy 396 & 427
Chevy 454 thru 512
Chrysler Hemi
Chrysler 273, 318, 340 & 360
Chrysler 361, 383, 400, 413, 426, 440
Ford 289, 302, Boss 302 & 351W
Ford 351C & Boss 351
Ford Big Block

BROOKLANDS RESTORATION SERIES

Auto Restoration Tips & Techniques
Basic Bodywork Tips & Techniques
Basic Painting Tips & Techniques
Camaro Restoration Tips & Techniques
Chevrolet High Performance Tips & Techniques
Chevy Engine Swapping Tips & Techniques
Chevy-GMC Pickup Repair
Chrysler Engine Swapping Tips & Techniques
Custom Painting Tips & Techniques
Engine Swapping Tips & Techniques
Ford Pickup Repair
How to Build a Street Rod
Land Rover Restoration Tips & Techniques
Mustang Restoration Tips & Techniques
Performance Tuning - Chevrolets of the '60's
Performance Tuning - Pontiacs of the '60's

BROOKLANDS MILITARY VEHICLES SERIES

Allied Military Vehicles No.1 1942-1945
Allied Military Vehicles No.2 1941-1946
Complete WW2 Military Jeep Manual
Dodge Military Vehicles No.1 1940-1945
Hail To The Jeep
Land Rovers in Military Service
Off Road Jeeps: Civ. & Mil. 1944-1971
US Military Vehicles 1941-1945
US Army Military Vehicles WW2-TM9-2800
VW Kubelwagen Military Portfolio1940-1975
WW2 Jeep Military Portfolio 1940-1990

25113

BROOKLANDS BOOKS

CONTENTS

BROOKLANDS BOOKS

ACKNOWLEDGEMENTS

Porsche cars are a subject of enduring interest to motoring enthusiasts, and this is certainly not the first time we have dealt with the Porsche 356 in a Brooklands title. However, when stocks of our earlier 356 book began to run low, we realised there was so much unused material in our files that it would be better to expand the book into a Gold Portfolio rather than simply to reprint it.

Brooklands Books provide an archive service for motoring enthusiasts, and in our endeavours we are supported by the original publishers of the road tests and other stories we reissue. In this book, we are pleased to record our gratitude to the managements of *Australian Motor Sports, Auto, Autocar, Autocourse, Autosport, Canada Track and Traffic, Car, Cars Illustrated, Classic and Sportscar, Foreign Cars Illustrated, Motor, Motor Life, Motor Racing, Motor Sport, Motor Trend, Performance Car, Popular Imported Cars, Road & Track, Small Car, Speed Age, Sporting Motorist, Sportscar Graphic, Sports Car Wheel, Sports Car World, Sports Cars Illustrated, Thoroughbred and Classic Cars, Top Gear* and *World's Fastest Sports Cars.*

R M Clarke

The 356 deserves a special place in the affections of all Porsche enthusiasts, for it was the first car which the company produced by itself. Ferdinand Porsche had been a well-respected engineer and designer for many years before that, and his company had been employed on all kinds of design consultancy and other contract work. But the 356 was the first Porsche proper.

It wasn't at all surprising that the 356 should have depended so heavily on VW Beetle components. Porsche, after all, had designed the Beetle and knew what to expect from its running gear. Moreover, the Porsche company was far too small to build a complete car from scratch: running gear had to be bought in from outside.

Nevertheless, the 356 was no kit car, but a homogeneous whole right from the beginning. There were those who questioned its on-the-limit handling (the weight of the rear-mounted engine could provoke sudden oversteer), but no-one doubted that in normal use it would out-handle and out-accelerate anything else on the sports car market at the time. The Porsche was also much more expensive than run-of-the-mill sports cars, but customers all over the world considered it was worth the extra. By the time production ended in 1965, more than 76,000 had been made and the profits had secured the company's future as a car manufacturer.

Ownership of a 356 these days is a costly business, because the cars have kept their value as enthusiast interest has remained high. For those who cannot afford the real thing, several small companies have made a living out of building replicas. The articles in the book explain what the 356 phenomenon was - and is - all about, and will probably make many more converts to the cause of one of the most fascinating sports cars ever made.

James Taylor

AUTO TRIALS

THE PORSCHE 1500

FROM 1932 to 1939 some of the finest racing and sports cars in the world came out of Germany. These cars were perfection in themselves, and many of us now realize the tremendous propaganda effect of the continued Nazi-sponsored victories on the people of Europe. One man played a large part in the designing of these supreme race cars—Dr. Ferdinand Porsche. In addition to his amazingly successful racing creations, Dr. Porsche was commissioned (in 1935) to design a "people's car" that every German citizen could afford. This project was brought to a successful conclusion design-wise, with the resulting Volkswagen remaining basically unchanged to the present day. Although the outward appearance offered a challenge to the esthetically minded, the engineering was considerably advanced. The good doctor would have liked to do more along these lines, but Hitler's political and military ambitions turned Porsche's talents to military vehicle design.

Photos by Jack Campbell and E. Rickman

After the war Dr. Porsche spent some time in prison camp before turning back to his drawing board and designing the car which carries his name. At this time, any plans to actually build the car were only dreams, so there was little reason to design for low production costs or to take short cuts in any way. Unfortunately, Dr. Porsche died shortly after the first hand-made model was completed, but his son and namesake took the plans and constructed the car exactly as it was drawn, adding only those improvements (such as curved glass windscreens) which were not known when the car was designed. The writer had the good fortune to see and drive this car at its second public appearance in 1948. Even then, with its modified Volkswagen 1100 cc engine, the car had amazing performance.

by Dick van Osten

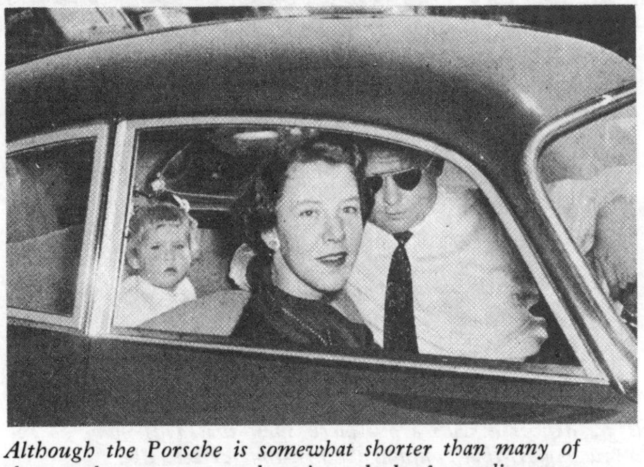

Although the Porsche is somewhat shorter than many of the popular sports cars, there is no lack of traveling room. Editor van Osten, Mrs. van Osten, and two-year-old Jacqueline show that this is one sports car that is practical for the average-size family

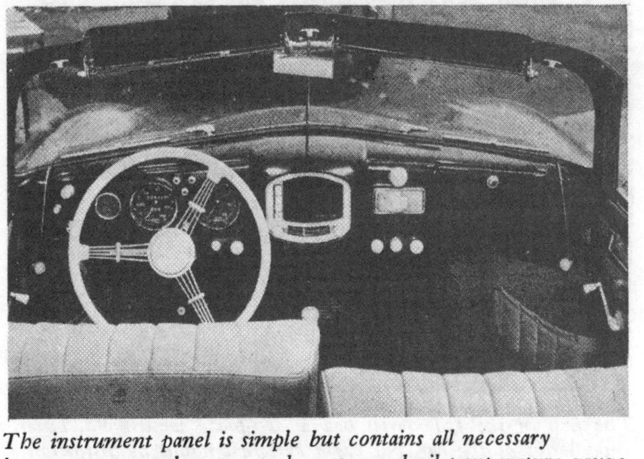

The instrument panel is simple but contains all necessary instruments: speedometer, tachometer, and oil temperature gauge. Generator action, oil pressure and "high-low" beam position are indicated by colored lights. The radio has two bands and is standard equipment on the 1500 models

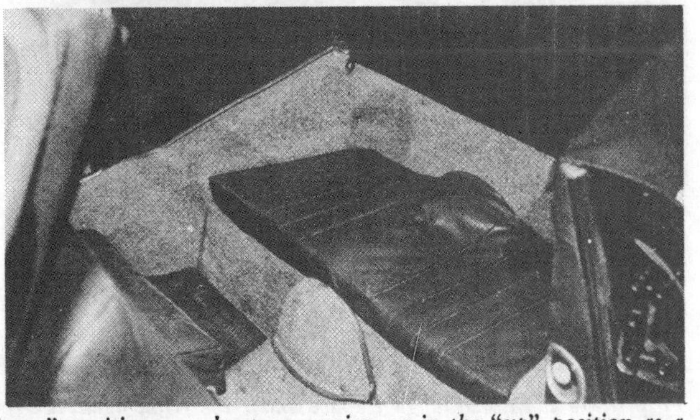

On the later model convertibles, the rear seat can be used in the "down" position as a luggage carrier, or in the "up" position as a back rest for additional passengers

Quality, Performance, and Economy Are Featured In One of the World's Most Interesting Sports Cars

The coupe which I tested was lent me by Bill Pollack, our Advertising Manager. The speedometer read 3740 miles and, according to Bill, the car was well broken in. The engine was absolutely stock and still carried the original Bosch plugs and points. To prepare for the tests, the car was given an ordinary tune-up that included a valve adjustment, oil change, and lube.

riding the rails

The term so popular among owners of fine cars that "she handles like she was on rails" could not have a better example than the Porsche. With its 83-in. wheelbase it has achieved a degree of ground adhesion that far surpasses any car in its wheelbase class. But make no mistake! This is not the type of car that Mr. Average Man can hurl around the first time he steps behind the wheel. The Porsche requires a different technique that is alien to most of us; but, once mastered, the car will do your bidding with an absolute minimum of effort. The basic key to success in handling a Porsche is to use about half the effort you usually use in driving.

The trailing-arm suspension with laminated torsion bars serves as an ideal independent suspension for this car. To many, the front suspension may feel soft, but this is in keeping with one of Dr. Porsche's favorite theories that "the wheels have to work if they are going to stick to the road." In spite of a soft floating ride, the car will corner as flat as a Bugatti addict's hat. The rear suspension is swing-axle type with laminated torsion bars, interestingly achieved without the use of sliding-spline universals. One end of the axle is flattened like a screwdriver and fits into a keeper in the differential. This allows a full 360 degrees of flex. The rear suspension on the Porsche follows the Continental theory of softer suspension in the rear than in front. The net result of all this gives the Porsche absolutely fantastic handling at any speed. However, it is at its finest in extremely high speed corners. A word of caution is advisable here. At high speeds a swing-axle arrangement, braked severely in a tight fast turn, can spin you around so fast you'll be looking for the gold ring. Also, you may find that another gear and some throttle give the answer. Don't get me wrong, the Porsche is not "squirrelly"; it is one of the most forgiving cars I have ever driven, but don't try to play "hero driver" without some practice.

The riding qualities of the Porsche approach those of the finest luxury automobiles on the market today. The ride has not been sacrificed for handling, or vice versa. A blending of the two has given this car an excellent ride that will leave the driver and passenger both rested and relaxed on the longest trips.

balance!

The argument of front *vs.* rear engine location will go on forever, but here is some food for thought. Dr. Porsche once said that it does not make any difference where the engine is located as long as it is light. The Porsche engine weighs 160 lbs.! By placing this light power unit in the rear, the designer can lower his frontal area to a point where the car performs

The first of the 1500 series had a two-piece windshield. Later models are delivered with a one-piece affair that adds much to the good looks of the car, but has a certain amount of distortion (from a few angles) that confuses the first-time driver. This unit is designed to "pop out" in the event of a severe head-on accident

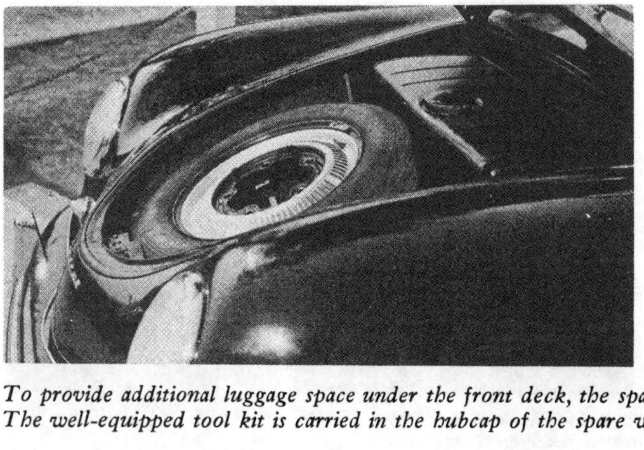

To provide additional luggage space under the front deck, the spare wheel has been repositioned in current production models. The well-equipped tool kit is carried in the hubcap of the spare wheel

After the engine has been removed, maintenance is no problem. All major components and accessories are easily reached. Although there are not too many Porsches on the highways of the U.S. as yet, parts are in good supply

A convertible model is very popular with the outdoor type. A ride in either one of the two body styles will surprise you by the complete lack of wind noise

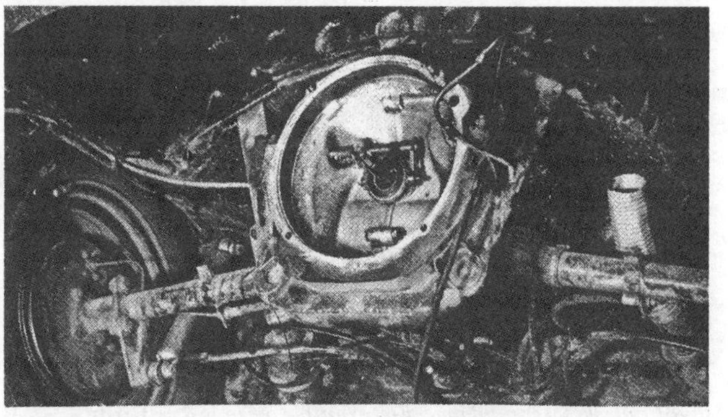

The engine is easily accessible by jacking up the rear of the car. Normal time for removing the entire unit is 25-35 minutes

PORSCHE 1500

aerodynamically without brute horsepower. The weight of the car I tested was 1730 lbs. with 770 lbs. on the front and 960 lbs. on the rear axle. This is just about the ideal weight distribution for acceleration and braking. During recent tests on a Porsche conducted by a Southern California aircraft company it was discovered that at high speed this weight differential reduces due to the frontal design. At 60 mph there is a 175-lb. downward air pressure on the front wheels which gives an approximate 50/50 weight distribution. This air pressure increases with the top speed and gives the car its feeling of absolute stability at high speeds.

The Porsche steering "feel" remains quite constant at all speeds. It is positive, light and fast with a complete absence of road or wheel shock.

it's fast!

The top speed runs were made with two different drivers on a level, measured, quarter mile at sea level with an outside air temperature of about 65 degrees. I expected to clock slightly over 100 mph, so it was quite a shock when the little 1488 cc (90.8 cu. in.) engine reached that figure with no apparent effort and kept on going! The speedometer was off 5 mph at 60, but was on the nose at 100 and on up. The other driver and I both managed to hit the maximum speed of 111.11 mph on both an east and west run. Conditions were ideal for this speed run, as it was made early in the morning with cool, moist air and the car running perfectly. Five miles an hour were probably added to the top speed by the perfect wheel balance, a typical detail of this car: all Porsches come from the factory with the wheels and tires in a perfect state of dynamic and static balance. Dr. Porsche once said that improper wheel balance can add or subtract 500 engine rpm at top speed!

acceleration and braking

The table of performance illustrates the wonderful acceleration of this car. A large part of its performance is due to the weight distribution and the fact that the opposed engine seems to have a large amount of low speed torque in spite of its short stroke (2.95 in.). The Porsche's brakes leave little to be desired. Stopping a car in 192 ft. at 60 mph is more than adequate. There was no brake fade during all of our tests, and the brakes pulled evenly with no tendency to lock wheels at any speed unless it was done deliberately.

porsche engine

The Porsche engine supplied with all models imported into this country is a 1488 cc, four-cylinder, horizontally-opposed, air-cooled unit constructed of magnesium alloys and aluminum. The cylinder barrels themselves are worthy of mention in that they are entirely aluminum *without* steel liners. The interior of the cylinder is hard-chromed with a knurling process that provides tiny oil "wells" in the cylinder wall. This process seems impervious to wear, as I recently examined an engine that had been run for 30,000 miles (including racing) and there was no trace of a ring "ridge" at either extreme of the piston travel. Cooling is achieved through a turbine fan mounted atop the engine and driven by a belt from the crank. Cooling does not depend on any forward motion; therefore, the car runs at relatively the same temperature regardless of speed. All components of the engine are easily accessible and, in the event that the engine does have to be removed, the standard time for the job is 25 to 30 minutes.

Transmission and differential gears are located in a single housing, which is fitted to the frame by special flexible mounts. Power is transmitted from the engine through a single-plate dry clutch. The gears for third and fourth are helically cut to insure silent operation. Driving pinion and ring gear of the rear axles are spirally cut. Gear shifting is effected in third and fourth speeds through gear pins, while first, second and reverse employ a change in position of the straight-toothed spur gears.

The Porsche uses a platform chassis of pressed steel welded to form a box section. The longitudinal members are built up as large, thin-walled sections to provide maximum resistance under great stress. In combination with the sheet-steel body, an extraordinary torsion-free and bend-resistant unit has been achieved by this construction principle.

ah-h-h, comfort!

The seats in this little car are nothing short of fantastic. The Germans love their comfort and the seats would satisfy even the most tender bones. They are semi-bucket, fully adjustable, and finished in a variety of fabrics, plastic, or leather. The passenger seat is supplied with a reclining adjustor which allows a simple turn of the adjusting wheel to alter the back angle, allowing you to lie back and sleep on trips.

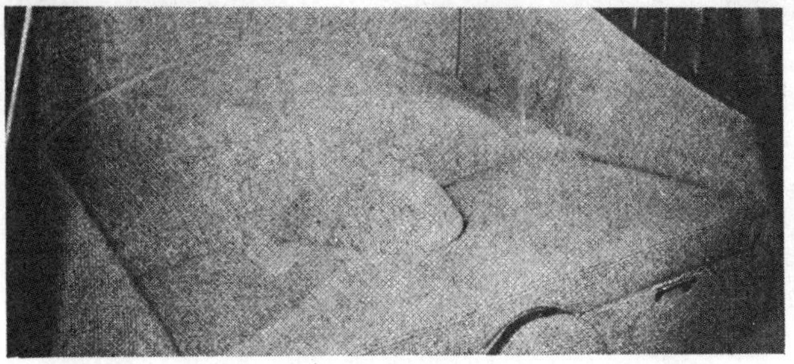

The coupes come with either fabric or plastic upholstery that blends beautifully with the cars' exterior finish. Luggage strap loops are standard equipment

The beautifully finned cylinders have an interior coating of hard chrome applied directly to the serrated aluminum walls

Many think the Porsche engine is just a modified Volkswagen powerplant. This is not true although many of the parts bear a slight outward resemblance. For example, here is a cast-iron Volkswagen cylinder on the left, a Porsche cylinder on the right. The only similarity is that they are both round

There is ample head and leg room for a six-footer plus. Getting in and out of a Porsche is a problem for first timers, but Porsche undoubtedly felt that the time actually spent getting in and out, as compared to the time spent in the car, did not warrant ruining a good design.

all this and economy too

In any high performance automobile the purchaser is usually happy as long as he has the fine performance and handling that are characteristic of a sports car. If the car also has economy, it is a bonus not generally found in this type of machinery. In our tests I was not particularly interested in economy, so we did not run any actual flow-meter tests. However, following our usual procedure, I filled the tank, covered 329 miles (including six top speed runs, acceleration and braking), drove highway averages of 70-75 mph cruising, and did approximately 75 miles of city driving. At the completion of the test the tank was filled and it took exactly 11 gallons—or an average for the whole test of 33 mpg. From which you can infer that at ordinary highway speeds mileages around 40 mpg would not be uncommon.

The Porsche comes equipped from the factory with radio, heater, seat regulator, and finned aluminum brakes. Accessories, available at special request, are custom luggage, passenger head rests, window washers, magnesium wheels and special sumps which add one-and-one-half quarts to the normal two-and-one-half capacity.

quality

In summation, I think that the most frequent comment I have heard about the car is its unmistakable quality. From the gentle "click" of the door to the smooth paint, from the handling ease to the engine's performance, the Porsche reflects genius in design and pride in craftsmanship. Production is limited, at the moment, to about 90 units a month, but this is not a car that can be stamped out by automatic machines. Although it is not a low-priced car (approximately $4284 for the coupe and $4560 for the convertible, plus local taxes and license), it is a car to which every owner can point with pride, one of the rare sports cars that makes the owner feel that he has cheated the factory by paying so low a price.

In the near future, after its introduction at the Paris Show, the new Porsche will come with larger brakes, headlights modified to comply with U.S. state laws, better bumpers for U.S. parking, and a synchro-mesh transmission. In addition, there will be a somewhat simplified model (without accessories) called the "America," developing 55 bhp at 4400 rpm with a 6.5:1 compression ratio to sell around $3395 for the coupe and $3645 for the convertible. Another model to be called the "Super" will develop 70 bhp at 5000 rpm with an 8.5:1 compression ratio. This model will sell for about the same price as the current line.

GENERAL SPECIFICATIONS

CHASSIS

Front Suspension: Independent w/laminated transverse torsion bars

Rear Suspension: Independent, swing-axle type w/laminated torsion bars

Frame: Platform-type chassis, semi-unit construction

ENGINE

Type: Four-cylinder, horizontally-opposed, air-cooled, located in the rear, roller-bearing connecting rods

Bore and Stroke	(84x74 mm) 3.41x2.95 in.
Bore/Stroke Ratio	.88
Displacement	(1488 cc) 90.8 in.
Maximum Bhp	61 @ 4800

DRIVE SYSTEM

Transmission: Manual floor shift, crash-type (on test car), four-speed with final ratio in fourth 0.8:1

DIMENSIONS

Wheelbase	83 in.
Tread	Front: 50.75 in. Rear 49.25 in.
Overall Length	152.5 in.
Overall Width	65.25 in.
Overall Height	51.25 in.
Road Clearance	7 in.
Weight (test car)	1730 lbs.
Weight/Bhp Ratio	28.3

TABLE OF PERFORMANCE

ACCELERATION TRIALS (SECONDS)

(Checked w/5th wheel and electric speedometer)

0-10 mph	1.1
0-20 mph	2.6
0-30 mph	4.5
0-40 mph	7.1
0-50 mph	11.0
0-60 mph	15.4
Standing Start 1/4-mile	18.5

TOP SPEED

(Clocked speeds over surveyed 1/4-mile)

Fastest one-way run (reached in both dir.)	111.11 mph
Average of four runs	106.13 mph

BRAKE STOPPING DISTANCES

(Checked with electrically operated detonator)

30 mph	51 ft.
45 mph	109 ft. 9 in.
60 mph	193 ft. 3 in.

The low build of the 1½-litre Porsche is emphasized by Bolster standing directly behind it. In standard form this little machine will exceed 90 m.p.h.

JOHN BOLSTER TESTS

THE PORSCHE "1500"

As regular readers are well aware, AUTOSPORT has already presented a road test of the Porsche, written by no less an expert than "Gatso". Nevertheless, I have had quite a few letters asking for my own personal views on the car, probably because I have carried out most of the tests that this journal has undertaken. The numerous and continuing successes of the marque in competition have focused attention upon it as a high performance machine, and consequently I accepted an invitation from the French concessionnaires to have a run in the car.

The Porsche that was placed at my disposal was not the "Super", which is generally used for speed events. This model differs from the normal machine which I tried in having a special engine, tuned to give 70 b.h.p. at 5,000 r.p.m. on a compression ratio of 8.2 to 1. The standard power unit develops 55 b.h.p. at 4,400 r.p.m. on its 6.5 to 1 compression ratio. I am told that both engines are equally long-wearing and robust, but that the "Super" is neither so flexible nor so quiet as the less highly-developed version. This one would expect, though I cannot speak from experience.

The design of the car is well-known, with its independent suspension, by torsion bars all round, and its stressed body-cum-chassis, which gains most of its rigidity from a central backbone. The air-cooled, flat-four engine is mounted right at the back of the vehicle, and the drive goes forward to a four-speed, all-synchronized gearbox, and back again to the final drive. The engine is thus behind the swing axles, and the all-indirect gearbox in front of them.

"Luggage" space is almost entirely occupied in the front by the spare wheel and the fuel tank.

To go into a few details, the four cylinders have a bore of 80 mm., and the stroke is 74 mm. (1,488 c.c.). The operation of the inclined valves is by pushrods, and the cooling of the finned heads and barrels is by forced draught from a centrifugal blower. The gear ratios are very pleasantly spaced, at 3.5, 4.9, 7.9 and 13.9 to 1. This is a compact machine, with a wheelbase of 6 ft. 11 ins., a front track of 4 ft. 2¾ ins., and a rear track of 4 ft. 1¼ ins. The fixed-head coupé weighs 15¼ cwt.

On the road, the good torque of the engine in the lower and middle ranges, allied with the well-chosen gear ratios, gives lively acceleration. With its small size, and the good visibility conferred by the short, sloping "bonnet", this is an ideal car for the rapid negotiation of traffic. The steering is very quick, the brakes are powerful, and it would be difficult to imagine an easier gearchange. In spite of the relatively moderate power output of the standard engine, the small frontal area and well-streamlined form of the body allow the maximum speed to build up to 95 m.p.h. on a fairly long straight. Third speed is good for 71 m.p.h., and on second the ultimate velocity is 50 m.p.h.

The two questions I am most often asked about the Porsche concern the noise level inside the body, and the effect of the rear engine on road-holding. As regards noise, let

CONTINUED ON PAGE 111

MAURICE GATSONIDES gives his

PORSCHE 150(

An Enthusiast's Car Demanding Cap

★

"In the hands of a good driver, the Porsche 1500 Super is a force to reckon with in competitions", writes AUTOSPORT'S *Continental correspondent, Maurice Gatsonides.*

★

IT was some time ago that I had my first experience of the Porsche car, that German thoroughbred which has come into the limelight so strongly in recent years with a series of performances in rallies and races which would be considered formidable even for a car of twice the engine size. Mine was but a short try-out of the marque, and one which probably impressed my passenger more than it did me. The not so new demonstration car had rather bald tyres, and the road was wet from a mild shower—ideal circumstances, indeed, to test the truth of those stories about a Porsche being dangerous on a slippery road.

A big open square, free from traffic, with a tarred road surface, was the ideal spot. A burst of acceleration, a turn of the wheel and yes . . . the tail whipped round. Not only did the car execute a nice *tête-à-queue,* but we turned through a full 720 degrees before coming to a standstill. Nor could anything be done either with steering wheel or throttle to alter things. My panicky passenger, the agent for the make, to whom I had given no warning of my "test", only regained his speech after I had made a turn round the block and was approaching the same square again, this time somewhat slower, to see whether I could keep the car under control. However, as I didn't wish to frighten the poor man too much, I ceased my "tests" and awaited a better opportunity.

This opportunity came a few years later, but to square things up, it was a test of 5,000 miles in three weeks, including the Sestriere Rally. Climbs to 6,000 feet, night driving through the wintry Alps and Apennines, fog, frozen ruts in the snow, high speeds on hot Italian autostradas and the same on iced German autobahnen; all this was quite enough to gain a well-founded opinion of the test car.

This time the car was a 1,500 Super with which Porsche's Competition Manager, Huschke von Hanstein, had crossed Europe in all directions for a couple of months. I knew Huschke from the 1937 Liége-Rome-Liége trial in which I then participated for the first time. In that terrible holocaust only seven out of 43 cars finished, the starters including six "works" Auto Union sports cars. Von Hanstein and Bund were driving a Hanomag, and they just managed to keep in front of my Riley Kestrel. Thus, when I met von Hanstein again we were old acquaintances, which was perhaps why there were no protests when I explained my objectives in making so abnormal a road test.

My first impression of this Porsche was very favourable. From the Porsche works, just outside Stuttgart, it is only five minutes to the autobahn, which took me along 400 km. of beautiful twin-track road in the direction of Holland, with an interval of only 40 km. These 250 miles went in exactly three hours. Here and there where the sun had not penetrated a thin layer of ice occurred. I had to be careful then, but very quickly I got accustomed to the direct steering: which is very sensitive. The steering is very light and the car with its short wheelbase follows even the tiniest movement of the wheel immediately. Here I am touching upon one of those features for which the Porsche is sometimes blamed. People used to an "American" type of steering will have to be extra careful. When they follow their "normal" reactions they will undoubtedly give the wheel far too big a turn. At this maltreatment the Porsche is easily induced to slide, and many such drivers will lose all confidence in the car and call her dangerous.

As soon as one is accustomed to this very direct steering, it is a real pleasure

CLEAN FRONT: With an air-cooled, rear-mounted engine, no radiator complicates the smooth, rounded nose of the Porsche. Two body types, a saloon and a drophead coupé, are built.

essions of the

SUPER

ndling

★

PLATFORM: (Right) This picture clearly shows the unconventional construction of the chassis.

★

to steer the car with two fingers at 100 m.p.h. Neither is driving tiring, for the engine is very quiet. Up to speeds of 80 m.p.h. conversation is possible without raising one's voice in the slightest degree. At higher speeds whistling of the wind round the windscreen begins, notwithstanding the fact that the outsides of the screen are strongly curved for the last 10 ins. These curved ends cause a refraction which is stronger when sitting near the screen, but long-legged drivers, sitting further back, will not experience any trouble.

To revert to this first long trip: after leaving the autobahn and crossing the German-Dutch frontier I drove home in the dark, arriving hours before the appointed time, a very unusual procedure! When the account was made up and the time for stops had been deducted, I had covered 670 km. in 6 hrs. 13 mins., averaging 107.5 k.p.h. (67 m.p.h.). First thing next morning was to refuel to ascertain the fuel consumption. I had done those 670 fast kilometres on 68 litres of fuel, which gave me 9.9 km. per litre, or 28.3 m.p.g.—almost unbelievable!

The 75-octane Dutch fuel caused some pinking in the Super's engine, tuned for 80-octane Premium petrol. This was easily remedied by adjusting the ignition, which theoretically diminishes the urge. The difference, however, was quite negligible.

The rather exacting Sestrière Rally with speed tests in the mountains along many up and down grades proved the brakes fully adequate for their work. The drums are bigger than before and are of light alloy with steel liners. Sometimes the brake linings gave off a smelly warning that they were doing

IN THE MAKING: (Centre, right) "Gatso" and Huschke von Hanstein study the Porsche assembly system. Chassis-cum-body unit is pushed along on small three-wheeled trolleys, attached trays containing all requisite components.

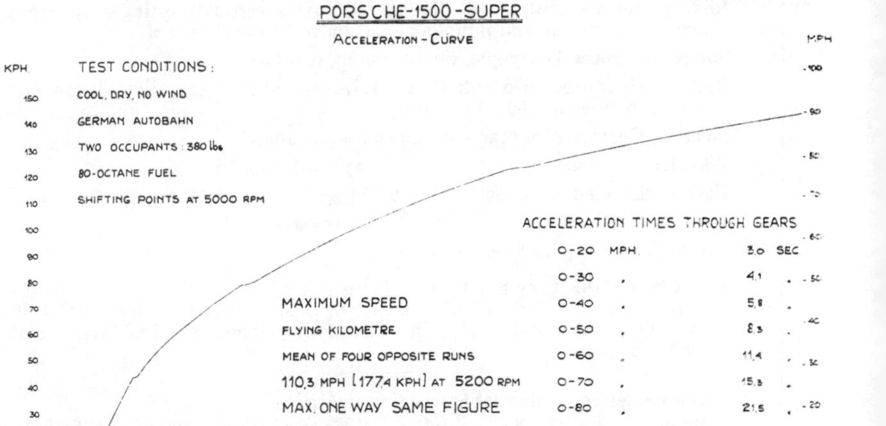

The Porsche 1500 Super—*continued*

their utmost, but at no time did brake fade occur.

My test-car had the new gearbox, in which the synchronization of the gears takes place through a new Porsche patent (Italian racing car builders are very interested). This system is both fast and foolproof, and one can change gears quickly without double-declutching at all speeds.

One or two minor faults should be pointed out. The lights, possibly adequate for other types, are certainly not strong enough for the speeds possible with the Super. The test car had a big quick-filler petrol cap which leaked. As the fuel tank is built right over the legs of the occupants of the car, this leaking resulted in a strong smell of petrol. Rear seats are sufficient for two children, or for luggage, but will not even take one adult.

Luggage space in the front, between spare wheel and petrol-tank, is very small, and only a very small bag will find a place there. Travelling with two people up, however, all luggage can be put in the rear, on the seat, and then the Porsche 1500 Super is ideal; very fast, with good road-holding, comfortable, and very economical into the bargain.

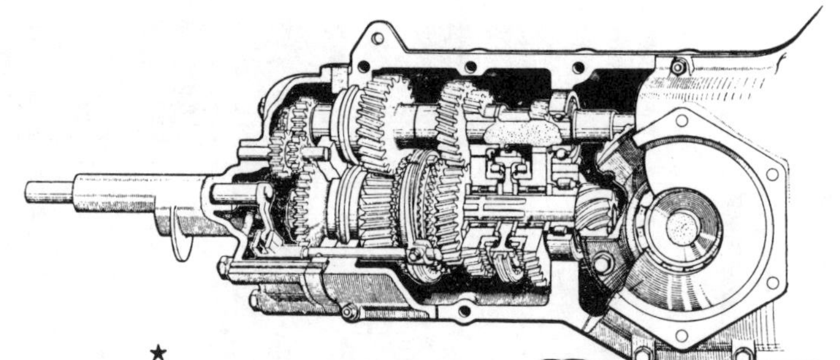

★

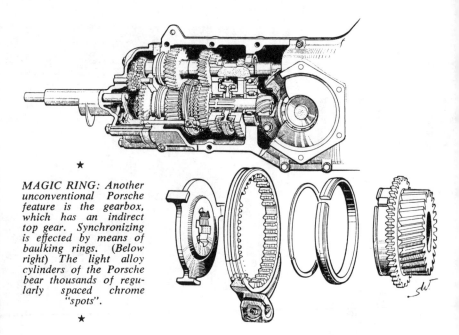

MAGIC RING: Another unconventional Porsche feature is the gearbox, which has an indirect top gear. Synchronizing is effected by means of baulking rings. (Below right) The light alloy cylinders of the Porsche bear thousands of regularly spaced chrome "spots".

★

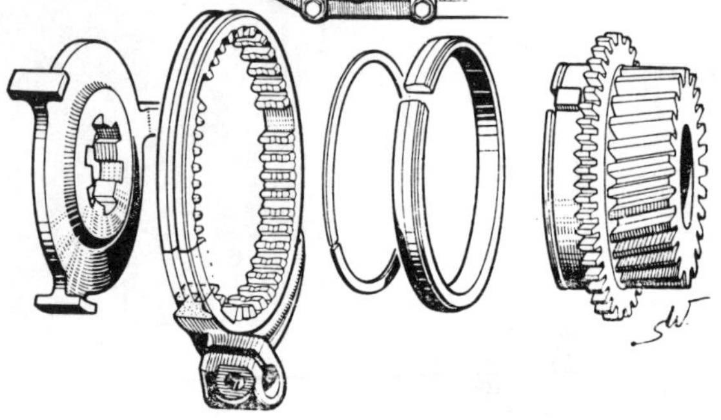

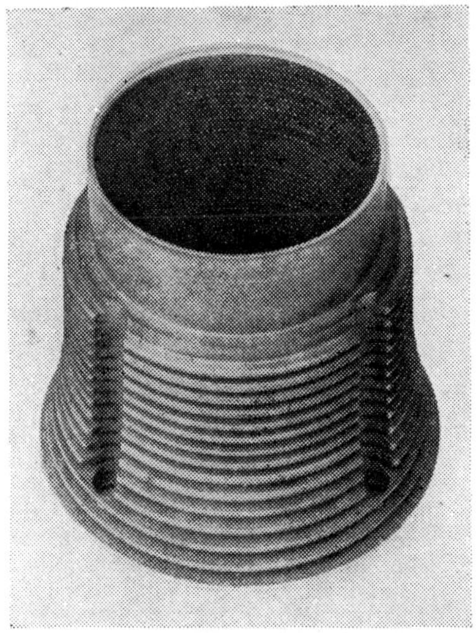

Like all fast cars, the Porsche may be difficult for people who have no sense of speed, as the steering is much more direct than on other cars. When cornering, the speed should be kept somewhat lower, but on the other hand, acceleration and top speed are of such high order that this can easily be made up again on the straights.

The air-cooled engine has a longer span of life than the car, owing to cylinder-walls with an interior coating of thousands of hard-chrome spots. These chrome spots are set integrally with the light-alloy cylinders, another Porsche patent.

Summing up briefly, the Porsche 1500 Super is a very remarkable sports car and, in the hands of a good driver, is a force to reckon with in competitions.

Official Prices, including tax and duty (as quoted by the Colbourne Garage, Ripley, Porsche concessionaires).

1½-litre hard-top, £1,971.
1½-litre convertible, £2,200.
1.3-litre hard-top, £1,842.
1.3-litre convertible, £2,070.
1½-litre Super hard-top, £2,147.
1½-litre Super convertible, £2,378.

TECHNICAL DATA

ENGINE	**1.1-litre**	**1.3-litre**	**1500**	**1500 Super**
Type	Flat 4-cylinder, air-cooled by fan, overhead valves. Mounted behind rear axle.			
Cyl. capacity	1,086 c.c.	1,286 c.c.	1,488 c.c.	1,488 c.c.
Bore	73.5 mm.	80 mm.	80 mm.	80 mm.
Stroke	64 mm.	64 mm.	74 mm.	74 mm.
Compression ratio	7:1	6.5:1	7:1	8.2:1
Max. power output	40 b.h.p. at 4,200 r.p.m.	44 b.h.p. at 4,200 r.p.m.	55 b.h.p. at 4,400 r.p.m.	70 b.h.p. at 5,000 r.p.m.
Con. rod bearings	Lead bronze shell bearings			Rollers
Carburetters	2 Solex 32 PBI			2 Solex 40 PBIC
Ignition	Bosch distributor, coil and plugs			

CLUTCH: Single dry plate, springloaded.

GEARBOX: Synchronized, helical gears, central gear lever. Ratios: 1st, 3.18:1. 2nd, 1.76:1. 3rd, 1.13:1. 4th, 0.815:1. Reverse, 3.56:1.

REAR AXLE: Spiral bevel final drive. Ratio: 4.375:1. Motive drive: Over oscillating axles to rear wheels.

CHASSIS: Frame: Welded pressed steel, box type.

Front wheel suspension: Two independent parallel arms with continuous square laminated torsion rods.

Rear wheel suspension: Oscillating half axles through spring stays, independently sprung with individual torsion rod to each wheel.

Shock absorbers Telescopic, double acting front and rear.

Brakes: Hydraulic, two cylinders on front brakes, light alloy drums with cast iron rings of 280 mm. diam.

Steering Gear: Worm gear with divided track rod.

Wheels: Steel disc. **Tyres:** 5.00 x 16.

Fuel tank: Under bonnet; capacity 11 gallons, with 1 gallon reserve.

Turning circle: 33 ft. **Wheelbase:** 83 ins.

Track, front: 50¾ ins.; **rear:** 49¼ ins.

DIMENSIONS: Length: 12 ft. 11 ins. Width: 5 ft. 5⅜ ins. Height: 4 ft. 3¼ ins. Ground clearance: 6¼ ins. Weight: dry: 1,684 lb.; including accessories: 1,782 lb. Permissible load: 858 lb. Max. total: 2,640 lb.

Speedometer correction table (reading in k.p.h.):

Reading:	80	100	120	140	160	175 (Max.)
True speed:	78	96	117	138	161	177

Road Testing the PORSCHE SUPER

high performance with comfort and economy

photographs by Rolofson

THE "dream car of twenty million people" may be a new Cadillac, but half a million Volkswagen owners dream of someday owning a Porsche! When the Porsche was first shown in the United States, in 1950, its 40 bhp and $4000 price tag fell fairly flat in spite of many good qualities. The advent of two 1488 cc models of 55 and 70 bhp respectively changed all of that in a hurry.

The 70 horsepower Porsche Super is an experience which we dare the twenty million dreamers to try. It will carry two people around town or on coast to coast trips in equal comfort, at equal speeds, and with far greater safety. Although we did not test the 55 horsepower Porsche America model, it too, will give the big American car owner something to think about, where only two people are to be transported. The top speed of the America, though substantially less than the Super, is still an honest 95 mph, a speed which can be maintained indefinitely so far as engine durability is concerned. Acceleration of the America is also excellent; a factory figure known to be conservative giving a zero-to-60 mph time of 13.9 seconds.

However this road test was on the more potent Super model and it far exceeded our expectations in every way. Factory literature gives the top speed as 100 mph. Our timed tests over a surveyed strip gave an average top speed of 107.6 mph, with a best one-way run at 108.3. Substituting the standard carburetor venturis with ones slightly larger and using No. 100 main jets instead of No. 85, we got one timed run at 111.1 mph. The carburetor changes also improved acceleration times to 60 mph and over the standing ¼ mile by .5 second. However, the acceleration data and plotted curve were obtained with standard carburetion as it was felt that few owners would tolerate the galloping idle (1200 rpm) and lumpy running below 2200 rpm which the "competition-tuned" carburetors gave.

While on the subject of idling characteristics, there has been a lot of comment on the irregular idle of the stock Super. There is no question about it being irregular, at about 800 rpm minimum speed. But strangely enough the engine never dies, and the instant the clutch is engaged the car moves away smoothly with absolutely no trace of fussiness. Common sense, with four excellent forward ratios, dictates a minimum rpm in each gear of about 1800/2000 rpm. In the ultra-high 4th speed, (which is actually an overdrive,) the acceleration and pulling power is smooth and responsive even at 2000 rpm, but 2nd gear is generally advisable for trickling through slow traffic. Using the gears is not at all unpleasant for an excellent syncromesh is provided and the gears are absolutely silent.

Out on the open highway 3rd gear can be used for any situation demanding extremely fast acceleration. Once we followed a truck at 45 mph, waiting for an opportuniity to pass. When the opening came, 3rd gear swept us around so quickly that we were ashamed of our timidity. Fifty to 80 mph in this gear takes only 14 seconds.

Normal cruising speed of the Super is almost anything you like. Even 90 mph felt very safe and comfortable and is well with-

Air-intake on the rear deck is the only clue to engine location.

Functional design is good looking, gives high speed with economy.

in the limits of reasonable piston speed. As a matter of interest, a piston speed of 2500 fpm is about equal to the timed top speed.

As expected, there is a slight amount of oversteer. This characteristic takes time and experience to get used to, but it certainly makes twisty roads easy to negotiate. On the other hand, the car was a little sensitive to steer in a straight line at speeds of over 100 mph, if any wind was blowing. In general steering was as good as any car we've ever tried and although it required only 2.3 turns lock to lock, parking was a simple matter, thanks to the lightly loaded front wheels. This weight distribution should also make the Porsche a cinch to drive on wet roads or on ice and snow—the antithesis of nose-heavy U. S. cars which require power steering to park and rear chains on snow.

The all-around performance of the Porsche is so good that it makes one wonder why any sports car need have an engine larger than 1500 cc (91.5 cu in.). The car's low drag factor is of course the primary contributing factor, since the horsepower required for an honest 100 mph is only 60. Our Tapley meter readings on the coasting tests recorded an average of 75 lbs/ton at 60 mph. Since the test weight was 1.09 tons, the sum of wind and rolling resistance force at 60 mph is only 81.8 lbs., one of the lowest we have ever found.

When you combine efficient streamlining with the comfort advantages of a fixed roof, the popularity of the open sports car appears to be on the wane. However, Porsche also can supply a convertible and a few roadsters have been built. The seats in this coupe appeared to be very comfortable, but after 6 hours of near-continuous sitting, the pleated leather left aches and pains which would make our vote go in favor of cloth upholstery. There is plenty of leg room and the reclining seat feature is something every car should have.

This particular car is the property of Johnny Von Neumann, Porsche and Volkswagen distributor for Southern California. Just back from two days of competition at Torrey Pines (full story next month), and with only 1400 miles on it, the test car gave no indication of rough use. Preparation for our road test consisted of installing original wheels and tires, re-converting the carburetors to stock, and a tune-up.

Wide-spread enthusiasm and booming sales are an indication that the Porsche is the answer for many who desire an outstanding sports car at a medium price. ●

Rear mounted engine is accessible for tune-ups, yet can be "dropped" in 20 minutes.

ROAD AND TRACK ROAD TEST NO. F-12-54

PORSCHE SUPER COUPE

SPECIFICATIONS

List price	$4395
Wheelbase	83 in.
Tread, front	50.8 in.
rear	49.3 in.
Tire size	5.00-16
Curb weight	1860 lbs
distribution	45/55
Test weight	2180 lbs
Engine	flat four
Valves	ohv
Bore & stroke	3.15 x 2.91
Displacement	90.8 cu in. (1488 cc)
Compression ratio	8.20
Horsepower	70
peaking speed	5000
equivalent mph	105.5
Torque, ft/lbs	79
peaking speed	3600
equivalent mph	76
Mph per 1000 rpm	21.1
Mph at 2500 fpm piston speed	108.8
Gear ratios (overall)	
4th	3.56
3rd	4.94
2nd	7.70
1st	13.9
R & T perf. factor	34.7

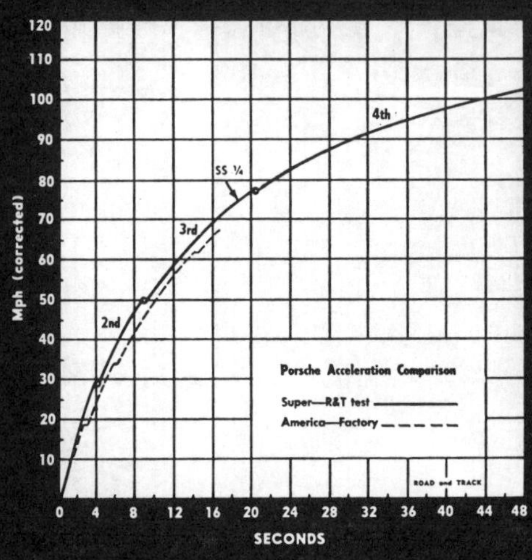

PERFORMANCE

Top speed (avg.)	107.6
fastest one way	111.1
Max speeds in gears—	
3rd	84
2nd	54
1st	30
Shift points from—	
3rd	78
2nd	50
1st	29
Mileage	22/28 mpg

TAPLEY READINGS

Gear	Lbs/ton	at	Mph
1st	560	at	22
2nd	440	at	39
3rd	250	at	54
4th	145	at	74

COASTING

(wind and rolling resistance)

75 lbs/ton	at	60 mph
40 lbs/ton	at	30 mph
25 lbs/ton	at	10 mph

ACCELERATION

0-30 mph	4.3
0-40 mph	6.4
0-50 mph	8.7
0-60 mph	12.4
0-70 mph	16.3
0-80 mph	22.5
0-90 mph	30.6
Standing start ¼ mile—	
average	18.9 secs.
best	18.4 secs.

SPEEDO ERROR

Indicated	Actual
10	11.7
20	21.2
30	30.3
40	39.2
50	48.9
60	58.6
70	68.4
80	78.0
90	88.0

Road testing a production class winner, the . . .

PORSCHE SPEEDSTER

photographs by Poole

THERE IS an automotive saying that "there's no substitute for cubic inches", but the modern Porsche either disproves this completely, or else it is the exception that proves the rule. Actually an abundance of "inches" is very useful in a heavy family car because the average owner uses and appreciates torque, not horsepower.

In a sports car, such as the Porsche, the engine is small, and the torque is proportionate. Yet, as we show in this road test, the latest Porsche 1500S speedster is capable of a very high performance. This result is due to an efficient engine, four useful gear ratios (all synchronized), and low overall weight. Common-sense design, thorough engineering and good workmanship contribute to the overall effect and insure customer satisfaction in terms of reliability.

The Porsche Speedster is available with a choice of engines, the model priced at $2995 having a 1488 cc engine rated by the conservative German D.I.N. method at 55 bhp. By the American S.A.E. rating this model, whose full name is the Porsche Continental 1500 Speedster, develops 66 bhp at 4400 rpm. However, our test was on the "Super" engined model (the 1500S), an alternative which costs $500 extra and which provides 70 D.I.N. bhp, or 84 bhp without accessories or exhaust system. By using a 1500S Speedster, with the more powerful roller-bearing type "Super" engine, it is possible to make accurate comparisons with the Super coupe which we road-tested in September, 1954.

Performance-wise, the Speedster being lighter by 70 lbs and benefitting from a revision of 3rd and 4th speed ratios, gives substantially better acceleration figures than those recorded for the Super coupe. Top speed however is about 4 mph less. (See the comparison table at left.)

Performance Comparison

	Speedster	Coupe
0-30 mph	3.6 secs	4.3 secs
0-40 mph	5.6 secs	6.4 secs
0-50 mph	7.4 secs	8.7 secs
0-60 mph	10.3 secs	12.4 secs
0-70 mph	14.0 secs	16.3 secs
0-80 mph	19.9 secs	22.5 secs
0-90 mph	29.5 secs	30.6 secs
ss¼ (best)	17.3 secs	18.4 secs
top speed	104 mph	108 mph
Drag factor, lbs	102	82
High gear perf. factor	39.3	34.7

The drag factor on the Speedster was taken by Tapley meter at 60 mph, with top down. The drag, with top and side curtains installed was not obtained for the simple reason that when 150 miles from home we discovered that the side-curtains were missing. We tried one high speed timed run with top-up and gave up that idea. It (the top) flaps viciously at anything over 70 mph. The average of two timed runs gave 100.5 mph, top down, with speedo reading 110. The factory gives the top speed as 104 mph and we have yet to find a German manufacturer who is not conservative in performance claims.

The Porsche has always been an exceptionally comfortable and easy-to-drive car. The Speedster is no exception, even with the rather "lumpy" idle of the Super engine. In town driving the engine revolutions can drop to as low as 2000 rpm in any gear, but 2500 rpm is recommended minimum speed. Engine noise is just a trifle more noticeable than in the coupe, at low speeds. The seats are extremely comfortable and the "squirming" room for legs, feet and elbows is especially noteworthy. There has been some comment on the lack of headroom in the Speedster, but the cars now being delivered have the seat frames mounted on 2" spacers which can be removed for tall persons. Unfortunately, over-6-footers will still find the headroom inadequate. The curved glass windshield is very low but nevertheless gives good wind protection with top down.

Any car with as much as 55% of the total curb weight on the rear wheels has a natural tendency to oversteer. We have never felt this characteristic was objectionable on any Porsche, nor have we ever found an owner who disliked this tendency. The 1955 Speedster incorporates, for the first time, a torsion

Unique engine placement allows y low seats and roof line, but high-speed cruising with top up and no side curtains is not comfortable.

Roomy cockpit and neat instrument layout.

type anti-roll bar. The front springs, which consist of laminated torsion bars, have been softened slightly by the removal of one leaf. When both front wheels strike a bump at the same time the resultant shock is slightly reduced as compared to earlier models. But when only one front wheel encounters a bump the anti-roll bar is also twisted. The result is a ride that is substantially the same as before. When the car starts to roll, as in a sharp corner, the bar twists, reducing the roll angle. At the same time the load carried by the outside tire is increased, which gives an understeering force.

The net effect of the new anti-roll or stabilizer bar (often erroneously called a "sway-bar") is that the new Porsche becomes a near neutral-steerer. Under some transient conditions our impression is that there is still a trace of oversteer, and like so-called conventional cars, the rear-end will break-away first when cornering beyond the limits of tire-to-road adhesion. The above applies only when the tires are inflated per factory recommendations with 4 to 5 psi more air in the rear tires than in front. Equal tire pressure front to rear, will convert the neutral-steer to a slight but noticeable oversteer. Adjusting the rear torsion bars to give one or two degrees negative camber is said to give a slight understeer. We did not try it, but can believe it. In short, the steering characteristics of the Porsche can be varied to suit the owner's own desires, a unique and most desirable feature.

The car used for this test was supplied to us by Competition Motors, Porsche distributors for eleven Western states. Just three days before, it had won the 1500 production race at Willow Springs, driven by Erich Bücklers (see page 25).

In conclusion, the Porsche Speedster with either powerplant is a most desirable machine. Its new low price will make it possible for a host of long-time admirers to step-up and buy.

The rear-mounted flat-4 engine is air-cooled.

ROAD AND TRACK ROAD TEST NO. F-4-55

PORSCHE 1500 S SPEEDSTER

SPECIFICATIONS

List price	$3495
Wheelbase	82.7 in.
Tread, front	50.8 in.
rear	49.2 in.
Tire size	5.00-16
Curb weight	1790 lbs.
distribution	45/55
Test weight	2150 lbs.
Engine	flat-four
Valves	pohv
Bore & stroke	3.15 x 2.91 in.
Displacement	90.8 cu in. (1488 cc)
Compression ratio	8.20
Horsepower	84
peaking speed	5000
equivalent mph	96
Torque, ft/lbs.	79
peaking speed	3600
equivalent mph	69
Mph per 1000 rpm	19.2
Mph at 2500 fpm	99
Gear ratios (overall)	
4th	3.87
3rd	5.36
2nd	7.70
1st	13.9
R & T performance factor	39.3

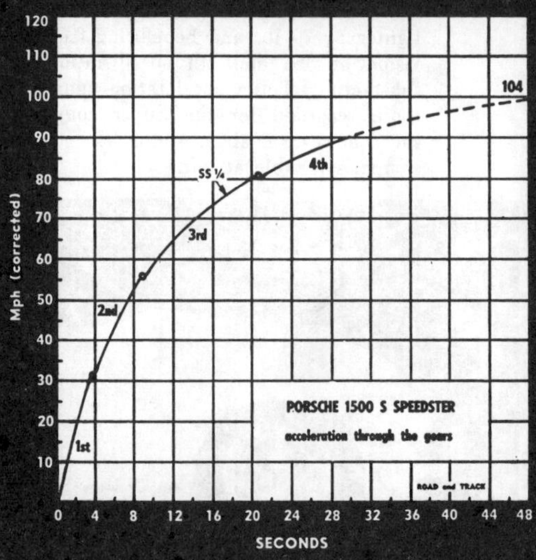

PERFORMANCE

Top speed	104
average (top down)	100.5
Max. speeds in gears—	
3rd (5800)	85
2nd (5800)	59
1st (5500)	31
Shift points from—	
3rd (5500)	80
2nd (5500)	56
1st (5500)	31
Mileage	20/27 mpg

ACCELERATION

0-30 mph	3.6 secs.
0-40 mph	5.6 secs.
0-50 mph	7.4 secs.
0-60 mph	10.3 secs.
0-70 mph	14.0 secs.
0-80 mph	19.9 secs.
0-90 mph	29.5 secs.
Standing ¼ mile-	
average	17.4 secs.
best	17.3 secs.

TAPLEY READINGS

Gear	Lbs/ton		Mph	Grade
1st	off-scale		—	—
2nd	470	at	35	24%
3rd	320	at	50	16%
4th	210	at	65	11%

Total drag at 60 mph, 102 lbs.

SPEEDO ERROR

Indicated	Actual
10	10.6
20	19.2
30	27.7
40	37.0
50	46.6
60	56.0
70	65.0
80	74.4
90	83.5

"First of all I was taken on a conducted tour of the factory, with full permission to photograph anything I liked. . . ." A view of the assembly shop, where surgical conditions of cleanliness prevail, as throughout the Stuttgart works.

JOHN BOLSTER TRIES A PAIR OF PORSCHES

A Visit to Stuttgart, and impressions of a 1600 "Super" and a "Carrera"

ON the morning after Le Mans, most people lie late abed. Not so this busy journalist, however, and by nine o'clock the Dauphine was making its usual rapid and silent progress towards Paris. Some three hours later, the car was locked up in a garage at Orly, and Bolster was staggering aboard a Lufthansa aeroplane, in which he instantly fell asleep. At Frankfurt-am-Main, he was awakened by an air-hostess, who made guttural German noises in his ear. The somnambulist was guided to another, smaller plane, and soon he was sleeping his way to Stuttgart.

The reason for all this haste was exciting enough. I was to have the loan of a Porsche "Carrera", with the four-camshaft engine, for one whole day, and on the morrow, I was to take over a 1,600 "Super". Early in the morning, I was waiting outside the factory for the doors to open and reveal "my" Porsche. Well, wouldn't you?

First of all, I was taken on a conducted tour of the factory, with full permission to photograph anything I liked (in contrast to another well-known Stuttgart car manufacturer!). Let me say, at once, that I was immensely impressed with what I saw. For instance, every mechanic has to undergo an apprentice's course lasting *four years.* The whole process of building cars is done under surgical conditions of cleanliness, and each man has his tools laid out on a felt pad in a predetermined order; there are no loose spanners on the bench or on the floor.

Every engine has at least four hours on the test bench, during which records are made of every facet of its performance, such as dynamo output at all speeds, for instance. Unlike the practice of other manufacturers, Porsche b.h.p. figures are always taken with the dynamo and cooling fan "on load". The four-camshaft engine for the Carrera and the Spyder has a test bench routine involving 48 hours of running. All steering gears are run in for a lengthy period on a special machine, which operates night and day. Every finished car then has 10 hours testing on the road.

It will thus be seen that in this works, the standards of the best Edwardian *marques* are still observed, though they have long been forgotten elsewhere. You would think that, with all this trouble, the Porsche would be a good car, and how right you would be!

THE CARRERA, Porsche's production competition car, with 1,498 c.c. four-overhead camshaft engine giving 100 b.h.p. at 6,200 r.p.m., which Bolster found "was perfectly docile and well-behaved throughout". On the left, the completely functional and unadorned frontal aspect. (Below) The side view, showing how compact this 6 ft. 11 ins. wheelbase, 16½ cwt. car is.

Although I was to test the Carrera and the 1,600 Super on separate days, it will be easiest, I feel, to describe them in a single narrative. The point is that the chassis and bodies of both cars are identical, and only the power units differ. Thus, a double description would be tedious.

Porsche bodies are of pressed steel construction, and are made outside by a large mass-production firm. They are incorporated with a rigid box-section frame, and the whole presents an exceedingly solid structure. Having regard to its very small size, the little coupé is in fact quite a heavy car. The front wheels are on trailing arms, and at the rear there are swing axles. Torsion bars, laminated in front, are the suspension medium, and the dampers are telescopic. Since last year, the rear dampers have been re-positioned, and now have a vertical instead of an inclined location.

The short engine is behind the swing axles at the extreme rear of the car, and the four-speed, all-synchromesh gearbox is ahead of them. Both engines are flat-fours, with air-cooling by forced draught. They are equally compact, and the Carrera, in spite of its complexity, is about 15 lb. lighter than the Super.

The Super is a relatively straightforward unit. It has pushrod-operated overhead valves, but differs from the standard type in having roller-bearing big ends, and pistons which provide a compression that is one ratio higher.

The Carrera has a slightly de-tuned version of the famous engine from the 550 Spyder. It has four shaft-driven overhead camshafts, two plugs per cylinder, and two double choke, downdraught carburetters. Very much oversquare, it has a capacity of 1,498 c.c., and has a continuous output of 100 b.h.p., or 115 b.h.p. if you take off the fan and dynamo. It does its best work in the 6,000 r.p.m. band, and naturally produces little power at low speeds.

The Super is a complete contrast. With a large stroke and a capacity of 1,582 c.c., it has a much flatter power curve. It develops 75 b.h.p. (88 b.h.p. without fan and generator), but in the middle of the range it gives considerably more power than the four-knocker job. There is a real surge of power at 3,500 r.p.m., and one normally drives between 3,500 and 4,500, though I plead guilty to touching 5,500 r.p.m. in top.

THE 1600 *SUPER:* (*Above*) *The view most ordinary road motorists will see of this* 1,582 *c.c.* 75 *b.h.p. coupé—a model which Bolster, a past Porsche critic, found "completely without vice".*

(*Left*) *"The driving position of the Porsche is superb" says the author, while "all the controls are correctly placed and work beautifully".*

As a competition car, the Carrera is obviously the job, but for road work I prefer the Super. The latter is, in fact, the quicker of the two from a standstill to 60 m.p.h., taking about a level 10 seconds compared with the 10.4 or so of the "racer". Of course, the Carrera has more "steam" once the revs rise, and has 10 m.p.h. more maximum speed. Nevertheless, it requires almost constant use of the gear lever, while the bigger engine is surprisingly flexible.

The Carrera is a perfectly practicable touring car, and is not excessively noisy for a sporting vehicle. I took a delightful journey in it, which embraced every sort of road condition. Leaving Stuttgart, I joined the Autobahn, which I followed almost as far as Karlsruhe. The traffic was heavy in places, but that 90 m.p.h. third gear gave me the mastery of anything on wheels. When, on occasion, the rev-counter swung around the 7,000 mark in top gear, the little low coupé gave a tremendous impression of sheer speed, the next obstruction suddenly seeming to fly towards one, though the powerful brakes were always able to cope.

Turning off the Autobahn, I made my way to Baden Baden for lunch. The best motoring journalists seem to eat their way round Europe, but I must confess that menus written in German are largely incomprehensible to me. I therefore chose the dish with the longest and most unpronounceable name, and it was delicious. However, I can never get over the sorrowful, couldn't-care-less attitude of the typical German waiter, especially after the friendliness and encouragement of his opposite number in France.

After lunch, I took the Carrera into the Black Forest, where the road winds steeply, up and down hill, with every sort of surface and corner. Owing to a "helpful" German, who didn't know his *links* from his *rechts*, I got thoroughly lost but visited some wonderful old villages. It was a memorable day's motoring, in a car which, in spite of its competition background, was perfectly docile and well-behaved throughout.

The next day, I performed another enjoyable tour in the Super, which is a quieter and more flexible car. Perhaps its most remarkable feature is the top gear acceleration above 80 m.p.h., and the way it flashes past the "hundred" mark seems quite unnatural for a 1½-litre machine. First and second speeds have similar ratios to those of the Carrera, but the greater torque of the bigger engine makes this car easier to take off the mark. Third and top are higher, for lower r.p.m. Owing to the crowded state of the Autobahn, I was unable to take the necessary series of readings in both directions to construct the usual graph, but the car feels definitely livelier than last year's model.

It is, however, in suspension and road-holding that the new Porsche shows the greatest improvement. That "tail-heavy"

(*Continued on page* **28**)

SPECIFICATION AND PERFORMANCE DATA

Cars Tested: Porsche 1600 Super fixed head coupé, price £2,138 including import duty and P.T. Porsche Carrera fixed head coupé, price £2,866 including import duty and P.T.

Engines: (Super) Four-cylinders 82.5 mm. x 74 mm. (1,582 c.c.). Flat-four, air-cooled with pushrod operated inclined valves. Plain main crankshaft bearings and roller big ends. 8.5 to 1 compression ratio. 75 b.h.p. at 5,000 r.p.m. Two Solex downdraught carburetters. Coil and distributor ignition.
(Carrera). Four-cylinders 85 mm. x 66 mm. (1,498 c.c.). Flat-four, air-cooled with four overhead camshafts driven by two vertical shafts. Roller main and big end bearings. 9 to 1 compression ratio. 100 b.h.p. at 6,200 r.p.m. Two twin-choke Solex downdraught carburetters. Twin-plug ignition with two distributors and two coils.

Transmission: Single dry plate clutch and four-speed (all synchronized) gearbox with central control, in unit with rear-mounted engine and spiral bevel final drive.
Ratios: (Super) 3.60, 5.00, 7.79, and 14.07 to 1. (Carrera) 4.85, 5.40, 7.79, and 14.07 to 1 (other ratios optional).

Chassis: (Both). Welded pressed steel box type frame, reinforcing pressed steel body. Independent front suspension by trailing arms and laminated torsion bars. Swing axle rear suspension with circular torsion bars. Telescopic dampers all round. Bolt-on disc wheels, fitted 5.60-15 ins. Michelin X tyres on Super; 5.90-15 ins. Continental tyres on Carrera. Hydraulic brakes, 2L.S. in front, 123 sq. ins. braking surface.

Equipment: 12-volt lighting and starting. Speedometer, rev-counter, temperature and fuel gauges, oil and ignition lights, radio, heater, and all usual equipment.

Dimensions: Wheelbase, 6 ft. 11 ins.; track, front 4 ft. 3½ ins., rear 4 ft. 2 ins.; overall length, 12 ft. 11½ ins.; width, 5 ft. 5½ ins.; height, 4 ft. 3½ ins. Turning circle, 36 ft. Weight, (Super) 16 cwt. 73 lb.; (Carrera) 16 cwt. 58 lb.

Performance: (Super) at 5,500 r.p.m. Top 110 m.p.h., 3rd 79 m.p.h., 2nd 51 m.p.h., 1st 28 m.p.h.
(Carrera) at 7,200 r.p.m. Top 120 m.p.h., 3rd 95 m.p.h., 2nd 66 m.p.h., 1st 37 m.p.h. (*see text*).

MPRESSIONS **by Hans Tanner**

PORSCHE CARRERA

he Carrera Porsche on Bob Said's lawn at his home, Pound Ridge, with Hans Tanner at the wheel.

PORSCHE, the name, has been associated with motor racing since the time f the Auto-Unions, designed by Dr. orsche. In the immediate post-war period e four-wheel drive Grand Prix Cisitalia was lso his design. However, those cars alone ere not Dr. Porsche's only claim to fame, e was responsible for the design of many mous Mercedes models and the highly successful Volkswagen, which in turn was the asis for the Porsche sports and touring cars.

The Porsche factory in Stuttgart, now nder the management of Dr. Ing Ferry orsche, son of the famous designer, prouces no less than seven different engines for orsche cars. These engines are the 54 hp 100 cc, the 60 hp 1300 cc, the 65 hp 1300S, 2 hp 1600 cc, 86 hp 1600S, 137 hp 1500 RS pyder, and the 115 hp 1500GS. The last ngine (officially the Type 356/1500 Grand port "Carrera") is the newest addition to e Porsche range.

The Carrera is a direct development from e racing Spyders (Type 550/1500 Renn port "Spyder") that have included amongst heir class wins, Le Mans and the Pan-merican Road Race. All the Porsche designs share many components, including a rankcase, cylinder barrels and cooling ystem, camshaft and valve train. The "S" ngines all have Hirth roller-bearing crankhafts and special connecting rods, whereas he normal engines use the same crankshaft, onnecting rods. The Carrera 1500 GS ngine also has dual overhead camshafts, win-choke Solex carburetters, two plugs per ylinder and a separate distributor for each et of plugs.

This air-cooled engine has four horizonally opposed cylinders, and the combustion hambers are fully hemispherical with inlined overhead valves, two plugs to each ylinder and dual overhead camshafts for ach group of cylinders. The engine has a ore and stroke of 85 mm x 66 mm giving capacity of 1498 cc with a compression atio of 8.7 to 1, and develops 115 hp at 6200 pm, with maximum torque at 5500 rpm.

The overhead camshafts are driven by hafts and bevel gears, and the main cam rive shafts are connected by splines. Such hanges as may be desired in compression ratio and cylinder height can be made without modification to the cam drive. The large blunt lobes of the cams act on finger type cam followers. The exhaust valves are sodium cooled and their heads are higher at the centre than at the periphery so that if a piston should hit a valve it will take the blow at the centre.

Cylinders and heads are cooled by means of ducted air that is force-fed by a fan driven by an adjustable pulley on the crankshaft. An oil cooler is also fitted in the path of the air stream so that all oil passes through it before reaching the bearing surfaces. Copper tubing runs through all drilled oilways in the crankcase, cylinder barrels and heads are lined with copper tubing.

A single oil pump controls both the oil feed and the scavenging, and a magnetic filter is incorporated in the bottom of the sump for the extraction of metal particles. The cylinders are light alloy castings without ferrous liners, but instead the bores are chromium plated, lightly scored to encourage a film of oil to adhere, a system which was adopted from German motorcycle practice.

The engine has twin choke Solex carburetters as standard equipment but can be fitted with twin choke Webers, at additional cost, for competition work. The Webers naturally require different manifolding and linkages but cause a marked improvement in acceleration and response to throttle whilst not increasing the maximum power output. Dual ignition is credited with giving an increase of at least ten per cent on total power output. One distributor feeds one plug per cylinder so that should one distributor fail the car can still be kept running on all four cylinders with the other distributor.

The Carrera is a combination of this engine and, either the Dropheadl or Speedster frame and body unit of the 356 series. The only changes made in the 356 bodies are in a wide view rear window with panoramic vision, a drop of the frame floor by several inches, and an entirely new instrument panel. The "chassis" has undergone several changes. Wheels were reduced in size from 16 in to 15 in. Suspension has been made considerably softer. A reduction in noise has been achieved by means of rubber cushioning of the engine, padding of the engine compartment and by undersealing the frame. The stabiliser is new, and the rear shock absorber system is changed. Steering gear and front axle geometry has been improved with a strengthened joint on a new track rod and a hydraulic shock absorber has been incorporated in the steering mechanism.

The engine is at the rear, behind the back axle, the clutch is single dry plate and the gearbox has synchromesh on its four forward speeds and reverse. First gear ratio is 1 to 3.182, second 1 to 1.765, third 1 to 1.227, fourth 1 to 0.96 and reverse 1 to 3.56. Two different additional sets of gear ratios are available on request.

The final drive is by spiral bevel gears with bevel gear differential over swinging half axles ; rear axle ratios available are 7 to 31, 8 to 35 and 7 to 34.

The welded pressed steel box frame has twin trailing arm front suspension with adjustable double transverse torsion bars of square section and integral hydraulic telescopic shock absorbers and an anti roll bar. Rear suspension is by swinging half axles and radius arms with one round section torsion bar on either side, again with integral hydraulic telescopic shock absorbers. The brakes are hydraulic on all four wheels with a mechanical parking brake on the rear wheels. The brake drum diameter is 11 inch and the brake shoe width is 1.57 inch with a total effective braking surface of 122 sq in.

The wheels are steel disc with drop centre 4.50 x 15 fitting tyres of 5.90 x 15. Wheelbase is 6 ft 11 in, front track 4 ft 2¾ in, rear track 4 ft 1¼ in, the total length of the car being 12 ft 11 in, total width 5 ft 5½ in. The drophead has a total height of 4 ft 3 in. whilst the Speedster is 3 ft 11½ in, ground clearance is 6.3 in and the turning radius approximately 36 ft. The dry weight of the drophead is 1780 lb, whilst the Speedster weighs 1670 lb. The oil tank holds 14-17 pints, the transmission 4.4 pints and the fuel

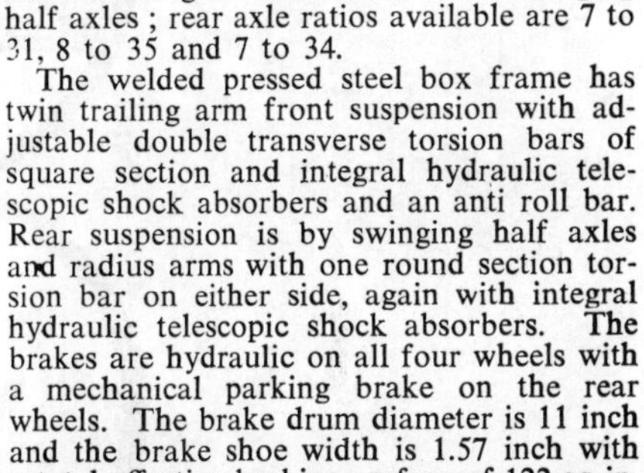

Plug changing is not easy on the Carrera owing to the size of the twin-camshaft covers.

tank 11½ gallons of which 1 gallon is the reserve. Technically a truly unusual and interesting specification.

I was able to test the first Carrera drophead in the USA belonging to Bob Said. This car, was finished metallic blue with blue leather trimming and light grey leather adjustable seats.

The instrument panel included only the necessary dials—a petrol gauge and oil thermometer were combined in the same instrument dial. A rev counter indicated up to 8000 rpm with the area from 6000 rpm to

CONTINUED ON PAGE 55

driving around

with walt woron

TO QUOTE FROM THE LYRICS of a favorite song in *South Pacific,* "There is nothin' quite like a dame." And as far as I'm concerned, that can also extend to include the Porsche, of which there is also nothin' quite like.

It's not that the Porsche is necessarily the epitome, but the *feel* of this car just isn't duplicated. The healthy rumble of the engine sounding from the rear, the absolutely effortless gearshifting, the gliding over the worst dips and bumps, the feather-light steering and the secure roadability combine to make a package that's so desirable I have to fight off the urge to buy a Porsche each time I drive one. (I may succumb yet!)

I won't insult the intelligence of long-time readers of MOTOR TREND with a detailed description of the Porsche, because it's been around in a basically similar form for eight years now. Whether it'll ever greatly change is known only in the mind of Ferry Porsche in Stuttgart, Germany. Right now it's aerodynamically perfect and until a whole new (and better) chassis concept comes along, there's no reason to shuffle the cards.

There are three basic body types and each can be fitted with one of three engines. This does not include the very hot Spyder that did so fantastically well at Sebring, and about which there will

. . . In that perennial pick of sports car aficionados .

PHOTOS BY OTTO ZIPPER

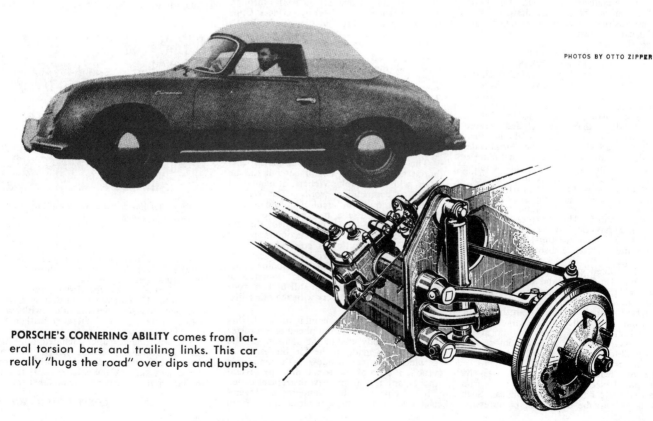

PORSCHE'S CORNERING ABILITY comes from lateral torsion bars and trailing links. This car really "hugs the road" over dips and bumps.

be a separate report in a future issue. The bodies are the coupe, convertible, and Speedster (virtually a roadster). The four-cylinder air-cooled engine in 1600 form gives 60 horses, in 1600S form pumps out another 15, and in Carrera dress (1500cc) gives a healthy 100. Prices vary from $3215 in the Speedster 1600 to $6215 for the convertible Carrera.

The 1600 convert that was loaned to me by Sam Weill of Los Angeles' Competition Motors is in about the middle of the price scale—$4065. (All prices are f.o.b. Los Angeles.) This one, for many reasons, is my favorite Porsche. I like the extra insulating qualities you get from the thickly padded top; the faint siren whine coming from the transmission-differential gears is less pronounced than in the coupe, for example. I like the fantastic ease with which you can put down the top; no power assist, yet you do it all with one hand. The workmanship and detail finishing is impeccable; oh, that our workmen took such pride! Then, of course, with top down you have as open a car as the Speedster; with top up and windows rolled shut you have a completely weatherproof coupe.

Performance-wise, this particular convertible was somewhat faster than the 84-hp '55 Speedster I reported on in July, 1955. This can best be explained by the fact that the convertible's engine was well broken-in. Whereas the Speedster engine had probably no more than 500 miles on it, the convertible's engine had gone over 5000.

The best acceleration time with two aboard was 13.3 from a standstill to a true 60 mph, 19 flat up to 72 mph, at which time the Porsche crossed the quarter-mile mark. The *average* of the four best runs (two each in opposite directions to cross out wind differences) was 13.9 for 0 to 60, 19.2 elapsed time for the quarter, doing 70.5 mph when crossing the mark.

After numerous practice runs I found that the best times could be had by revving to around 3000, with slight blips of the throttle to prevent the engine from loading up, then easing out the clutch pedal instead of popping it. Shift points were at 4700 in each gear, though third gear didn't peak until after passing the quarter-mile mark. Peak speeds in each gear (just short of the redline marking from 4500-5000 rpm) were 23 mph in first, 47 mph in second, 75 in third, and 100 in fourth.

The convertible is undoubtedly not as quick as a Speedster because of its added weight (1870 pounds curb weight vs. 1672 pounds for the Speedster). There is also another strange thing about this breed of cat in that there's probably more variation between individual cars than any other make.

In driving the Porsche, one recommended shifting practice is the constant use of the gears to make sure that whenever you dump on it you've got the revs in the torque range (the multiple green stripes on the tach). If you haven't, shift down. Lugging in too high a gear won't do the engine any good, nor will you like the lack of acceleration that you get in too high a gear.

The slight bucking you encounter when decelerating is due to the fact that the engine is trying to get down to its normal rpm idle of 800, but loads up, causing slight surges between 800 and 1200 revs. It can be avoided by disengaging the clutch or throwing the gearshift into neutral. This, incidentally, is recommended whenever you stop in a Porsche. The reason is to prevent wear on the clutch throw-out bearing, and applies as well to other cars.

From a Porsche, even though you drive it hard and mostly around town as I did this one, you can get double the mileage you'd get from the cars twice its size. The only drawback I can see to the Porsche is that its bumpers aren't adequate for protection against the "play-it-by-ear-parkers" that infest our country's streets. Oh well, I suppose I could again get used to picking out those parking spots where no one could possibly back in. To have a Porsche in my garage, it'd be well worth it!

the Porsche

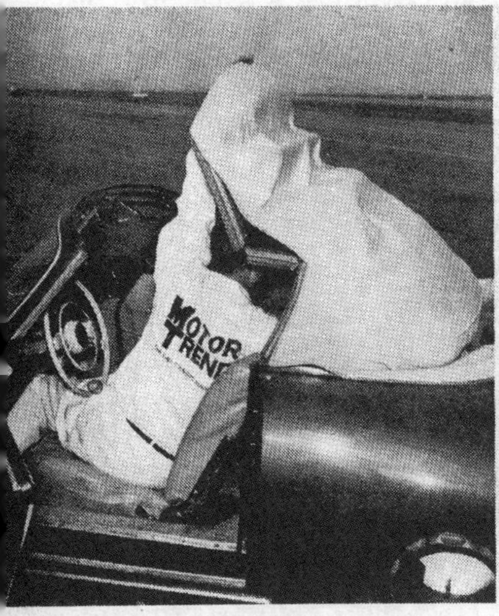

TO PUT TOP DOWN, unsnap two fasteners, and while still sitting in seat, fold top to stowed position.

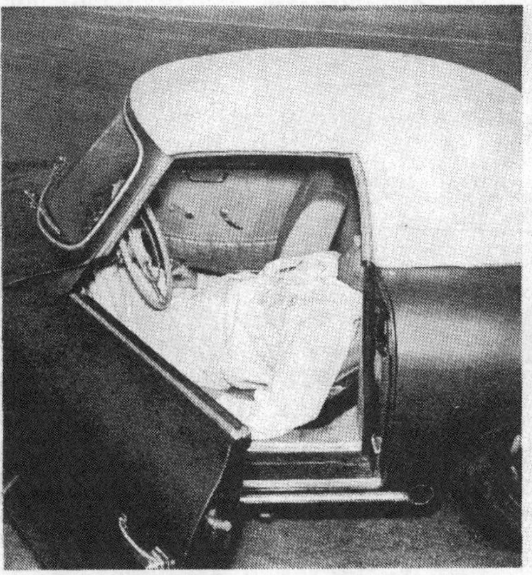

FOR A SNOOZE along the roadside, release the catch at the hinge point of seat-back, let fall to reclining position.

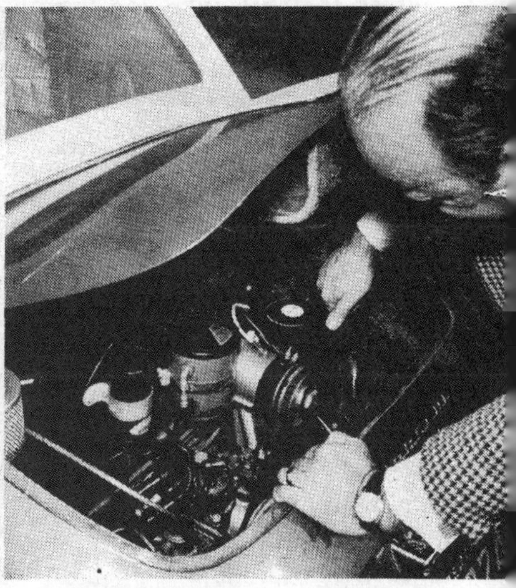

TUNING THE ENGINE or working on it topside is easy, though compartment is tight.

PORSCHE 1600-SS

M-TEST

BY BOB ROLOFSON

IN ALL FAIRNESS, I must start off by admitting that I have been a Porsche-hater for lo these many years. Therefore, it was with misgivings that I wheeled a 1600 Super Speedster from the spotless confines of Competition Motors in Hollywood. Some 14 days later (under much pressure) I reluctantly returned the beautiful little car – a fresh convert to the ever-growing congregation of avid Porsche worshipers.

It seems that while I have been nursing memories of the old unpredictable post-war models, Dr. Porsche has been busy rearranging the innards of his silver spoons without carving up the exterior. Capitalizing on the example set by Daimler-Benz, Dr. Porsche has been using his racing teams to develop the touring Porsche. By rearranging the chassis member, the Porsche engineers have been able to mount the rear shocks (à la Spyder) into a vertical position, improve steering geometry and add a hydraulic steering-damper, use new tie rods with reinforced linkage, and a new type stabilizer. In addition, the windshield is larger, the floor is lower for easier entrance, the dash is uncluttered, with instruments in a hooded grouping directly behind the wheel. A trip indicator, combined starter-ignition switch, push-pull handbrake, an idling adjustment knob on the dash, and a headlight flasher on the steering wheel, complete the picture.

Contrary to the opinion that sports cars must have stiffer springing, Porsche has proven that roadability is improved through softer springing. This theory, combined with the 88-hp 1600 engine and the suspension components taken from the Spyders, has produced new improved handling characteristics. It is still a different breed of cat on the road. It can't be typed as mushy, tenacious, or like being-on-rails; it's just pure Porsche. At slow speeds the car handles on a curve like any other car, except that it is unusually stable. At speed, the car comes into its own. Instead of all four wheels tracking, the rear end begins to slide toward the outside of the curve . . . *begins* to slide. Unlike the older models this slide is not a sudden breakaway, but casual, controllable two-wheel drift which allows the driver to set the car up

PADDED, COMPLETELY SPRUNG SEATS are easily adjusted for both rake and legroom. These are bucket-type coupe seats, optional equipment at $45 extra.

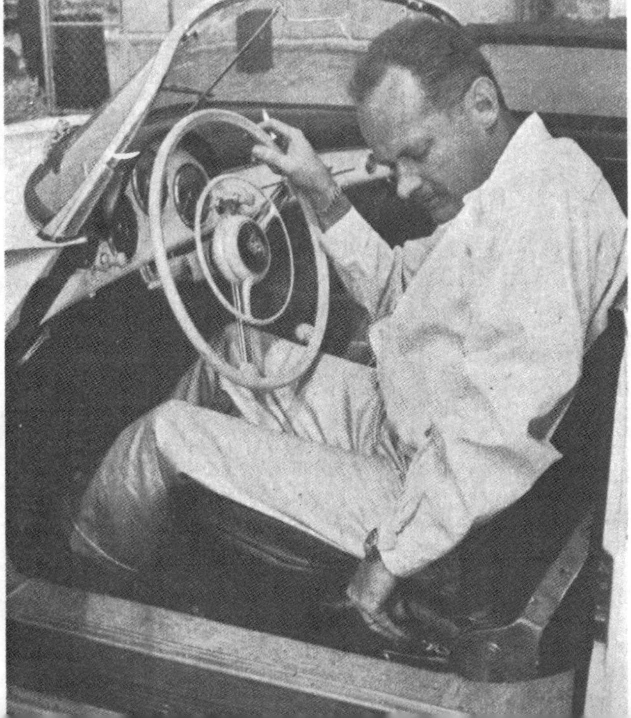

ACCELERATION
From Standing Start
0-45 mph 6.7 0-60 mph 10.1
Quarter-mile 18.3

Passing Speeds
30-50 mph 4.5, 45-60 mph 4.7, 50-80 mph 13.7

CRUISING SPEEDS
Maintains constant speed of 60-65 mph easily, 70 mph where legal

TOP SPEED
106.2 mph

FUEL CONSUMPTION
Stop-and-Go Driving, 24.9 mpg for 354 miles

Highway Driving, 28-30 mpg for 221 miles

Overall Average, 25.2 mpg for 575 miles
Fuel Used: Mobilgas

BRAKING
Withstood 19 slowdowns from 60 mph to 20 mph and one panic stop without fade or swerve.

THE LUGGAGE COMPARTMENT, located up front in place of the usual position of the engine, is difficult to use because of the forward-mounted spare tire. Note the tools.

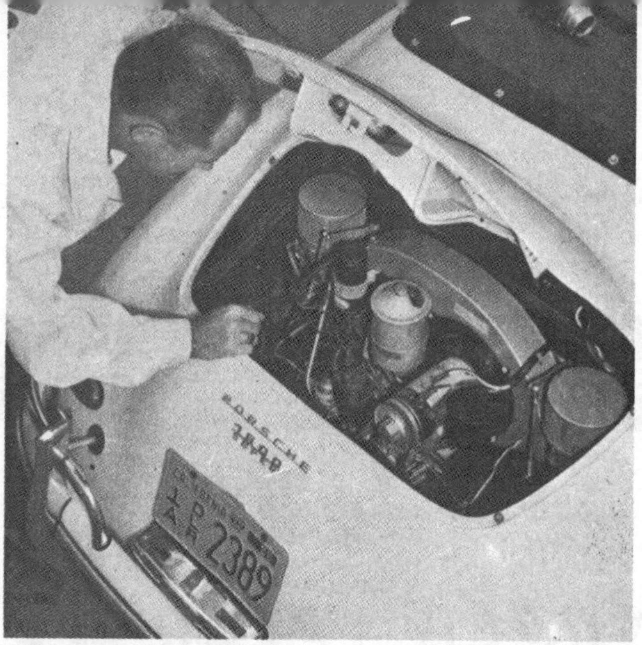

ENGINE ACCESSIBILITY leaves much to be desired because of the unusually small rear deck lid. The components themselves, however, do not require a very long reach.

on tight turns. A touch of the throttle, a slight turn of the wheel and the tail swings into line for straightaway acceleration. You find yourself going miles out of your way looking for curves to play with, and before long are deliberately forcing the SS into four-wheel drifts, just for the fun of it!

Aside from the actual fun of playing with the SS, it is a touring machine par excellence. Steering is of the fingertip variety – no need to grab and wrestle. On a flat section of the freeway the car tracked, hands off, for three-quarters of a mile! During my two weeks with the SS, the skies opened, and the California dew became much too heavy for pleasurable highway testing. However, in 354 miles of traffic driving the car averaged 24.9 miles to the gallon. This indicates that open road cruising between 60 and 70 mph should produce from 28 to 30 miles per gallon.

One of the criticisms of the older models was idling noise and vibration. The SS gurgles like a twin-screw Chris-Craft, with almost no vibration, and even at speed there is no objectionable noise in the cockpit. The four-speed all-synchro transmission works like a hot knife through butter, fully justifying its use by Ferrari and Maserati in their racing juggernauts. Common in Europe, but new in the U.S. is the dimmer switch on the steering wheel. Tapping the "horn" flashes the lights, the ring working the horn. A handy gadget for passing in competition and relieving some of the strain of highway driving at night.

On the negative side, it becomes quite a struggle shifting into reverse. The push-down and throw-over, while fighting a spring-loaded gate, is out of keeping with the rest of the car's operation. The top is the fastest and easiest "one man" manual canvas yet, but with it up a feeling of claustrophobia sets in immediately. Even when bending down and peering out of the rear and side openings, there are still two large blind spots on either side of the rear window.

The construction and finish of the Porsche (bodies by Reuter) are beyond criticism. From the solid whopp of the doors shutting, to the magnificent adjustable seats, the car is finished like a sample for the European auto shows. /MT

SPECIFICATIONS

ENGINE: Opposed 4, air-cooled. Bore 3.25 in. Stroke 2.91 in. Stroke/bore ratio .89:1. Compression ratio 8.5:1. Displacement 96.5 cu. in. (1582cc) Advertised bhp 88 @ 5000 rpm. Max. torque 86 lbs.-ft. @ 3700 rpm.

TRANSMISSION: 4-speed all synchromesh gearbox. Overall ratios: 3.18:1, 1.76:1, 1.13:1, 0.815:1.

CHASSIS: Front suspension – trailing links and transverse laminated torsion bars. Rear – swinging half-axles, transverse torsion bars and trailing arms. Brakes – two leading shoe front hydraulics, ribbed alloy drums with cast iron liners. Ross-type steering gear, with 33-ft. turning circle, 2¼ turns lock-to-lock.

DIMENSIONS: Wheelbase 82.7 in., overall length 135.0, overall height 51.0, overall width 65.0, front tread 51.0, rear tread 50.0, weight (dry) 1790 lbs.

PRICE (port of entry): $3715

ACCESSORIES: Coupe seats $45, side curtains $10.

THE TOP IS AS SIMPLE to raise as it looks. It gets our praise as the fastest "one-man" top ever seen on a sports car. When top is up, however, claustrophobia may set in.

WHEEL ROAD CHECK:

PORSCHE

1600

SUPER SPEEDSTER

There's Nothing Square About A Porsche!

WAY back in what now seems like the prehistoric days of postwar American sports car racing, this editor had his first encounter with a Porsche. It was a bloody affair, indeed. The event was Bridgehampton and this unsuspecting writer had been induced to pit an early MG against the combined Porsche talents of Koster, Doc Thompson and a few other throttle-jockeys who had already learned that even the smaller Porsches were potent road machines. From that overcast, gloomy day onward . . . we've been thoroughly convinced that there is absolutely nothing esthetically or socially square about the Porsche automobile.

A famout sports car personality once stated publicly, "The Porsche is the dream car of a million VW owners." There is room for disagreement here. The Porsche . . . and, more particularly, the new Porsche Super seems to be more the dream car for drivers currently enseated in Jaguars, Corvettes and other similarly-priced machinery. With drastic upheavals and major changes in what constitutes a sports car these days—as opposed to that theory of a few years back—the Porsche still remains almost a perfect combination

THE SECRET DESIRE of many sports car fans is this new, true "Hardtop Convertible" by Porsche . . . and, as each new one enters the streets, desire fans higher. Priced with the true convertible, the Porsche Hardtop offers a more practical all-weather car. Convertible top may be had as an option.

of GT model and out-and-out race car. It is one of the few remaining sports cars which still claims enough calmness for marketing, enough snarl for a class or overall win in its general category. As for the Porsche Spyder—if it had another 500 cc. and two thumbs, it would probably take over the world.

For this Road Check, VW-Porsche distributor John Von Neumann and Regional Manager Sam Weill, Jr. loaned us a 1958 Porsche Super Speedster—equipped with 1600 cc.; white paint, black coupe-type seats and some 5000 miles on the dial. The car had been tuned by Hollywood, California's Competition Motors and, although the car had seen a great deal of "test" duty, it ran like a Swiss watch at an International Trade Fair.

The most exciting aspects of this 1600 Super were (a) the coupe seats and (b) the roller-bearingless engine. First, the seats.

Whatever upholstering master assembles the Porsche coupe seats . . . he manages to combine the elegance and solidity of the Bugatti "bucket" with the functionalism and form of the famed Ferrari passenger-model seats. The individually-controlled Porsche coupe seats are deep and comfortable; providing adequate support for back and thigh through mile after tiring mile of traveling or racing. The knob-controlled adjustments are many and the driver (or passenger) can select a position ranging from secretarial chair to chaise. For the tall driver, it's entirely possible to recline completely, still retaining control of the steering wheel (although the wisdom for this type of posture would seem to be in some question.) In short, the seats provide ecellent support, fine lateral stability on the tightest of bends and a series of excellent positions which aid in removing road kinks during travel periods. These seats are a long whoop and holler from the conventional bucket-type normally associated with the Speedster model and the editors feel that any Speedster which will be run for normal driving should be equipped with this optional extra. For those who prefer the "harder" way of life, Speedsters are available with lighter, smaller bucket seats and a savings of approximately $125.00. Let it be pointed out here, however, that the coupe seats are not really *needed*. The Porsche—in all models—glides rather than rides over even the roughest of countryside roads.

The most exciting change for the 1958 Porsche 1600 Super lies within the rear engine compartment. The Super,

NEWEST PORSCHE SUPER SPEEDSTER is completely unlike earlier "tricky" Porsches, stays glued in turns on pebble-strewn dirt roads. Note 4500 rpm reading on tach as staffer enters corner.

THIS IS THE WAY the Porsche Super came out of the corner (left). Car is stable and rock-steady despite treacherous stones and dirt road.

long-desired for its extra push, but long-derided for troublesome roller bearings, now delivers 88 bhp utilizing standard aluminum bearings. The change in personality is as drastic as a stripper at a literary tea. The new Super is all Lady on the outside still a Tigress in the bustle department.

The 1958 Super engine features a new carburetion setup which utilizes two dual-throat Zenith downdraft carburetors instead of the usual single-throats on previous models. Whether it is the new carburetion set up, the new bearing material, the redesigned shift mechanism (which reduces travel from gear to gear) or a combination of all three . . . the new Super Speedster scurries and hurries once that throttle is kicked. Moving out from a stoplight, the Super scrunches down, pulls off the line with a firm squeal, storms to 30 mph in a little over 3 seconds, to 60 mph in a shade under 11 seconds. This may not be too rapid by comparison with the FI Corvette, but it is doing nicely, thank you—for a conventionally-fed flat-four of only 96.5 cubic inches.

With the new gear ratios, the Porsche winds to the redline in a hurry in first, delivers its best power punches in second and third gears. Winding to 5500 rpm in each gear, the Super hits 28 mph in first; 51 mph in second, 80 mph in third, and with topand side curtains in place, turned a best two-way average of 107.20 mph.

One word of warning to the tall ones . . . beware that top on high speed runs! The fluttering and flapping on your crew cut seems to be the German version of the Chinese water torture. Open, the Speedster windshield is definitely low for the six-footer, but seems nicely placed so that air-flow goes up and over and the pukka sports car cap stays firmly in place. The Speedster is very definitely a car designed for top-down, windowless driving. Weather protection is sketchy but of quality manufacture and our test Speedster went through two of Southern California's most severe rainstorms without seeping a drop through body or top. The easily-in-and-out (Continued on Pg. 28)

HIGH-ANGLE PICTURE illustrates width and depth of new rear window and general bustle-back feeling. Hardtop fits so smoothly it gives car impression of being fixed top coupe. Note new wind vents in front windows. Announced as "optional" on coupes and hardtops, spokesmen later indicated only hardtops would sport them.

BENEATH A SHINY POSTERIOR beats 88 rugged horsepower. New Super powerplant features dual 2-throat carbs, abandonment of roller bearings. Super Speedster scoots to 60 mph in less than 11 sec. (see road check this issue).

(ROAD TEST PANEL)
PORSCHE SUPER SPEEDSTER

Acceleration

0–30 mph	3.2 sec.	0–60 mph	10.8 sec.
0–40 mph	5.3 sec.	0–70 mph	14.5 sec.
0–50 mph	7.5 sec.	0–80 mph	19.1 sec.

TOP SPEED .... 107.20 mph (average)
GASOLINE MILEAGE .... 24/29 mpg (for all tests)
SPEEDOMETER ERROR .... 6% optomistic @ 60 mph
TRANSMISSION .... 4-speed, all-synchronized

1st	14.1	3rd	5.00
2nd	7.81	4th	3.91

ENGINE
4-cylinder, 4-cycle flat four, horizontally opposed, air cooled (by fan).
HORSEPOWER
88 bhp (SAE)
96.5 cu. in. overhead valve (in V)
Bore–3.25 in.
Stroke–2.91 in.
Carburetion–Two dual-throat downdraft carburetors
Compression Ratio–8.5:1

DIMENSIONS
Wheelbase–82.7 in.
Tread–51.4 in. F/50.1 in. R
Width–65.6 in.
Height–48.0 in.
Road Check Weight–1994 lbs.
Weight Dist.–44% F/56% R
Steering Ratio–1:14.15
Turn Radius–36 ft.
Ground Clearance–6.3 in.

A THING OF BEAUTY despite its "Ivy League" cap is the Porsche Speedster. Even with larger coupe-type seats, six-footers are most comfortable in the torso and leg department, just so-so overhead. For 1958, car features strangely-designed hub caps, raised exhaust tips as major exterior changes.

sidescreens are, unfortunately, one piece plastic and, when in place, prohibit any outside signaling or newspaper purchasing. The Porsche's turn signals are evidently well located, however, and we safely negotiated tight, slippery traffic without a physical encounter—or the threat of one—at any time. And, although the Speedster seems virtually as waterproof as a watch on a television commercial, visibility does suffer when top and side curtains are in place and the fine agility factor of the Porsche—so useful in city driving—is lost because of lost vision. This should very definitely be number one on the things-to-do list at Stuttgart for next year.

Inside the car, the Speedster has plenty of leg, elbow and shoulder room for two adults in front, for two young-type youngsters or a litter of Siamese kittens in the rear. The larger coupe-type seats definitely occupy some of the valuable cockpit space, but their obvious advantages overpower any logic or attempt at logic about "more space." With the top down and side curtains stowed, that behind-the-seats area is completely full and it's only with top up that the young 'uns can clamber into the back seat. By the way, kids seem to enjoy riding in the Porsche more than just about any other car. Might be the diminutive overall dimensions which intrigue them in their Lilliputian world.

The Porsche features a new ZF steering gear in conjunction with the 1956 hydraulic steering damper and the car steers more easily, actually seems to have lost a great deal of its famed oversteer characteristic. Steering is now exteremely light and easy at all speeds but without the "delicacy," which can be so treacherous in the upper mph range. In tight corners and bends, the Porsche snuggles down and putta-puttas through with little trace of any bad steering characteristics and it is only when a tight turn is taken a bit too hastily that the 56% weight on the rear wheels begin to come around without permission. SC WHEEL'S testers utilize, among other courses, a 23 mile stretch of dirt-and-rock road which winds through one of Southern California's longest canyons. Driving this course at varying speeds and in various gears, the staff found that the Porsche stayed glued to the curves even when skating on pebbles and rocks. On the few bends where the car did come out-of-shape, a wheel correction and some throttle quickly pulled the rear end politely back into line. Several of the pictures on these pages were taken on the above-mentioned course at speeds generally considered much too rapid for this type of road—in any car. Not so, for the Porsche.

Because there was some dissatisfaction with the visibility, the too-tight top and the side curtains of the Speedster, SC WHEEL also drove the new Porsche Super Hardtop model. Designed to supplement and, eventually, replace the Porsche Convertible, the new Hardtop features a removable metal top slightly similar in configuration to the fixed top of the DKW Coupe. The top causes the Porsche (standard convertible body) to look quite a bit different; a little more elegant, a little less sporty than other Porsches. The top is fastened onto the windshield by three convertible-type hasps and to the back of the car by two unique clamps. In place, the top fits snugly, gives the car fixed head coupe appearance. The convertible top is also available as an option but those drivers who have long yearned for just a little more space in their Porsche will do without it.

The new Hardtop Super was the unanimous choice of WHEEL staffers for the true boulevard-type sports car, the Speedster for competition purposes (naturally!) in production class. At one time, the mighty Porsche was considered quite a bit overpriced for its size and horsepower output. Today, as prices rise on other sports cars—and as Porsche continues to improve its already near-legendary performance and handling—the Porsche begins to change classification from expensive sports car to best-buy sports car.

Speedster, coupe or hardtop . . . Normal, Super, Carrera, GT or Spyder, there seems to be a Porsche for every need and every payment book. The MG may well have started the postwar sports car movement in this country—but many experts are agreed that the Porsche is the car that keeps it going.

◈ ◈ ◈

CONTINUED FROM PAGE 18

feeling has gone, and the average driver would not be conscious that this is a rear-engined car. The suspension feels harder than before, and a much steadier ride is given at speeds over 100 m.p.h. The car also handles better in fast bends.

The Super was completely without vice, but the Carrera had one disconcerting habit. On the type of concrete road with a central join, the car would take charge for a moment on crossing the black line obliquely. As the Super did not exhibit the tendency, and the chassis were identical, it was obvious that the difference was due to the tyres. The Super had Michelin "X", and these are certainly the tyres to use on a Porsche. The Carrera had tyres of another make, which may be better for racing, but do not compare for ordinary road work. The "X" tyres transmit a little more road noise under certain circumstances.

The driving position of the Porsche is superb. One has a bucket seat that gives support in all the right places, and also that lateral location which is so necessary for fast cornering. Not only is there ample fore and aft adjustment, but the back of the seat may be set in a moment to any preferred angle. All the controls are correctly placed and work beautifully. This is, above all, a *driver's* car.

Under the front bonnet, the petrol tank and spare wheel occupy most of the space. The rear seat is so "occasional", however, that it is no hardship to fold it up and use the back compartment for luggage. The car is beautifully made throughout, and no decoration mars its fine lines.

I admit that, in the past, I have not been a Porsche enthusiast, because I did not like the handling characteristics of the earlier models. The latest version is so greatly improved in this respect that I have pleasure in withdrawing my previous criticism. In England, this is an expensive car, because purchase tax is charged on top of import duty. Nevertheless, there's nothing quite like a Porsche, and for the man who can afford it, it is a most desirable possession.

Porsche Carrera Speedster

Smooth aerodynamic coachwork lends much to the performance of the Porsche. As this picture shows, there are few concessions towards styling in the transatlantic manner.

A SPORTS car fitted with properly designed seats is immediately impressive to the true enthusiast. It is well known that first class sporting drivers are fussy to the point of being faddish about seats and driving positions. But how strange it is that very few manufacturers take the trouble to fit seats which give maximum support under fast driving conditions. All over the world, the abominable bench seat has given rise to a situation where enthusiastic drivers will welcome almost any type of separate bucket seat. But it does not follow that any old individual seat will give good support. The Porsche Carrera, we are glad to say, has the finest seats we have ever sampled on any production sports car as yet submitted for test. Yet these seats were not luxuriously upholstered foam rubber and leather affairs. They were cloth covered, firm and almost hard, but so nicely shaped in armchair style that driver and passenger were never called upon to expend effort in trying to resist side thrust when the car was cornered quickly. In a high performance car this really does mean a great deal. We would go so far as to say that no fast car can be properly controlled if the driver has to depend to any extent upon his grip on the wheel to remain upright. If the driver is forced to use the steering wheel almost as a passenger might use a grab handle, then the car cannot be considered as being under complete control.

We feel that the very fine seating arrangements in the Porsche enabled us to extract maximum performance from the car in a relatively short time. On other occasions we have collected sports cars from manufacturers and have been forced to spend some considerable time in adapting ourselves to the seating layout, and in gathering experience in a makeshift manner. The Porsche, on the other hand, was taken straight from the factory to the autobahn near Stuttgart and driven, in fairly heavy traffic at dusk, at speeds in excess of 110 m.p.h. within half an hour after collection. This, it should be understood, was no great feat of driving skill as it would be fair to say that we are by no means given to taking undue risks when driving strange vehicles. That the Porsche could be driven so quickly after relatively little experience is a tribute to the driving position and the seating arrangements—to say nothing of mechanical excellence. The car is certainly compact, but there is a good range of seating adjustment. The easy to handle wood rimmed steering wheel and sensitive steering response promote immediate confidence. And the gear lever is positioned so that the driver does not have to lean forward when making gear changes.

The Porsche engine and transmission arrangements are, of course, very well known. The flat four horizontally opposed 1½ litre power unit used in the Speedster is actually similar to the engine of the Spyder car, with twin overhead camshafts on each bank of two cylinders. A pair of double venturi Solex downdraft carburetters are fitted and there are two plugs in each cylinder, with a dual ignition system. The crankshaft is of the built-up type with roller main and big end bearings. Dry sump lubrication is a further feature. The output of this Carrera engine, although high, has been reduced slightly as compared to the Spyder unit, to ensure long life and reliability. In terms of installation, the only real difference between the Speedster and the Spyder cars is that in the latter the power unit is fitted ahead of the rear axle centre line, whereas the touring car adopts the standard Porsche layout.

As far as the Porsche company is concerned the Carrera Speedster is a touring car. The Spyder is a *production* sports racing car. But the performance of the "touring" Speedster is literally fantastic when we consider that the engine capacity is a mere 1½ litres. One point, which should be immediately obvious, is that the Carrera Speedster complies with FIA Grand Turismo class requirements. Yet the car is capable of reaching 125 m.p.h., whereas other stark and thinly disguised sports racing cars which may, or may not, be capable of such speeds are certainly not eligible for the Grand Turismo class. The Porsche is also perfectly at home in city streets. The engine is quiet and smooth enough to run at 25 m.p.h. in top gear if either by manipulating the throttle pedal or by actuating the supplementary over-riding control lever beneath the steering wheel. It is seldom necessary to make use of this latter control. After a little practise the driver can select various gear ratios by adjusting the position of the throttle pedal.

It should be appreciated that, as far as the Rolls Royce is concerned, automatic gearchange depends entirely upon road speed and the position of the throttle pedal. That is to say, if one moves off gently on a light throttle opening the car will go through the lower ratios and will select top gear at approximately 25 m.p.h. But if one intends to make utmost use of the considerable acceleration available, opening the throttle wide from a standstill, the intermediate ratios will be held longer, to some 20 m.p.h. in first, 42 m.p.h. in second, and 62 m.p.h. in third gear. Progressive opening of the throttle has the effect of varying these maximum intermediate gear speeds. As compared to a non-automatic system the only "unusual" feature of the Rolls Royce transmission mechanism becomes evident when the throttle is released when accelerating hard. This brings about an immediate change into top gear. Thus, it is possible to accelerate rapidly to, say, 35 m.p.h. in first and second gears and then, by momentarily closing the throttle, engage top gear. This system also works in the opposite manner. When cruising at any speed below 60 m.p.h. in top gear a lower ratio can be engaged by depressing the throttle pedal fully.

THE steering column mounted control lever is merely a limiting device. The quadrant is marked N-4-3-2-R and by placing the lever in position 2 the driver limits the gearchange mechanism to the use of 1st and 2nd gears. The same thing applies with the lever in position 3. The car will make use of all three indirect ratios but the change into top gear will not be made unless the maximum permissible r.p.m. in third gear is exceeded. Some drivers prefer to leave the control lever in position 3 when driving in town. This, to a certain extent, prevents almost continuous automatic gearchanging. But we found it possible to drive at speeds below 30 m.p.h.—almost entirely on top gear—by deliberately maintaining very light throttle openings. Naturally, this considerably betters fuel consumption.

A feature of Rolls Royce cars is that all controls, major and minor, work with unimpeachable precision. The brake and throttle controls—there is no clutch pedal, of course—are delightfully smooth, and it cannot be said that any physical effort is required to steer the car. The famous Rolls Royce mechanical brake servo is still used on the Silver Cloud car, although some improvements have been made recently. As has been mentioned, the brakes on this car are, we believe, unequalled on any other production type car manufactured anywhere in the world. This may appear to be a somewhat sweeping statement

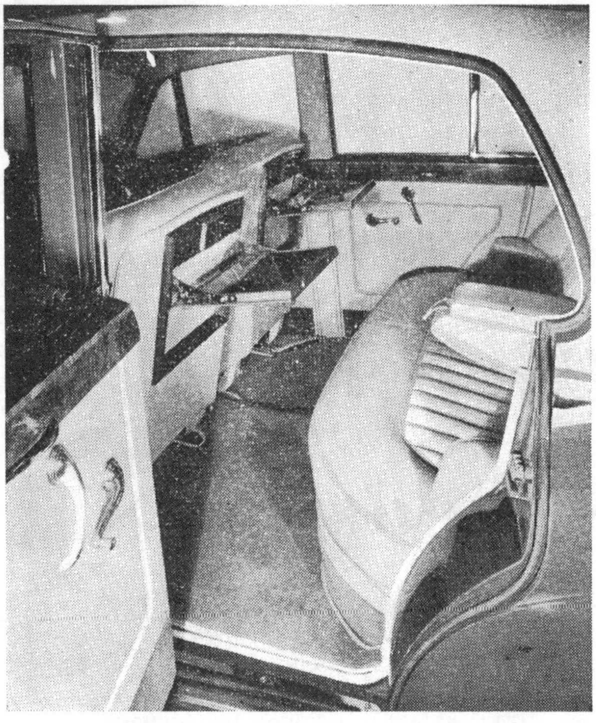

View of the rear compartment showing the picnic table extended. The duct for hot or cold air in the compartment can be seen on the floor behind the far seat

but it is perfectly true that the features most open to criticism on many modern cars can be traced directly to unworthy braking systems. Unfortunately, the fact is that one seldom appreciates this point until there is an opportunity to sample the Rolls Royce braking system. Perhaps in very much the same way that Messrs. Jaguar were able to exploit fully the benefits to be gained from the use of disc brakes at Le Mans we were able to motor the Silver Cloud on roads typical of the West of Scotland at speeds which, at first, seemed almost unbelievable. If we were asked to select one feature of the Rolls Royce for personal praise we would undoubtedly choose the braking system.

ON the other hand, there is one point we would criticise. The heating and ventilation arrangements on the Silver Cloud are not quite in line with the other quality fitments of the car. It is obvious that, when arranging the system, the intention of the designers was to produce a foolproof arrangement. However, there is one distinct snag. To appreciate this, it is necessary to describe the

The superb finish of the 4,887 c.c. six cylinder Rolls Royce power unit is a tribute to British craftsmanship. Note that the automatic gearbox is in unit with the engine. The circular device on the tailshaft housing is the renowned Rolls Royce mechanical brake servo. The twin S.U. carburetters are of the latest HD 6 type

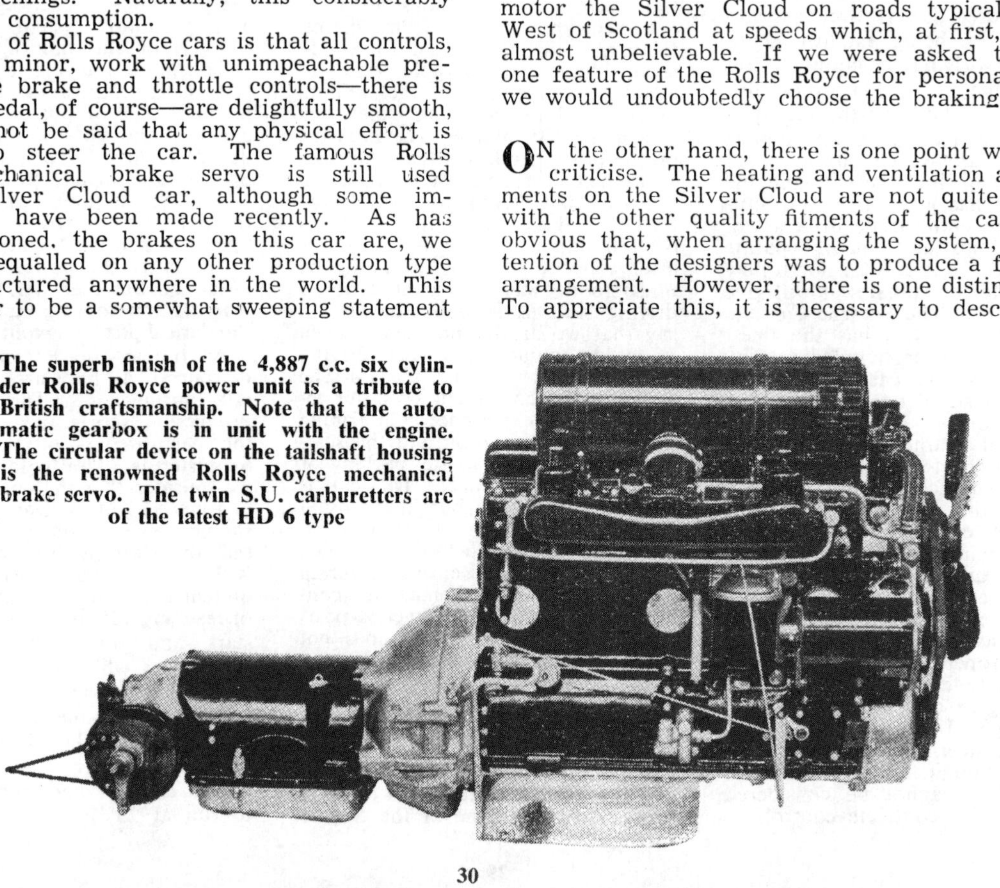

Back squabs of the front seat are capable of independent adjustment and the folding arm rests move with the squabs

complete system. There are two separate heat exchanger units, one each for heating and demisting systems. These units are housed in the front wings and are brought into operation by servo assisted controls on the instrument panel. The general idea is that one can adjust the temperature of the passenger compartment without opening any of the main door windows, by having hot air flowing through the heater unit and cold air coming through the demister ducts, or vice versa. The controls of each separate unit provide for three possible variations in terms of air flow, the first position relying on the speed of the car to force air through the various ducts. Further movements of the control switches actuate two-speed boost fans. Now it is obvious that the system is comprehensive enough to cater for wide temperature variations, but the snag is that one must constantly fiddle with the controls. Whilst one can ostensibly control the *airflow* through the two systems, the temperature of the incoming air is either hot or cold. It would seem that a suitable admixture of hot and cold air could be obtained, but in practise this is not so. What is really required is some means of varying the *temperature* of the incoming air, as opposed to controlling the flow of same.

As an excuse for dealing at length with this subject it may be said that the rest of the car is well-nigh perfect. The six-cylinder engine, which has overhead inlet and side exhaust valves, is a masterpiece of detail design. Rolls Royce have forsaken carburettors of their own design and now fit two of the latest type HD 6 S.U. instruments, which are fed from a gigantic 18 gallon fuel tank by twin electric pumps. For such a large car fuel consumption is not really excessive. By not exceeding 50 m.p.h. it is possible to obtain 20 m.p.g. and when driving hard this figure drops only to some 14 m.p.g.—a big advance on the 7-8 m.p.g. of the larger pre-war Rolls Royce cars.

TO sum up, the high standard of finish both in respect of mechanical and coachwork details is superb. There is no other car in the world—even at the price of £5,386—which can offer such all-round quality. And, regardless of the price mentioned, the car offers *true* value for money and the cost is entirely justified.

MECHANICAL SPECIFICATION

Engine.
Cylinders—6.
Bore—95.25 mm.
Stroke—114.30 mm.
Cubic Capacity—4,887 c.c.
Valves—Overhead inlet, side exhaust.
Compression Ratio—6.6 to 1.
Max. Power—Not published.
at ,, ,,
Carburettors—Two S.U. type HD 6.

Transmission.
(Automatic gearbox)
Top gear—3.42 to 1
3rd gear—4.96 to 1
2nd gear—9.00 to 1
1st gear—13.0 to 1
M.P.H. per 1,000 r.p.m in top gear—24.8.

Chassis.
Brakes—Hydraulic, with Rolls Royce servo assistance.
Brake drum diameter—11¼ inches.
Friction lining area—240 sq. ins.
Suspension, front—Independent, coil springs.
rear—Semi-elliptic.
Shock absorbers—Rolls Royce hydraulic, electrical control.
Tyres—8.20 x 15.
Wheels—Bolt-on steel disc.

Steering.
Steering gear—Cam and roller.
Turning circle—42 feet.
Turns of wheel, lock to lock—4½.

Dimensions.
Wheelbase—10 feet 3 inches.
Track, front—4 feet 10 inches.
rear—5 feet.
Overall length—17 feet 8 inches.
width—6 feet 2¾ inches.
height—5 feet 4¼ inches.
Dry weight—36¾ cwts.

PERFORMANCE FIGURES

Weather—Fine and dry. Temp. approximately 50 deg. F.

Fuel—Premium grade.

Speedometer Correction—

Reading -	20	30	40	50	60	70	80	90	100
Timed speed	19	29	39	49	59	70	80	90	100

Maximum Speeds—

Gear.	M.P.H. (Normal and Maximum)	
Top	Mean 103.3 m.p.h.	Best 104.2
3rd	Max. 65.	
2nd	Max. 40.	

Acceleration (time in seconds)
(With automatic gearbox control in normal position).

10-30	3.4 secs.
20-40	4.0 ,,
30-50	6.4 ,,
40-60	8.8 ,,
50-70	8.8 ,,
60-80	12.0 ,,
70-90	16.0 ,,

From rest through the gears (automatic control).

0-30	4.8 secs.	0-70	18.7 secs.
0-40	7.0 ,,	0-80	25.8 ,,
0-50	10.2 ,,	0-90	34.9 ,,
0-60	13.7 ,,		

Fuel Consumption—
Driven hard—14.0 m.p.g.
Normal—17/19 m.p.g.
Fuel tank capacity—18 gallons.

Price—Basic, £3,590. Purchase tax, £1,796 7s 0d. Total, £5,386 7s 0d.

(The Rolls Royce Silver Cloud used during this test was kindly placed at our disposal by the Clyde Automobile Company Ltd., Renfrew Street, Glasgow.)

necessary. And of course there is no cooling water to boil away at traffic halts.

IT cannot be said that the car is as easy to enter as a Rolls Royce limousine. But at least one can open a door and get into the driving seat in a reasonably orthodox manner. Embarrassing situations which call for acute bending and wriggling movements do not arise, and one need never fear that lady passengers may demand compensation for damage to any unwisely exposed expanse of nylon. These considerations apply when the Speedster is driven as an open car. When the hood must be raised access to the driving compartment is sharply restricted. It is not impossible to get into the car, but a certain technique must be evolved. It is, however, perfectly easy to raise and lower the hood from the driving seat, so that the difficulties of entry and exit are minimised. In fine weather it would perhaps be advisable to fasten the tonneau cover over the compartment at the rear of the seats, to keep dust out of any luggage carried, but when this is done it is not then possible to raise the hood from the driving seat. In changeable conditions it is much better to leave off the tonneau cover. It is then easy to reach over the seats and catch hold of the hood irons, and the top can be erected in a matter of seconds.

In terms of road performance we would like to make it clear that this particular Porsche car does *not* oversteer. It cannot be denied that there were Porsche machines which had to be handled with care until their characteristics were understood, but the Carrera Speedster exhibits no such trait. The handling of this car has actually been improved by making the steering mechanism less sensitive to very small movements of the wheel. The steering is still admirably sensitive by the best of standards but the car is not liable to react violently to the less skilled actions of the novice driver. No special technique, such as was required with certain other rear engined cars, is necessary with the Carrera Speedster model. To anyone who has never driven a modern sports car with softly sprung four-wheel independent suspension the Porsche would indeed be a revelation. On the autobahnen, which are not always smoothly surfaced, we discovered that bumps which would rock a more normally suspended sports car on its rebound stops became smoother as speed was increased. It was in fact possible to cruise this $1\frac{1}{2}$ litre motor car at a true 100 m.p.h. for long distances on the autobahn, and, the greater the speed, the smoother the ride.

THE Speedster is a thoroughly enjoyable car to drive. It is neither difficult to manage nor yet is it "temperamental." Starting is easy, but one must be careful not to jiggle the throttle pedal when the engine is warm. The car performs well immediately after a cold start and but for the fact that it is advisable to allow the oil to warm up slightly before driving really hard it would appear that maximum output is readily available. In town driving no special precautions need be taken to prevent overheating or plug oiling or any of the other maladies common to high performance cars of not so very long ago. The gearbox is so pleasant to use that there

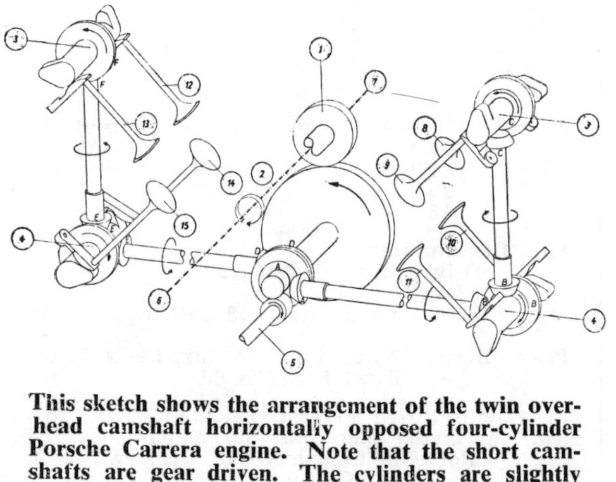

This sketch shows the arrangement of the twin overhead camshaft horizontally opposed four-cylinder Porsche Carrera engine. Note that the short camshafts are gear driven. The cylinders are slightly offset when viewed in plan.

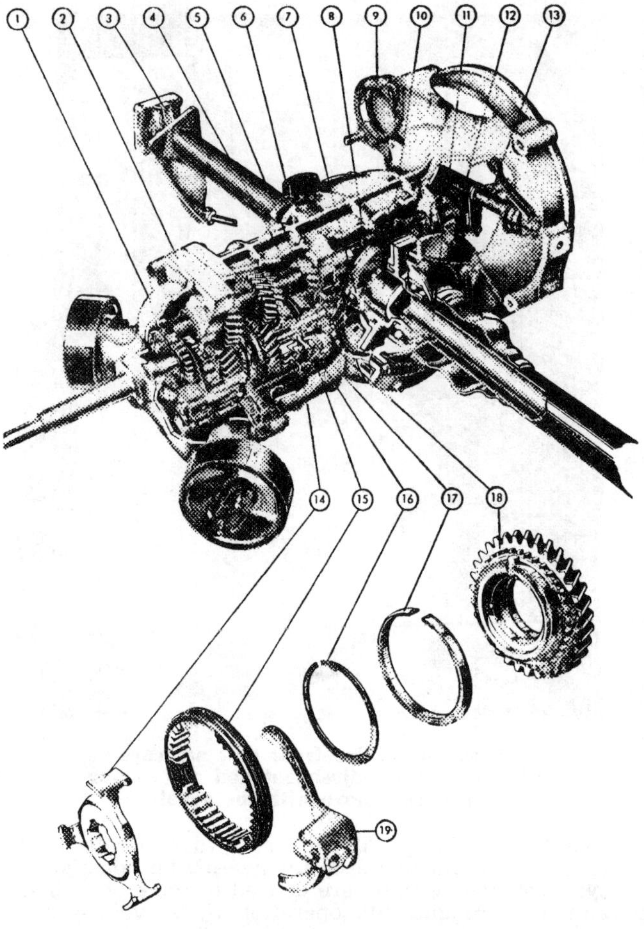

The transmission system is an outstanding feature of the Porsche. This cutaway drawing shows the general arrangement. Numbered parts are as follows:—1 Starting handle housing; 2 Layshaft carrier; 3 Axle shaft; 4 First motion shaft; 5 Gear cluster and synchromesh assembly; 6 Breather and oil filler; 7 Differential star pinion; 8 Crown wheel; 9 Starter motor housing; 10 Differential cage; 11 Axle shaft; 12 Input shaft; 13 Clutch withdrawal mechanism; 14 and 15 Synchronising hub and dog clutch; 16 Lock ring; 17 Synchronising baulk ring; 18 Gear assembly

is some tendency to make unnecessary use of the lower ratios when driving in traffic. The car will pull very nicely at indecently low speeds in top gear. Exhaust noise on our test car was perhaps just a little too loud and sporty. Not loud enough to cause comment on the Continent, but loud enough to make progress in Britain embarrassingly conspicuous. The exhaust note from the Carrera engine is in fact rather unusual. At low speeds the note is reminiscent of the burble produced by the famous Ford vee 8 engine. But during acceleration, and as engine speed approaches the 6,000 r.p.m. mark, the Speedster's two short tail pipes emit a screeching crackle similar to the noise made by small multi-cylinder racing motor cycle engines. From the driving seat, with the hood down, the general noise level is fairly low. When cruising at high speeds the wind seems to carry most of it away. When the car is used with the top up, the driving compartment becomes much noisier. A whine from the cooling fan and some transmission noise can be heard. The electric fuel pump fitted on the test car also made some rather peculiar noises occasionally.

All things considered, and even at the price of approximately £2926 including British purchase tax and import duty, the Porsche Carrera Speedster is a remarkable motor car. The engine, gearbox and transmission system, steering, suspension and brakes exhibit innovations of the highest standards in engineering. The car is good to look at and is extremely well finished, if not so luxuriously equipped as the other Porsche models. There is, of

The low overall height of the Speedster can be gauged from this picture. The sweeping tail line of the car is also seen to advantage.

course, no other *production touring car* available at any price which will equal the performance offered by the Porsche. Comparisons tend to be odious, but we might say that the only other machine which might, in the Grand Turismo class, challenge the supremacy of Porsche is the 1½ litre Maserati. In terms of sheer performance the British built Lotus is certainly capable of matching the Porsche, but it is not substantially cheaper to buy, it suffers badly in terms of utilitarian value, and would not be accepted as a Grand Turismo entry. We do not normally make such comparisons in our road test reports. On this occasion we make the exception only to illustrate what may happen in the very near future if the European Free Trade scheme is agreed upon. The fully equipped Porsche Carrera Speedster, with its 125 m.p.h. performance and beautiful twin overhead camshaft engine would then be available in Britain for several hundred pounds less than the cost of the fast, but stark, Lotus Le Mans 85 model.

A cockpit view of the Carrera Speedster. The wood rimmed steering wheel is very pleasant to handle and the instruments are easily read at high speeds

MECHANICAL SPECIFICATION

Engine
Cylinders—4 (horizontally opposed).
Bore—85 mm.
Stroke—66 mm.
Cubic Capacity—1498 c.c.
Compression Ratio—9 to 1.
Valves—Overhead, twin camshafts on each bank.
Maximum Power—115 b.h.p. at 6,200 r.p.m.
Carburettors—2 double choke Solex downdraft.

Transmission
(All indirect ratios, final drive ratio—4.428 to 1)
Top gear (s/m)—0.815 to 1 (overall 3.613 to 1)
3rd gear (s/m)—1.13 to 1 „ 5.00 to 1
2nd gear (s/m)—1.76 to 1 „ 7.793 to 1
1st gear (s/m)—3.18 to 1 „ 13.70 to 1
Alternative ratios—4.875 and 4.375 to 1.

Chassis
Brakes—Hydraulic, 2 LS on front.
Brake drum dia.—11 inches.
Friction lining area—122 sq. ins.
Suspension, front—independent, trailing links, laminated torsion bars rear—swinging half axles, torsion bars.
Dampers—Hydraulic telescopic.
Tyres—5.90 x 15 Super Sport.
Wheels—Bolt-on steel disc (wire wheels and knock-off hubs optional).

Steering
Steering gear—Worm and nut, divided track rod, with steering damper.
Turning circle—36 feet.
Turns of wheel, lock to lock—2¼.

Dimensions
Wheelbase—6 feet 10½ inches.
Track, front—4 feet 3¼ inches.
rear—4 feet 2⅛ inches.
Overall, length—12 feet 11¾ inches.
width— 5 feet—5½ inches.
height— 4 feet.
Dry weight—15 cwt.

PERFORMANCE FIGURES

Weather—Warm and dry, light winds. Temp. approx. 65 deg. F.

Fuel—Premium grade.

Speedometer Correction
See text. Performance check by revolution counter readings.

Maximum Speeds

Gear	M.P.H. at 6, 200 r.p.m.
Top	125 m.p.h.
3rd	90 „
2nd	70 „
1st	37 „

Acceleration (Time in seconds)

M.P.H.	Top	3rd	2nd	1st
10-30	—	—	5.0	3.2
20-40	—	5.5	4.9	—
30-50	8.1	6.2	5.0	—
40-60	8.5	7.0	—	—
50-70	9.9	8.0	—	—
60-80	11.7	10.0	—	—
70-90	16.6	—	—	—

From Rest through the Gears

0-30	4.0	0-70	14.9
0-40	5.7	0-80	17.4
0-50	7.8	0-90	24.2
0-60	10.8	0-100	33.0

Fuel Consumption
Driven hard—25 m.p.g.
Normal—28/30 m.p.g.
Fuel Tank Capacity—11½ gallons.

Price: Basic—£1950. Purchase Tax—£976 7s 0d. Total £2926 7s 0d.

(The Porsche car used in this test was kindly placed at our disposal by Dr.-Ing. h.c. F. Porsche, Stuttgart-Zuffenhausen.)

LOW SEATS of the Porsche are bounded by sides and high hood line. Quick slope of the hood results in good visibility and little wind blast.

Test Guide To The

PORSCHE LINE

Porsche's Super Speedster Scoots Through Test to Uphold the Family Tradition of Quality and True Sports Driving Fun

AERODYNAMIC design is exemplified in the 1600 Super Speedster roadster. Many will prefer the convertible to the roadster for the added advantage of roll-up windows. Quality of manufacture is extremely high throughout the entire line.

HERE IS A CAR THAT IS EASY TO CORNER AT SPEEDS. PUTTING IT INTO A DRIFT OR CONTROLLED SLIDE IS HELPED BY REAR ENGINE.

REAR VIEW of the four-cylinder engine which gives some observers the impression of a combined aircraft and motorcycle power-plant. Red-lined between 5000 and 5500 rpm, it revs up considerably faster than a comparable aircraft engine.

CARBURETION of the rear engine Super Speedster is ably handled by dual Webers. Access to the engine area is a bit awkward.

EXTREMELY large brakes exhibited not a bit of fade throughout test period. Brake drums are ribbed aluminum, cast iron liners.

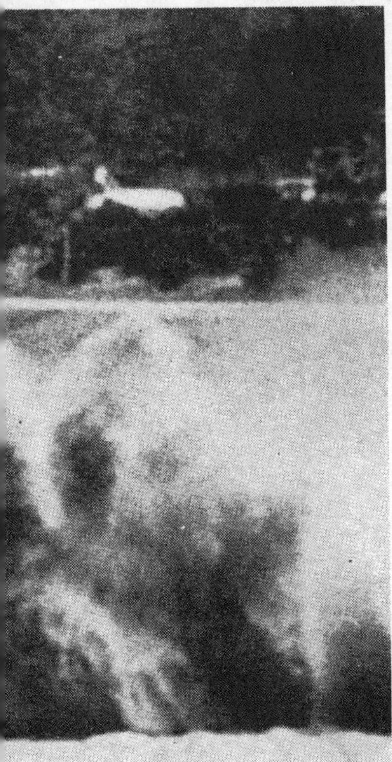

SHOULD the happy day ever occur when an overanxious merchant holds a "Dollar Day" sale of sports cars, the counter handling Porsche products will be one of the first to sell out of merchandise. Here is an automobile which is first on the list of a good percentage of enthusiasts. If it were not for a fairly prohibitive price and limited production there would be many more scooting around America today.

During the course of its test the 1600 Super Speedster roadster displayed a new brand of handling. Being a rear engine car it has its natural oversteer tendencies but, once the novice driver realizes that the rear end breaks away with ease, he'll be able to control drifts and slides much more easily with the Porsche system than with the conventional front-engine car. In relation to its Volkswagen cousin the Porsche's handling is improved because of the elimination of the camber in the rear wheel suspension. This refinement does away with the tendency of the inside rear wheel to cant in turns.

Crossing railroad tracks is another experience that makes one wonder about the relationship of extreme weight to smooth ride. The Porsche weighs only 1700 lbs. but it floats its way across a grade crossing like a ballet dancer while the Detroit fullbacks rumble beside it. This advantage is not due entirely to engineering but also to basic sound construction.

After a number of miles of traveling the driver begins to appreciate the stopping ability of the car. It carries big, safe brakes that don't know how to fade. This is due to a combination of factors: aluminum-ribbed brake drums with cast iron liners plus stamped wheels which contain a good number of ventilating holes.

Passengers sit low in the Porsche. The sides come up and around and the hood is practically at eye level. But that hood slopes down quickly to afford excellent visibility. The road test roadster was fitted with optional bucket seats which proved that they were worth more than the $45 extra cost. They hug their guests in real comfort and prevent sliding in turns and fatigue in tours. They are easily adjusted for leg and back comfort.

A bad feature of the roadster is the definite feeling of confinement with the top up. The driver feels as if he is peering out of a tunnel and, with the side curtains added, one has all the visibility of the jockeys of Sherman tanks and Rose Parade floats.

Instrumentation includes a big speedometer, tachometer, oil temperature and gas gauges and warning lights for the generator and oil pressure. Lights are dimmed by pushing the horn button while the inner wheel ring sounds the horn. This is a European innovation that takes some driver adjustment but it soon proves quite handy in night driving.

A small gripe as far as the dash accessories go is the lack of an ash tray and a lock-up type glove compartment. Roadster and convertible drivers in particular have a real need for a safe storage spot for valuables while smokers find it close to impossible to push out an arm with every flick of ashes.

The air-flow shape of the Porsche body, which seems to defy design modification, is such that driver and passenger miss the heavy blast of air which is common in some sports roadsters. The shape of the car and the windshield seem to deflect the main stream of air high above the driving compartment to avoid this tendency. With top down, too, the noise level is low and highway conversation is possible, but, with top up and on coupe versions, the old rear engine noise jinx pops up again.

For driving fun the gear box is great. All four gears are synchromeshed and their close ratio selection goes without criticism. The appearance of this transmission in a number of Europe's top

GUIDE TO THE LINE

SUPER SPEEDSTER ROADSTER $3615

SUPER HARDTOP $4280

SUPER COUPE $4115

SUPER CONVERTIBLE $4365

SUPER SERIES New York prices are quoted. These four cars carry the 88-hp pushrod engine shown at right above. Other power is 70-hp pushrod engine and 115-125 Carrera overhead cam engine (left above). Approximately $2000 separates the latter variations.

UNLIKE the Volkswagen, camber to the rear wheel suspension has been eliminated. Handling is improved because of this feature.

Test Data

Test Car: 1958 Porsche 1600 Super Speedster
Body Type: two-door roadster
Basic Price: $3615 (New York port-of-entry)
Engine: four-cylinder opposed, air-cooled
Carburetion: dual Webers
Displacement: 96.5 cubic inches
Bore & Stroke: 3.25x2.91
Compression Ratio: 8.5-to-1
Horsepower: 88 @ 5000 rpm (minimum)
Horsepower per cubic inch: .91
Torque: 86 lb.-ft. @ 3700 rpm.
Test Weight: 1700 lbs. without driver
Weight Distribution: 42 per cent on front wheels
Power-Weight Ratio: 19.32 lbs. per horsepower
Transmission: four-speed, synchromesh all gears
Rear Axle Ratio: 3.18-to-1
Steering: 2.25 turns lock-to-lock
Dimensions: overall length 135 inches, width 65, height 51, wheelbase 82.7, tread 51 front, 50 rear
Springs: torsion bar
Tires: 5.60x15
Gas Mileage: 26.9 mpg (city and highway average)
Speedometer Error: Indicated 30, 45 and 60 mph are actual 28, 42 and 55 mph, respectively
Acceleration: 0-30 mph in 3.7 seconds, 0-45 mph in 7.2 and 0-60 mph in 11.4 seconds

ALTHOUGH TOP GOES UP EASILY IT CERTAINLY CONFINES THE CAB. SIDE CURTAINS ADD TO THE EFFECT OF BEING INSIDE A TURTLE SHELL.

OPTIONAL extra comfort seats are among the most luxurious offered today. They adjust for greater comfort and good support.

racing cars is one of its best recommendations.

The engine of the Porsche, as the rest of the chassis, is related directly to the Volkswagen. But the Porsche powerplants naturally are of large displacement and hopped-up to a great degree. Some reports have it that horsepower ratings are only a minimum guarantee of the factory. Hand work by master mechanics personalizes the power of each engine and many have been found way over their advertised horsepower rating.

Engines of three strengths are found in the Porsche line. The road test roadster was powered by the 88-hp middle member of the trio. The other engines are the 70-hp junior model of the same pushrod engine and the 115-125-hp Carrera overhead cam engine.

Good acceleration times are due in large part to the low weight factor. Cruising, passing and top speeds are about on a par with some current American passenger cars.

The overall impression of the Porsche's high quality might best be summed up in examining the makers' attention to little details. Zerk fittings are used on door hinges to assure positive lubrication as opposed to the American dependence upon capillary action for the oil. Little wire clips support each tire valve stem to prevent centrifugal force from throwing them against the wheel rims.

From these little features to good power, quality and craftsmanship the Porsche has all the elements of pleasurable sports driving.

THE LINEUP—Four body styles and three engine variations are the building blocks of the Porsche line. The 1600, 70-hp and the 1600 Super, 88-hp series are available in roadster (Speedster), coupe, hardtop and convertible coupe variations. The high powered Carrera engine is offered in the Speedster and Gran Turismo and convertible coupes.

PRICES — New York port-of-entry prices range from $3215 for the 1600 Speedster to $5915 for the Carrera convertible coupe. Additional prices will be found with accompanying illustrations.

DISTRIBUTION — The Hoffman-Porsche Car corporation of New York handles the Porsche national dealer network. The main complaint voiced so far has been the lack of products per dealer. Parts and service policies are patterned after the efficient Volkswagen methods.

THE MANUFACTURER — The 1950 initial production of the Porsche was not the introduction of that name to the automotive world. Dr. Ferdinand Porsche, through long associations with Austro-Daimler, Daimler-Benz and Steyr, had established himself as one of the industry's all-time great designers. His most famous innovations are the Volkswagen, the Auto-Union racing car, torsion bar suspension and the car that bears his name. Since his death in 1951 the family concern has been managed by his son. Quality continues high with a reputation for stability and slow craftsmanship.

THE FUTURE — The Porsche is the dream car of enough enthusiasts throughout the world to insure the fact that it will remain popular and basically unchanged for a long time to come. •

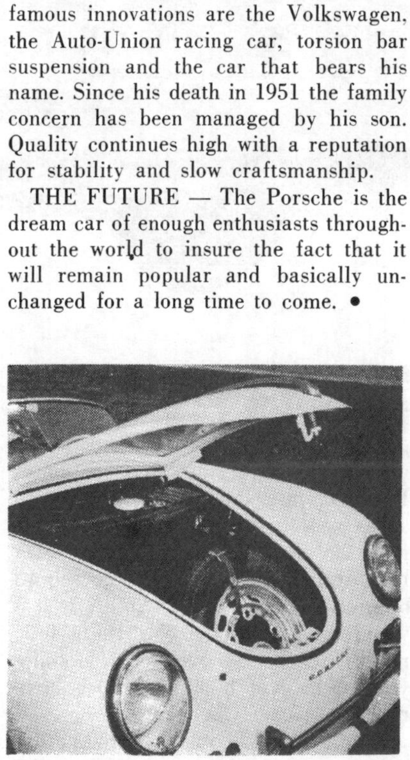

GAS TANK and spare tire take up nearly all usable room under the hood. Only other area for storage is behind the front seats.

The new Porsche 356A/1600 doesn't look different from older models, but they are not sisters under the skin, where mechanical wonders are even better than before.

STUTTGART SIZZLER '58

SPEED AGE
EXPERT TEST

By JOHN BENTLEY

WHEN the first squat and humpy little Porsche coupé growled to a halt outside Max Hoffman's Park Avenue showroom one day in 1950, sportscar aficionados were, perhaps, not suitably impressed. "What?" they exclaimed. "Only 1100 cc and 40 bhp, and it costs over $4,000? It just won't sell over here. Well – a few, maybe, just as a novelty; but nothing you could ever build up into a business."

Sure, the air-cooled, horizontally-opposed engine mounted snugly at the rear was interesting; torsion-bar suspension was a good idea, too. And one had to admit that Dr. Porsche's brainchild *pour le sport* was a beautifully finished machine. But for that kind of money, not even a synchromesh box? It didn't add up.

The car's seductiveness was of a kind that grew with every mile, I recall—I was among those that drove the trailblazer – but it had some disturbing faults such as a tendency to pitch unduly and to become so front-end-light at speed that the car felt as though it were being driven on ice.

Eight years ago, this was, when the factory's production rate was one car per diem. It is now 12 times greater, with the bulk of output still earmarked for the U.S., the bhp developed by today's equivalent model is 75% higher; numerous refinements have been added, including the finest and fastest synchromesh transmission in the world. Yet, in spite of devalued dollars, the price has actually come down.

However, the significant thing about all this is that the basic design of the Porsche has not changed one whit in all these years. Nor, for that matter, have its structure and shape departed from principles which were absolutely right in the first place.

As a four-time Porsche owner

A couple of friends dropped by during test with their own white Porsches, useful for comparison. Test car is at left, older coupe in center, 1500 Speedster at the right.

(though not since 1954), I took on the assignment of road-testing the latest 1600 coupé with more than passing interest. The car made available to SPEED AGE through the courtesy of Hoffman-Porsche of New York, U.S. distributors, was beautifully finished in white lacquer with red leather upholstery, and showed signs of meticulous servicing. It was too new, however, to permit the repeated use of maximum revs. The performance figures could, therefore, stand some upward revision for a fully broken-in engine. Maximum speed attained, for instance, was a corrected 90 mph (4,500 rpm) which still left quite a bit in hand. Momentary acceleration under light load, going up through the gears, is harmless enough; continued lugging at peak rpm in fourth gear can ruin a new engine.

The body shell of the latest 1600 coupé is, of course, identical with those of the Super and Carrera coupés, but no less interesting is the fact that it has not changed dimensionally in years. The test car had the same generous 50-inch door-to-door interior width as my 1954 Porsche, the same armchair seats of lavish proportions and comfort. Each is of 21½ inches maximum width and depth, with a deeply-upholstered back 22 inches high. A simple control knob permits the seat back to tilt downwards 45° from the vertical, providing passenger or driver with couch-like comfort—especially in view of the enormous amount of legroom from seat edge to bulkhead floor – no less than 25 inches in a straight line.

Before taking the wheel of our test car, I duly noted the 1958 modifications for use as points of reference, and these make an impressive list. Included among the major ones are a completely new cam-and-roller steering assembly of ZF manufacture, fitted with a damper; new Zenith twin-choke carburetors; a short-throw gearshift; an improved clutch; softer suspension; and cast-iron cylinder barrels instead of the former chrome-lined aluminum ones.

It may be said, right away, that the use of cast-iron cylinders (as in the VW) has no detrimental effect on the running of the 1600 Porsche engine, nor does it pose any cooling problems. These barrels are about 70 pounds heavier than the aluminum cylinders retained on the Super, but against this they can be rebored just like any conventional engine block (and are cheaper to produce, of course). It is no longer necessary to buy a new barrel with a matching piston when replacements are needed. No doubt, satisfactory cooling stems in part from the fact that the 1600 engine is only mildly stressed and has a low rpm peak and a moderate compression ratio.

SPECIFICATIONS:

ENGINE & CHASSIS

CYLINDERS	4 OPPOSED
BORE	3.25 IN.
STROKE	2.91 IN.
DISPLACEMENT	96.5 CU. IN.
COMPRESSION RATIO	7.5:1
MAXIMUM OUTPUT (HP @ RPM)	70 @ 4500
VALVES	OVERHEAD PUSHROD
CARBURETORS	TWIN ZENITH 32 NDIX DOWNDRAFT
TRANSMISSION	FOUR-SPEED ALL-SYNCHROMESH
OVERALL RATIOS	
LOW	13.68
SECOND	7.79
THIRD	5.00
FOURTH	3.61
REAR AXLE RATIO	4.43
MPH PER 1000 RPM (FOURTH)	20.00
TURNING DIAMETER	36 FT.
STEERING	ZF WORM GEAR
STEERING WHEEL TURNS (LOCK TO LOCK)	2.6
TIRE SIZE	560 x 15
BRAKE LINING AREA	122 SQ. IN.
WEIGHT (CURB)	1,921 LBS.
FUEL TANK CAPACITY	13.6 GALS.

DIMENSIONS

WHEELBASE	82.7 IN.
TREAD (FRONT)	51.4 IN.
TREAD (REAR)	50.1 IN.
OVERALL LENGTH	155.8 IN.
OVERALL WIDTH	65.6 IN.
OVERALL HEIGHT	51.5 IN.
GRAUND CLEARANCE	6.3 IN.

PERFORMANCE FACTORS

ACCELERATION THRU GEARS (SECONDS)	
0-30 MPH	5.0
0-40 MPH	7.1
0-50 MPH	10.6
0-60 MPH	13.8
30-50 MPH	7.8
MAXIMUM SPEED (MPH ESTIMATED)	100
MAXIMUM TORQUE (LBS/FT @ RPM)	82 @ 2,800
BHP PER CU. IN.	.72
LBS PER BHP (TEST CAR)	27.44
PISTON SPEED FT/MIN @ PEAK RPM	2,182
MILEAGE, ALL TESTS	27.81 MPG

NOTES: Weather: warm, dry, no wind. Speedometer correction: at 60 mph read 65 mph—8.3% fast.

lie new cast-iron cylinders, steering assembly and carburetion, and suspension, for brand-new performance.

Rear elevation of Porsche is clean as ever. Innovation is exhausts through bumper guards, a la Detroit.

Front compartment houses gas tank and spare tire. "Luggage space" is just about big enough for tool kit.

No sooner did I occupy the driver's seat in the test car, and inhale the aroma of new paint and leather, than memories came flooding back about this compact jewel of a machine. Starting on the Zeniths presents no problem in any weather, if you follow instructions. Since it was a cold start, I depressed the gas pedal fully, and the engine fired at once when I turned the key, then quickly settled down to a steady 700 rpm idling rhythm.

The latest oil temperature gauge, by the way, is no longer calibrated in degrees centigrade. Variations in oil temperature readings (which always seemed to err on the high side) bothered conscientious drivers a good deal. Not generally known is the fact that the gauge element records the oil temperature as it comes out of the engine, not as it leaves the oil cooler. This makes quite a difference, and on occasions has cost a driver a race because he feared for his engine. So now the gauge simply consists of a wide green band with a very narrow red one at the extreme right. Anything in between is safe.

First impressions as you drive the Porsche 356A/1600 coupe follow one another in quick succession. The clutch has a relatively short travel, but grips smoothly and easily and does not (as sometimes formerly) slip when abused. The shift lever, stiff with newness on the test car, was nonetheless a joy that invited constant use. Gone is that long forward swing from second to third; the much shortened travel and positive feel allow very fast up- and downshifts that do justice to the unique Porsche system of radially-sprung synchro rings.

Right away, too, you notice the difference in the ride, which is appreciably softer than formerly, yet retains all the desirable characteristics of firm suspension. There is no mushing or leaning, yet by the same token one feels far less shock on a rough surface than with a big domestic sedan. Negotiating the local horror which passes for a road and which is nothing more than a casually filled mass of half-washed-out bumps, rills, potholes and dips, my 4,000-pound family Behemoth practically shakes itself to pieces at 30 mph. The same stretch, negotiated in the Porsche at a good 10 mph faster, brought only the faintest jounce and was so free from discomfort one would have thought the road had been resurfaced overnight. How was this done in a machine with a wheelbase of under 83 inches and a laden weight of

PORSCHE 356A/1600 TEST

Under the familiar exterior improved gearshift, clutch

Engine compartment (left) and interior (above) are standard Porsche. All changes for '58 are out of sight.

around 2,100 lbs? Well, the front torsion springs are now softer and at the same time slightly huskier. This permits an increase of up-and-down wheel travel without sacrifice of stability. Also, the shocks are relocated to a near-vertical position, as in the racing Spyder.

The steering of the latest Porsche is another bewitching characteristic created by the works engineers with almost uncanny skill. It is not "featherlight," as might be expected; nor (in spite of the extra 2½° of caster action borrowed from the Spyder) does it have a "wilful" self-centering action. The caster is there, to help you recover from any sudden and violent change of direction; and there is just enough "weight" to the steering to give one a feeling of positive control without any sacrifice of quickness. That ZF box is a wonder, and its use in conjunction with a hydraulic damper and a front stabilizer bar creates a new concept in the steering of a rear-engine car. The 1600 Porsche now literally neutral-steers, and even if a driver handles it foolishly it will not break loose on a turn any sooner than a machine with a conventional front-mounted engine.

This is not hearsay. I made repeated tests on winding sections notable for tight reverse turns, and over every type of road surface. On firm paving, the rear end clung tenaciously and gave ample tire-squeal warning before it broke loose. Even then it was a simple matter to recover with the usual combined steering correction and throttle application. Over a loose surface, the Porsche responded like any front engined car with a sensible weight-distribution. It corrects just as easily, too. The hydraulic damper seems to absorb every vestige of road shock before it gets anywhere near the steering wheel; and at 90 mph the car is so steady that it can easily and safely be steered with one hand.

Perhaps, because I have always liked Porsches, I find it easy to enthuse over their design features; but it would be hard not to praise the steering and handling of the Type 356A, which are presumably identical in the Super and the Carrera, since all are "cast in the same mold."

One other delightful performance feature of the 1600 is the vastly improved carburetion resulting from the twin-choke Zeniths. Low down the range, especially, the car is unrecognizable. It will haul away from 10 mph in third gear and 15 mph in fourth gear without complaint or hesitation, even when the throttle is kicked down. Bearing in mind that fourth is a permanently built-in .815 overdrive which automatically raises the rear end ratio, this is all the more remarkable. The less complex throttle linkage apparently remains unaffected by engine temperature variations, and throttle response is instantaneous at all times, with plenty of "dig" low down the range. In view of the acceleration cam used with this engine, its eagerness is understandable; but even so it is interesting to note that the 1600 with a modest 70 bhp and 3.63 axle ratio is only about 6/10ths of a second slower from zero to 40 mph than the 115 bhp Carrera using a 4.29 ratio.

Cruising speed of the 1600 coupé is purely a matter of individual taste. The engine is as happy at 80 mph as at 60—and at a mile a minute, certainly, mechanical and wind noise are so slight that you can carry on a conversation in normal tones, or listen to the radio with the volume turned low. This is a great deal more than can be said of some other imported sports cars in the Porsche price bracket. At high rpm, engine noise in some of them is so deafening that above 70 mph conversation becomes impossible.

To highlight some of the other attributes of the 1600, the brakes are (as might be expected) superb and perfectly even; throttle and brake pedals are so located that it is easy to heel-and-toe by resting one's heel on the gas pedal and the toe on the brake; and the finish and instrumentation of the car, while functional and practical, could hardly be better. A gas gauge is combined with the oil temperature dial; the centrally located tachometer is redlined at 5,000 rpm but calibrated to 6000; the speedometer reads somewhat unnecessarily up to 120 mph, but also indicates tenths of a mile on the odometer—a useful rally feature. Calibration in five mph divisions, however, is both confusing and inaccurate.

Other niceties include the crash-pad effect of the leather-upholstered dash; provision of a rheostat for variable illumination of the dials and a cigar lighter; and a useful glove compartment with a lid. There is also a grab handle built into the passenger side of the dash.

By no stretch of imagination could the Porsche coupé be called anything more than a luxurious two-passenger machine. Yet that folding rear seat comes in right handy either as a luggage platform or a space in which to park a couple of eight-year-old children. As a seat, it is 14¼ inches deep, with a 15-inch back and about 40 inches of overall width. However, the gearbox hump cuts off a foot width of usable seat space, and upholstery is kept to a minimum, although eight inches of knee room are available with the two front seats normally located.

As a luggage platform, the folded rear seat provides a deck for about eight cubic feet of luggage. This will easily cover the needs of two people on a two-week holiday.

The sensible bumper guards and rails featured on all Porsches except the Gran Turismo Carrera Speedster and coupe are continued unchanged and provide a useful parking safeguard on busy streets. But the new Detroit-style exhaust outlets, discharging through the bumper guards, seem incongruous in a machine the very essence of which negates all the styling absurdities perpetrated on Domestic Iron. Improved ground clearance results, it is true, but the pipes have to be contorted into right-angled doglegs to match the outlets. In a 96 cu-in. engine you cannot afford to squander power through needless back-pressure—especially since Porsche never lost a sale in eight years because of the regular exhaust system with projecting pipe stubs.

Probably not since the days of the Bugatti has any sports car exerted upon its owner the dynamic kind of fascination peculiar to the Porsche. And for the many who are susceptible to that fascination and can think of automobiles only in terms of Porsches, the $3,665 price tag is by no means excessive. It is, in fact, not much to pay for mechanical bliss. ●

PORSCHE PEDIGREE

Year	Type	Model	Displacement (c.c.)	Output	Max. Speed	(in secs.) 0-60
1950	356	1.1 liter	1086	40 @ 4000	85	18.0
1951	356	1.3 liter	1286	44 @ 4000	90	17.1
1952	356	1.5 liter	1488	55 @ 4400	96	14.9
1953	356	America	1488	55 @ 4400	100	14.7
1953	356/1500S	1500 Super	1488	70 @ 5000	107	12.4
1954	356/1300	1.3 liter	1290	44 @ 4200	90	16.3
1954	356/1300S	1300 Super	1290	60 @ 5500	95	15.5
1955	356/1500	Continental	1488	66 @ 4400	98	15.0
1956	356/1600	1600	1582	70 @ 4500	100	13.8
1956	356/1500GS	Carrera	1498	110 @ 6200	120	11.5
1956	356/1600S	1600 Super	1582	88 @ 5000	105	10.5
1958	356A/1500GS	Carrera GT	1498	125 @ 6400	125	11.1

The sleek 1600 is dwarfed by the imposing sign at the entrance to Kindberg

The Porsche type 356A/1600 super hardtop

tested by Edward Eves

A sample of wintry conditions outside the Zweirad-museum at Neckarsulm

IN common with its progenitor, the humble KdF wagen or " Volks," the Porsche has always been a car which attracts proponents as rabid as its opponents, which seems to be a sure sign that it is a vehicle of some character.

Undoubtedly as soon as he had conceived the People's Car, Dr. Porsche the Elder had ideas about making a sports version based on the mechanical organs of the VW. Actually the first Porsche must have been built almost alongside the prototypes of the latter vehicle, for when the Axis race, from Rome to Berlin, was mooted in 1939 a special racing coupé FW was prepared for this event. It is history now that the race was never held, but the car survived the War and appeared in races in Austria after the cessation of hostilities. The external appearance of this racer bore the strongest of family resemblances to the Porsche as we know it today and beneath its streamlined body could be found the flat-four air-cooled engine, swing axles and trailing link suspension of the homely VW.

The first fifty post-war Porsches were built at Gmuend in Austria and were unique in that they had aluminium bodies. This was 1950; in the middle of that year, after only three months of production in Austria, it was possible to move to Germany and production started at Zuffenhausen, a suburb of Stuttgart, with a steel bodied car. The excellent performance of the car, due almost entirely to its good streamlined shape, immediately attracted attention. In those days it was not without its faults: soundproofing was elementary, the wonderful Porsche synchromesh box had not been thought of and the cable operated brakes had all the shortcomings of that system. Moreover, the virulent oversteer which the car possessed made it somewhat lethal in the hands of the innocent, starting a legend which persists to this day. As the years passed the VW production parts which made up the running gear were replaced one by one with components which were more suited to the purpose, and the engine was progressively increased in capacity from 1100 c.c. in 1950 to its present capacity of 1600 c.c. At the same time modifications to the suspension and steering geometry step by step eradicated the car's rather sudden handling characteristics, a most important point, as the firm were making a big drive to capture some of the American market and a vehicle with understeering characteristics was essential. By the end of 1955 this had been achieved by a combination of rear wheel camber and toe-in, front anti-roll bar and a change of wheel size. This is basically the car as we know it today, with initial understeering changing into a final oversteer, a combination considered by many experts as the ideal.

With all this history at the back of my mind I was overjoyed when Huschke von Hanstein suggested that I might like to take the opportunity to use a 1600 Super for a short holiday between races. Naturally I jumped at the offer, for the Super seemed to offer some of the possibilities that the ordinary 1600 just lacked, and I promptly decided the proper thing to do was to take the car to the country of its birth, driving to Vienna by the busy main road through Linz and returning via Weiner-Neustadt, Bruck and Bad Ischl, a twisty mountain road which would make an excellent contrast to the Autobahn between Stuttgart and Salzburg.

Arriving at the factory in Zuffenhausen I was invited to park my 403 in the orchard behind the main offices and take a look at the latest thing in 1600 Supers. At the last Frankfurt Show a number of important modifications had been made with the idea of improving the usability of the car. Improvements in bearing materials had made the use of a plain bearing crankshaft a possibility and the Hirth roller bearing crank had been abandoned. In the carburation department a double choke Zenith 32NDIX had been fitted with resultant gains in bottom and middle range torque while in the handling department a Ross type recirculating ball steering box of ZF manufacture had been adopted. The gearchange movement had been reduced and a new clutch gave lower pedal pressures. The cylinder barrels were of aluminium with chromium-plated bores and, compared with the straight 1600 the head had larger valves and gas passages. The output of the Super motor remains unchanged at 75 b.h.p. at the relatively modest speed of 5,000 r.p.m.

The new hardtop converts the Cabriolet into a very practical coupé with improved visibility compared with the

Porsche production line. The bodies enter at the far end of the building, circumnavigate the factory and drive away at the end

The volume of each cylinder head is carefully checked to ensure even running

standard Coupé; over-centre clips hold it in position and rubber seals effectively prevent the ingress of rain under conditions of high speed driving, as I was to discover. Seated in the comfortable driving seat with Reutter adjustable back, the two-spoked steering wheel is found to be set sensibly low and near enough to the dashboard to permit an arms-stretched driving position without making it difficult to reach the pedals when the seat is in the appropriate position. A full-circle horn ring sounds adequate, high-pitched, Bosch horns, while the centre " horn-button " flashes the head-lamps for signalling on the Autobahn, a feature that we shall look for in future English productions now that we are going to have motor-roads of our own. Instruments, directly in front of the driver and seen through the upper sector of the wheel, are on the left a combination instrument incorporating an oil temperature gauge (very important), a petrol gauge and warning lights for oil pressure and dynamo charging. In the centre is a revolution indicator calibrated up to 6,000 r.p.m., a large green sector between approximately 2,500 r.p.m. and 5,000 r.p.m. indicating the best driving range while a red sector from 5,000–5,500 r.p.m. condones a speed which must not be held for more than a few minutes. To the right is the speedometer with total mileage and trip indicators. Under the dashboard is an inappropriate pull-and-twist umbrella-type handbrake lever which I never mastered, a retrograde step from the older type which was a horizontal pull-on lever with a ratchet, this is situated on the left (for LHD). In the centre of the under-dash is a nicely finished petrol tap control with three positions, on, off and reserve. The tank holds 11½ gallons.

Both the engine compartment and luggage compartment lids are released from the inside of the car by cable controls. The luggage room under the bonnet is so shallow that only small articles can be stowed inside, but the backrest of the rear seat folds down and is suitably backed to stow quite large cases; straps are provided to hold the luggage in place during hard driving. When luggage is not being carried the space in the tonneau is sufficient for two large people on short journeys or two small people on long journeys, but really the

A mouth-watering sight for many an enthusiast: Carrera engines awaiting the call to duty

Engine assembly is effected by a track system which carries the unit from fitter to fitter. The completely individual method formerly adopted has been discontinued

A pause amid beautiful country near Bad Aussee. As can be seen a new road is under construction

Porsche is best regarded as a high speed touring car for two people with lots of baggage space. Unladen, 59 per cent of the weight of the car is on the back wheels. With two people on board and some luggage in the front compartment, plus a full tank, the weight distribution approaches 50/50 but as soon as the tonneau is stacked up with heavy cases the main weight moves rear-ward again. This disadvantage is not over-apparent in use.

The first leg of my journey to Vienna was along the Autobahn to Salzburg and on this 225-mile stretch I was able to calibrate the speedometer and gain some idea of the maximum speed. My first impression was of the excellent directional stability. It was quite possible to operate the stopwatch and steer with one hand at the maximum velocity of 107 m.p.h., an indicated 180 k.p.h. on the speedometer, which had a 4 per cent optimism at that speed. This was attained over the kilometre, covered in 20·9 seconds. More important than the maximum was the ability of the car to accelerate from 35 to 75 m.p.h. in 10 seconds, using third gear and to cruise at an easy 90 or 95 m.p.h. on a whiff of throttle with 100 m.p.h. always available, even on gradients and against strong head winds; a performance not feasible with the ordinary 1600 model.

Mention of the gearbox must not be forgotten, the Porsche split-ring synchromesh enables changes to be made as quickly as the hand could move. Only between first and second could snatch changes produce any noise and this was achieved only twice. The reduced movement of the gearchange lever, which is also a little thinner than the previous type, has made the change a little more stiff than of old when there was a greater mechanical advantage and it could literally be thrown from one gear to another.

A night stop in Munich enabled me to complete and airmail copy and by 11.30 a.m. I had found my way onto the undulating Munich-Salzburg autobahn. The wet surface enabled me to discover that oversteer has been eliminated at touring speeds and I was soon confidently drifting the little car round the rather sharp swerves that are a feature of this section of autobahn. The undulations were something of a temptation, too; on one downhill stretch I was startled to see 6,000 r.p.m. and 200 k.p.h. come up! I gently eased off.

Once through Salzburg and into Austria, the road to Linz becomes narrow, long-winded and tiresome—or it would be in a less virile motor car. The surface is smooth but very wavy, there is a steep camber and all of the corners are pavé. As the weather consisted of a heavy downpour this promised to be a good test of the stability of the Porsche. Although the road abounded with lorries—not to mention the Sheik of Kuwait and his retinue in sheik-size Cadillacs, off to visit Vienna—the lively acceleration in second and third enabled all of these hazards to be dealt with in comfort and it was possible to make experiments in tail-end breakaway on the paved corners. After starting rather gingerly I found that the Michelin X tyres enabled me to use speeds that I would have employed in the dry and I must admit that I never did get the back-end really swinging. During all this the screen-wipers never faltered and no trace of rain came through the joints of the hardtop.

Dusk found me in Vienna and the Porsche became a town car for a few days while I explored the delights of this beautiful city. In this role it was just as able as at high speed on the Autobahn, the only disadvantages being the difficulty in getting into and out of its 51 inches of height gracefully, and the rather vulnerable side panels which protrude further than one imagines.

Leaving Vienna towards Weiner-Neustadt the road is wide and straight, through open country, and a strong cross-wind revealed a tendency for the car to wander at speeds of more than 80 m.p.h., but there was nothing vicious about this. Towards Bruck the road became winding and mountainous and the Porsche really came into its own. Using second gear with its 55 m.p.h. maximum, the tremendous torque unstuck the tail to just the amount desired and the joy of twitching the car right and left through hairpins became insidious. The brakes, two leading shoe front and single cylinder rear, of Teves manufacture, were fully up to their job and at no time was there any suggestion of fade.

The Austrians are not unaware of the origins of the Porsche and one gets many a smile and a wave. This was most apparent in Bad Aussee where, when I parked nearby, the policeman on point duty left his post and found me a hotel! From Bad Aussee it was a gentle day's run back to Stuttgart and I was able to check that hard driving had in no way impaired the performance of the car by repeating my tests on the Autobahn.

Summing up, my own view is that the appeal of the Porsche is first of all, to the intellect, by reason of its conception. By the combination of good shape and a high-torque engine pulling a high gear a car has been produced which runs effortlessly at high speed with a low fuel consumption—over the whole of the test it was 31 m.p.g.—and a minimum of wear and tear on the working parts. In practice careful development has eliminated most of the faults endemic to the rear-engined layout and resulted in a car as satisfactory to use as it is to contemplate. I was indeed sorry to hand over the Super to its rightful owner.

For my own purpose, that of long distance, high-speed travel with economy this car approaches the ideal. If these features were not enough, the beautiful construction and finish alone would justify ownership.

Performance. Porsche type 356A 1600 Super Hardtop.

Maximum speed		107 m.p.h. (172·5 k.p.h.)
Mean time over flying kilometre		20·8 secs.
Fuel consumption throughout test		31·8 m.p.g.
Acceleration:	0 – 50	7·8 secs.
	60	11·9 secs.
	70	16·3 secs.
	80	21 secs.
	100	34·6 secs.
Maxima in gears:	1st	30 m.p.h.
	2nd	53 m.p.h.
	3rd	80 m.p.h.

The above speeds with B type gears, using maximum of 5,500 r.p.m.

Weight and dimensions (Makers' figures):

Length and width	12 ft. 11¾ in. × 5 ft. 5½ in.
Height	51·5 in.
Wheelbase	6 ft. 10¾ in.
Track	51·4 in. front; 50·1 in. rear
Weight (dry)	16 cwt. 16 lbs.
Fuel capacity	11½ galls. including one reserve

CORVETTE *OR* PORSCHE

YOU'VE REALLY STUCK YOUR FOOT IN IT NOW." "How's that?" I asked. "It can't be done. You can't compare a Corvette with a Porsche. How unlike can two cars be?"

Briefly that was the feeling among some of the MT staff members when we decided to compare these two sportscars. On the surface they would seem to defy comparison. But dig a little and see how much alike they really are.

Both are in the $4000 price class. The Porsche Convertible D (replaces the Speedster) is slightly under—$3745 delivered on the West Coast. Our 250-hp soft-top Corvette rolls out in Los Angeles for $4375 including heater and four-speed gearbox.

Both are priced in the $4000 class. One is Europe's best sportscar in this category; the other America's best — and only — sportscar. How do they compare in handling, ride, performance?

by Wayne Thoms

Cost of fuel injection, $484, has not been included. (Although our test car carried an injection system, it does not materially affect overall performance. See "Sam Hanks Tests Four Corvettes," MT, March 1958.)

The obvious difference in the cars is power. No one denies that the Corvette has pure brute force available—power which makes the Porsche's 70-hp standard engine seem puny. But that force has to be transmitted to the ground, converted into forward motion, stopped, turned, controlled — sometimes by persons who don't fully realize the potential dangers involved. The result is that for all practical purposes a lot of that horsepower becomes excess—an unusable excess. We're not knocking the Corvette. It's an exciting handful of performance which is not duplicated for the money, even from countries where labor is considerably cheaper than in the U.S.

Let's see how the two cars stack up, point by point, in areas where they are comparable.

How well are they put together?

We enter two schools of body building—steel vs. fiberglass. If you have definite feelings against fiberglass, consider revising

Corvette Convertible

your views. Corvette's 'glass work is smooth and every bit as functional as steel. During minor prangs it will come off unscathed, absorbing amounts of energy which would dent steel panels. Our only objection is to a certain amount of flexing around door jambs which means a few creaks and groans, apparently congenital in fiberglass construction. Panels match properly, doors close in a satisfying fashion; it is a carefully constructed automobile.

The Porsche is a masterpiece of precision fitting and close tolerances in its body construction. The wonder is that any coachbuilder can work so accurately. There aren't many cars in the world that are turned out free from visual defects, but the Porsche approaches perfection as nearly as can be.

After squeezing inside, what?

They're both sportscars and require a technique for entry and exit. It is really no problem and is, in truth, not as difficult as exiting from the rear door of some domestic '59s parked alongside a curb.

Visibility in both is perfect with tops down, limited in the rear quarter areas with tops erected. Designers of both cars kept the driver in mind when vital instruments were installed. Speedo, tach and the rest of the gauge layouts are clearly visible through the wheel.

Seating is a critical factor in sportscars. The consensus was that Porsche's well-upholstered, fully-reclining bucket seats are almost too good. They offer excellent support but tend to be overly soft, especially as compared to seating in previous year models. Individual seats in the Corvette are comfortable but could use added support under the knees. Both cars would benefit from adjustable steering columns. To obtain arms-out seating in the Corvette, for example, the seat must be run so far back that it is nearly impossible to fully depress the clutch.

How easily do they start?

Both engines turn over easily, starting quickly hot or cold. The Porsche has no choke, but a husky accelerator pump shoots big charges of raw gas through the carbs, giving a rich choke

Porsche Convertible D

effect. Porsche carburetor heating is different. A pair of thermostatically controlled tubes blow hot air directly on the carburetors as the engine warms up.

How are they for city driving?

Both cars are good traffic machines requiring different driving techniques. We must give a slight edge to the Porsche here because quicker, lighter steering makes moving through tight traffic less of a chore. We found that most of the Porsche's city work was in second and third gear in order to avoid the overdrive fourth and to keep the revs in the "happy zone" above 2500 rpm. Torque from the Corvette is so fierce that the engine can loaf along in fourth, say at 20 mph, and pull away smoothly, although third is a more satisfactory traffic gear. Pushing the Corvette through town, the sensible driver will rarely exceed 2500 rpm.

How about open-country driving and high-speed handling?

Being forced to choose one of these cars in which to make a cross-country trip would be difficult. Both of them are capable of speeds far in excess of any legal speed limit. The Porsche will cruise all day long at 90 mph—comfortably; so will the Corvette—even faster. And make no mistake. This Corvette will handle. It corners flat and can be jockeyed through a hot turn with surprising ease.

Firmly suspended, as good handling sportscars should be, these two cars vary considerably in riding qualities. The Corvette rides harshly with a substantial amount of pitch and chop on rough roads. The same routes are gobbled up by the Porsche's four-wheel-independent suspension with a minimum amount of shock transmitted to driver and passenger.

Match the two cars on a tight mountain road where the Corvette's torque and acceleration can't be utilized and you'll probably get there quicker in the Porsche. It just hangs on better in the turns. If this mountain road should be downhill, the Porsche's brakes will outlast the Corvette's. The Germans have installed brakes that stop in a hurry and refuse to fade. Corvette's standard binders are more than adequate for normal use but for competition or extremely hard use, the optional

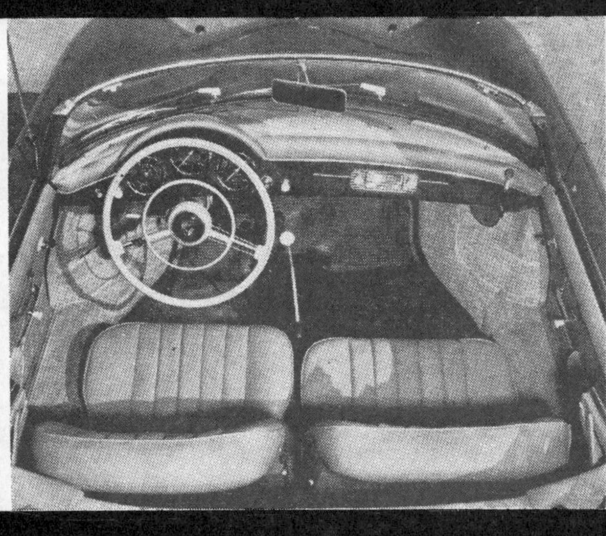

Acceleration

	Corvette	Porsche
0-60	7.8 secs.	15.2 secs.
Quarter-mile	15.7 & 90 mph	19.9 & 67.5 mph
30-50	4.2	5.9
45-60	3.2	6.1
50-80	6.8	19.6

Top Speed

(Test cars, estimated)	120 mph	105 mph

Handling

(Comparative times around 3.3-mile Riverside Raceway road course)

2 min. 32 secs.	2 min. 47 secs.
Avg. 78.5 mph	Avg. 71 mph

Fuel Consumption

Stop-and-Go Driving	14.3 mpg	24.5 mpg
Highway Driving	14.9	35.0
Overall Average	14.6	29.7

(Fuel Used: Mobilgas Special)

Cerametalix lining is a must. Because it works best when hot, it is not recommended for idling around the city.

Both cars are blessed with four-speed, all-synchro gearboxes. Porsche takes justifiable pride in theirs but we prefer the Corvette's. It's smoother, faster and has a shorter throw between gears—qualities which rank it with the best in the world.

How about fresh air, heating and defrosting?

Here is an area where Detroit engineers, attuned to the luxury requirements of their customers, have an edge on overseas sportscar designers. Porsche has a perfectly good hot air heating and defrosting system, better than most other sportscars. The Corvette has a flexible system of heating, ventilating and defrosting which will warm up sub-zero days or take the edge off a nippy Southern California night with equal ease. It has been designed with passenger comfort in mind rather than installed as something which works but which no true enthusiast will be using anyway.

Did someone mention fuel economy?

First of all, sportscars shouldn't be purchased for economy. The nature of their use—fast acceleration, high speeds, use of intermediate gears—precludes good mileage figures. The Porsche is an economical exception with open-road, fast cruising figures of 35 mpg and mileage in congested areas averaging 24.5 mpg. Combining the Corvette's city and open-road fuel consumption gave us 14.6 mpg—really not too bad for 283 cubic inches constantly begging to be opened up.

Where do I put the suitcases?

There is luggage space enough for two persons in both cars. The Porsche stows it behind the front seats, occupying the occasional rear seat. A conventional trunk in the Corvette will take about the same amount of material as the Porsche. There is a very limited amount of space under the Porsche front hood.

How about service?

The Corvette's obvious advantage is parts and service from thousands of Chevy dealers across the country. Porsche service, often combined with Volkswagen, is fairly good but the dealer distribution will never approach Chevrolet's. Corvette's high-

performance V8 gets expensive to maintain when the owner insists upon the ultimate in performance. On the other hand, the specialized nature of Porsche maintenance has kept repair prices high. It adds up to the fact that sportscars are luxury items with upkeep prices to match.

Which one is the best buy?

Depends on what you want in a sportscar. Both have a lot to offer. If getting a lot of performance from a precision-built, small-displacement engine is intriguing, then the Porsche is the answer. If you like the idea of having one of the world's fastest accelerating sportscars, then pick the Corvette.

MT staff members became extremely partisan—on both sides of the fence. Feelings were evenly divided except for one nameless male who refused to choose, insisting that he would be happy only with both cars.

The truth is that both are excellent buys. They're sturdy, reliable, comfortable and above all, fun to drive. What more can you ask of a sportscar? **/MT**

CORVETTE

ENGINE: Ohv V8 with rockers. Bore 3.88 in. Stroke 3.0 in. Stroke/bore ratio .78:1. Compression ratio 9.5:1. Displacement 283 cu. in. 1 4-bbl. carburetor. Dual exhaust. Advertised bhp 250 @ 5000 rpm. Bhp per cu. in. .88. Piston speed @ max. bhp 2500 ft. per min. Max. torque 305 lbs.-ft. @ 3800 rpm.

TRANSMISSION: Manual shift, 4-speed all-synchromesh. Ratios 2.20:1, 1.66:1, 1.31:1, 1.00:1.

CHASSIS: Welded box section frame with I-beam X-member. Front suspension—Independent ball joint, with long and short control arms, coil springs and tubular shock absorbers. Rear—Solid axle, with outrigger-mounted semi-elliptic leaf springs and tubular shock absorbers. Axle torque taken by radius rods. 6.70 x 15 tires. Steering—Saginaw semi-reversible worm and ball bearing, 3.7 turns lock-to-lock, ratio 21.0:1. Rear axle—conventional, ratio 3.70:1.

DIMENSIONS: Wheelbase 102 in., overall length 177.2, overall height 51.6, overall width 72.8, front tread 57, rear tread 59, rear overhang 42.4.

PRICE: Factory-suggested retail price of test car equipped with heater and four-speed gearbox—delivered Los Angeles, $4375 plus taxes.

PORSCHE

ENGINE: 4-cylinder opposed, air-cooled, ohv with rockers. Bore 3.25 in. Stroke 2.91 in. Stroke/bore ratio .9:1. Compression ratio 7.5:1. Displacement 96.5 cu. in. (1588cc). Advertised bhp 70 @ 4500 rpm. Bhp per cu. in. .73. Piston speed @ max. bhp 2180 ft. per min. Max. torque 81.2 lbs.-ft. @ 2800 rpm.

TRANSMISSION: Manual shift, 4-speed all-synchromesh. Ratios 3.09:1, 1.76:1, 1.22:1, 0.85:1.

CHASSIS: Pressed steel welded in box section, unit body-frame construction. Front suspension—Two transverse torsion bars and trailing arms, anti-roll bar, tubular shocks. Rear—Swing axle, transverse torsion bars and trailing arms, tubular shocks. 5.60 x 15 tires. Steering—ZF worm gear with hydraulic damper, 2¼ turns lock-to-lock, ratio 16.0:1. Standard rear-end gears 4.43:1.

DIMENSIONS: Wheelbase 82.7 in., overall length 155.8, overall height 51.5, overall width 65.6, front tread 51.4, rear tread 50.1.

PRICE: Suggested retail price of test car equipped with heater (standard) and four-speed gearbox (standard)—delivered Los Angeles, $3745, plus taxes.

PHOTOS BY BOB D'OLIVO

CAREERING ABOUT IN A

THE CARRERA IS "COMFORTABLE, FAST, WELL-BRAKED AND GREAT FUN"

IT'S an extremely stable, fast, sports car. It's a touring car with vast comfort in the seats. It's both easy to use in any kind of traffic and particularly annoying to get going in the morning. No, it's not three or four cars, but one Porsche Carrera De Luxe 1600GS.

"My" Carrera test car from the Stuttgart factory was all these things, occasionally simultaneously. As a De Luxe it was the "tame" version but the car wasn't completely standard in this guise. In addition to serving journalists, the car is used as personal transportation by Huschke von Hanstein, the Porsche race boss. He has made some changes in it.

As extras the car features a metal sun roof, stone guards on the headlights and a head rest on the passenger's side. This was on the right incidentally, as the car is based in Germany. These items added much to the pleasure but did little about the performance.

Two factors that did affect performance were the Michelin X tyres and the out-size fuel tank. The tyres made quite a bit of difference in the handling of the car as you approached the limits. They also seemed to increase a waltz motion in the tail when caught by high cross-winds on the German *autobahnen*. A pressure increase helped somewhat.

The fuel tank, too, made a difference in handling, as well as in acceleration runs. The De Luxe Carrera is fitted with an 11½-gallon tank as a rule. Apparently wanting greater range, Hanstein had this car equipped with the GT Carrera tank of 17½ gallons.

Apart from increasing the range, the full tank undoubtedly contributed to our rather disappointing acceleration figures. It had a noticeable effect on cornering but the amount would be almost impossible to pin down.

If this were a sports-race test, some method of equating these factors would be necessary. But I decided to handle this car in exactly the manner prescribed by Porsche. It is not meant to be a racing car—they have Spyders for that. Rather it is a fast tourer—particularly in the heavier De Luxe version—and supposedly capable of crawling through traffic with no ill-effects on car, driver, or traffic.

A racing car test would be invalid on the roads in any case, and there is plenty of opportunity to appraise a tuned Carrera on any Continental track, so we can leave such matters aside.

We will take Porsche at their word and see what the Carrera can offer the average driver—with money, of course—as transportation around town and an occasional highway jaunt.

This isn't a car on which to generalize but we can credit it with good marks for its purpose, on a broad front, before delving into the highlights and the annoyances that appeared while we enjoyed the car. To my amazement, despite Porsche claims, the car was extremely docile in traffic.

On one occasion it crept through a holiday throng without a murmur and ticked happily all the while. But then I found a stretch of open road ahead and stepped down hard—only to find myself waiting. I had discovered the first drawback to crawling in a Carrera.

Non-stock items showing in the front view include the headlight stone guards, the sliding roof panel and the head-rest on the co-driver's side. The car doubles as race boss von Hanstein's private transport and has a few personal items

Maximum torque on this car doesn't appear until 5,000 r.p.m. and you might just as well forget all figures much below 3,700 if you want to move out smartly. Below that the car takes its own time until the needle hits the green field of the tachometer, starting at 4,000.

In speed terms, the car lacks that push in the small of the back that you might expect, when below 60 m.p.h. in third gear, as an example. You have to change-down to move.

It would be interesting to count the times you change gear in a Carrera for a given town stretch. I have an idea it would be more often that necessary—even when keeping

PORSCHE

by

SLONIGER

ON TEST

PORSCHE CARRERA 1600GS

the revolutions up. The Porsche-designed synchronized gearbox is too renowned for me to labour the point. The lever is right where you want it, always, and the throws from gear to gear are short and crisp.

In another respect the driving position was not entirely to my liking. Fairly long movements on the clutch and brake pedals mean that a man of average height must sit more forward than he would like in relation to the steering wheel.

The pedals themselves are perfectly placed in relation to one another and heel-toeing is like gear-changing. You do it just for fun.

The steering feels very precise and is naturally fairly direct at 2¾ turns from lock to lock. With the large tank full of fuel it tends to be slightly heavy at low speeds, however.

I know it doesn't matter to the performance, but I would like to see a steel and wood steering wheel in a car of this sort. The plastic is nice but somehow out of keeping.

Interior finish is right up to the best standards, with good use of leather for doors and seats. For the latter it is combined with cord on the Reutter models. This prevents sliding, in conjunction with an ideal shape.

The seats hold you in place laterally and provide just the right support for my taste. The backs recline and the passenger can take a very pleasant nap under way. An optional head rest on the Carrera made this even easier.

In the back, the occasional bench provides enough room for adults on short journeys but little more. It, too, is well-padded leather, but leg room is hardly extensive.

When a Carrera carries the GT tank, as this one did, the space behind the seats is about the only place for luggage. There is almost more room in the glove compartment than in the nose, since the spare and tank pretty well fill things.

A Porsche dashboard is plain, painted metal and nothing is added for the Carrera. The top is padded and glare-free.

SPECIFICATIONS

PERFORMANCE

Through the gears:

0–30	...	...	4.4 sec.
0–45	...	...	8.1 ,,
0–60	...	...	12.0 ,,
30–60	...	...	8.6 ,,
60–100	...	...	25.3 ,,

Maximum speeds: top, 115.3 at 6,500 r.p.m.; third, 84; second, 57; first, 33. Speedometer error, 8.8 per cent. Fuel consumption: Main roads, 22.7 m.p.g.; speed and acceleration testing, 19.8 m.p.g.; mixed city and country, 19.1 m.p.g.; overall average for 547 test miles, 20.5 m.p.g. (Imp.).

ENGINE

Four-cylinder, air-cooled, horizontally-opposed, twin overhead camshafts on each bank. Bore: 87.5 mm. Stroke: 66 mm. Capacity: 1,587.5 c.c. Compression ratio: 9.5 : 1. Two twin-choke downdraught Solex 40 PJJ-4 carburetters. Power Output: 105 DIN h.p. at 6,500 r.p.m. Torque: 88.9 ft./lb. at 5,000 r.p.m.

TRANSMISSION

Four-speed, fully Porsche synchronized, floor control. Ratios: 1st, 11 : 34; 2nd, 16 : 31; 3rd, 20 : 27; 4th, 25 : 24.

SUSPENSION

Front: Two longitudinal trailing arms, two transverse square torsion bars, anti-roll bar. Rear: Swinging half-axles, radius arms, one round torsion bar on each side. Hydraulic telescopic Koni dampers all round.

STEERING

ZF worm with divided tie-rod; steering damper. Ratio: 1 : 16. Turns, lock to lock, 2¾. Turning circle: 36 ft.

BRAKES

Hydraulic with 11-in. drums. Two leading shoes at front, leading and trailing at the rear. Total area: 122 sq. in.

DIMENSIONS

Wheelbase: 6 ft. 10½ in. Track, front: 4 ft. 3⅜ in.; rear, 4 ft. 2 in. Length: 12 ft. 11¾ in. Width: 5 ft. 5½ in. Height: 4 ft. 3¼ in. Ground clearance: 6⅜ in. Empty weight: 18 cwt. 69 lb. Tyres: 165 × 15 Michelin X (5.90 × 15).

CAPACITIES

Fuel tank (test car carried enlarged GT tank): 17.5 gallons (Imp.). Crankcase: 14 pints.

PRICE

£3,061, including purchase tax.

Just about room for a toothbrush. Although the car is a de luxe model, it carries the G.T. fuel tank of 80 litres (17.6 Imperial)

Little room left over to work on a Carrera engine in place. Spark plug changes require the agility of an asbestos octopus

The view most people get of the Carrera. Tip-offs to its hidden power include the double air intake grille's in the engine lid, the free exhausts (normals and Supers have the pipes incorporated in the bumper overriders) and the word Carrera, of course

Instrumentation was both good and bad in the Carrera. The rev.-counter occupies the centre of three dials, right in front of the driver. It is flanked on one side by a speedometer that includes trip counter and a fair degree of optimism. On the other side the fuel gauge and oil-temperature indicator share a dial. Oil pressure and generator have to be satisfied with lights, a mistake to my thinking in a car of this class and price.

An umbrella-type grip under the dash works the hand brake. It was very effective in holding the car, yet it just doesn't seem as handy as a fly-off floor type.

As for the heater—I can't report one way or the other. The car has a petrol model since hot air was insufficient, but ours wasn't working.

Starting a Carrera is not accomplished from one second to the next. The starter switch is in the key unit and it turns over readily, but the car won't respond.

Five to ten minutes were normally required to bring the engine to life in the morning and even warm starts take some doing. You first let the electric pump stop clicking, then tramp on the throttle pedal two or three times. With the pedal fully down, you then let it turn over. When the engine catches, it idles smoothly at 1,000 r.p.m., more or less.

The lack of acceleration at low revolutions has been covered. This lack was responsible in part for our poor acceleration runs. Poor, that is, for a Carrera. The only way to move the car forward quickly is to run the engine up to 5,000 r.p.m. and slip the clutch. This is fine for measurements but tends to produce a burned boot smell before long.

In fairness to Porsche, I want to state that the test car is apparently not one of their better examples. Even Porsche admits that this particular car is deficient, when compared to others of the series. This only makes you wonder the more that they offer it for tests.

During top speed runs the lack was again apparent. While the book on a Carrera De Luxe speaks of a possible 7,200 r.p.m. for short bursts, the test vehicle wouldn't go over 6,500, regardless of the distance. The speedometer would read 125 m.p.h. but the true top speed was only 115.3.

Porsche insists, incidentally, that the car is running with the standard rear axle ratios, although the behaviour led me to suspect that Hanstein had fitted others for some reason.

With the motor in full cry behind you conversation is well nigh impossible. So is thought. This was hard to understand on the De Luxe model, although they might want to save the weight of soundproofing in the GT.

At the same time, I don't want to leave the impression that this car wouldn't move. With only 1,600 c.c., a top speed of 115 m.p.h. is certainly worth remembering. A steady cruising range above a true 100 m.p.h. is easy. As a fast touring car—the Porsche claim—the car has plenty of potential.

Naturally enough, braking is an important matter with a car this fast—even when it hugs the road like a Porsche. This was another realm where the Carrera earned full credit.

To test the stopping power I ran the car up to 60 m.p.h. six times and then brought it to a stop as rapidly as possible without locking the wheels. These runs were made as quickly as possible after one another and followed immediately by two stops from 75 m.p.h. Most machinery would at least show fade when treated this way but the Porsche sailed through.

On a third run from 75—added out of curiosity—there was a very slight spongy feeling but it disappeared before it could be measured in terms of pedal travel.

The GT Carrera, incidentally, uses the larger Spyder drums in the front. In addition, Porsche recently raced a special car with their own form of disc brakes in front, They pay a good deal of attention to halting in Stuttgart.

Weight distribution in the Porsche is 42/58 per cent front and rear and some oversteer is to be expected. It wasn't really noticeable in the test car until close to the limit. With the X tyres this limit is something you approach very warily.

In the area of handling, there is little to add to what is often said about Porsches. Considering the Michelin tyres and the large fuel tank, my observations would be too specialized to apply to a normal Carrera De Luxe.

On the final night, one further criticism arose. The lights are not at all adequate for a car of this speed capability. The high beams barely suffice for 100 m.p.h. and the dipped lights are about as much use as a miner's helmet. The horn could be louder as well.

To sum up, a most pleasant week: the car is truly a fast tourer. It is comfortable, fast, well-braked and great fun—perhaps the most important single point. It is also noisy and a problem to start but the bad points are lost amongst the good.

It is not a racing car—an opinion in which Porsche concurs—but the sort of machine any driver with a love of motoring would enjoy. ★

Driver's eye view of the instruments. The tachometer is where it belongs, in the middle, flanked on the right by a speedometer in kilometres per hour. A daily mileage count is included. Oil temperature (top) and fuel gauge fill the left dial, with warning lights for generator and oil pressure. The two pull switches above the rev.-counter on either side each control a half of the twin ignition. Lights and choke are the large knobs below them

Interior with the exceptionally fine adjustable seats. No frills but everything needed is right in front of the driver

Porsche A New Super 90

ANOTHER notable German car manufacturer to rely on evolution rather than revolution for the coming year is Porsche. There are no major changes in basic design, but an entirely new model, the Super 90,, is announced.

Except for the famous RS and RSK sports racing cars, there are four basic styles of body—the coupé, the roadster replacing the former convertible, the hardtop which has a "notched back" bodyline, and the drop head coupé.

Into these cars three variations of engine may be installed, all of 1,582 c.c. capacity. These are the 60 b.h.p. so-called "ladies' engine," the 75 b.h.p. Super and the new Super 90, developing 90 b.h.p. at 5,500 r.p.m., running at a compression ratio of 9 to 1. The latter differs from the Super in having slightly larger induction pipes and inlet-valves, higher valve lift and a different exhaust.

Rear suspension has been improved by the addition of an auxiliary spring between each swinging half-axle and the gear-box casing, similar in principle to that of the new Mercedes sixes.

Externally, a restyled front end is the most notable feature. The wingline has been raised appreciably at the front, and the head lamp lenses are now set higher and given less incline. The bumper is higher and more massive overriders have been added. New standard feature on the 1960 models is a rear window demister. Brake drums now have 72 light alloy axial fins for better cooling.

The gear lever has been cranked backwards to bring the knob more naturally to the driver's hand, and the already excellent synchromesh for all forward speeds has been improved to make it impossible to override the mechanism.

The occasional rear seat, hitherto in one piece, is now divided into two separate seats, the deeply curved backrests of which may be folded forward individually, so that additional luggage may be carried in the rear, even when one rear seat is occupied.

The four-o.h.c. model Carrera will continue to be built to special order.

Left: Raised wing line to match the higher mounting of the head lamps is new, as are individual miniature seats at the rear

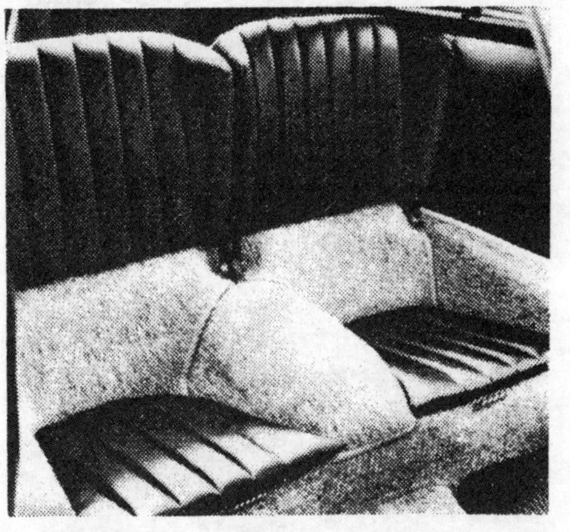

CONTINUED FROM PAGE 19

Porsche Carrera

7500 rpm red-lined. The mph counter read up to an optimistic 180 mph.

To test the car I drove it on the magnificent highways round Pound Ridge, New York and also round Bob Said's own small testing track. Along the newly finished New York State throughway, one of America's finest highways, I was unable to rid myself of all the frustrations of driving a sports car in the US and drove at a splendid 60 mph to avoid the police chasing me. However, I was immediately conscious of driving a car with real performance but in almost complete silence and without that violence which is usually associated with 120 mph cars. With the hood up and the windows closed the silence of the car could be compared with that of the more expensive luxury American Detroit productions. Steering was superlative, quick, light and devoid of play. As I drove through the twisty but well surfaced roads through Pound Ridge I had the impression of complete stability at all speeds, although I did take some time getting used to the car on the sharper bends. As it was impossible to attempt any fast runs on the main highways or along the strictly police-controlled multilane parkways, I took the car several miles out of Pound Ridge, where there were some excellent straights and a little speeding could be done without running over the local judge's toes.

At speeds up to 90 mph the comfort was equal to an American car without that rubbery feeling. Over that speed the suspension became a little harsher, but it was difficult to believe that we were travelling at 100 mph, again because of the lack of noise and the smooth ride. The brakes are in keeping with the other excellent features of the Carrera, they are the same type that were originally fitted on the Liege-Rome-Liege rally winners, employing the two leading shoe system with a large bimetal drum. Braking at speeds above 100 mph is as good as at 10 mph—slowing the car down smoothly yet rapidly without ever locking the wheels or pitching the driver out of the car.

The gearbox is a dream, Porsche's patent synchromesh nearly changes gear itself going up whilst racing down changes can be made by the simplest crash box technique. The Carrera lends itself easily to drifting techniques but requires some practice for anyone new to the car, due, of course, to the rear engine. Once the technique is mastered, however, the Porsche Carrera quickly becomes a remarkably agile high performance car. Several speed runs were made, and although conditions were unfavourable to high speeds 121 mph was reached on one of the runs.

The car that I drove was fitted with twin choke Solex carburetters and had a definite two stage acceleration effect, there being good initial acceleration and another sudden surge at the 5000 rpm range, which I believe to be a particularly useful asset.

PORSCHE
FOR 1960

FRONT AND REAR EXTERNAL DIFFERENCES IN '60 PORSCHE, LEFT, ARE QUICKLY APPARENT. BUMPERS AND HEADLIGHTS ARE RAISED.

drivereport: Wayne Thoms

a few points closer to perfection

IN THE WONDERFUL WORLD of automobiles, money will buy almost anything—luxury, ostentation, speed, handling, bigness (or smallness), economy or its lack. There is only one element that has become increasingly difficult to buy—perfection. Not that any car is perfect; that would be asking too much because the choice of an automobile is a highly personal decision. However, there are a handful of cars today that approach perfection, blending many desirable elements into one vehicle that comes as close as is possible to filling its intended purpose.

We believe that the Porsche is one of these cars. Year after year its engineers have followed a pattern of slow, steady evolution. Refreshingly, the manufacturers have never made change an end in itself. This year's Porsche, with its minor sheet metal changes front and rear, nearly appears to contradict the plan. In fact, it does not. Whether or not you like the external styling changes—raised headlights and front fender line, extended front end with a shark-like nose, raised and restyled bumpers front and rear—is really not important. The changes were made for a purpose. Porsche designers felt that higher bumpers would offer greater protection from the American drivers who park by ear. (Actually, the new bumpers are still on the flimsy side and probably are no better or worse than last year's.)

Inside, the changes are both functional and significant. Replacing the single-purpose turn indicator is a flat lever which is turn indicator, high-low beam selector and headlight flasher. Steering wheel is dished while the horn ring has been removed in favor of the old-fashioned center button. The most important single change, which more than compensates the styling purists who feel that traditional Porsche lines have been aborted, is in the shift lever and linkage. The lever is sturdier and slightly shorter, while the throw between gears is shorter and considerably easier. We understand that the entire linkage has been redesigned more along the lines of the Volkswagen which always has shifted more easily than the Porsche. Underneath, the ever-adequate brakes are now more so with the addition of cooling fins.

Our test car from Competition Motors, a Roadster (last year it was called the Convertible D), was equipped with the normal engine, 70 hp at 4500 rpm. At $3650, Los Angeles p.o.e., it is the lowest priced Porsche in the line but is representative of the entire series. The Super engine with 18 more horses adds to acceleration and top speed, but handling is identical. (Very shortly we will see the new Super 90, about 105 hp and with a transverse leaf spring below the swing axles to aid high-speed cornering.)

Describing the feeling of security that a Porsche imparts to the driver is not easy; it really must be experienced. Perhaps one reason for this safe sensation is the way driver and passenger sit dead-center in the unitized body-chassis. Too, the individual semi-bucket seats provide back and thigh support which keeps the driver in a comfortable, natural position behind the wheel.

Porsche acceleration with the normal engine is not startling. Inasmuch as there is no difference in car weight, horsepower or gear ratios for this year, there will be no difference in performance. Last year's Convertible D test showed:

0-45 mph	8.9 secs.
0-60	15.2
¼-mile	19.9 and 67.5 mph

But figures don't tell the whole story. The Porsche just feels absolutely efficient as it whisks through traffic or rolls along the highway at an easy 80 mph with an honest 100 potential. And the knowledge that a more reasonable cruising speed, say 65, is giving 35 mpg is reassuring. It eats up twisty mountain roads with no brake fade and goes around turns at speeds that leave other cars floundering for more roadway. (Porsche hasn't been plagued with that skittish rear for some time.) Rough terrain is soaked up in the Porsche torsion bars in a way that is uncanny for a car with only an 82.7-in. wheelbase. Steering is light and precise with a ratio that is quick but not so sudden as to require difficult micrometer movements of the wheel in fast bends.

Apparent to the most casual examiner is the precision of Porsche's coachwork. Roadster bodies are built by Drauz with coupes and cabriolets assembled by other coachbuilders. The standards of assembly must be among the highest in the world. On many cars tolerances often build up at final assembly so that doors, for example, have huge gaps where no gaps should be. Not so on the Porsche. Everything fits and works smoothly.

We have always enjoyed reporting on the Porsche because it needs no apologies. It does all the things its designers intended and does them so well that it sets itself apart among sportscars of the world.

GEAR LEVER IS SHORTER STURDIER WHILE INTERIOR ARRANGEMENT IS THE SAME EXCEPT FOR NEW WHEEL, TURN INDICATOR LEVER.

Non-stock items visible in front view of our test car are headlight guards, roof panel and headrest on passenger's side. Car doubles as personal transportation for racing-team manager von Hanstein, who selected these extras.

Clues to the car's identity offered by a rear view are dual air-intake grilles, free-hanging exhaust pipes and the "Carrera" inscription.

PORSCHE CARRERA 1600 GS

If we told you that driving a 1.6-liter Porsche Carrera was great sport, it would be the truth. If we told you, further, that the twin cam coupe was a pain on more than one occasion, it would be equally the truth. Should this seem a paradox, so is the car!

The vehicle we picked up at the Stuttgart factory, was a "Deluxe"* 1600 GS—the tame version, in other words. While this is the firm's lend-out test horse, between tests it doubles as private transportation for Porsche race boss Huschke von Hanstein. It carries an extra or two for this job that affect its operation.

Such items as the sliding metal roof panel and head rest for the passenger did not influence performance. On the other hand, the car was fitted with Michelin X tires—the French jobs with the steel cords. The standard equipment is Continentals. As everybody must know by now, the X tires at speed do strange things to any car and particularly to a rear-engined model. You have better bite than with many another tire but when the limit is reached there is less warning. I should better say, no warning. Additionally, the tires seemed to increase tail-wag in high cross-winds when run at the factory recommended Michelin pressures.

A second non-stock item to affect the test car was the fuel tank. Normally a Deluxe Carrera carries 13-2/3 gallons in the nose. The GT models take on 21 gallons per refill. Hanstein apparently likes longer stretches between stops and his car has the larger tank. The greater weight had something to do with rather disappointing acceleration times—the tank was full when we started—and also made some difference in handling.

Such factors would color a sports-racer test but we had decided not to run one of those anyway. It is no secret that a well-prepared Carrera can leave most cars in its class behind. In fact, a German gentleman named Walter has a model that seemingly owns the class. But the Porsche factory contends that the Carrera—particularly a Deluxe model—is not primarily a race car. They suggest a Spyder for speed-happy people. Porsche insists that the Carrera is simply a fast touring car that can also be lugged through traffic at will.

Okay, so we took them at their word and investigated how the car stacks up for everyday use and the occasional

Sloniger sees room only for toothbrush with 21-gallon GT tank installed. Bet you could squeeze in a shaving kit too! Normal tank has 13½-gallon capacity.

Neat appearance of Carrera engine compartment is always impressive. As usual, it takes asbestos arms and 3½ hours to change sparkplugs, a fairly frequent chore.

Interior of Carrera is typically clean. Beautiful upholstery and fine adjustment of the backrest make seating a pleasure. Tester experienced slight trouble getting proper wheel and foot control adjustment.

Rear seat is inadequate for carrying adults for more than the shortest hops, as knee space is practically nil; trio of moppets would find ample room, however.

Driver's-eye view of the well laid-out instrument panel shows the centrally-located tach. Note that recommended rpm range is between 4000 and 7000!

VEHICLE: Porsche Carerra

TEST and TECH

MODEL: 1600 GS DeLuxe
PRICE: $5930 POE

PERFORMANCE
0-30 .... 4.4 sec.
0-45 .... 8.1 sec.
0-60 ....12.0 sec.
Standing ¼ mi.—N.A. @ mph
Top Speed—115.3 mph
Test Circle—N.A. mph
Speedo Error—8.8%
Av. Temp.—
Test MPG's—17.1 av.

WEIGHTS & MEASURES
Wheelbase—82.7 in.
Tread—fr.—51.4 in.
rr.,—50.1 in.
Height—51.5 in.
Width—65.6 in.
Length—155.8 in.
G. C.—6 in.
Curb Weight—2095 lbs.
Test Weight—2095 lbs.
Distribution—Front—43%

Test Weight—2095 lbs.
Distribution—Front—43%

REFERENCE FACTORS
BHP per Cu. In.—1.1
Weight/BHP Ratio—19.95
Piston Speed @ peak—
2806 ft. per. min.
Brake Area per lb.—.058

ENGINE
Type—4 cyl., 4 cycle, flat-opposed, (gohc) air-cooled
BHP—@ 6500 rpms
Torque—88.9 ft. lbs., @ 5000 rpm
Bore & Stroke—3.44 in. x 2.59 in.
Induction—2 dual-throat solex
Electrical—12v. Twin Distributor Ign.

CLUTCH
Type—Single Disc, Dry
Dia.—7 in.
Actuation—Mechanical
T.O.B.—Ball Bearing

TRANSMISSION
Type—Integral, Full-Synchro
Ratios 1st—3.09 3rd—1.35
2nd—2.21 4th—0.96

DIFFERENTIAL
Type—Spiral Bevel
Ratio—3.57
Drive Axles—Swing, Single-Joint

STEERING
Type—2F Worm
Ratio—16 to 1.
Turns L to L—2.75
Turn Circle—36 ft.

BRAKES
Type—Hydraulic Duplex/Simplex
Drum Dia.—11 in.
Lining Area—122 sq. in.
Test Results—Excellent

TIRES
Type—Tube
Size—5.90 x 15

CHASSIS
Frame—Integral Pan
Body—Steel, Welded
Front Sus.—I.F.S., Torsion Bar, Trailing Arm
Rear Sus.—Torsion Bar, Trailing Arm, Koni Tube Shocks

CAPACITIES
Crankcase—N.A. qts.
Cooling—N.A. qts.
Gas Tank—21.1 gal.*
*Spl. GT Tank

rapid highway jaunt. In other words, how would it do for the average owner?

In general the answer was: pretty well. Some annoyances developed, as we shall see, but the fun was certainly there in large measure. Amazingly enough, the Carrera showed absolutely no inclination to be balky in heavy traffic. It ticked along like its far-distant cousin the VW.

Then the road opens up ahead of you. You step down hard—and wait. Here is the rub to lugging a Carrera.

The green field on the tachometer begins at 4000 *rpm*. For purposes of go you might just as well ignore everything much below that figure. Maximum torque comes in at 5000, so there isn't much push below, say, 3700.

As less than 3000 revs the car definitely takes its time about moving up. Then the needle hits the green field and you feel the push in the small of your back. To put it in figures: don't drop much under 60 *mph* in third, for instance, and expect good acceleration without downshifting.

Of course, shifting is hardly a problem with the Porsche gear box. It is axiomatic by now that few cars have as precise a gate. The proof of the Porsche-designed synchro system is found in the number of builders around Europe who pay good money for the right to use it. The lever sits right were your hand expects it and the throws are short and crisp.

While on the subject of driving position, we might as well mention one space ratio that didn't suit. The clutch and brake pedals have fairly long throws. For a man of medium height the seat has to be at least two notches forward of full-rear to use the pedals properly. However, we would like the seat all the way back so we can drive with outstretched arms. So the wheel-pedal distance is too long for our taste. On the other side of the ledger, the pedals themselves could hardly be placed better in relation to each other. Heel-toeing is so éasy that you do it just for fun.

The steering proper is very direct. This is no car to play with, after all, with its true top speed of well above a hundred. The feel of steering is very much "part-of-the-car", although a full tank (the big one) does make it slightly heavy at low speeds. It's very small matter, incidentally, but I would want some sort of a sport steering wheel on aesthetic grounds. The plastic model just doesn't seem to match the nature of the beast.

As for the interior, it would be hard to fault anything, except maybe rear seat room and who expects that? The occasional bench back there will take a couple of people briefly. With the GT tank up front, the bench back will spend more time folded forward for luggage. I figure you can just about get one toothbrush—without case—in the nose after the 21 gallon tank and spare tire are fitted. But the car had Reutter cord and leather seats that must rank with the best. They aren't full buckets in a race sense but still support just the right spots. In addition the backs recline to various positions so the passenger can nap. The test car had a headrest on that side to complete the comfort.

Below a padded-top, the dashboard of a Carrera is plain, painted metal, but the instruments sit in the right places. The rev counter is right in the middle, flanked by the rather optimistic speedometer with trip indicator, and a dial with oil temperature and fuel gauges. For a car of this price it seems odd that amps and oil pressure are only covered by lights.

The hand brake has an umbrella handle, under the dash on the left. It proved very efficient in holding the car but a fly-off floor type would be more in keeping with such a machine. We can't report on the heater—a gas model—since (1) it was warm when we had the car, and (2) it didn't work anyway.

This brings us to a trip in the GS. Just the turn the key past "on" and you have the starter. Just? Here I came to one of the most annoying habits of this race-bred engine when put to everyday use. It would regularly refuse to start for five to ten minutes in the morning and was obdurate for lesser periods at any time. The proper procedure is to wait until the electric fuel pump stops clicking. Then hit the gas pedal a couple of times and hold it all the way down. Then keep cranking. It always caught eventually and idled smoothly around 1000 *rpm*.

We have already commented on the lack of push at low revs. This is partially responsible for the acceleration times. They were a disappointment, frankly. But to get moving in a hurry is to wind it up to 4500-5000 and slip the clutch By the end of our test, the car smelled like a burned boot.

It's only fair to say that this test job doesn't seem to be the best of the new 1.6 Carreras around. I've heard more than one comment on its below-par go and our times bear out the theory that it could be better. It is a mystery why the factory uses it for a test hack. Even Porsche admits it is a little on the minus side.

This applies to our top speed runs too. While the speedometer was quite willing to climb up to the advertised speed of 200 *kph* (125 *mph*) the watches weren't so charitable. Our average of 115.3 was just plain all it would drag out with a long run.

The book on this car speaks glibly of 7200 *rpm* for short bursts, yet we couldn't nudge the tack needle past 6500. Suspecting some rear end by-play, we asked Porsche about it, but they insist that the ratios are standard. Shifts during the acceleration runs were kept within the green field where the maximum torque is found, because that's where the average driver—average with a Carrera?—would run.

When the car is traveling at full cry you can hardly hear yourself think inside. On the GT model where weight is an important factor we could understand this, but some soundproofing wouldn't make that much difference in a Deluxe.

We don't want to give the impression that the car won't go. After all, 115 from 1600cc is certainly no small achievement. Measured against the production of racing Carreras, this seems under the mark. But for a fast tourer, as Porsche claims it to be, the achievement was excellent.

When a machine moves that fast—even one hugging the road like a Porsche—it is doubly important that it stop. Here the Carrera really earned the gold star. Our AS test consists of six hard stops from 60 *mph*, just short of locking the wheels. They follow one another just as fast as you can get back to 60—reasonably fast in this car. If you have any brakes left at this point, the editor says, "now try two from 75 *mph*." As a rule, road cars today will be pretty well without brakes before this. Then you see how long it takes them to recover at a steady 40 *mph*.

Frankly, I don't know how long it would take the Carrera brakes to recover. I never really got them to fade in the first place. The six stops didn't even faze the Carrera. After two from 75 a very critical foot might detect the slightest bit of sponge. Just for good measure I ran another from 75 immediately—still a little sponge, compared to normal, but excellent compared to many other cars. It was gone before we got back to cruising speed.

Incidentally the GT has larger Spyder front drums and the factory recently raced an experimental car with their own design of disc brakes up front. Stopping is hardly likely to be a Porsche problem for some time.

It hardly seems necessary to go into Porsche road holding at this late date. Weight distribution front/rear is 42/58 but oversteer didn't bother me until near the limit. Then watch out. When those Michelins tires finally break loose the tail goes by very rapidly.

One last criticism before I close: the lights are definitely inadequate for the speed of the car. At night the high beams barely reach far enough to make the cruising speed logical. When you have to dim, it's like driving into a coal mine. The horn could blow louder too. You come up on normal cars pretty fast.

I think the word "normal" as regards other cars is the best comment on a Carrera. It is definitely not normal in that it is well up to the task of true fast touring. The car is comfortable, rapid, well-braked, and best of all great fun. It. is also noisy and reluctant to start, but the good far outweighs the bad.

It is not a race car—but Porsche doesn't think so either. A Porsche Carrera 1600 GS is a specialist's car—the kind that makes you wish you could afford to be a specialist too. •

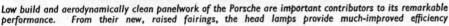

Low build and aerodynamically clean panelwork of the Porsche are important contributors to its remarkable performance. From their new, raised fairings, the head lamps provide much-improved efficiency

The *Autocar*

ROAD TESTS

1769

Porsche Super 75

UNIQUE in character and deportment is the Porsche; ever since the make's introduction 10 years ago it has defied convention and proffered a quite individual form of motoring. Even experienced drivers who choose to buy one must take some pains to appreciate its qualities and abilities to the full; once the techniques have been mastered there are few cars indeed which provide such a satisfying and intriguing form of road travel.

It has been said of some rather dull but very well made cars that they represent a triumph of engineering over design; of the Porsche it might be said, not unkindly, that it has become a triumph of development over design. When first presented to the public it was not an altogether good car on the road; it called for more than average skill—even courage—to get the best out of it. Over the years, various modifications to the suspension and steering gear have given the car progressively more orthodox handling characteristics.

As a result, behaviour of the Super 75 recently tested was found noticeably more predictable than that of its predecessors, and it took a driver appreciably less time to become at ease with the new model after handling more humdrum machinery. Despite this concession to orthodoxy, the Porsche character remains almost as strongly defined as ever.

For 1960 the Porsche "face" was lifted—quite literally—by raising the head lamp fairings several inches, and bringing up the front and rear bumpers to match. Whether this has improved the look of the car is a matter of personal taste, and no concern of a road test. Certainly the new position of the Bosch head lamps (which satisfies legal requirements in all States of the U.S.A.) has greatly improved their combination of range and spread on main and dipped beams, to such an extent that they are now of outstanding efficiency, even by today's generally high standards. Their settings can be adjusted without removing the rims.

Perhaps the most interesting basic difference between the engines of the current Super models (75 and 90), as distinct from the present standard 1600 and superseded Super, is that they now have four separate cylinder barrels of light alloy, of which the bores are faced with hard chrome. These have the particular advantages of light weight and quick heat dissipation. Net maximum power output of the Super 75 is 75 b.h.p., the gross figure (in test house conditions, without cooling fan and auxiliaries) being 88 b.h.p. While the Super's highest torque figure of 88 lb. ft. is slightly greater than that of the standard 1600, it is achieved at considerably higher r.p.m.—3,700 instead of 2,800—so that one cannot expect quite the same tractability at low crankshaft speeds.

Any 1,600 c.c. coupé which can accelerate from a standstill to 90 m.p.h. in appreciably under 30 sec (28.8 to be exact) and reach a mean maximum approaching 110 m.p.h. must be considered a sports car; yet in many respects this Porsche has a Jekyll and Hyde character, being almost ideal day-to-day transport for two, in or out of town. It is completely docile, has light and precise controls, and is endowed with most of the creature comforts demanded of a strictly touring car these days. Moreover, there are no slapdash crudities to be found, either of components or their assembly. Doors, for instance, open and close with satisfying ease and quietness, and are effectively sealed against dust, rain and draughts. Despite the car's low build, they do not foul high kerbs when opened.

In only one serious respect does the sporting side of the Porsche predominate; considerable engine noise enters the driving compartment, of a type which would certainly disturb some occupants—others, perhaps, scarcely at all. Its main source derives from the carburettor intakes, each cylinder drawing its mixture through an individual choke in one of the dual downdraught Zenith carburettors. Each carburettor is protected by a small air filter which provides little or no silencing; there appears to be plenty of space for larger air-cleaner/silencers to be fitted. Moreover, provision on the new Porsches of heating ducts to keep the rear window mist-free also entails a local reduction in sound-insulation.

No rich-mixture devices are fitted for cold starts; instead, one is instructed to depress the throttle pedal two or three times (to operate the accelerator pumps) before turning the starter key, and in very wintry weather to hold the clutch out of engagement. This works well enough and, once started, the engine is not given to stalling, although it is obviously wise to let it warm a little before moving off. Thereafter, engine compartment temperature, acting on a thermostatic control, is made to open or close valves in heater tubes leading to each carburettor. A slight low-speed flat-spot in the test car was overcome by increasing the

Spare wheel and fuel tank occupy much of the nose. A fine quality tool kit includes a tyre pressure gauge; the mechanical jack is particularly quick and light to operate when lifting, and has instantaneous release

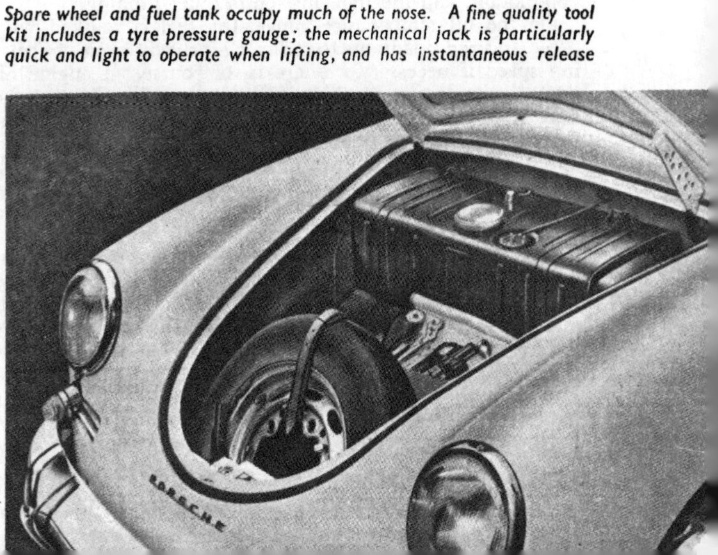

Porsche Super 75 . . .

Although the back window is necessarily shallow, it is near enough to the driver to allow him a fuller view than might be expected. Swivelling panes in the door windows are new

engine's idling to the rather fast rate recommended by the manufacturers—700 to 900 r.p.m.

A cranked gear lever of new-to-Porsche design sprouts from a point in the floor nearer to the driver than did its predecessor; it is also shorter (with correspondingly reduced movement) and more rigid. While the change is light and crash-proof, it demands depression of the clutch pedal to the full extent of its long travel. The clutch itself is smooth, progressive and light to operate.

Each forward gear engagement is assisted by the famous Porsche synchromesh of the self-servo baulk ring type, and the gearbox mechanism as a whole is fully in line with the high mechanical standard of the rest of the car. It has entirely suitable ratios—second, for instance, allowing a maximum of over 50 m.p.h., yet providing rapid acceleration, from, say, 10 m.p.h. in city traffic. When driving hard on the open road one must keep a watchful eye on the tachometer, since the makers' recommendations for maximum revolutions are all-to-easily exceeded, power being maintained in strong measure right up to the limit of 5,500 r.p.m.

As an indication of this, to accelerate in third from 60 to 80 m.p.h., in the face of increasing wind and rolling resistances, takes only 2 sec longer than between 30 and 50 m.p.h., the figures being 8.9 and 6.9 sec respectively. The ability, in second gear, to reach 50 m.p.h. from 30 in only 4.3 sec allows the Super 75 to escape from most opposition. These figures seem the more remarkable when one takes account of the car's considerable weight—just over a ton with two up, as tested.

There is an organ-type throttle pedal, so that one can "heel-and-toe." Brake and clutch pedal levers are carried on low pivots, which give a more direct and natural arc of movement than the pendant type.

A traditional virtue of the Porsche is its easy running at high cruising speeds, brought about by a combination of high overall gearing and the quietness with which the streamlined body cleaves through the air. The Super 75 can maintain a constant 100 m.p.h. with remarkably little commotion, and the transmission is quiet-running.

On the oil temperature gauge, the dial is marked with green and red quadrants to indicate a prudent limit of cruising speed if necessary. There is, of course, an engine oil cooler and, despite much hard driving on the test car, the needle never approached the red section; excessive oil temperature would result only from cruising too near maximum speed in very hot weather, or from some mechanical fault such as a slipping fan belt or wrongly timed ignition. The cooler is by-passed through a pressure relief valve when the oil is cold.

For those accustomed to travelling long distances on high-speed motorways, the recorded fuel consumption of 25 m.p.g. at a constant 90 m.p.h. is well worth bearing in mind, especially since the Super 75 does not require the most expensive grades. The overall consumption of 29.2 m.p.g. for 1,114 miles included the performance testing and a number of fast journeys, as well as some city commuting. By avoiding speeds in excess of 60 m.p.h. and full-throttle acceleration, a typical journey average of 35 m.p.g. was recorded.

Drawing from the lessons and experience of a vigorous works racing department, the Porsche designers have evolved a production private car with handling qualities which enable it to compete very successfully in rallies without modifications to standard specification. Carrying only 42 per cent of its weight (unladen) on the front wheels, and having a wheelbase of under 7ft, the Porsche naturally differs considerably in feel from cars with more orthodox layouts. It has all-independent suspension, by superimposed parallel trailing arms at the front, and by swing axles at the rear. When travelling fast the ride is soft by sports car standards; it is a little firmer at low speeds when there is sometimes a characteristic lateral rocking motion—difficult to define—suggesting rather restricted vertical wheel movements. The short wheelbase also makes the car prone to pitch on poor surfaces, noticed particularly at night when the head lamp beams lift and drop in sympathy.

Whatever the terrain, there is a wonderful sense of unity about the car's whole structure (in which the steel body and boxed frame are welded together), with no apparent flexing or rattling of its separate components.

For really fast cornering, the absence of roll and almost uncanny individual wheel adhesion displayed by the new car combine to make it outstandingly fast and safe on winding roads. It maintains these leech-like qualities to a remarkable degree (aided by Michelin X tyres) on a damp surface, and remains both stable and predictable. It has been said that the new rear-end geometry has made this the first Porsche which could be drifted round a bend, and any over-steer tendency could pass unnoticed in normal use. Tyre squeal is almost unheard with these Michelin tyres, nor is one hindered by wheelspin on full-power starts from rest.

Very quick response and lightweight action of the steering add much to one's pleasure and confidence when driving the car fast on cross-country journeys; road shocks are absorbed by an hydraulic steering damper. A light touch on the wheel is all that is necessary for such sensitive control—indeed, too firm a grip is best avoided.

The test car's engine and transmission were carried on prototype, rather flexible mountings of a new pattern which resulted in some weave at high speeds on the straight. Although calling for some concentration, this directional instability in time ceased to be a worry as one became accustomed to it. It is understood that all production cars imported into this country will have the old-pattern mountings, and a similar car with these was tried later and found to run true with much less correction.

Aluminium brake drums with transverse ribbing and cast steel inserts are fitted. The brakes are powerful and well balanced, and have good properties of endurance when put to hard use. On the debit side, they were somewhat rough on the test car, particularly at low speeds, as though the drums were distorted. Pedal pressures are quite moderate, and reaction to pedal movement is progressive. The T-handle parking brake is able to hold the car on a 1-in-3 gradient. In addition to speedometer (with trip mileage recorder) and tachometer, there are gauges for oil temperature and fuel level, as well as the usual indicator

In the back are two seats for children—or for one adult sitting sideways with head bowed. Their backrests can be folded forward to form a luggage platform. New for 1960 are the dished steering-wheel and cranked gear lever. The accessible fuel filter bowl which can be seen below the facia does not obstruct the driver's legs, as might appear. There are full-length map pockets in the doors, and a locker in the facia

lights. On this car the speedometer was erratic above 70 m.p.h. By night a rheostat controls the intensity of instrument lighting and, since the instruments are overhung by the padded brow above the facia, there are no reflections in the screen. A cigarette lighter is a standard fitting.

The dished steering wheel has three spokes arranged in T-formation so that they do not obstruct the driver's view of his instruments when the car is travelling straight. There is plenty of room for the thighs beneath it, and clear vision above it. Mounted on the steering column is a multi-purpose finger-tip lever to operate the direction signals, to raise or dip the head lamp beams and to flash these for signalling by night or day. Master switch for side and head lamps is a push-pull knob, rotated to regulate instrument lighting. A reversing lamp is lit with reverse selected and the head lamps dipped. The steering wheel boss is pressed to sound a single-note horn—not as effective as the ring it replaces, and in this case calling for too much pressure.

Standard fittings include a hand throttle, which can be locked in any position, and foot-operated screen washers. The self-parking screen wipers are rather noisy. Beneath the facia is a convenient three-way fuel tap—giving, Off, Main and Reserve positions. The tank holds 11½ gallons, including one reserve, allowing the Porsche well over 300 miles between refills. Twelve fuses for the electrical services are also located under the facia. A typically ingenious feature is that the rear-view mirror has an eccentric mounting, and can be turned to suit short or tall drivers.

Softly padded sun visors with wire frames have been a notable Porsche feature for several years. Conforming with American requirements, the windscreen is of laminated safety glass. Both front seats have adjustable backrests, which can be made to recline fully if the seats are pulled right forward. Cushions and backrests are trimmed in a serviceable, smooth plastic, and are contoured to give real comfort and proper support against side forces. They remain entirely restful on long journeys, when the ability to change position by altering the backrest rake is of considerable value.

Although the scuttle is a little high, the steep, downward slope of the short bonnet helps to provide a good field of vision, the road being visible within a few feet of the car's nose. On this latest model, swivelling window panes in the front doors have added to the front pillars' effective thickness, which some habitual Porsche owners might regret. Gone now are the previous under-scuttle fresh air vents.

Interior heating, supplied from the engine cylinders, is admitted via an adjustable valve, just forward of the gear lever, and soon becomes effective after a cold start. Although no exhaust fumes entered the car, the atmosphere remained fresher in cold weather if one of the hinged rear quarter windows was kept open. The new demisting ducts to the back window were not very effective during short journeys, proved a great boon once they had time to clear the whole glass.

There is plenty of room for maps and the other odds and ends one carries in a car—a locker in the facia, full length pockets in the doors, little receptacles at knee level, just forward of the screen pillars—and even coat hooks. The new rear seats with folding backrests provide extra room for occasional passengers, and with these folded down the Porsche has abundant luggage space to supplement the small compartment in the nose. A particularly neat washable

In its practically dust-proof compartment, the flat-four engine is accessible for most routine maintenance, but the sparking plugs are difficult to reach, and tappet adjustment must be tackled from beneath the car. The ducted cooling fan is attached to the forward end of the belt-driven dynamo

Porsche Super 75 . . .

plastic lines the roof, and there are practical rubber mats on the floor.

Greasing requirements are quite moderate, at 1,500-mile intervals, and the owner's handbook is unusually comprehensive, including sectioned and exploded views of engine and transmission, as well as graphs of road speed against engine speed in all gears, power output and acceleration. The fine tool kit in a plastic bag includes a dial-type tyre-pressure gauge and spare fan belt. Incidentally, Porsche owners are proud of the fact that service engineers familiar with the make can remove the engine complete in under 15 minutes. Within the sump filter gauze, incidentally, is a magnet to collect any iron and steel particles. A towing eye is attached to the front of the chassis.

This Porsche has an almost animate personality and is a car with which one could never become bored. A road express for travelling far and fast, it is built with such precision that one would expect long service without more than routine attention.

PORSCHE SUPER 75

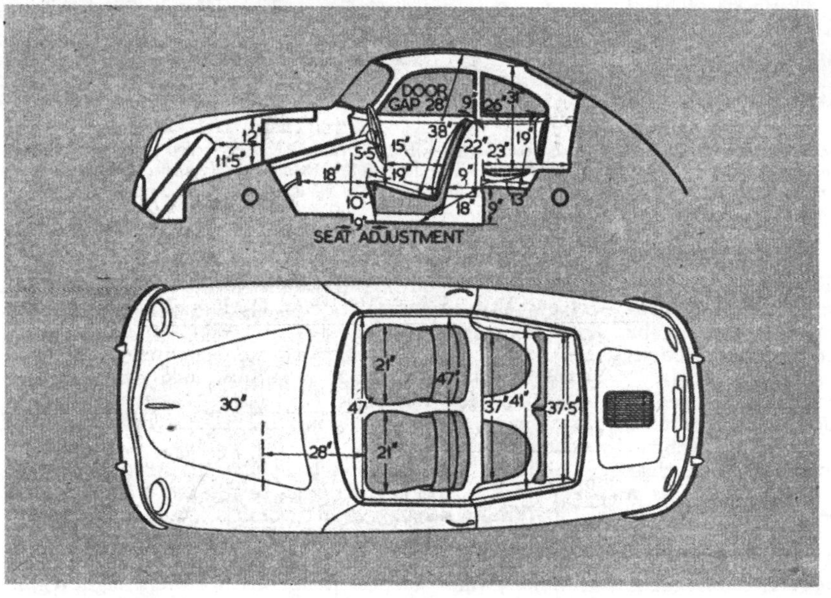

Scale ¼in. to 1ft. Driving seat in central position. Cushions uncompressed.

PERFORMANCE

ACCELERATION TIMES (mean):
Speed range, Gear Ratios and Time in Sec.

M.p.h.	3.61 to 1	5.01 to 1	7.82 to 1	13.69 to 1
10—30 ..	—	—	4.9	—
20—40 ..	—	7.8	4.4	—
30—50 ..	10.7	6.9	4.3	—
40—60 ..	11.0	7.3	—	—
50—70 ..	11.6	7.9	—	—
60—80 ..	12.8	8.9	—	—
70—90 ..	14.3	—	—	—
80—100..	21.9	—	—	—

From rest through gears to:

30 m.p.h. ..	3.2 sec
40 " ..	5.6 "
50 " ..	7.8 "
60 " ..	11.4 "
70 " ..	15.6 "
80 " ..	20.6 "
90 " ..	28.8 "
100 " ..	41.7 "

Standing quarter mile 18.1 sec.

MAXIMUM SPEEDS ON GEARS:

Gear		M.p.h.	K.p.h.
Top ..	(mean)	108.8	175.2
	(best)	110.0	177.1
3rd ..	.. ..	80	128.8
2nd ..	.. ..	52	83.7
1st ..	.. ..	29	46.7

TRACTIVE EFFORT (by Tapley meter):

	Pull (lb per ton)	Equivalent gradient
Top	210	1 in 10.6
Third	315	1 in 7.0
Second..	470	1 in 4.7

BRAKES (at 30 m.p.h. in neutral):

Pedal load in lb	Retardation	Equiv. stopping distance in ft
25	0.20g	151
50	0.52g	58
75	0.85g	35.5
90	0.92g	32.8

FUEL CONSUMPTION (m.p.g. at steady speeds):

	Top Gear
30 m.p.h.	50.0
40 "	44.0
50 "	38.8
60 "	35.6
70 "	32.2
80 "	29.4
90 "	25.0

Overall fuel consumption for 1,114 miles, 29.2 m.p.g. (9.67 litres per 100 km).

Approximate normal range 27-35 m.p.g. (10.5-8.1 litres per 100 km).

Fuel: Premium grades.

TEST CONDITIONS: Weather: Dry, overcast. 0-5 m.p.h. wind.

Air temperature, 44 deg. F.

Model described in *The Autocar* of 11 September, 1959.

STEERING: Turning circle:
Between kerbs, L, 33ft 2in; R, 32ft 10in.
Between walls, L, 34ft 11in. R, 34ft 7in;
Turns of steering wheel from lock to lock, 2.2

SPEEDOMETER CORRECTION: M.P.H.

Car speedometer ..	10	20	30	40	50	60	70	80	90	100	110
True speed.. ..	10	18	28	39	50	59	68	73	81	90	100

DATA

PRICE (basic), with coupé body, **£1,563.**
British purchase tax, **£652 7s 6d.**
Total (in Great Britain), **£2,215 7s 6d.**
Extras: Radio, **£32 19s 3d** (including tax).

ENGINE: Capacity, 1,582 c.c. (96.5 cu. in.).
Number of cylinders, 4.
Bore and stroke, 82.5 × 74 mm (3.25 × 2.91in.).
Valve gear, o.h.v., pushrods.
Compression ratio, 8.5 to 1.
B.h.p., 75 net at 5,000 r.p.m. (B.h.p. per ton laden, 74.1).
Torque, 88lb. ft. at 3,700 r.p.m.
M.p.h. per 1,000 r.p.m. in top gear, 20.0.

WEIGHT (with 5 gals fuel), 17.25 cwt (1,932 lb).
Weight distribution (per cent): F, 42.0; R, 58.0.
Laden as tested, 20.25 cwt (2,268lb).
Lb per c.c. (laden), 1.43.

BRAKES: Type: Porsche drum.
Method of operation, hydraulic.
Drum dimensions: F and R, 11in. dia., 1.57in. wide.
Swept area: F, 108.5 sq. in.; R, 108.5 sq. in. (214 sq. in. per ton laden).

TYRES: 5.60—15in. Michelin X.
Pressures (p.s.i.): F, 18.5; R, 23.0 (normal). F, 21.5; R, 25.5 (fast driving).

TANK CAPACITY: 11.5 Imperial gallons, including 1 reserve.
Oil sump, 8.8 pints, including filter.

DIMENSIONS: Wheelbase, 6ft 10.7in.
Track: F, 4ft 3.4in.; R, 4ft 2.1in.
Length (overall), 13ft 1.7in.
Width, 5ft 5.6in.
Height, 4ft 4.4in.
Ground clearance, 5.9 in.

ELECTRICAL SYSTEM: 6-volt; 75 ampére-hour battery.
Head lamps, double dip; 45-40 watt bulbs.

SUSPENSION: Front, independent, parallel trailing arms, transverse laminated torsion bars, anti-roll bar. Rear, independent swing axles with compensating transverse leaf spring, transverse round-section torsion bars.

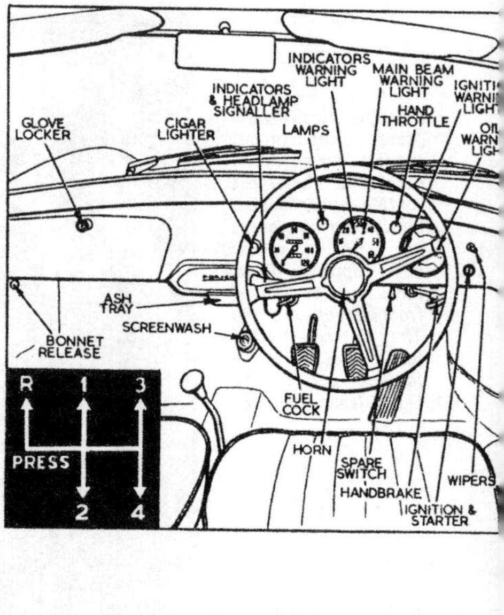

BEST OF THE REST *Germany*

New coupe body for 1960 marks first radical change for Porsche since firm began early production in 1949.

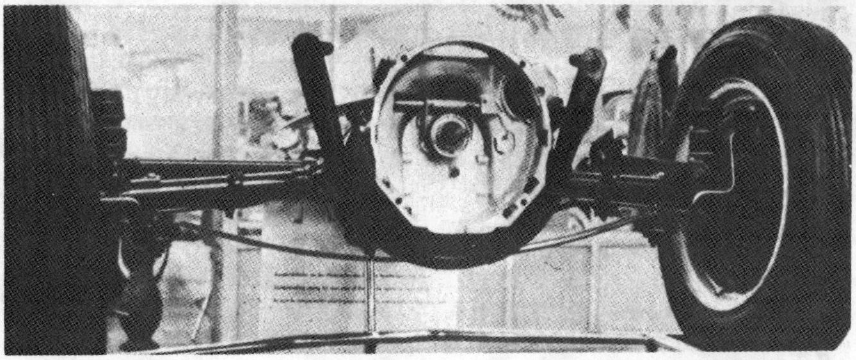

Super 90 features transverse leaf spring under swing axles to reduce rear roll, and diminish remaining small oversteer.

Rear of roadster has higher bumper for better protection against Detroit cars.

The interiors have been redesigned with dished steering wheel, new shift lever.

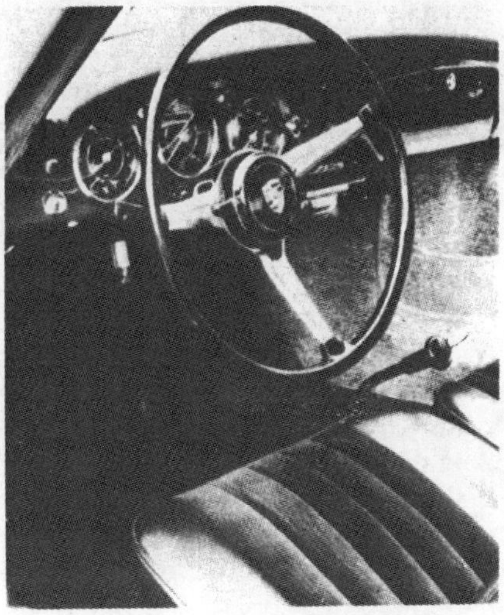

PORSCHE SUPER 90

Although the Super 90 is new this year, it was well in contention for Sports-car of the Year—not surprising because everything Porsche turns out seems to be outstanding. Actually, the Carrera would probably have received the nod for runner-up over the Super 90 except for the factory's production plans for the Carrera. The Carrera Deluxe will be available on special order only. In plain facts, write the factory and send money. About 50 Carrera GTs will be built with special lightweight coupe bodies for racing – some by an Italian coachmaker, although they will look the same as production cars. Accordingly, since the Carrera is no longer generally available, it was passed over in favor of the Super 90.

The 90 develops 90 DIN hp, about 105 bhp, from its 1582cc engine. While this reaches into race car output, the reliability is excellent. All that is asked is that revs be kept up; in other words, no lugging. Its big advantage over the Carrera is the fact that the 90 uses a plain-bearing crankshaft in a pushrod engine. Maintenance is within the reach of any owner. The overhead-cam Carreras are quite expensive to repair and maintain. If price is a consideration, the Porsche is probably the world's best buy.

228
Z-208

Road Research Report: PORSCHE 1600 and SUPER 90

► In the days when it was first created from VW cloth, the Porsche was irrefutably one of the most advanced automobiles in the world. By building a new lightweight, streamlined container for two atop the basic Volkswagen chassis, it had proved possible to extract more performance and better handling. Once this was done, the only limits to further improvements were the VW components – specifically engine, gearbox and brakes. Since those days the Porsche has been kept competitive by steady, careful replacement and improvement of the parts inherited from the People's Car. This painstaking, near-religious devotion of Porsche engineers to their pet product has been rewarded by an automobile that is, in every important way, supremely satisfying.

In 1960, though, the limiting factor has become the over-ten-year-old body. On September 9, 1959 Porsche announced the first *major* revision of this classic shell, dubbing it the 356B. Though this change was long overdue – and, in a sense, still insufficient – it was obviously made with great trepidation on the part of the Porsche staff. In shape and utility the 356B's body is now substantially improved, but the chassis and engine changes – especially the Super 90, the ultimate development of the original engine – continue to outpace the body's progress. Evaluation of Porsche's new clothes isn't an easy matter, because the changes are subtle, as they have been for a decade. To assess them properly, SCI put 8,000 miles on two kinds of Porsches on two continents. This Road Research Report tells the story.

EXTERNAL ALTERATIONS

Porsche admits that the increase in bumper heights (by about 4 inches in front and 6 in back) was brought about by the needs of the American market. This change plus the higher, heftier bumper guards gives sufficiently good protection to dispense with the tubular over-riders formerly regarded as "musts", but Porsche owners still don't have ironclad protection against traffic damage. In particular the elongated front parking light lenses protrude far enough to be vulnerable. Porsche bumpers have long featured a narrow rubber strip around the periphery; inspection shows that the newer cars have a firmer synthetic insert that's less likely to crack and deteriorate. At the back, the exhaust pipes joggle through S-bends to get to the exits, which are integrated with – and which quickly discolor – the rear bumper guards.

Though, as always, an illuminated location for a rear license plate is provided (body to be drilled to suit), Porsche dealers have had to affix front plates at the outer edge of the bumper, where they quickly became dented and even more unsightly than when new. Transatlantic co-operation is likely to result, soon, in a front plate mounting arrangement similar in location to the taped-on placement on our white 1600 R.R.R. car. As the bumpers moved up, so did the headlights. They're now less susceptible to damage, and they're enough higher to improve lighting effectiveness markedly. As the Porsche publicity release said, "This has become still more important recently since many Porsche drivers travel long distances at night to avoid crowded highways during daytime". When fog lights are installed, they'll be hung below the bumper where stray upward rays will be completely shielded from the driver's eyes.

SUPERB SEATING

There are many more detail changes inside the 356B. To discuss them we have to step inside, a process which, in itself, isn't easy. Opened by pushbutton, the door easily swings wide and is held there by an ingenious rubber tongue which catches the front edge of the door as it hinges into the bodywork. Each door has a lock, integrated with the opening pushbutton.

Once a door is locked from the outside, it can't be opened by means of the pushbutton – no matter how often it's opened from the inside – unless it's unlocked with the key again. Locking from the inside is accomplished by the usual upward door handle movement.

Getting into the Porsche is made difficult by the body's basic design. The door's forward edge is more to the rear – away from the toeboard – than is usual nowadays, calling for real retraction of the legs while swinging them in. The concept of a relatively narrow "cab" atop a wide basic body, so integral with the Porsche's aerodynamic layout, produces a relatively thick door and a very wide door sill that's awkward to step over. Even long-time Porsche owners find it hard to avoid dirtying a trouser leg on the outer edge of the sill.

The Reutter seats have plenty of fore-and-aft travel in a range that leaves generous leg room back of the wide, corrugated-rubber pedals. There's also surprising room for heads and elbows inside this compact coupe, thanks in part to the way the inner panel of the door slopes away to the outside. The medical advice that has contributed to the seat's contours shows up in the fine support given to the small of the back and to the shoulders, as well as in the nice degree of firmness that fights fatigue on long trips. Equally effective against weariness is Reutter's adjustment for the seat back's angle. Clever padding of the seat and a deep scoop to the back combine to hold driver and passenger comfortably in place during moderate maneuvers, in spite of the inherent smoothness of the artificial leather upholstery.

New in the 356B is a rear seat back that's split down the middle, to allow just half to be folded down for luggage carrying while a third passenger "sits" beside it. This is actually a very workable arrangement for short trips, as we had occasion to discover during our testing. There are two apparent complications to this layout. One is that there's no latch or catch to hold the seat backs in the upright position, leaving them free to fold forward when the car decelerates. This is academic when the rear rider is an adult, but with a child back there it could be dangerous. The other is that straps are definitely needed to hold luggage in place – also to keep it from flying forward under braking. Porsche does provide suitable strap anchors and straps are an optional extra.

NEW CONTROLS

As usual, the size, height, angle and distance of the Porsche steering wheel are ideal for most drivers. Entirely new for '60, the wheel's design elicits mixed reactions. Its three spokes, stamped from flat sheet metal, are made to look like castings with perforated centers – or some such. Some staff members liked the design; others felt that the attempt to simulate some other material was very unlike Porsche – that they might better have used flat, polished spokes. There was some hope that Porsche's patented hydraulically-damped telescopic steering column would be fitted to the 356B's, but this wasn't possible. In its stead the wheel is given a "deep-dish" shape.

Everyone agreed that the new black steering wheel rim was a complete pleasure to handle. Its thickness and diameter are just right; its black color does cut down on reflections in the windshield (as advertised), and there are even little dimples under the spoke junctions that provide a very pleasant tactile sensation. Handy at the left of the steering column is a new lever which does double-duty, controlling both the directional signals and the headlight dimming. Unlike many other such controls, it's very logical and easy to use. Flipped forward, it switches on high beam. When you're driving fast, keeping your eyes on the road, it's easier to check which beam you're using by quickly touching the lever than it is to glance down at the blue dashboard light. The European Editor suggests that a further forward push on the lever could sound the horn, for convenient signalling at night.

All the dashboard knobs have been made black instead of white, giving a "richer" feel to the interior. The windshield wiper switch is on the left side of the dash, where it's easily reached, but it suffers by having a small knob and a stiff action. We had occasion to drive the Porsches in spotty weather, switching the wipers on and off frequently, and were soon wishing we had a handy toggle switch. The wipers themselves are fast and efficient, and are supplemented by a washer system which is a standard Porsche fitting.

DIALS, POCKETS AND AIR FLOW

As always, the black-faced instruments are simple but adequate in graduation. They're easy to read by day – though they're too low for really quick glance-analysis – and the rheostat control selects the illumination you want at night. In addition to the tach and speedometer (naturally with different graduations for 1600 and Super 90), dials indicate fuel level and the general range of oil temperature. Also on the dash is a hand throttle, intended for a fast idle during warmup. Whether it's deliberate or not we don't know, but this control is so adjusted that it will not cause the engine to over-rev, even if you pull it all the way out with a fully-warm powerplant. It runs up to about 4800 rpm but no more! On a level road it can be used to cruise at about 50 mph in top gear.

Many things about the Porsche make it ideal for long trips, but one of its nicest features is the multitude of places to put maps, manuals and similar traveling equipment. The lockable glove compartment is roomy, though its opening fails to pass one of the SCI tests. (A Rolleiflex camera won't go in.) There are deep pockets in both doors and in the cockpit sides under the dash. One of the items that's usually stowed here, the Porsche owner's manual, is a real model for other manufacturers. Both graphically and informatively it's excellent.

Over the years VW and Porsche heaters have been developed to produce more and more heat, and on

*(Text continued on page **72** data overleaf)*

New transverse finned brake drum will be regular equipment on the 1600, 1600 S and Super 90 Porsches. In each case the stopping power of the new drums matches the speed and power.

"A thing of beauty is a joy forever." Old-line Porsche owners may bemoan the passing ot the now classic body style, but on sober reflection will realize that the increased height of the bumpers will enable the 1960 model to fend for itself when left unattended on city streets. The high-set head lights are also a functional change giving better illumination for high-speed driving.

PORSCHE Super 90 Coupe

ENGINE:

Displacement ....96½ cu in, 1582 cc
Dimensions ....Four cyl, 3.25 x 2.91 in
Compression Ratio ....9.0 to one
Power (SAE) ....102 bhp @ 5500 rpm
Torque ....99 lb-ft @ 4300 rpm
Usable rpm Range ....1500-5800 rpm
Piston Speed ÷ $\sqrt{s/b}$
@ rated power ....2840 ft/min
Fuel Recommended ....Super-premium
Mileage ....15-23 mpg
Range ....205-315 miles

CHASSIS:

Wheelbase ....82.7 in
Tread, F,R ....51½, 50 in
Length ....158 in
Suspension: F, ind., trailing arms, lam. torsion bars; R, ind., swing axle, torsion bar.
Turns to Full Lock 1⅓
Tire Size ....5.90 x 15
Swept Braking Area — drum ....218 sq in
Curb Weight (full tank) ....2080 lbs
Percentage on Driving Wheels 57%
Test Weight ....2400 lbs

DRIVE TRAIN:

Gear	Synchro?	Ratio	Step	Overall	Mph per 1000 rpm
Rev	No	3.56		15.79	4.7
			—		
1st	Yes	3.09		13.70	5.4
			75%		
2nd	Yes	1.77		7.82	9.4
			56%		
3rd	Yes	1.13		5.01	14.7
			33%		
4th	Yes	0.85		3.77	19.5

Final Drive Ratio: 4.43 to one.

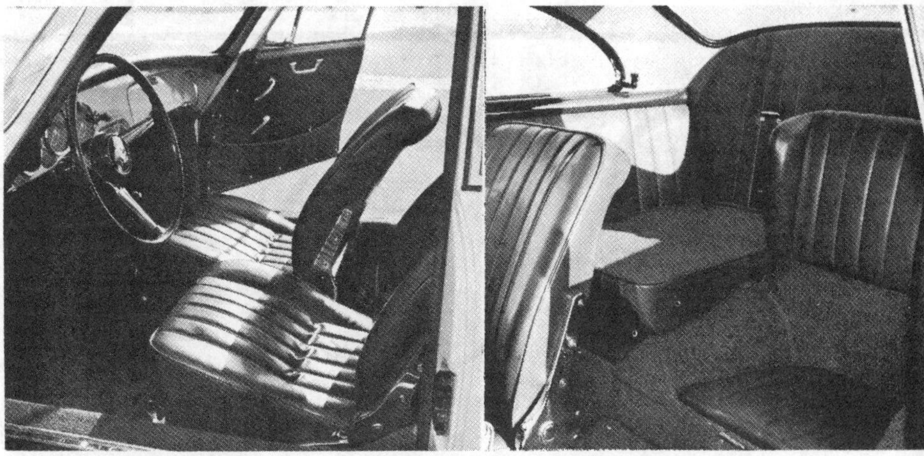

1960 Porsche boasts a dished steering wheel as well as a new gear shift lever. The rear split-seats—another '60 change—allow carrying one passenger and some baggage on the folded seat back.

Heater outlet on the 1960 Porsche. It provides warmth, but gets too hot to touch while doing it.

New German Dunlop sports tire was developed in cooperation with the Porsche factory. It's akin to the Italian Cinturato in construction.

Road Research Report: PORSCHE 1600 and SUPER 90

Factory Office — Porsche of America, Inc. 527 Madison Ave. New York 22, N. Y.

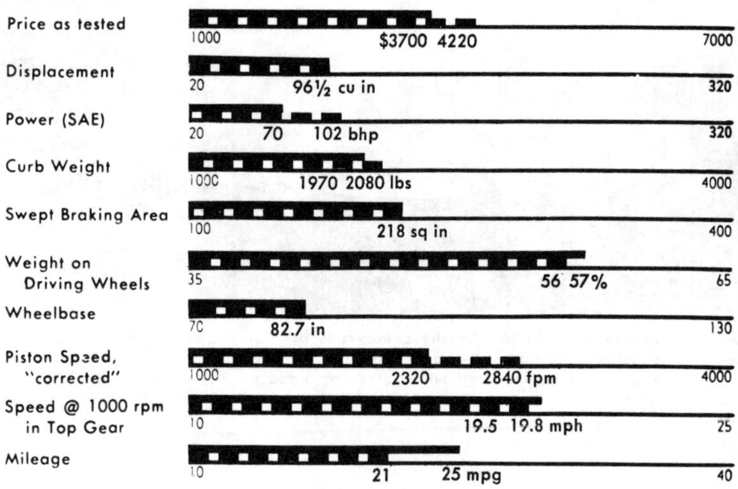

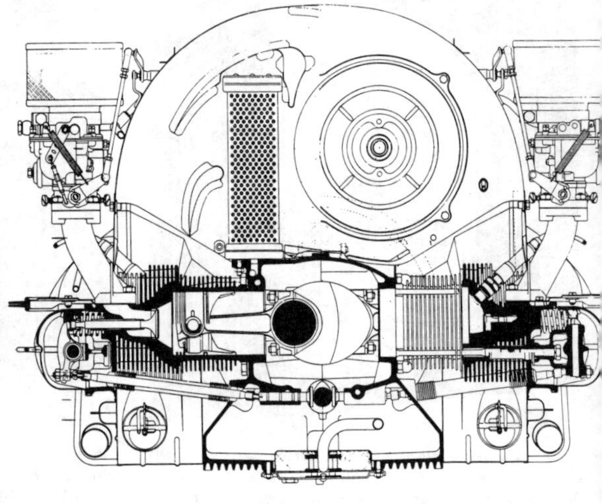

Normally the engines are shown at ⅛ scale but due to space limitations, this cross-section of the Porsche 1600 engine is 1/10 scale

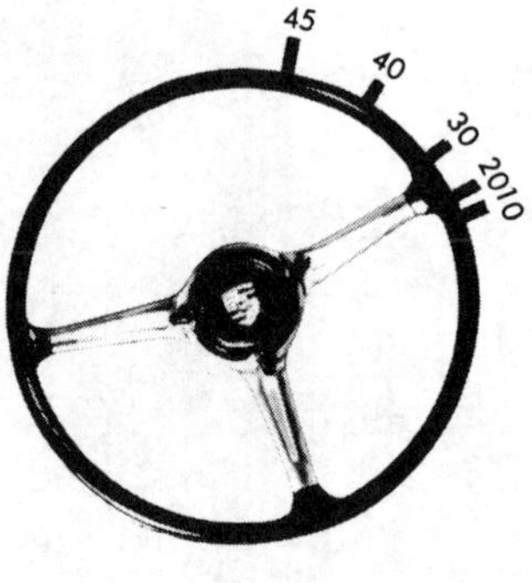

1600
Steering Behavior

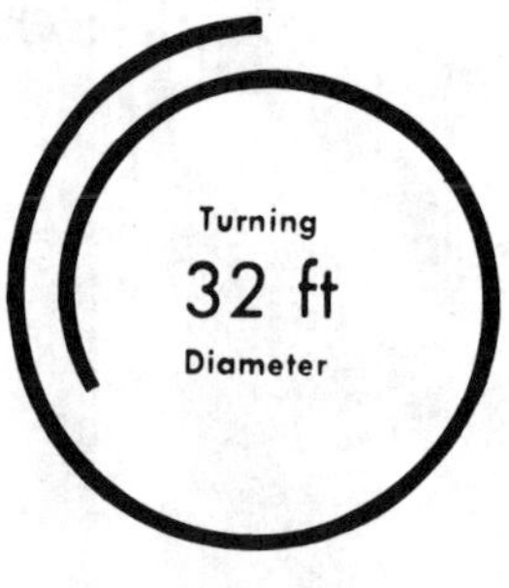

Turns to Full Lock

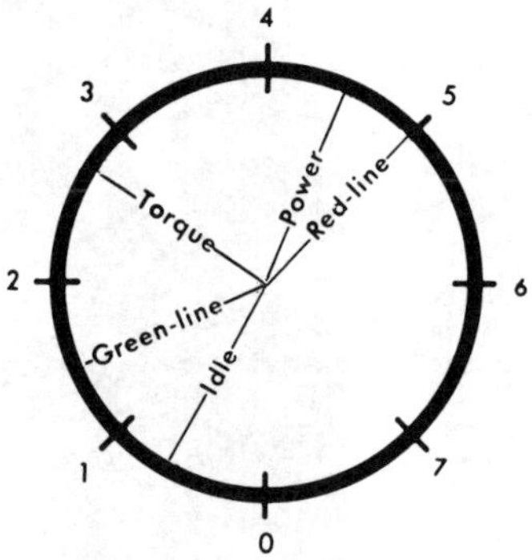

Engine Flexibility

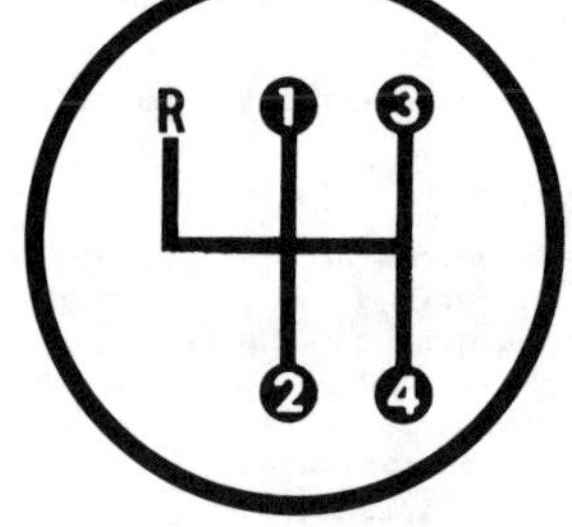

Shift Pattern

ENGINE:

Displacement	96½ cu in, 1582 cc
Dimensions	Four cyl, 3.25 x 2.91 in
Compression Ratio	7.5 to one
Power (SAE)	70 bhp @ 4500 rpm
Torque	81 lb-ft @ 2800 rpm
Usable rpm Range	1400-5000 rpm
Piston Speed $\div \sqrt{s/b}$ @ rated power	2320 ft/min
Fuel Recommended	Regular
Mileage	21-29 mpg
Range	290-400 miles

CHASSIS:

Wheelbase	82.7 in
Tread, F,R	51½, 50 in
Length	158 in
Suspension: F, ind., trailing arms, lam. torsion bars. R, ind., swing axle, torsion bar.	
Turns to Full Lock	1⅓
Tire Size	5.60 x 15
Swept Braking Area—drum	218 sq in
Curb Weight (full tank)	1970 lbs
Percentage on Driving Wheels	57%
Test Weight	2270 lbs

DRIVE TRAIN:

Gear	Synchro?	Ratio	Step	Overall	Mph per 1000 rpm
Rev	No	3.56		15.79	4.6
1st	Yes	3.09	—	13.70	5.2
2nd	Yes	1.77	75%	7.82	9.2
3rd	Yes	1.13	56%	5.01	14.4
4th	Yes	0.82	39%	3.62	19.8

Final Drive Ratio: 4.43 to one.

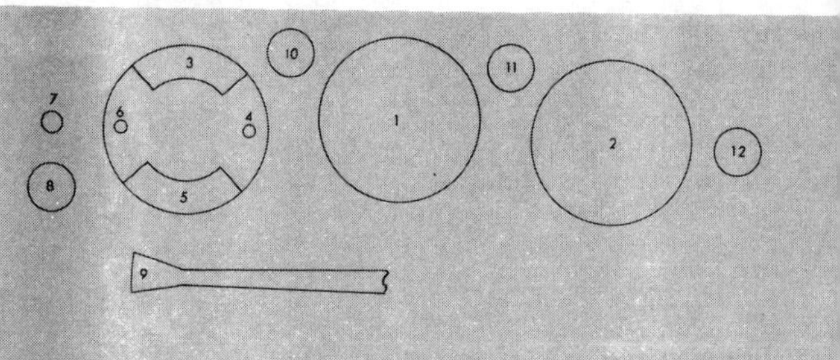

1	Tachometer	5	Fuel Gauge	9	Turn Signal/Dip Switch
2	Speedometer	6	Generator Light	10	Hand Throttle
3	Oil Temperature	7	Windshield Wiper	11	Light Switch
4	Oil Pressure Light	8	Ignition/Starter	12	Cigarette Lighter

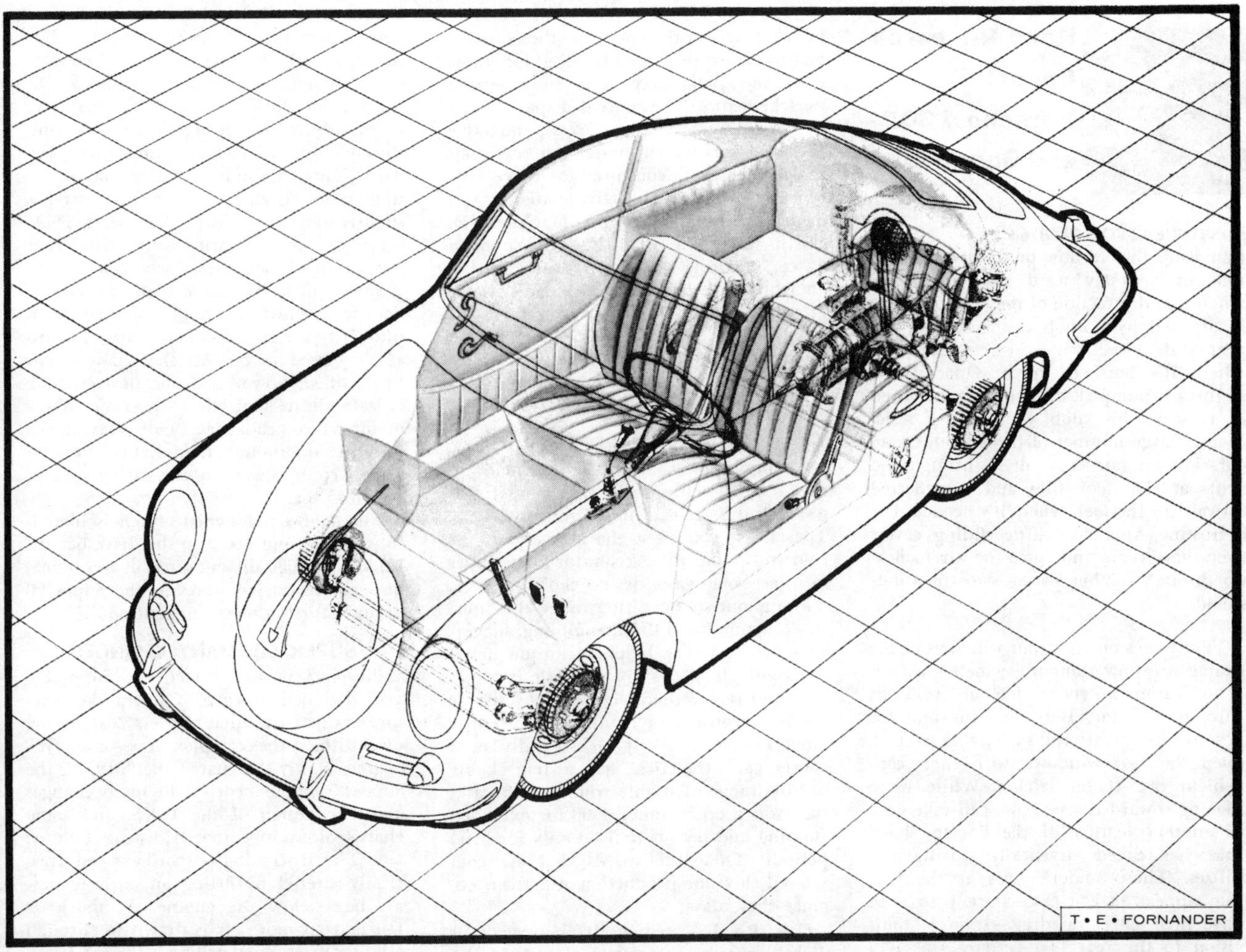
T • E • FORNANDER

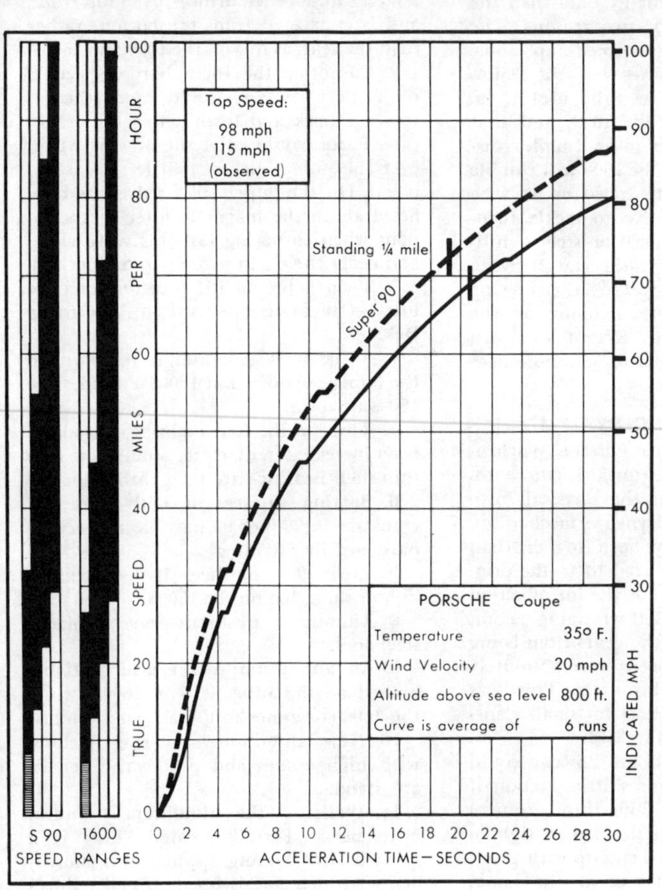
Top Speed:
98 mph
115 mph
(observed)
Standing ¼ mile
Super 90
PORSCHE Coupe
Temperature 35º F.
Wind Velocity 20 mph
Altitude above sea level 800 ft.
Curve is average of 6 runs
TRUE SPEED MILES PER HOUR
INDICATED MPH
S 90
1600
SPEED RANGES
ACCELERATION TIME—SECONDS
0 2 4 6 8 10 12 14 16 18 20 22 24 26 28 30
0 20 40 60 80 100
30 40 50 60 70 80 90 100

Road Research Report Porsche 1600 and Super 90

CONTINUED FROM PAGE 68
that score they're now pretty good. But it remains very awkward to control the amount and direction of the heat. Amount is adjusted by a knob at the base of the gear shift lever, very close to the floor where it's hard to reach. Quantity of warm air pumped into the car is varied by twisting this knob, which has a ridiculously large number of turns from On to Off. The air normally enters through two vents at the door sills, and is deflected forward to the feet, where it's needed. For defrosting, you close little sliding covers over these vents and force the air to flow up through further passages to the windshield.

Vent panes on the front windows of the coupes are now standard, which makes it a lot easier to get a flow of fresh air through the car. Both for this and for best heater operation it's advisable to crack open the rear windows, with their convenient over-center latches. While we're looking toward the rear, we can take note of another feature of the Porsche body that has dated drastically during the Fifties. Those smooth lines at the rear that appear so efficient — since proven to have little effect on drag — severely limit vision to the rear. To be sure this is a built-in feature of the coupe only, which is regarded as the "classic" Porsche by most fans of the make. But it indicates how useful a new body shape could be.

OUTSIDE OPENINGS

An inside knob unlatches the trunk lid, which has a finger-operated safety catch like a conventional alligator-type hood. Both this safety catch and the concealed hold-open mechanism tend to baffle service station attendants who, while searching for the right position, sometimes apply metal-bending force to the hinges. Why would they be opening it anyway? To get at the fuel filler, a big cap that's easy to put on and remove, and through which the gasoline level is readily visible. There's a small cavity for soft luggage between the tank and the spare tire, which is leather-strapped in place. The battery is down below and behind the tire, and is held down by the spring clips that retain its fiber-board cover. Also to be found in the trunk of a new Porsche is a can of the proper paint and a tool kit that is as complete as you'll find these days.

Another knob, behind the driver's seat, pops open the engine lid. It may or may not be intentional, but the small size of this vented trap door expresses the official Porsche factory service philosophy: If something goes wrong, stop. Get out of the car, and walk or ride to your nearest VW or Porsche dealer. Do *not* fool with it yourself. There are very full instructions for basic mechanical work in the owner's manual, but this is only to guide those servicemen who may never have seen a Porsche before. The concealed spark plugs, the limited engine room access, the valve rocker covers down under the car — all design features conspire to make the Porsche a car that actively discourages owner maintenance. This heightens an existing impression that this is not so much a "car" as it is a compact, sealed-for-life "machine for traveling" that needs such attention seldom, and then only from the hands of skilled technicians. One excellent attribute of the Porsche's engine room: It's so well sealed off that water and dust seldom intrude to foul the engine's workings.

DILIGENT PERFORMER

No important change has been made in the 1600's engine since that model was tested and described in SCI for May, 1958. To start it you twist the key, and if it's cold you pump the accelerator a few times to inject some gasoline; no choke is fitted. Throughout its operating range the "normal" engine has a deep, rumbling, bigger-than-life feel that bespeaks torque in all the right places. Its 850 rpm idle is rough in sound rather than feel, and its response to the throttle is generally quick. For a modern engine, though — especially in a sports car — the 1600 has a remarkably narrow range of usable rpm. Porsche asks that you keep it under 4500 for extended running and take it to 5000 only for brief periods. These are speeds that are considered slow for production American engines these days.

Our Road Research 1600 turned in slightly poorer performance data than the May, 1958 car did, for two reasons. The 356B seems to have picked up some poundage — almost 100 — over the 356A, and the earlier car was fully broken in. Top speed is almost identical, and that same heartening ability to hold high cruising speeds is evident. The 1600 will rumble along at any speed up to 80 or 85 with enough power in reserve to tackle turnpike-type grades. Its speed on steeper hills is held back by the ratio gap between second and third gear; you're either revving high in second or just hanging on the torque peak in third. Except for such hilly conditions, the ratio selection does a good all-around job.

NEW SHIFTING SYSTEM

Recently the famous Porsche synchronizer was redesigned, toward two ends. One was reduction of the physical force needed to engage the synchro mechanism, which had previously been higher than desirable; this was reduced to ¼ the original value. The other was the introduction of a more powerful self-wrapping action which would prevent the gears from being engaged until their speeds were absolutely and completely synchronized. This was also accomplished, at least for small transmissions like that in the 356B.

With these things done, Porsche could have achieved a lighter shifting action if it had kept the old long-throw control linkage, but instead it decided to tighten up the shift pattern and end up with about the same necessary forces at the knob. Most drivers will be pleased by the firmer, more direct feel of the new linkage, but the increased blocking of the revised synchro has some less happy side effects. On shifts from third to second, for instance, if you don't double-clutch that "slicing through butter" feel just isn't there any more. Though the new system may prove to be more durable, we regret that it takes slightly longer to shift a 356B than a 356A. When the box is warm, swift shifts from top to third and *vice versa* can be extremely quick, but those really important ones from third to second and then down into first just aren't as beautifully smooth as they used to be. All the changes will be justified, however, if the new gearbox is less delicate and offers the owner fewer maintenance headaches. Before leaving the transmission, though, note that the Porsche Spyder continues to use the earlier type of synchronizer.

The 356B's redesigned clutch is incredibly smooth and takes up the drive beautifully. The 1600 doesn't affect it too much, but making racing starts in the Super 90 brought forth a most pungent odor.

SUPER 90: MANY CHANGES

Porsche's newest model, the Super 90, was designed to give Carrera-like performance at considerably less cost to the owner than the complex four-cam "GS" engine. Newly designated the "619/7", the Super 90 engine incorporates many changes over the design of the 1600S, and some chassis alterations too. A listing follows.

1. The air-cooling system has been drastically altered by fitting an entirely new air box below the engine. As much as ten percent more air is drawn in through a larger unscreened orifice at the top front, and is exhausted from the bottom rather than the rear, as it is on the 1600 and 1600S.

2. Cornering the 1600S hard, especially on airport courses, would cause the oil to surge back and forth across the crankcase. Foam would enter the oilways whenever the pump sucked a little air instead of oil. On the Super 90, a valve has been fitted above the magnetic filter in the oil pan; when cornering fast this valve closes and keeps the oil in two separated pockets.

3. Twin Solex 40 PII-4 carburetors are fitted — the same type used on the Carrera Deluxe.

4. A 200 watt generator is standard on the Super 90; 1600 and 1600S Porsches use 160-watt units.

5. Three of the four main bearings have been increased in diameter 5mm. New-type thin-shell bearings are used throughout.

6. Bearing surfaces of both cam and crank on the Super 90 have been specially hardened by nitriding.

7. Super 90's flywheel is five pounds lighter than that on the 1600S.

8. Aluminum pushrods have replaced steel ones.

9. An aluminum rocker arm assembly is used on the Super 90 and 1600S, while the 1600 continues to use a steel assembly.

10. New aluminum four-ring pistons, with high domes and deep valve reliefs, are standard.

11. Walls of the aluminum cylinders have been "Ferral" treated. This is a sprayed steel coating applied over molybdenum which speeds break-in and reduces

oil consumption. The famous chromed walls are continued on the 1600S; the 1600 still has cast-iron cylinders.

12. Valve springs are stiffer.

13. Intake and exhaust ports are bigger.

14. A heavy-duty fan/generator drive belt is used.

15. A new soft iron gasket has been fitted between the end of the crankshaft and the belt pulley.

16. Connecting rods throughout the Porsche line have been redesigned as a result of the Super 90's requirements.

17. Super 90's and Carreras are fitted as standard with a single-leaf compensating rear spring, which is available for other Porsche models on special order.

BREAK-IN AND BRAKES

SCI's European Editor has purchased one of the first Super 90's, and has this to say about break-in: "I was told at the factory to use 5000 rpm from the very beginning — with the aside that 'our engines ask to be beaten; break them in fast and they'll be fast later on'. Taking this advice, 5000 rpm was never exceeded in the first 2500 miles, though the owner's manual suggests a limit of 4000 revs. Now, after 5000 miles, my Super 90 is running smooth and sweet and is commencing to have that 'loose' feel that indicates it'll be a fast car."

One of the most impressive of the Super 90's several outstanding qualities is its *smoothness*. The engine is smooth at 600 rpm idle — smooth all the way up to its safe maximum of 5800 rpm. How safe is this maximum? One Super 90 engine has been run at 5800 for over 200 hours continuously, at the factory. Cruising speed on the road is an effortless 100 mph, and even 110 can be maintained indefinitely whenever conditions allow. Acceleration feel — and the actual statistics — is like that of the Carrera, and even the noise at top revs takes on that Carrera-like growling throb.

All 356B Porsches have been fitted with new brakes, of which the most novel features are stronger drums with lateral finning, new labyrinth seals between drum and back plate, and a robust and extremely efficient new braking lining — Energit 999. On our test Super 90, these brakes were superb. From 100 mph to rest one feels that a giant hand is pulling the car to a stop. In 5000 miles we experienced no brake troubles whatsoever, and encountered no fade under Alpine conditions. The 1600's brakes were good—more than up to the car's performance — but when used very hard they tended to vibrate annoyingly, a symptom that's not unique to our particular test 1600.

FINE ROADHOLDING

The 1600 carries on a Porsche tradition of extraordinarily good roadholding. Most all sports cars will show some ability to cling to corners on a reasonably smooth road surface; under these conditions the Porsche shows no impressive superiority. In fact until you're used to the car it can have a "squirrelly" feel that's deceptive. If the recommended standard tire pressures are used, the 1600 is very, very sensitive to side winds on open highways, and it's only somewhat better with the higher fast-touring pressures (21 psi front, 26 psi rear) that we used through our testing.

But it's on the bumpy back roads that this car really performs wonders. You find yourself searching for serpentine, climbing, diving and winding byways just to exploit the astonishing agility of this car. The surface doesn't matter; the bumpier it is, the more the Porsche likes it. If severe ripples break the tires loose, the wide tread and supple suspension usually succeed in clamping them to the road again before the car has moved sideways more than a few feet. So solid and so secure does this car feel over the most atrocious roads, in fact, that many owners may tend to overstress the automobile without knowing it. In a sense, then, the Porsche reputation for chassis fragility may be attributable to severe driving that results from its solid feel!

Our Steering Behavior evaluation revealed the remarkable design job that's been done by Porsche in the last decade. The 356B very gently but very definitely understeers up to the breakaway point, at which it's the back that wants to leave the scene first. Unfortunately we weren't able to test the Super 90, with the compensating spring, on our 400-foot circle, but expectation would be that it would understeer still more. We'll publish a Steering Behavior chart for comparison as soon as a test can be arranged.

SUPER 90 HANDLING

Generally, the Super 90 does seem to have a slight cornering edge over those Porsches not fitted with the compensating spring. The difference was clearly demonstrated a year ago at the Nürburgring when a factory coupe was raced with the Super 90 engine and special springing. Changing from a non-compensated car to the Super 90, factory driver Edgar Barth was able to cut several seconds from his previous times. "It just corners faster," says Barth, "and you feel that you can throw it about in complete safety." Adjustable Koni shocks are also standard on the Super 90.

Our discussion of the Super 90 wouldn't be complete without a word about the German Dunlop sports tire that's being fitted to all Super 90's and Carreras now. Developed in collaboration with Porsche, it's of the Michelin X breed with metal threads in the carcass and very flexible sidewalls that carry a portion of the tread pattern. For high-speed driving the recommended pressures are 20 psi front and 24 psi rear. The tires are virtually silent and only begin to protest audibly when the car is cornering at the extreme limit.

WHAT MORE COULD YOU ASK?

Throughout this Road Research Report we've discussed the way all the component parts of the Porsche operate. What may not be evident here — and what is surely evident when you step inside the car — is the loving way all these parts are put together. Though production of Porsche cars has increased greatly since the tentative days in the early Fifties, they've still been able to maintain a quality level that's exemplary. If you want a superb machine for traveling fast in comfort, one on which you can rely completely, the Porsche has few peers in its price class. In every way that really counts, both automobiles examined this month are excellent sports car buys.

—SCI

POWER AT A PRICE

TO BE FULLY APPRECIATED, the Porsche Super 90 must be considered a highly-specialized model. It's neither fish nor fowl in that it's much healthier than the 1600 Super, but lacks the real Gran Tourismo performance of a G. T. Carrera. Price and docility are the obvious entities that keep it from approaching the latter yet make it a more palatable purchase. Basically, the Super 90 is a hot-rodded version of the normal bushing-bearing 1600. By means of the "Three C's" (cam, carburetion, and compression ratio) the 90 develops 15 more horses than the Super, 30 more than the Normal. Handling changes have been incorporated with the increased power by the addition of a compensating spring in the rear suspension, and the results are *very* interesting.

Sole (obvious) exterior engine changes appear to be the replacement of the Zenith dual-throat carburetors of the Super with Solex 40's of the same type. The latter, however, have bigger throats and venturis along with a jetting arrangement that lends itself to high-performance work and tuning. A half-point increase in compression ratio over the Super engine and a higher-lift camshaft combine with the breathing improvements to move horsepower, torque, and rpm range up a considerable percentage. These modifications work out extremely well, yet the engine remains very docile. In fact, we'd hazard that it's tamer in traffic and lower speed ranges than the 1600 Super. The high torque and wide rpm range combine to give the impression of many more cubic inches than there actually are. Getting off the mark fast from a standing start takes some practice, however, as the big carburetors can't be dumped open too fast. Once the biggest chunk of inertia is overcome, you can go to the floor with the pedal and start moving out very fast indeed. In fact one of the most impressive things about this engine is the feeling of torque — sheet push in the shoulders — that one gets on booting the throttle with the tach in the green zone. As is the case with all Porsches but the likes of the GT Carrera, there isn't the feeling of wild acceleration from a standing start, but once under way it comes on with increasing force. The effect of this is that, unless one is used to this particular Porsche characteristic, speed builds up far faster than one would believe possible. After one of these seemingly mild starts, the first look at the speedometer can come as something of a shock since that instrument may well be telling you that you are unwittingly breaking every speed law in the book. More than one Porsche pilot, SCG's Editor included, has on occasion found himself trying to explain this phenomenon to an unsympathetic arm of the law.

Aside from the individualities of the Super 90, changes wrought in Porsches over the past few years are not too outwardly apparent but amazing in effect. Gone is the lightness in the steering and the unpredictable oversteer that often found you looking back in the direction from whence you had come. The steering is now firm and lets the driver establish a "feel" of adhesion. Another item that's altered is the formerly delicate shift mechanism that, under any misuse, would warp or break any place from the handle clear in to the synchro rings in the transmission. All of this is beefed up and a tad stiffer. The lever is more conveniently placed and the throw is shorter, eliminating the former long reach to third. Gone are the days of the one-finger shifts, but we'd rather have it this way.

The clutch is light, smooth, and takes a positive bite without that all-in, all-out feeling. Detail improvements have been made to eliminate the former tendency to snap clutch cable ends in such inconvenient places as dark country roads or mid-town Manhattan during rush hours. We found it necessary to abuse the clutch some to obtain maximum acceleration readings and found it far stronger than in previous models, the Carrera De Luxe included.

The brakes are potent and smooth with better than average balance and virtually nil fade. The only possible objection was a slightly spongey pedal feel that was probably more due to arm length than any other factor. Required pressure was quite light and the resulting stops from any speed were phenomenally strong.

While the handling of the newer Porsches in general is vastly improved, the characteristics of the Super 90 are different as well. The compensating spring, consisting of a single transverse leaf that centers under the gearbox and connects — through rubber biscuits — to the trailing arms, enables the spring rate to be softened slightly but stiffens roll-resistance. Result: it's strictly a flat cat in a corner. To improve adhesion the German Dunlop Sports tire is made standard equipment. It is a soft, high-tread skin very similar to a motorcycle tire and provides maximum bite in the wet or around low-velocity corners. We felt, however, that they made the Porsche become squirrely in fast, dry corners as they seem to squeegee under maximum load. But we should first state that the "90" isn't cornered like a Porsche! Normal procedure with a Push-ee is to "drive it in," letting the front end plow to compensate for the rear coming out. In the S-90 that technique will net you a trip through the tules. It must be set into a drift attitude before the corner and varying amounts of power applied. Regardless of technique, the car would only negotiate a corner smoothly when it was quite a bit below its actual limit. With harder racing tires installed, the breakaway would probably be gradual, any drift or slide more controllable. Applied to normal road usage, however, the effect is fantastic. You just crank the wheel, brace yourself, and watch it make the turn. This test gave us one more example, as though we needed one, that when one is going racing, a racing tire should be used, and when touring is contemplated, there's nothing like a touring tire.

The ability to soak up both long and short bumps is amazing in the "new" Porsches. This has always been a long suit for Porsche, but it's even better now and even the slight tendency to pitch, caused by the short wheelbase, has been virtually eliminated.

Seating is different, at least in the roadster, in that one seemingly sits higher, in a more chairlike position. (To some it's desirable but classic Porsche pushers may prefer the old, down-in-the-car seating, reduced visibility and entry difficulty notwithstanding.) There's lots of room in the cockpit both laterally and longitudinally — but not necessarily vertically; a six-plus footer could just bump his head on the top bow.

In the lighting department there is another change and, in our estimation, not necessarily a desirable one. After turning on the lights with the usual

(continued on following page)

Numeral 90 tagged to Super nameplate is the only clue to the identity of the potent newcomer to Porsche family.

Only slight revisions in styling have been made since the Porsche design originated in the early post-war period.

PHOTOS BY PAT BROLLIER

Nose into the inside of the turn, the Super 90 barrels through a decreasing radius, downhill bend like flat cat.

Driving techniques with the Super 90 are quite different from those of standard versions; this one really drifts.

Touring comfort with rollup windows and added visibility of new top styling are bonuses for Porsche purchasers.

New seats have more cushion than old speedster buckets, and less cradling.

Engine compartment remains starkly simple, and offers good accessibility.

POWER AT A PRICE

dash switch, we washed the windshield eight times before the fact sunk in that there was no dimmer switch on the floor, only the washer pedal. The dimmer is on the steering column and is operated with the left hand. Once the operation is mastered it is no particular handicap, but is seems to us that the change was not necessary — it's just something more for already busy hands to do.

Except for this one item, however, Porsche has done its usual neat job in the small control department. All the various knobs, now black instead of the former ivory that was almost an identification mark of *any* German car, are well placed and simple in their push-pull operation. The instruments, too, are well placed in such a way that there is only minimal eye-shifting from road to dash and back again to check operating conditions. In the left group there is a fuel level gauge and an oil temperature indicator which, unfortunately, doesn't give the actual temperature but merely lets you know if things are hot, cold or something in between. The center instrument is the beautifully marked tachometer that has been the mark of a Porsche virtually since the beginning. In addition to the usual numbers and gradations it, like all Porsche tachs, is marked with green, striped red and solid red zones. For the benefit of those unfortunate enough to be unfamiliar with the Porsche in any guise, these zones indicate various running and/or power conditions. The green zone is the area in which full throttle may be used, particularly in top gear. You can run below this engine speed but the power isn't there and max throttle should not be used. The light red area tells you that you're approaching peak power and that you're above safe cruising speed — momentarily yes, steadily, no. The red zone is the same as the red-line on any tach — it means roughly: Watch it, bub, or you'll run out of valves, gears, rods or something else equally expensive if you go much higher.

As it is, with the S-90, engine speeds can be taken about 800 rpm higher than with the other versions. In terms of performance this gives somewhat more range than is the case with the other pushrod versions. The car is a healthy cut above the 1600-S and several rungs up the ladder from the 1600-N. It is roughly equivalent in push to the Carrera DeLuxe, though not in terms of rev range, since even this mildest of four-cam engines will turn willingly to 7000 rpm and 6000 revs is pushing hard in the case of the stock rocker-box versions. However, the S-90 can sustain con-

*(continued on page **88**)*

PORSCHE ENGINE OUTPUT COMPARISON CHART FOR:
SUPER 90, SUPER, NORMAL

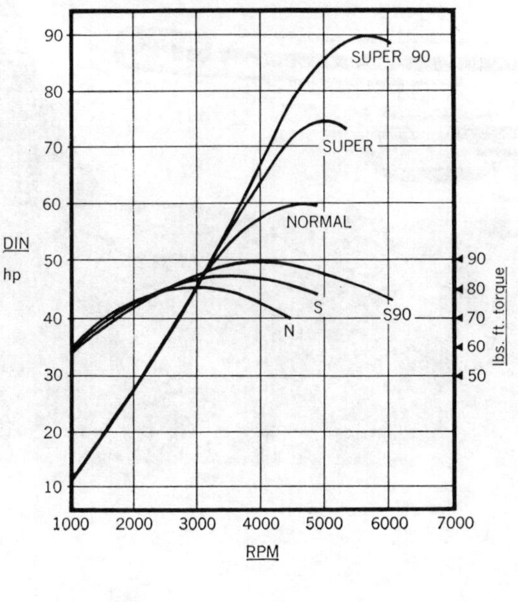

ROAD TEST/1
TEST DATA

VEHICLE	Porsche	MODEL	Super 90
PRICE (as tested)	$4375 POE (West Coast)	OPTIONS	None

ENGINE:

Type	Flat 4-cylinder, 4-cycle, air-cooled, bushing-bearing
Head	Alloy, hemispherical chambers
Valves	Pushrod-rocker actuated, single cam
Max. bhp	102 @ 5500 rpm
Max. torque	89 lbs. ft. @ 4300 rpm
Bore	3.25 in. 82.5 mm.
Stroke	2.91 in. 74 mm.
Displacement	96.5 cu. in. 1582 cc.
Compression Ratio	9.0 to 1
Induction System	2 dual-choke Solex 40 PJJ-4
Exhaust System	Direct port-to-muffler, dual outlet
Electrical System	6v single distributor ignition

CLUTCH:	Single disc, conv. pressure plate	**DIFFERENTIAL:**	Spiral bevel
Diameter:	7⅛ in.	Ratio:	4.43 to 1
Actuation	cable	Drive Axles (type):	Swing, enclosed
TRANSMISSION:	Integral with differential, full-synchro	**STEERING:**	ZF worm-and-peg
		Turns Lock to Lock:	3
		Turn Circle:	36 ft.
Ratios: 1st	3.09 to 1		
2nd	1.76 to 1	**BRAKES:**	Drum or Disc
3rd	1.13 to 1	Diameter	11 in.
4th	0.85 to 1	Swept Area	218 sq. in.

CHASSIS:

Frame:	Pressed steel, welded box section
Body:	Semi-unit, steel
Front Suspension:	Ind., trailing arm, torsion bar
Rear Suspension:	Ind., swing, trailing arms, torsion bar
Tire Size and Type:	5.90 x 15, Dunlop SP

WEIGHTS AND MEASURES:

Wheelbase:	82.7 in.	Ground Clearance:	5.9 in.
Front Track:	51.4 in.	Curb Weight:	2010 lbs.
Rear Track:	50.1 in.	Test Weight:	2310 lbs.
Overall Height:	51.6 in.	Crankcase:	5.5 qts.
Overall Width:	65.7 in.	Cooling System:	(air)
Overall Length:	157.7 in.	Gas Tank:	14.7 gals.

PERFORMANCE:

0-30	4.0 sec.	0-70	14.6 sec.
0-40	6.0 sec.	0-80	18.8 sec.
0-50	8.1 sec.	0-90	24.0 sec.
0-60	9.7 sec.	0-100	29.5 sec.

Standing ¼ mile 19.0 sec. @ 84 mph — Top Speed (av. two-way run) 110 mph

Speed Error	30	40	50	60	70	80	90
Actual	28	38	48	58	67	77	86

Fuel Consumption Test:	16 mpg	RPM Red-line	5800 rpm
Average:	27 mpg	Speed Ranges in gears (Green zone):	
Recommended Shift Points:		1st	0 to 30 mph
Max. 1st	30 mph	2nd	26 to 58 mph
Max. 2nd	58 mph	3rd	45 to 85 mph
Max. 3rd	85 mph	4th	55 to 112 mph

Brake Test: 80% G Average, over 8 stops
Fade encountered on 8th stop

REFERENCE FACTORS:

BHP per Cubic Inch	1.06
Lbs. per bhp	19.45
Piston Speed @ Peak rpm	2667 ft./sec.
Swept Brake area per lb.	0.108 sq. in.

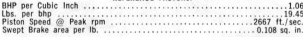

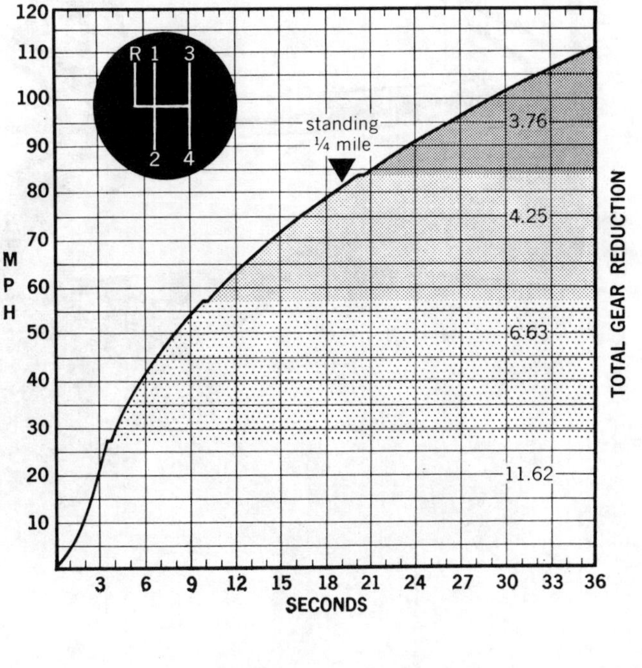

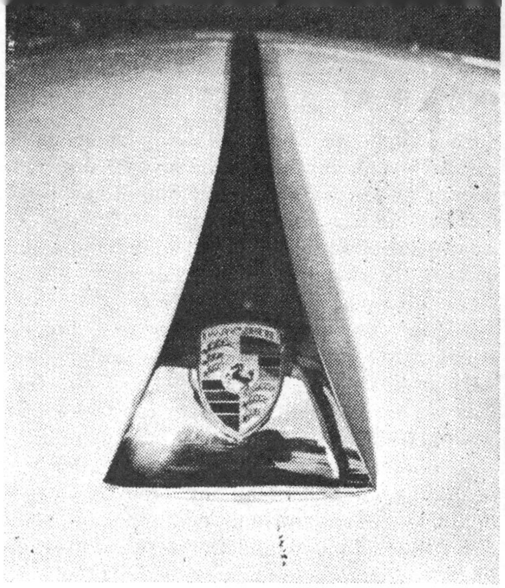

The sign of the new Porsche with chrome centre bonnet strip sweeping outwards towards the horizons.

A PORSCHE WITH PFFT! By CLYDE HODGINS

THE JEKYLL AND HYDE SUPER 1600

S.C.W. FULL ROAD TEST

JUST after Doug Blain left for England, Tony Litt, manager of Arnold Glass' Capitol Motors in the Sydney suburb of Artarmon, rang and offered the use of one of his client's Porsche Super 90's for a SPORTS CAR WORLD test.

I thanked Tony for his trust in our reputation of looking after fabulous cars in our care, but I could not agree with his views on salesmanship of the latest 356B Porsches. (Now don't get me wrong. Tony is a mighty salesman. The last four times I've visited his showrooms I have nearly ended up trading in my Matador red Prefect — on, in this order, a Renault Gordini, a Simca Monthlery, an ordinary Porsche 1600 and lastly, a Datsun Fair Lady.

I told Tony, "I am happy any time to drive a Porsche Super 90 round NSW, even with big ads on the sides as at the race meetings, but I think you would be spoiling me and the readers of SCW. Last January Doug Blain tested the Porsche 1600. Now you want to make me a full Admiral without being a captain in the interval. I would like to test a 1600 Super first, then test the Super 90 a month or two later, otherwise no one would buy a 1600 Super."

Herr Litt answered, "Agreed. We have a demonstrator in the 1600 super model, which is Arnold's personal car. You can pick it up Thursday afternoon and keep it till the weekend, when we are likely to sell it."

This was slap bang in the middle of the credit squeeze and the extra tax payment. But I knew Tony was fair dinkum as I had missed out on several used Healey tests by leaving the vehicles at Capitol's Haymarket branch over the weekend.

I've always admired the Porsche which, I used to tell "unconscious" spectators in the outback during the Round-Australia Trials, were actually VW racing cars. To the uninitiated, this was sufficient, but any car lover, at least, knows the sight and sound of the Porsche. Then if he has been a little luckier, he will have driven one, or if he owns one — well, all his Christmas presents have come at once.

I had driven the new model 1600 Super several months earlier for another test and then described myself as a greatly frustrated "young" man. I only had the car for 24 hours, compared with 36 hours on the SCW test. Anyhow, on that occasion it rained all the time, so that I was unable to see what it could open out to. Also, the time factor kept me confined to near-Sydney traffic with 3000 revs going to waste in the rear engine compartment.

Arnold's Porsche was a black one, with a bench type seat and white wall tyres as extras. I would have really gone to town about having to take color pictures of a black car, but in a Porsche color does not seem to matter. Like a night prowler, it could be seen and heard scampering in the night and brought to life several country towns on our southern run to Pullitop (near Wagga) and return.

I edged my foot on to the accelerator pedal, in reverse gear out of the garage, while telling Tony that I would be certain "police bait" in such a car. As I moved off he replied, "No chance. The police will leave you alone. They consider only sensible people buy Porsches. They say a person would not spend the money needed for a Porsche if he just wanted to show off."

On my way home to Bondi I found that a Porsche driver was to drive within himself, forgetting about the others on the road. If you try and outspeed them (which can be done on 99 percent of occasions) then you will end up without a licence or in a casualty ward — for even the wonderful road-holding qualities of the Porsche will not be a guardian angel.

With a Porsche you know you are good, so there is no need to show it. Our test, though fitted into 36 hours, had been designed to even out-test the Porsche, just what SCW followers would like to do if they had the vehicle, time and petrol money available.

Two friends were going down to holiday at Pullitop, so we decided four of us would make the trip down, with only two coming back when the full SCW test strip would be used. With the addition of the bench seat, Porsche say their car can become even a five seater for shorter journeys. We wanted to try it out. Earlier in the day I had twice monkeyed round to open the tiny luggage compartment, which however also houses the most important petrol tank of 11½ gallons. But this was the sore point in the Porsche armor during the next 24 hours.

When we reached our departure point at midnight the bonnet would not come undone no matter how we tried. So it was three passengers in the front with the fourth person, plus baggage in the back compartment.

Though the suburbs were deathly quiet at this time I had to be rather restrained in fourth gear. The easily read Porsche rev counter has green lines running from 3000 up to 5000, which is the recommended driving range. All the Porsches do 20.3 mph at 1000 revs. So to do 3000 and not strain the 1600 Super, you would have to do 60.9 mph. Not for us round the Sydney suburbs!

We sat on 2000 revs (or 40.6 mph) where possible. Then if revs dropped due to traffic interrup-

(Above) the front bonnet compartment, with hardly any room for luggage after fitting the petrol tank and spare tyre. (Below): The engine room.

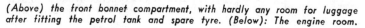

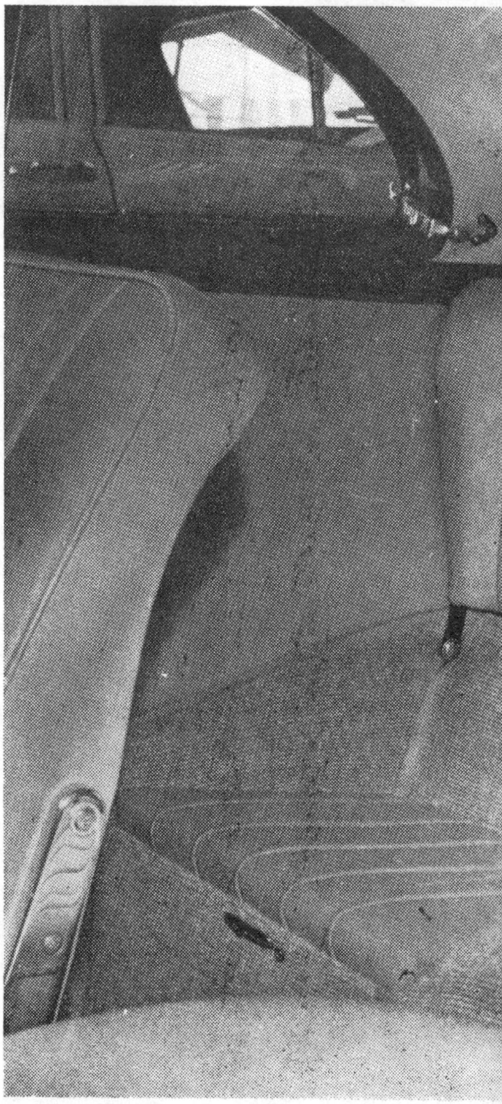

Both seats lay right back, with two occasional seats at the rear, which can be folded down to take more luggage.

tions, a swift change down was made.

It is not till on the open road that you appreciate the Porsche. During the dark I was content to use a mere 3000 revs and cruise at 60 mph, when steering was featherlight with no trace of either under or oversteer. Of course, the extra load probably helped. As the Porsche flew across the sunrise I eased up to 4000 revs, or 81.2 mph, which I felt was an ideal cruising speed with four persons aboard, till we reached our destination. Incidentally tyre pressures on the run down to Wagga were 20 lb up front and 24 in the rear, as recommended by the factory for fast cruising.

My three passengers found the Porsche even comfortable enough to fall asleep. It could not have been the fatigue on such a short run which was covered leisurely yet at a good average of 55 mph.

On stopping for breakfast we looked up the Porsche book about opening the bonnet and then realised this apparently was one of the failings of these fabulous machines. The book told what to do in case of bonnet catch breaking or sticking. You had to pull out a rubber stopper near the left front wheel and insert a bent piece of

Old and new lines of the Porsche, which now has higher headlights for improved night driving.

Interior of the Porsche with the bench type seat (note the vee for gear lever movement) at £25 extra, as on the model we tested.

wire. Apparently it had happened before on this Porsche as the rubber was out. But the wire did not work, so we continued our journey with some misgivings about petrol supplies.

About 20 miles from Wagga the 1600 Super cut out due to a lack of fuel. I switched to the emergency tank of one gallon and drove cautiously to see that it lasted out the distance.

Next problem was to find someone in Wagga to open the bonnet. Knowing there was no Porsche agent I drove to the VW people, as I thought they probably had faced the same problem many times. There I was told that with VW's you cut straight through the bonnet motto, which can be replaced at a small cost. But surely not with a Porsche!

Finally after a lot of fiddling a giant mechanic gave it a tug sideways and it came open. We filled up without closing the bonnet, leaving it on the first latch. This allows you to get your fingers inside to push back the second catch.

Out on the Oldham's station, where our friends were to holiday, the unmade roads really tested out the suspension — at slow speeds, thank you. It proved what I have thought before — that the Porsche has every attribute of the VW for Round-Australia trials.

Where the Porsche really glories — at dawn and open, bitumen roads facing you for miles and miles. This was just outside Wagga.

Driver's eye view . . . with speedo, rev counter, oil-temp and petrol gauges.

Even with four people aboard and a fast average, the 1600 Super had given 34 miles per gallon. On our run home we gave the Porsche its workout on the SCW strip and it was not lacking. Our top speed was a timed average both ways of 108.8 mph. Other people claim this same vehicle has done 115 mph, but I was quite happy with our figures.

During our run home rain fell continually, and the Porsche gave us several thrills on tight corners. But this was soon corrected by lowering the tyre pressures to 16-20.

Nothing is lacking on the Porsche instrument panel. There is a combined oil temperature gauge, as well as lights for generator and oil pressure. The tachometer, which is red lined at 5000 revs (compared with 4500 on the ordinary 1600 and 5500 on the Super 90) also carries the high beam indicator (blue) and turning indicator (red).

The speedo carries total mileage as well as a trip meter. There is an ash tray, cigarette lighter, two side map pockets and a small glove compartment. Two pull buttons on top of the dash are for lights and a hand throttle. The heater tap is centrally situated on the floor, just in front of the gear lever — a la VW. Windscreen washing is foot controlled and the handbrake (which I felt was a little hard to use) underneath the steering wheel.

Summing up, the Porsche 1600 Super is an ideal buy for any young man who wants added prestige with top performance. And it's not confined to the young, either. On the Saturday morning I returned the 1600 Super to Tony Litt he was just completing the sale of a blue Porsche to the managing director of a big Sydney company. Later I saw the car on the Pacific Highway with its oldish owner not the least perturbed about the power he might unleash if he put his foot on the wrong pedal by mistake. #

PERFORMANCE

TOP SPEED:

Two-way average	108.1 mph
Fastest one way	109 mph

ACCELERATION:

(test limit 5000 rpm)
Through gears:

0-30 mph	4.2 sec
0-40 mph	6.9 sec
0-50 mph	8.3 sec
0-60 mph	13.5 sec
0-70 mph	17.5 sec
0-80 mph	23.2 sec
Speed at end of quarter	75

MAXIMUM SPEED IN GEARS:

(factory figures)
(at 5000 rpm)

I	27 mph
II	46 mph
III	72 mph
IV	99 mph

SPEEDOMETER ERROR:

30 mph actual — indicated 30.5 mph
40 mph actual — indicated 40.5 mph
50 mph actual — indicated 50.5 mph
60 mph actual — indicated 60.0 mph
70 mph actual — indicated 70.5 mph
80 mph actual — indicated 80.4 mph

TAPLEY DATA:

Maximum pull in gears:

I	515 lb/ton at 21 mph
II	465 lb/ton at 37 mph
III	295 lb/ton at 55 mph
IV	190 lb/ton at 77 mph

BRAKING:

Fade: Nil
Stopping distance from 20 ft — 16 ft 9 in (very safe)

CALCULATED DATA:

Weight as tested (2 men), cwt	20¼
Max bhp (nett)	75
Max torque (nett lb/ft)	86
Bhp/litre	47.4

SPECIFICATIONS

PRICE:

£2880 (inc tax). Roadster about £200 less; hardtop about £100 more; Blue, Black and Silver Colors £35 extra.

ENGINE:

Type: Four cylinders, flat four, horizontally opposed, air cooled (in rear)

Valves	Overhead in V
Cubic capacity	1582 cc
Bore and stroke	82.5 x 74 mm
Compression ratio	8.5 to 1
Carburettors	2 dual downdraught Zenith 32 ndix
Fuel pump	AC mechanical
Max power	88 (gross) at 5000 rpm
Max torque	86 lb/ft at 3700 rpm

CHASSIS:

Type: Seamless pressed and welded steel box type, one piece with body.

Wheelbase	6 ft 11 in
Track, front	4 ft 3½ in
rear	4 ft 2 in

Suspension:
Front: Longitudinal, swinging (trailing) arms.
Rear: Swinging half axles, radium arm guided (longitudinal).
Springing: Torsion bar, stabiliser at front.

Shock absorbers ... adjustable koni

Brakes:
Type: Front, Duplex; rear, single cylinder.
Operation: Hydraulic.
Steering: ZF worm gear, divided tie rod, damper.

GEAR RATIOS:

I	11.2
II	7.8
III	5.0
IV	3.6

All synchromesh.

GENERAL:

Length overall	13 ft 2 in
Width	5 ft 5½ in
Height	4 ft 4½ in
Test weather	fine, no wind

All test runs made on dry, bitumen-bound gravel road with driver and one passenger aboard. All times average from runs in opposite directions ,using a corrected speedometer.

ANY ANGLE SHOWS THE SUPER 90 AS A CAR OF EXCELLENCE, BUILT TO PRODIGIOUS STANDARDS OF CRAFTSMANSHIP AND FINISH.

Rear end styling has remained almost unchanged since Porsche's inception in 1950. Improvements have gone on under the surface.

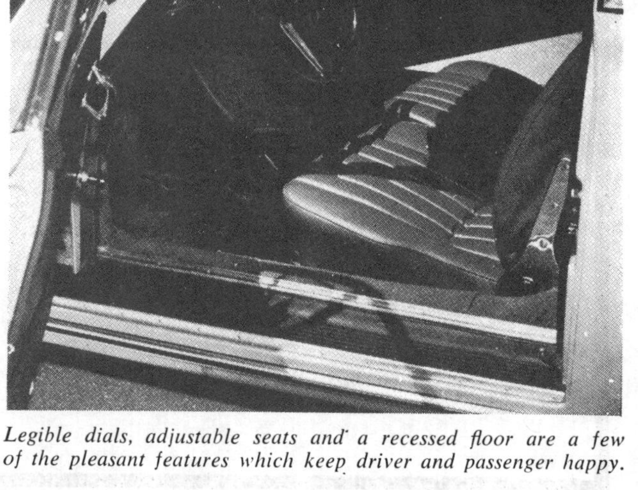

Legible dials, adjustable seats and a recessed floor are a few of the pleasant features which keep driver and passenger happy.

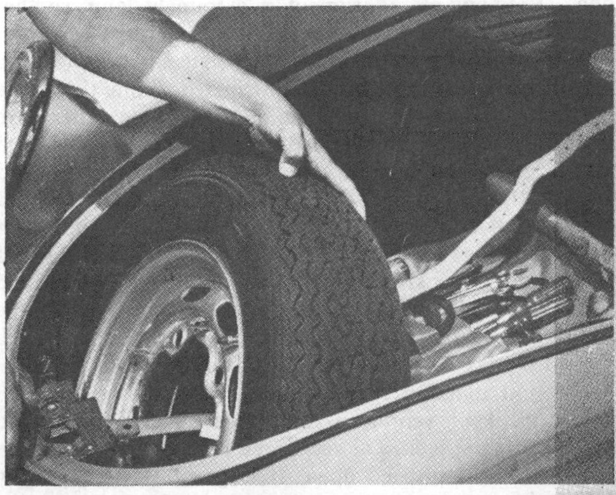

Essentials cut down under-hood storage space, but luggage may be carried in the rear seat compartment.

Engine room is uncluttered and accessible. Twin Solex carburetors flank the vertical fan shroud.

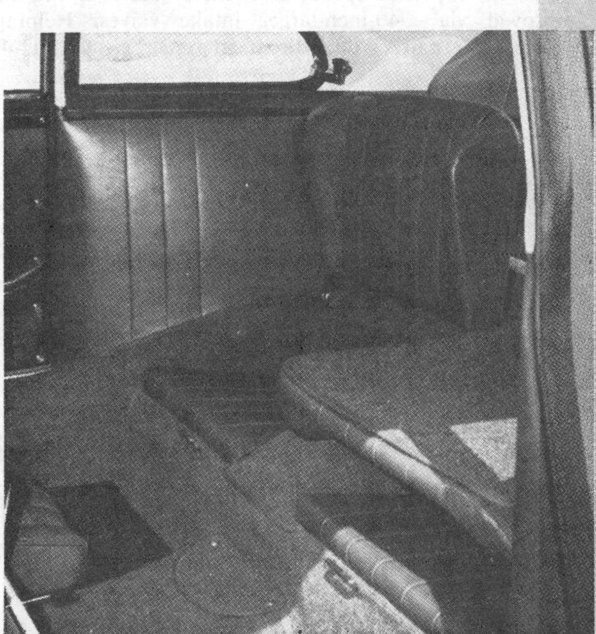

Two adults can ride here for short periods. The seat backs fold, forming a level area for stowage.

PORSCHE

SUPER 90

With its more powerful engine, this new model adds to Porsche's laurels for performance, handling, safety

WHAT CAN THEY DO as an encore?" asked an old-line Porsche enthusiast, awed and a little stunned after his first drive in a Super 90.

It's a legitimate question. The new Porsche, and particularly the Super 90, has reached such an incredibly high state of development that it would seem very difficult, if not impossible, to improve it materially. But that's what Porsche fans have been saying each year for years. And every year the Porsche folks come up with something better, although in all fairness it should be pointed out that '60 was the year of the big change, marking the 356B series (restyled body and interior) and the introduction of the Super 90 engine.

We have no intention of projecting Porsche's future progress; rather the task is to report, explain and criticize Porsche's top performer in their production line, the Super 90.

The "90" refers to 90 DIN horsepower, a German rating roughly equal to 102 SAE bhp. This is the most powerful pushrod engine Porsche has ever produced, providing (with considerably more tractability) almost the same performance as the four-overhead-cam Carrera Deluxe – not to mention lowered cost. (The Carrera is no longer considered "production" because only a handful are being built with special bodies for race car owners.)

Anyone familiar with the Volkswagen has a pretty good idea of how the Porsche operates, even if he has never been close to one of the more exotic sports machines. Not that there is any mechanical interchangeability (although there was once); it is simply that the Porsche also employs an opposed, aircooled Four for power – rear-mounted,

ROAD TEST

by Wayne Thoms

driving swinging axles. All-independent suspension is through torsion bars, and the body is part of a unit structure on a platform chassis. Porsche proved long ago that all these elements can be blended into a delightful entity while the skill Porsche employs in the process has become virtually an auto industry standard.

Our test vehicle, a coupe in traditional silver-gray with red leatherette interior, was provided by D. D. Michelmore, a Reseda, Calif., Porsche dealer and race driver who takes great pride in his product. Well he should, for the Super 90 coupe can best be described as luxury motoring for the discriminating gentleman. (And except for the engine, tires and one suspension variation, the Normal and Super Porsches are identical to the "90." Because of these similarities, anyone contemplating Porsche ownership can get an excellent idea of the entire line from our experience.)

What is luxury motoring? In this context it's a trim, utterly comfortable two-passenger automobile. Built for extreme high-speed touring, it includes enormous safety factors through precise handling and braking, yet the car is equally at home in city congestion and on the race course. In fact, we found it quite remarkable that the Super 90, designed as it is to be competitive as a racing sports car on demand, should be so docile in traffic. This is a good place to say, "Yes, we have heard the stories about the '90' being noisy, temperamental and unreliable. In our opinion, they are untrue with a capital NO."

Much of Porsche's attraction must be credited to non-mechanical areas – that is fit, finish and scientifically engineered comfort. Quality control is such that body panels match to seemingly impossible tolerances. There are no areas of sloppy workmanship in the Porsche. Exterior paint jobs are of consistently high quality and there is even a quart can of the body color included with each car for touch-up.

Seating has gone through various phases of refinement. Today's coupe seats appear similar to earlier models, but the difference comes after a day at the wheel. Designed with the help and advice of medical consultants, the seats support the back and thighs in a mildly contoured bucket that may be reclined at will during a protracted stretch of driving. Fore-and-aft adjustment is extremely long, so that any size driver should be able to find comfort.

Seat-to-window relationship is such that all-around vision is excellent, even though we anticipated limited viewing to the rear because of the acute window slope. There are rear seats, miniature buckets with split backrests that fold into a large or half luggage shelf. At 13 inches wide by 13 deep by 20½ high, the seats are suitable for adults – but they lack kneeroom. One adult is comfortable on short hauls or the seats are perfect for children. The shelf formed by the folded backrests is the major luggage area and measures 35 inches wide, 23 deep and 12 inches high to the base of the quarter windows. The under-hood space, well occupied by gas tank and spare tire, is quite limited.

We found that the coupe is one of the few sports cars that can be kept ventilated, draft-free and quiet of wind roar at touring speeds. The technique is to run with the rear quarter windows pivoted open. It is generally unnecessary to open either door window or vent pane. Here is a tip that should be obvious but is not. With side windows down, there is a terrific drumming set up at highway speeds. It can be killed instantly by cracking open the rear quarter windows. Hot air heating/defrosting is excellent in moderate temperatures. We can't vouch for extreme cold (when the engine would run cooler).

At the center of the instrument cluster is the tachometer, and this is what gives the car away as a different sort of Porsche. The shaded red segment begins at 5500 rpm (the Normal starts at 4500). This means that the needle can swing into the area once in a while for very brief periods. At 5800 rpm commences a solid red band that ends at 6000. Inside this area you are strictly on your own. You say you never rev that high? A careless downshift will put you there rather quickly – and there *may* be no sudden loud noises. If the only symptom is a loss of power, the best you can hope for will be bent pushrods. Don't permit that description to frighten you off; the Super 90 is easy to drive sensibly.

The "90" engine differs from Normal and Super in several specialized areas that are worth knowing about. First, it is better cooled through a revised air intake system which permits high, sustained speeds with more safety. Breathing is improved via .040-inch-larger intake valves. Helping feed them are a pair of dual-throat Solex carbs – 40 PJJ-4.

Impeccable handling, even on reverse-banked curves, is assured in any Porsche. Front-end styling changes came about in 1960. Headlights were raised and trim altered.

PHOTOS BY BOB D'OLIVO

Compression is up through the use of new high-dome, four-ring aluminum pistons. Rocker arm assembly is aluminum rather than steel. Valve springs are stiffer. The flywheel is five pounds lighter than the Super's. Cam and crank bearings have been nitride hardened. Cylinder walls are Ferral coated, a process which speeds break-in and reduces oil consumption. (The Super continues with chrome walls.) Three of the four main bearings are larger by 5mm than other models.

There are two other deviations of considerable importance (in their own right and because they may be adapted to other models). One is a simple ball check valve built into the breathers of the rocker covers. Should any oil ride up to the breathers during a hard corner, it can't get out. The other is what the factory calls a centrifugal oil valve located in the magnetic-mechanical oil filter. Local Porsche hot rodders call it an anti-slosh valve. It keeps up a constant supply of oil rather than an occasional burst of air and foam during tight, fast bends. It replaces the pan baffles often added for racing.

As we said, the engine is extremely docile at low speeds. It idles nicely at 800-900 rpm and will take off from low revs in the higher gears – although the practice is not recommended. However, it will stumble if the throttle is really kicked open while the engine is under load at low rpm. For example, it is noticeably more difficult to start from rest on an uphill grade with the "90" than with the Normal. As speed increases, there is a "coming alive" feeling that turns on about 4000 rpm. The "90" doesn't ever feel as if it wants to run out of revs. A close eye on the tach is strongly recommended.

The three characteristics which can do so much for sports car handling – steering, shifting and clutch action – are completely satisfying. Steering is very light, requiring a sensitive touch. The shift mechanism was revised in '60. It received a sturdier lever with a more solid feel and less slop. The Porsche synchro retains its famous reputation for slicing through the gears. What can be said about the clutch? It's very light in its action and it's positive in its bite – just as it should be.

continued

PORSCHE SUPER 90

2-occasional-4-seater coupe

ODOMETER READING AT START OF TEST: 1400 miles

RECOMMENDED ENGINE RED LINE: 5800 rpm

PERFORMANCE

Acceleration (2 aboard)

0-30 mph	4.1 secs.
0-45 mph	7.4
0-60 mph	12.9

Standing start ¼-mile 19.5 secs. and 76.5 mph

Speeds in gears @ 5800 rpm

1st	30.1 mph	3rd	78.3 mph
2nd	52.2 mph	4th	107.3 mph

Speedometer Error on Test Car

Car's speedometer reading	35	51	57	70
Weston electric speedometer	30	45	50	60

Miles per hour per 1000 rpm in top gear .... 18.5 mph (actual meter reading)

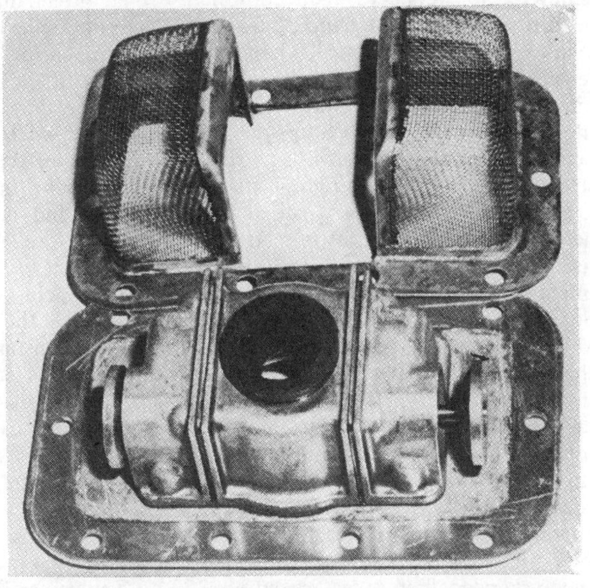

A system of baffles and screens keeps oil from sloshing in the sump. This device is particularly helpful in racing.

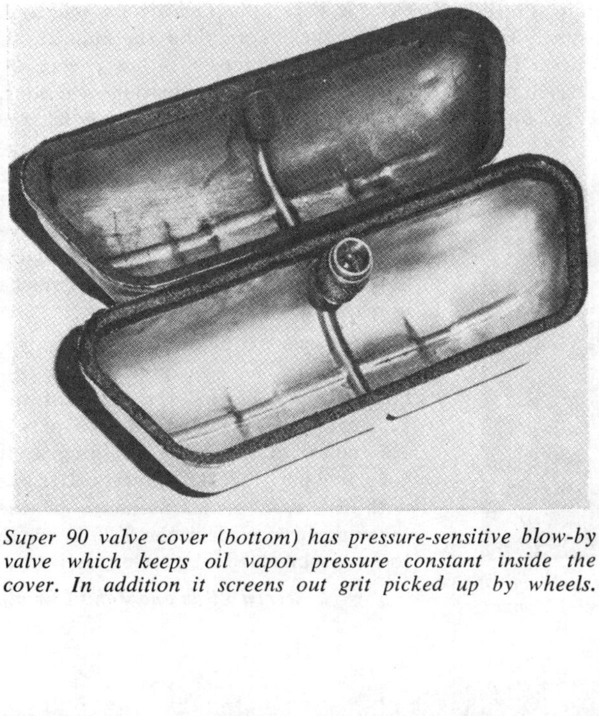

Super 90 valve cover (bottom) has pressure-sensitive blow-by valve which keeps oil vapor pressure constant inside the cover. In addition it screens out grit picked up by wheels.

SPECIFICATION FROM MANUFACTURER

Engine

Ohv, opposed 4-cyl., aircooled
Bore: 3.25 ins. Stroke: 2.91 ins.
Displacement: 96.5 cubic inches
Compression ratio: 9.0:1
Horsepower: 102 @ 5500 rpm
Ignition: 6-volt battery/coil

Gearbox

4-speed, all synchro, central floor lever

Driveshaft

Transaxle

Differential

Spiral bevel gear
Standard ratio 4.428:1

Body and Frame

Seamless, pressed and welded steel box frame with unit body
Wheelbase 82.7 ins.
Track, front 51.4 ins., rear 50.1 ins.
Overall length 157.7 ins.
Dry weight 1980 lbs.

Suspension

All independent
Front: 2 longitudinal trailing radius arms (designed as suspension arms); 2 transverse square torsion bars, stabilizer bar, adjustable Koni tubular shocks

Rear: Swing axles guided by longitudinal radius arms (designed as spring supports); 1 round torsion bar each side; 1 compensating spring as anti-stabilizer; adjustable Koni tubular shocks

Wheels and Tires

Slotted steel disc wheels, Dunlop SP braced tread, 6.60 x 15 tires

Brakes

Hydraulic drums — Duplex-type front, Simplex-type rear
Front and rear: 11-in. dia. x 1.57-in. width

Porsche Super 90

continued

Once up at cruising-touring-racing speeds, everyone wants to know how the Super 90 corners. It corners very, very well, the result of two obvious items that differ from the less potent models. Mounted below the rear axles – and attached to them as well as the transmission housing – is a compensating spring. It is a single leaf which counteracts the effects of the front stabilizer bar. It has no appreciable effect during normal, straight-line, smooth-road driving.

The factory says: "This compensating spring allows (you) to take bends at a still higher speed, since the tendency . . . to oversteer is reduced, which in turn will reduce the trend of the rear axle to veer off the course." They claim fewer steering corrections with slower, more predictable breakaway while taking a bend at too high a speed. Also better directional stability on rough straightaways. They are right, as usual.

Secondarily, handling is aided by a new German Dunlop SP braced tread tire. Its 165 x 15 dimensions (approximately 6.60 x 15) compare to the Supersport tires on the Super – 5.90 x 15. With a soft sidewall and around-the-edges tread, it sticks like glue, allowing the car to be wheeled around corners at *near* racing speeds without the slightest feeling of discomfort and almost no tire noise. Our initial impression of roadholding was excellent. Then we found only 14 pounds front, 16 pounds rear in the tires. Pumping them to the recommended high-speed pressures, 25 and 28 front and rear, seemed to help handling but it was difficult to pin down. How the tires would react under true racing conditions we could not determine. Anyone planning to race should conduct his own experiments.

There is one relatively inexpensive accessory that is of extreme benefit for serious competition. A limited-slip differential is available for about $150, and we are told by drivers who have used it that it's great. Of course, they agree that you have to learn to drive all over again, at least through the corners, but it is practically guaranteed to cut seconds off lap times.

Porsches have always had adequate brakes. In '60 they were improved with finned drums. They stop beautifully and there is only one word of caution that does not appear in the owner's manual: if possible, don't apply the parking brake while the drums are hot. They'll cool out egg-shaped and provide an annoying low-speed braking characteristic for the life of the car.

In the area known as ride, the Porsche is without compromise. Because the wheelbase is short there must be some attendant choppiness, but it has been minimized with Porsche's wonderful suspension. It is a great temptation to take the car through rough terrain at better than sensible speeds – just to feel how well the suspension soaks up road imperfections. In a related area, the Porsche has a most unusual noise level. Wind noise is nil – but because engine noise comes from the rear and because it is mingled with the high-pitched note of the cooling fan, some people feel the car is disagreeably noisy.

Fuel consumption is going to jump all over the scale, depending upon how the car is driven. Regular city traffic and steady use of indirect gears will drive it down as far as 16-20 mpg; the open road and steady cruising will pick it up to the factory rated 27.7 mpg – unless the top speed of 112-115 mph is utilized too often.

The Super 90 coupe carries a $4600 price tag on the West Coast. Whether this is excessive rests completely with what a prospective owner wants. Attempting to be completely objective and weighing all sides, we firmly believe that it is not too high a price for the car. In relation to the overall market the "90" comes up an excellent buy. •

Porsche Super 90 dash fascia is dominated by tachometer, which is redlined at 5400 rpm. Above 5800 rpm, solid redline begins, marking area of extreme danger.

POWER AT A PRICE

continued from page 77

sistently tighter revving than can the lesser varieties, thanks to a new cooling layout that hauls in far more air than is the case with 1600 and 1600-S. Other changes, unseen but nonetheless present, that allow harder usage are such niceties as nitrided bearing surfaces on both crank and cam, a lighter flywheel, stiffer valve springs, light alloy rockers, bearing diameters larger by five millimeters on three mains, an improved oil system, about which more in a moment, and last but by no means least, a new cylinder liner. Rather than the usual chrome used on the Supers, the walls of the S-90 cylinders are Ferral-treated which means that a steel coating sprayed over molybdenum is applied as a lining material. This is easier to break in than chrome plate and has less tendency to polish, behaving more like a normal steel liner.

Getting back to that oil system mentioned above, a new sump filter is used on the S-90. Similar in action to the magnetic filters used in the others, the S-90 filter has one important addition. This is a centrifugal valve that acts to trap oil in the filter compartment on long, hard or fast bends, thus assuring a constant supply of oil to the pick-up. This eliminates one source of trouble endemic with racing Porsches which tended to sling oil in the sump to one side on hard turns, thereby delivering a charge of air or foam to the oil pump and thence to hard working bearings, instead of lubricant. The result of a diet of foam in bearings need not be elaborated upon here.

Actually no description of a group of parts or attributes can give a picture of their sum total, especially in this case. A Porsche is and always has been much, much more than the sum of its parts; the Super-90 is no exception. Since the first production versions, Porsche cars have been a yardstick for quality and, more, have in most instances managed to instill in their owners a pride of possession almost amounting to fetishism. To achieve this stature, a car must be a cut above lesser machinery and this the Porsche is in virtually all its forms.

In the case of the Super-90, the pushrod Porsche has been given a new dimension even beyond the scope of the four-cam versions, a dimension of usable power at a price. Combining as it does the push of the Carrera DeLuxe with the ease of maintenance of the other pushrod models, the S-90 is worth the wait involved in getting delivery.

Jerry Titus and John Christy

PORSCHE 1600 Super Coupe

Story by Mike Kable — Pictures by Geoff Bull

In recent years, few really fine continental sports cars have found their way to Australia in any great number. Prohibitive sales tax applied to so-called "luxury" vehicles is perhaps the principal reason why we are constantly denied the opportunity of seeing, let alone buying, the glamorous creations which help fill the glossy pages of overseas magazines. The few that do filter through become a centre of attraction everywhere — on the stand at a motor show, resting by a kerb in Melbourne or Sydney or almost hidden to view in the overcrowded tender area of a racing circuit. One notable exception is Porsche, which has been steadily carving a decent niche in the enthusiasts market since its introduction several years ago. Offered at prices which range from nearly £2,500 to well of £3,000, the demand is such that it is quite rare to see a new Porsche rest on a showroom floor for very long. So it goes without saying that given the chance, Australians will pay for a quality product — if it is available.

Indeed, quality is unmistakably written all over and inside Porsche. It positively exudes an air of refinement and typical German workmanship. Cost is forgotten in the shine of its flawless exterior and the expensive aura of its interior. Even after a thorough, three-day road test, the initial impressions remained, this time accompanied by a feeling of satisfaction which lingered on for several weeks. Liken it, if you like, to the glow of well-being which follows dinner at a god restaurant.

Porsche's real sales impact came last year with the introduction of the 356B range of 1600, 1600 Super and Super 90 coupes, roadsters and hardtops. In a little over 10 years, it was the only significant change and even then, not readily apparent to most people. But, as the official sales brochure says, Porsche concentrated on unseen engineering advancements — in performance, handling ease, comfort and safety. Despite the subtle changes in styling, it is quite evident in a direct comparison of the two models that the 356B is certainly the more handsome. The slim guards drop away sharply at teh front to a bumper bar which has been considerably improved by uplifting and neat, functional overriders. Gone is the rather distinctive "shovel-nose" appearance of the 356A.

Adding to the general impression of "uplift", headlights and the protruding parking lights have been raised to a level where more effective road illumination is possible. Air intakes for the brakes are located both above and beneath the front bumper, which with its strip insert of hard rubber is now in a much better position to absorb parking bumps and scrapes. From head-on, the frontal aspect is pleasing, jarred only by the large, ugly bonnet handle. Classical treatment of the rear is quite unspoilt by the plated engine air intake grille and a bumper set-up similar to that at the front. Another noticeable styling feature is the adoption of prettier hub caps emblazoned with the Porsche emblem and certainly more in keeping with the character of the car than the old plain, unornamented type which added to the general misconception of some that Porsche, after all, was just a "glorified" Volkswagen.

So much for the bodywork. Major mechanical alterations include 11-inch transverse finned alloy brake drums and the addition of a transverse single leaf spring to the rear suspension to do away with the occasional tendency of the earlier model to "break away at the back." Here, it is interesting to note that Porsche has retained these drum brakes on its new Formula One Car, being the only F1 manufacturer **not** to use discs.

For our test car, we turned to N.S.W. Porsche distributor Arnold Glass, who needs little introduction to A.M.S. readers. Actually, the jet-black 1600 Super coupe we tested had been used by him as personal transport and had covered some 4,500 miles when Capitol Motors' sales manager Tony Litt made it available. Before leaving the workshops, the car was prepared by Bob Becker, whom we discovered to be an original employee of the Porsche works at Stuttgart and consequently a most knowledgeable person on everything relating to the marque. The Super is the middle model of the range and

Left: "Cost is forgotten in the shine of its flawless exterior and the expensive aura of its interior." Against a background of Mt. Panorama the Porsche 1600 Super shows off its flowing lines and general air of elegance.

Below left: Cockpit is superb, the dished wheel a delight to use and the instruments easy to read.
Below: Looking through the engine hatch the accessibility of accessories is obvious.

develops 75 D.I.N. horsepower at 5,000 r.p.m. compared with the standard 1600's 60 D.I.N. horsepower at 4,500 r.p.m. Both engines have the same displacement of 1582 c.c. and the additional power of the Super comes from a higher compression ratio — 8.5 to 1 — a "hotter" camshaft and bigger-choke carburettors. Otherwise, there are few internal differences, though the Super does have light-alloy hard-chrome cylinder barrels and the 1600 cast-iron ones.

Entry into the Porsche through the wide, substantial doors requires dexterity but is simplified through practice. One has to perform a series of three or four movements rather than just stepping in and sliding the body onto the seat. This car was equipped with the optional one-piece bench seats and divided squabs with separate Reutter adjustment allowing for several types of driving positions. The two tiny rear "occasional" seats could not comfortably support adult passengers over long distances, but their squabs fold down to create additional luggage space. Seats and door trim are covered in top-grade synthetic leather while the thick woven corded carpets and rear seat backing should stand considerable abuse. A small hump housing wiring and heater controls does not intrude unduly into the generous floor space.

Cockpit comfort for both driver and passenger is superb, with the contoured seats giving exceptional support under all conditions — even when the car is sliding. Full-arm control finds the beautifully raked, three-spoked dished wheel a delight to use. The horn button carries the Porsche owner's "badge of office". Set into the steering boss is a plastic-tipped stalk which doubles as a directional switch and headlight lever — forward for high beam, backward for low beam. Vision through the upper half of the wheel takes in the three instruments — oil temperature, fuel gauge, generator and oil warning lights set in the multi-purpose dial on the right, tachometer directly above the steering column and speedometer on the left. All are calibrated in green on black and in top gear the steady speedometer and tachometer needles rise and fall in perfect unison, a feature all too rare in modern sports cars.

Though the facia is well underneath the padded windscreen sill, the gauges are easy to read in daylight or at night, when illumination can be controlled via a rheostat button. Apart from the normal switches, a ratchet hand throttle is provided for cold weather warm-ups and is an absolute boon, leaving the driver free to pack luggage and perform other tasks while the engine reaches operating temperature. The three-way fuel cock beneath the facia is a trap for the unwary as its ON position is with the handle pointing at AUF — German for on. Although the heater gives plentiful warmth, the regulator knob alongside the gearstick requires several turns from off to on. Hot air issues from vents set below the doors and closing of their flaps forces heat through the defroster passages to the windscreen.

Starting is by a three-way combination switch. There is no choke — three pumps of the throttle suffice in most cold-starting circumstances. However, we found the Porsche reluctant sometimes to start easily after a long run.

From the beginning, the Super's two-sided nature was apparent. Smooth in traffic, it will amble along in second and third gears without any harsh running. This excellent degree of flexibility contributes greatly towards keeping patience in check when on crowded roads. But the real joy of Porsche motoring comes at the de-restricting signs on clear, open highways.

In city driving, the biggest advantage is the synchromesh first gear which slides nicely into place under about 20 m.p.h. and leaves one ready for abrupt take-offs. The positive gear-change mechanism is almost beyond justifiable criticism. While the movement between gears is long, the action is a fluid one where the fastest possible changes can be made in the shortest possible time. And the gearlever has a good solid feel, being well placed in relation to the rim of the wheel. There is none of the sensations of lost motion usually associated with lengthy linkages on rear-engined cars and this also applies to the gentle clutch. The organ-type accelerator pedal has a lot of travel and does not transmit much vibration. Brakes are adequate for all occasions but our car suffered from an annoying squeal at low speeds.

Though the horizontally-opposed four cylinder engine emits typical air-cooled noises at low speeds, it is reasonably silent at high speeds — except for the roar of the fan. We point out that the noise level is quite unobtrusive inside the car with the two rear quarter windows open slightly on their hinges.

Driving the Porsche is a unique experience and this is due mainly to the exaggerated impression of sheer speed under heavy acceleration. When the power is turned on in first and second gears, the front comes up, the back goes down and the car shoots away rapidly. Actually, the accompanying set of timed figures reveal that acceleration through the gears is not remarkable by any standards. The feeling of speed can be probably attributed to several factors, namely the deep-down-inside seating position which makes one think he is in the cockpit of an aeroplane rather than a car, the way the bonnet falls way and gives such a wide view of the road and the way the car stands up on its rear wheels. When conditions permit, the Porsche can be cruised at 80 m.p.h. or higher with a commendable amount of safety. Incidentally, at this speed one has only to open the front quarter window to see just how efficient are the general aerodynamics. Doing this provokes a violent buffeting noise! The engine will still respond readily from 80 m.p.h. but would need a long wind-up to reach its claimed maximum of 110 m.p.h.

Roadholding is a contentious point with Porsche and it is interesting to note that most owners who throw caution to the wind in their first weeks of ownership generally wind up in trouble!

This car very definitely delivers messages when cornered hard or unwisely and needs a thoroughly precise hand on the wheel at all times. That is not to say it is unstable. On the contrary, adhesion is very good and the rear wheels hang on seemingly indefinitely. The whole point is that often the car is travelling far faster than you think and bends and curves loom up surprisingly quickly to trap you. Sawing wildly at the wheel induces trouble and in most cases, only a little correction is required to return the car to a straight line. It is quite easy with the Porsche to over-correct. The ride over all types of surfaces is in the incredible class and the body remains perfectly rigid on rough roads. Steering is silky-smooth with just the right amount of feel.

Touching on other points, there is little luggage room underneath the bonnet because of the space occupied by the 12.5 gallon fuel tank and spare wheel. The engine hatch is on the small side, but accessibility is not too bad. Setting tappets and changing plugs is a simple wheel-off, sit-down job rather preferable to standing up and leaning over the bonnet of a conventional car. Porsche does not skimp in its provision of tools and these include a special plug spanner, hub cap removal lever, tyre gauge and spare fanbelt.

The top sector of the curved screen is tinted and cuts a lot of sunlight dazzle. In wet weather the wiper action is ample and the screen-washers are operated by a control to the left of the clutch rather similar in action to a foot dipswitch. Apart from an alloy strip lined with rubber and a Reutter Coachwork badge, the body sides are free from ornamentation. Attention to detail has been carried on even to the large sliding ashtray, recessed to hold a cigarette, and a push-in lighter. Deep door pockets and a good-sized glovebox can accommodate a variety of odd-shaped objects and the main windows come fully open with 4½ turns of the handle. Wheels are slotted to give extra cooling air to the brakes. The square reversing light throws out splendid illumination and provided with the car is a comprehensive, easy to follow driver's manual printed on art paper (a real collector's piece !). An accessories handbook lists such thoughtful extras as a three-piece set of leather suitcases tailored to fit and be strapped in the rear, seat belts, 13 different types of radios, round leather head-rests to take the neck and shoulder fatigue out of travel, a luggage rack which screws into the engine air intake grille and straps to tie on two pairs of skis, touch-up paint pencils and chrome-plated wheels with knock-on twin-eared hub-caps (a la Carrerra).

On such a completely finished car, it is difficult to find any real faults. It has everything — and then some!

SPECIFICATIONS — PORSCHE 1600 SUPER COUPE

Engine: Four cylinder, horizontally opposed, 3.25 in. x 2.91 in. — 82.5 m.m. x 74 m.m. — 1582 c.c., 8.5 to 1 compression ratio, 75 b.h.p. at 5,000 r.p.m.

Transmission: Four-speed synchromesch. Rear axle ratio 4.428 to 1.

Tyres: 5.60 x 15 all around.

Weight: 2,150 lbs. with fuel, oil and one occupant.

Dimensions: Wheelbase 82.7 in., track (front), 51.4 ins., rear 50.1 ins. Length, 158 ins. Height, 52.4 ins. Width, 65.6 ins. Ground clearance, 5.9 ins. at lowest point. Turning circle, about 36 ft.

Steering: Porsche ZF worm gear with divided tie rod and steering damper. Two and a third turns from lock to lock.

Prices: 1600 coupe, £2,695. 1600 Super Coupe, £2,880. Super 90 Coupe, £3,230. Roadster approx. £200 less than coupe. Hardtop approx. £100 more than coupe.

PERFORMANCE

Speeds in gears at 5,000 r.p.m.:

First, 25 m.p.h. Second, 50 m.p.h. Third, 80 m.p.h. Fourth, 110 m.p.h. (claimed).

Acceleration:

0—20 m.p.h., 2.2 secs.; 0—30 m.p.h., 4.1 secs.; 0—40 m.p.h., 6.3 secs.; 0—50 m.p.h., 9.3 secs.; 0—60 m.p.h., 13.4 secs.; 0—70 m.p.h., 19.2 secs.; 0—80 m.p.h., 26 secs.

Acceleration in gears:

Second: 20—40 m.p.h., 5.1 secs.; Third: 30—60 m.p.h., 13 secs.; Fourth: 40—60 m.p.h., 13 secs.

(Conditions when tested fine, dry flat road).

PORSCHE PROTOTYPE

Impressions of an experimental car with the new 2-litre Carrera engine.

BY no means a new car nor even an up-to-date one, S-LP 389 is very much a works hack. Basically a 1960 (1,600 c.c.) car with the new 2-litre engine installed, it was detached after 19,000 miles of testing for a rapid international tour to show people what this new Carrera model will be like when it goes into production next year.

Memories of the early 1½-litre Carrera (with its background whirr from roller-bearing crankshaft and gear-driven overhead camshafts merging at high revs. with a strident exhaust note to produce an exciting surge of sound over a useful range between 4,000 and 7,000 r.p.m.), of the 1,500 c.c. cars of five years ago with their marked oversteer, of the fierce 2-litre coupés at Le Mans this year, all these combined to give a pre-conception which was to prove entirely false.

As usual when a very fast car is available for a very short time the roads were thoroughly wet. Some early and rather tentative experiments were made to find what would happen if the Continental Radial tyres were pushed too hard. Nothing happened except a considerable rise of driver morale; the car just motored round the corners and it was not until considerably later on that it was found that wet road understeer continues right to the limit (at least on slowish corners) with enough power in third to balance it nicely and enough in second to overbalance it thoroughly, so that a properly shaped seat and a steering wheel in just the right place for rapid correction are invaluable assets in retaining control of the situation. The steering has a remarkably positive, frictionless action which gives an unusual degree of feel.

With 10 miles' experience, a soaking surface, no practice and a mind divided between the car and a stopwatch, one can guarantee to make a fair hash of a standing quarter-mile. Nevertheless, one run with too much wheelspin and another with too little, gave a mean of 17 sec., using 6,500 r.p.m. in the gears. The rev. counter has a shaded red sector extending from peak r.p.m. (6,200 at which the engine develops 130 b.h.p. net) up to 7,000 at which a thick red line bars further progress. Mechanical noise from the new plain bearing engine, with its four chain-driven camshafts, intrudes very little and with the throttle eased right back for cruising speeds in the region of 100 m.p.h. the whole car is unusually quiet.

At low speeds the four large cylinders can be felt and a subdued but purposeful full-throttle exhaust note goes on rising until around 5,000 r.p.m., above which everything becomes remarkably quiet and smooth. Translating from the metric speedometer, 6,200 r.p.m. gives about 65 m.p.h. in second gear and 100 m.p.h. in third, which is a delightful gear for continuous use on winding main roads where this speed comes up extremely quickly between bends. In top, road conditions prohibited really fast motoring, but a reading of over 190 k.p.h. (about 120 m.p.h.) was seen on one slightly uphill stretch with the speed still rising quite quickly. A speedometer check at 60 m.p.h. revealed 5 m.p.h. "flatter," but there seems no reason to doubt the makers' claim of a maximum in the region of 125-130 m.p.h.

Even more impressive, however, is the extent to which the complex Carrera engine has been civilized in this latest version. It is extremely flexible and accelerates very strongly from low r.p.m. without any flat spots and with no steps in the power curve. At the end of 150 miles' fast motoring it ambled up the Great West Road towards Isleworth leaving a trail of worried fast-car owners who thought their machines ought to leave the traffic lights even more quickly than a perfectly ordinary-looking Porsche; and it idled amiably through the lunch-time traffic blocks without a trace of oiling-up. **Charles Bulmer.**

the continuing search for perfection

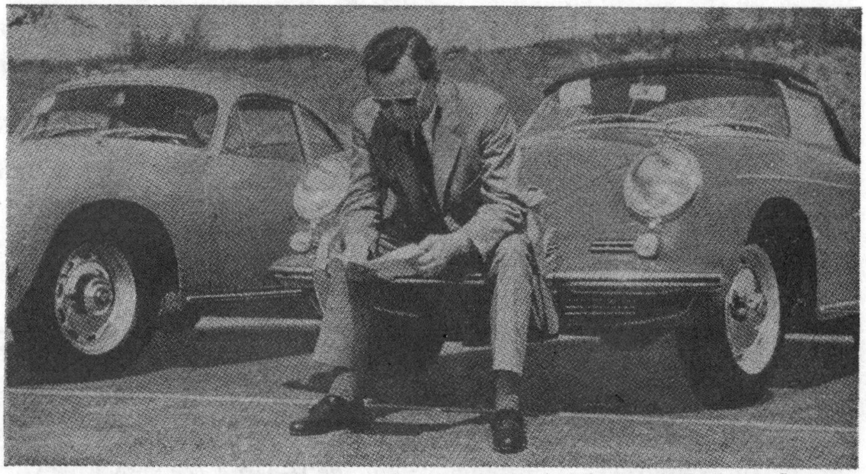

Ferry Porsche . . . present head of the Porsche factory in Stuttgart

A great sports car isn't built overnight. It is developed and refined through years of continuous designing, research, testing and competition. Such a sports car is today's Porsche. A car held in esteem by motoring connoisseurs the world over. A car whose performance has been proven through countless victories in the world's ruggedest races and rallies from LeMans to Sebring. A car whose technical advancements continue year after year—in a continuing search for even greater perfection.

A legendary engineering genius

Behind this aim stands the inventive history of two men . . . the late Professor Dr. Ferdinand Porsche . . . and his son, Ferry Porsche, the present head of the Porsche factory at Stuttgart.

Professor Porsche's engineering skill is a legendary story—from the moment he startled the automotive world with the revolutionary concept of his air-cooled, four-cylinder, valve-in-head engine back in 1912—to his "Dream and Do" development of a small, compact and economical "people's car" . . . which was the prototype of today's Volkswagen.

Milestones in automotive history

And, Dr. Porsche's pioneering work on racing cars are milestones in European automotive history, too. His 500 hp, rear-engined giants of the thirties broke a whole string of world records when they first appeared. By 1937 these cars had amassed 37 wins in 55 tries, and held 15 world and 23 class records.

In the late 1940's Professor Porsche and his son worked together developing the design for the Porsche 356—forerunner of today's Porsches. The first 50 of these cars were handmade with aerodynamically-designed aluminum bodies—and created a sensation in automotive circles.

Porsche's famed air-cooled rear engine

Over half-a-century later

Porsches are still creating excitement today—with their compact design—competition-proven air-cooled rear engines—fully-synchronized servo-mesh transmission—torsion-bar suspension and double-size brakes. All these features, and more, are characteristics of Porsche's development—a search for perfection that started over half-a-century ago. You'll find Porsches available in four models—coupe—hardtop—cabriolet—and roadster. Three engine versions, too. For further information, prices, etc. see your local Porsche Dealer . . . or write PORSCHE OF AMERICA CORPORATION, 527 Madison Avenue, New York 22, New York.

Craftmanship is the basis of Porsche quality

all it shares with other cars is the road.

PORSCHE

The Motor

MAKE: Porsche. TYPE: Super 75 Coupé.
MAKERS: Porsche K.-G., Porschestrasse 85, Stuttgart—Zuffenhausen, W. Germany.
Concessionaires: A.F.N., Ltd., London Road., Isleworth, Middx.

ROAD TEST • No. 20/62

DATA

CONDITIONS: *Weather: Dry, warm, negligible wind. (Temperature 64°-66° F., Barometer 30.1 in. Hg.) Surface: Dry tarmacadam. Fuel: Premium grade pump petrol (97 Octane Rating by Research Method).*

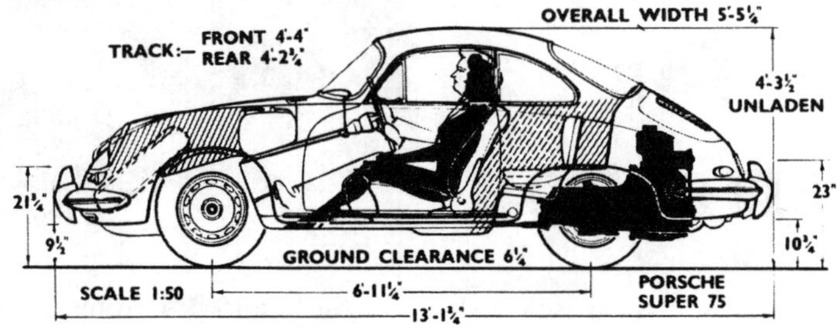

INSTRUMENTS

Speedometer at 30 m.p.h.	3% fast
Speedometer at 60 m.p.h.	4% fast
Speedometer at 90 m.p.h.	6% fast
Distance Recorder	2% fast

WEIGHT

Kerb weight (unladen, but with oil, coolant and fuel for approximately 50 miles) ...	17½ cwt.
Front/rear distribution of kerb weight	42/58
Weight laden as tested	21¼ cwt.

MAXIMUM SPEEDS

Flying Mile

Mean of six opposite runs	106.6 m.p.h.
Best one-way mile time equals ...	108.5 m.p.h.

"Maximile" Speed. (Timed quarter-mile after one mile accelerating from rest.)

Mean of opposite runs	100.3 m.p.h.
Best one-way time equals	102.3 m.p.h.

Speed in gears (at 5,500 r.p.m.)

Max. speed in 3rd gear	81 m.p.h.
Max. speed in 2nd gear	52 m.p.h
Max. speed in 1st gear	30 m.p.h

FUEL CONSUMPTION

51.5 m.p.g. ...	at constant 30 m.p.h. on level
50.0 m.p.g. ...	at constant 40 m.p.h. on level
47.0 m.p.g. ...	at constant 50 m.p.h. on level
41.0 m.p.g. ...	at constant 60 m.p.h. on level
37.0 m.p.g. ...	at constant 70 m.p.h. on level
35.0 m.p.g. ...	at constant 80 m.p.h. on level
30.0 m.p.g. ...	at constant 90 m.p.h. on level
24.0 m.p.g. ...	at constant 100 m.p.h. on level

Overall Fuel Consumption for 1,733 miles, 67.5 gallons, equals 25.7 m.p.g. (11.0 litres/100 km.).

Touring Fuel Consumption (m.p.g. at steady speed midway between 30 m.p.h. and maximum, less 5% allowance for acceleration) ... 35.8 m.p.g.

Fuel tank capacity (maker's figure)... 11½ gallons (Including 1.1 gallon in reserve)

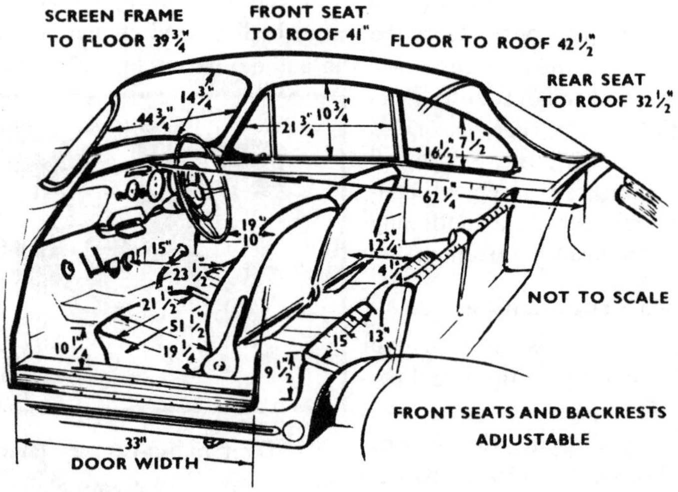

HILL CLIMBING at sustained steady speeds

Max. gradient on top gear ...	1 in 12.0 (Tapley 185 lb./ton)
Max. gradient on 3rd gear ...	1 in 7.6 (Tapley 290 lb./ton)
Max. gradient on 2nd gear ...	1 in 4.5 (Tapley 490 lb./ton)

BRAKES from 30 m.p.h.

0.98 g retardation (equivalent to 30½ ft. stopping distance) with 95 lb. pedal pressure.
0.87 g retardation (equivalent to 34½ ft. stopping distance) with 75 lb. pedal pressure.
0.55 g retardation (equivalent to 55 ft. stopping distance) with 50 lb. pedal pressure.
0.21 g retardation (equivalent to 143 ft. stopping distance) with 25 lb. pedal pressure.

ACCELERATION TIMES from standstill

0-30 m.p.h.	4.5 sec.
0-40 m.p.h.	6.8 sec.
0-50 m.p.h.	9.1 sec.
0-60 m.p.h.	13.5 sec.
0-70 m.p.h.	18.5 sec.
0-80 m.p.h.	23.1 sec.
0-90 m.p.h.	33.0 sec.
0-100 m.p.h.	50.4 sec.
Standing quarter-mile	18.8 sec.

ACCELERATION TIMES on upper ratios

	Top gear	3rd gear
10-30 m.p.h.	—	7.9 sec.
20-40 m.p.h.	13.1 sec.	7.7 sec.
30-50 m.p.h.	12.5 sec.	7.3 sec.
40-60 m.p.h.	12.9 sec.	7.7 sec.
50-70 m.p.h.	14.9 sec.	9.1 sec.
60-80 m.p.h.	15.8 sec.	9.6 sec.
70-90 m.p.h.	18.2 sec.	—
80-100 m.p.h.	28.0 sec.	—

STEERING

Turning circle between kerbs:

Left	31 ft.
Right	30 ft.
Turns of steering wheel from lock to lock	2½

Specification

Engine

Cylinders	4
Bore	82.5 mm.
Stroke	74 mm.
Cubic capacity	1,582 c.c.
Piston area	33.2 sq. in.
Valves	Inclined overhead (pushrods)
Compression ratio	8.5/1
Carburetters	Twin Zenith NDIX double choke downdraught
Fuel pump	Solex mechanical
Ignition timing control	Centrifugal
Oil filter	By-pass
Maximum power (net)	75 b.h.p.
at	5,000 r.p.m.
Piston speed at maximum b.h.p.	2,430 ft./min.

Transmission

Clutch	7.1 in. Häussermann s.d.p.
Top gear (s/m)	3.61
3rd gear (s/m)	5.01
2nd gear (s/m)	7.81
1st gear (s/m)	13.69
Reverse	15.77
Final drive	Spiral bevel gears, 31:7
Top gear m.p.h. at 1,000 r.p.m.	20.3
Top gear m.p.h. at 1,000 ft./min. piston speed	41.8

Chassis

Brakes ... Ate hydraulic drum brakes (2LS at front)

Brake dimensions 11 in. dia. by 1.58 in. wide drums front and rear

Friction areas: 121 sq. in. of friction lining operating on 218 sq. in. of rubbed drum surface.

Suspension:

Front: Independent by transverse laminated torsion bars, parallel trailing arms and anti-roll bar.

Rear: Independent by swing axles and transverse torsion bars.

Shock absorbers:

Front and rear ... Koni telescopic

Steering gear ... ZF worm and peg with hydraulic damper

Tyres ... 5.60—15 standard, 165—15 Dunlop SP (on test car) or Michelin X at extra cost

Porsche Super 75

SOMETIMES a test car reveals its personality rather slowly and a neutral first impression is succeeded by a growing like (or dislike). The Porsche, on the other hand, has an immediate attraction for most people; several passengers expressed this feeling spontaneously before completing their first mile. Essentially its charm springs from a very rare blend of first-class sports car virtues with touring car amenities and from the overall balance of its design. A surprisingly large percentage of the most desirable cars available have some features which fall far below the general standard—it may be noise, heavy controls, harsh suspension, an unpleasant gearbox, uncomfortable seats, a bad driving position, poor visibility, etc. The Porsche is not perfect and it does not reach the highest standards in everything but it does get the "above average" rating in more aspects than almost any other sporting or G.T. car we have tried.

In Brief

Price (including Dunlop SP tyres as tested) £1,707 plus purchase tax £641 2s 9d plus £18 14s 6d (tyre exchange) equals £2,366 17s 3d.

Price without extras (including purchase tax), £2,348 2s 9d.

Capacity	1,582 c.c.
Unladen kerb weight	17½ cwt.
Acceleration:	
20-40 m.p.h. in top gear	13.1 sec.
0-50 m.p.h. through gears	9.1 sec.
Maximum top-gear gradient	1 in 12.0
Maximum speed	106.6 m.p.h.
"Maximile" speed	100.3 m.p.h.
Touring fuel consumption	35.8 m.p.g.

Gearing: 20.3 m.p.h. in top gear at 1,000 r.p.m.

The 356B series comprises nine models, a permutation of three different body styles with three 1,600 c.c. engines of different power output. We had the intermediate engine giving 75 b.h.p. net, half-way between the 60 b.h.p. of the standard model and the 90 b.h.p. of the Super 90. The three bodies, all of which are mounted on a platform chassis of great rigidity, comprise a detachable hardtop, a detachable convertible and a fixed head coupé. The last, which we tested, is the traditional low-drag body, still very similar in shape to that of the first Porsche which was introduced in 1949 and which was based largely on Volkswagen mechanical parts.

Thirteen years of development have left few if any of the original components unaltered but the general layout remains the same with a rear-mounted air-cooled flat-four engine, swing axle independent rear suspension and front wheels mounted on twin parallel trailing links. The usual tendency for cars to grow in size and weight has been largely resisted and although increasing refinement has brought some weight penalty, this 17½-cwt. car is one of the very few machines available to a buyer who insists on luxury in a compact and agile form.

First impressions

The unusual comfort of the front seats confirms that correct shaping is more important than soft padding. The upholstery is quite hard but body weight is well distributed over its surface and the adjustable rake back rests support the whole length of the spine whilst also giving satisfactory location against substantial cornering forces. *The Motor* staff, who vary rather extravagantly in height from 5 ft. 4 ins. to 6 ft. 5 ins., had to admit that the fore and aft adjustment was entirely adequate.

A low floor is a desirable feature and although the pedals are

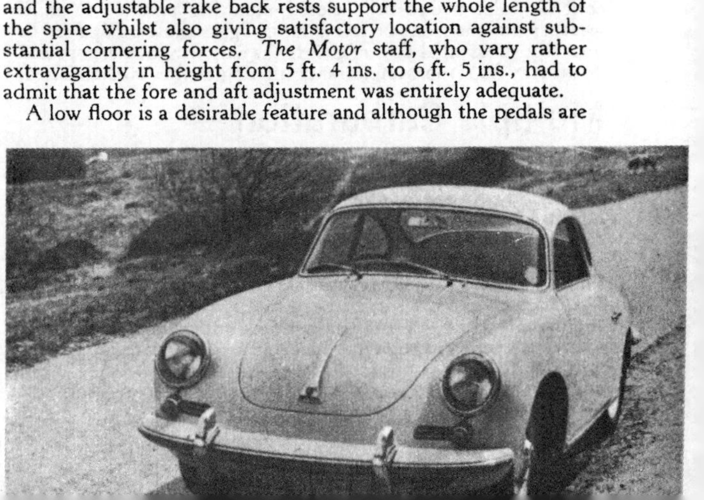

The rear engine allows a particularly clean frontal appearance. Performance and fuel consumption figures suggest that the impression of good aerodynamic shape is real and not illusory.

Porsche Super 75

spaced well apart an angled organ-type throttle allows easy and natural heel and toe operation of brake and accelerator; the left foot has plenty of room to rest when it is not working the clutch or the plunger type windscreen washer. A manual dip-switch is combined with the direction signals and headlamp flasher in a convenient finger-tip control projecting from the left of the steering column. The steering wheel is placed high enough to leave ample room above the legs and low enough not to interfere with an excellent view down the short sharply sloping bonnet. The rear view is also comprehensive and this latest Porsche, with front and rear windows enlarged since the end of last year, shows a useful improvement in all-round visibility over earlier models.

At night this visibility is maintained by powerful headlights with a good spread and in bad weather by extremely effective windscreen wipers, with a heavy contact pressure. Although variable wiper speed is no longer a novelty, these have the widest speed range we have yet encountered. The facia is neat and practical with well-separated switches and large, clearly marked instruments. No oil pressure gauge is fitted but there is an oil thermometer as a reminder that oil temperatures fluctuate more widely in air-cooled than in water-cooled engines. The instrument was not calibrated in degrees, but we never got the needle anywhere near the red warning sector even after quite a number of miles at or near maximum speed.

Road Impressions

The thoughtful design of the seats and controls makes a new driver feel at home very quickly and his acclimatization is accelerated by the Porsche gearbox, which for many years has set something of a standard by which others are judged. Long connections to the rear-mounted gearbox isolate the lever from engine vibration whilst introducing a degree of flexibility which is no disadvantage in practice. All four forward ratios have synchromesh and, perhaps because this car had done only 500 miles when we took it over, bottom gear was always heavy to engage, but the other changes were light, and very fast. An unusual and most attractive feature is the quietness of the lower gears which give maximum speeds of approximately 30, 50 and 80 m.p.h. at 5,500 r.p.m. It seems natural in the Porsche to run up to 5,000 r.p.m. (the beginning of the red sector on the rev. counter) quite regularly and not, as in most cars, only when in a desperate hurry; thus in ordinary driving one comes near to repeating the excellent acceleration figures shown in the data panel. The mean maximum speed of 106.6 m.p.h. was recorded with less than 1,000 miles on the clock and would probably improve appreciably after a lot more running in.

Obviously the smoothness of the flat-four air-cooled engine is a major factor in encouraging this sort of use; as heard from outside the car or by reflection from walls through open windows, the power unit is not quiet but its remote position and effective insulation prevent the direct transmission of mechanical sounds to the interior leaving only a deep-throated and not unpleasant combination of intake and exhaust noise. When throttled back for high-speed cruising most of this disappears and generally the engine has a relaxed air as though working well within its limits.

Wind noise round the very well-streamlined and well-sealed body is extremely low with all the windows shut; a separate cold air inlet makes fully closed motoring possible in mild weather but the front or rear quarter lights must be opened to induce a substantial flow of air. If the side windows are wound down very far, a most unpleasant buffeting airflow is established.

Multiple Carburation

We have said that the engine enjoys turning fast and a green sector on the rev. counter from 3,000-5,000 r.p.m. indicates the region in which the needle should be kept for high-speed motoring, but it is certainly not inflexible. Two double-choke downdraught carburetters provide a separate inlet tract for each cylinder and there is ample evidence that carburation is unusually clean. Smooth, even pick-up is possible from below 1,000 r.p.m. and the steady speed fuel consumption figures are particularly good. An 11½-gallon tank with a reserve tap and a touring fuel consumption of nearly 36 m.p.g. make a cruising range of 400 miles possible at moderate touring speeds. In our hands the car was driven as hard as possible nearly all the time

The interior is extremely well finished and very practical. There is a map pocket in each door, pockets in the sides of the scuttle and a glove box with a lock. Wide doors give easy access in spite of hill sills. The photograph below shows that the fuel tank (which has an enormous filler), spare wheel and tools occupy much of the available space. The bonnet lid has a release catch under the facia and there is no separate lock.

and with a good deal of rush-hour town motoring thrown in the overall figure of 26 m.p.g. was creditable. No rich mixture device is fitted—a few strokes of the throttle squirt in enough fuel from the accelerator pumps for cold starting and almost immediately the engine will idle reliably without use of the hand throttle provided.

Sensitive Steering

It is well know that early Porsches had the appreciable oversteer that is often associated with rear engines and swing axle suspension and which demanded considerable skill in fast driving. Suspension and tyre development have now eliminated premature rear-end breakaway and left a car which can be driven extremely fast on winding roads without exceptional technique. Drivers who prefer more understeer can have it if they order the modified rear suspension which is standard on the Super 90 and available on the Super 75 as a factory-fitted optional extra. This consists of a centre-pivoted transverse leaf spring which allows the use of thinner torsion bars giving a reduction in rear roll stiffness of about 20%. Our test car was not equipped with this extra spring.

In general, the high-geared steering is reasonably light if not, perhaps, as light as one would expect with a high-efficiency mechanism and only 7½ cwt. on the front wheels, but considerable effort is needed to hold it into a sharp corner taken really fast when self-centring is very pronounced. Textile braced tread German Dunlop SP tyres (an optional extra) may have been partly responsible for this but, in return, they grip the road tenaciously in wet or dry conditions. In the limit, it is still the back wheels which break away first but they do so fairly gently; this limit can be postponed to still higher speeds by cornering with the power on; with i.r.s. and 58% of the unladen weight on the driving wheels a good deal of power can be used with advantage even in the lower gears.

It is very noticeable that the Porsche responds best to those with a light, sensitive and relaxed touch and any attempt to grip the wheel and direct it forcefully results in jerky cornering and erratic straight-running. Normally it needs little correction at high speeds, but changing cambers, to some extent, and cross winds, to a considerable extent, can cause high-speed wander.

The roll stiffness is very great, the centre of gravity low and the rear roll centre high, a combination which diminishes lean on corners to a very small amount but introduces a characteristic lateral rocking motion into the ride as camber changes are followed closely and rapidly. Springing is comfortable but very firm so that there is some well-controlled vertical movement on ordinary roads but really bad roads are absorbed with unexpected ease; washboard surfaces, pot holes, bumps and ridges disturb neither its road clinging nor the monolithic feel which is an outstandingly pleasant result of a very rigid rattle-free structure and well-insulated suspension. This is one of the few cars where cornering speeds are indicated by the sharpness of the bend and not by the roughness of its surface.

The deceleration figures taken from 30 m.p.h. show that the brakes are powerful and fairly light but, although they proved entirely adequate for motoring in this country, they fall below the standards set by good modern disc brakes. At low speeds and low pressures they made a loud and rather gritty rubbing noise and when stopping really hard from fast cruising speeds high pedal forces were needed and a slight judder was observed. A rapid succession of hard stops from 60 m.p.h. produced increased pedal travel and some fade. The pull-out handbrake, mounted under the facia, is extremely powerful and held the car with ease on a gradient of 1 in 3, but it is rather awkward to release and tends to remain in a half-way position unless pushed firmly back.

Luggage room under the front bonnet is rather limited but there is plenty of room inside the car when the occasional seat backs are folded flat and luggage can then be secured by straps which are available as an extra. For short journeys it is quite possible to put two average-size adults in the rear seats provided that the front ones are pushed forward to give kneeroom.

In many ways a light small-engined car with a really high performance gives a keen driver the maximum satisfaction but, in this country at least, most of the vehicles which rival the Porsche for speed and agility lack its refinement comfort and carrying capacity. It is amazing that it still has so few competitors or imitators.

Carburetters, fuel pump, dynamo and ignition system are all very accessible. The upward-projecting outlets each side under the air cleaners supply warm air to the carburetter from the cooling system after starting. When the engine is hot a thermostat control cuts off the supply.

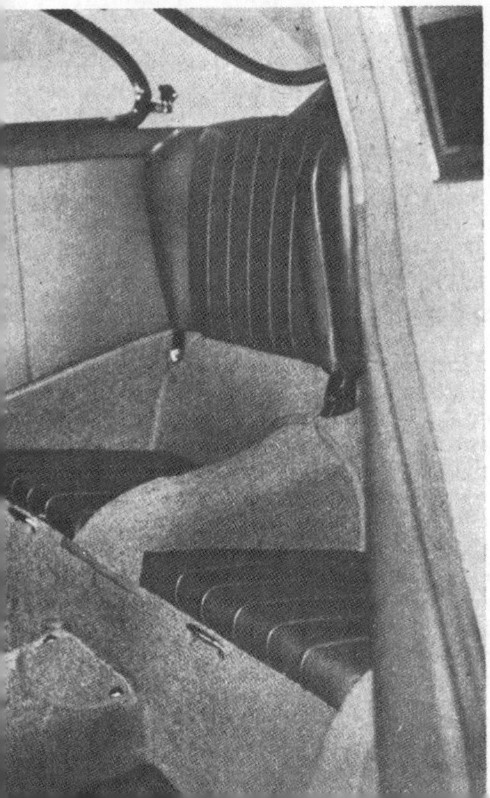

When these occasional rear seat backs are hinged downwards a flat carpeted floor extends across the back for luggage carrying.

Coachwork and Equipment

Starting handle ... ... None
Battery mounting ... ... In front luggage compartment
Jack ... ... Screw pillar type
Jacking points ... Under centre of car each side
Standard tool kit: Jack and handle, tyre pressure gauge, box spanner, 2 large and 1 small screwdrivers, wheelbrace, 4 double-ended spanners, pliers, ring spanner, tommy bar, contact-breaker tool and fan belt.
Exterior lights: 2 headlights/sidelights, 2 stop/tail lamps, 2 number plate lamps, reversing light.
Number of electrical fuses 12
Direction indicators ... Self-cancelling flashers
Windscreen wipers: Self parking, twin blade, variable speed electric.
Windscreen washers ... Foot operated plunger type
Sun visors... 2
Instruments: Speedometer, rev. counter, oil temperature gauge, petrol gauge, electric clock.
Warning lights: Generator, oil pressure, main beam, side lights, direction indicators.
Locks:
With ignition key ... ... Both doors
With other keys ... ... (1) gear lever (2) glove locker
Glove locker ... ... One in facia
Map pockets: One in each door and one forward of each door.
Parcel shelves ... ... None
Ashtrays ... ... One in facia
Cigar lighters ... ... One
Interior lights ... ... 2 in roof
Interior heater: Heating and demisting by hot air from engine cooling system with additional cold air intake. Provision for fitting optional extra petrol combustion heater.
Car radio: Optional extra, several British and German makes to choice.
Extras available: Seat covers, radio, Dunlop SP or Michelin X tyres, fog lamps, safety belts, rear compensating spring (if ordered with new car), straps for rear luggage compartment, leather upholstery, sunshine roof, luggage rack, etc.
Upholstery material Corduroy and leatherette
Floor covering ... ... Rubber mats
Exterior colours standardized: 7, plus 4 more at extra cost.
Alternative body styles: Cabriolet with detachable head or hard-top.

Maintenance

Sump: 10 pints, S.A.E. 30 HD (summer), S.A.E. 20 HD (winter). (Oil change only, 6 pints.)
Gearbox and final drive 6 pints, S.A.E. 90 hypoid
Steering gear lubricant... ... S.A.E. 90 hypoid
Cooling system capacity ... ... Air-cooled
Chassis lubrication: By grease gun every 1,500 miles to 12 points.
Ignition timing ... ... 5° before t.d.c.
Contact breaker gap ... ... 0.016 in.
Sparking plug type: Bosch W 225 TI or Champion L85.
Sparking plug gap ... ... .020 to .024 in.
Valve timing (with .04 in. tappet clearance): Inlet opens 17° before t.d.c. and closes 53° a.b.d.c. Exhaust opens 50° before b.d.c. and closes 14° a.t.d.c.
Tappet clearances (cold):
Inlet ... ... .004 in.
Exhaust... ... ... .006 in.
Wheel toe-in:
Front ... ... .04 in. to .12 in.
Rear ... ... Zero to .04 in.
Camber angle:
Front ... ... 0° 10′ to 1° 10′
Rear ... ... 0° 10′ to 1½°
Castor angle ... ... 5° ± ½°
Steering swivel pin inclination... ... 4½°
Tyre pressures:
Front ... ... 23 lb.
Rear ... ... 26 lb.
Brake fluid ... ... Ate blue
Battery type and capacity 6 volt 84 amp. hr.

CT&T ROAD TEST

PORSCHE 365B

A Superb Car, Now Better Than Ever

THE CAR

Porsche's 1962 lineup has shrunk from past years. There are still three engine options (70 h.p. 1600 normal, 88 h.p. 1600 Super and 102 h.p. 1600 Super-90), but the hardtop and roadster models are discontinued. Remaining are the coupe and cabriolet, the latter available with a removable hardtop. The hardtop coupe was short-lived and not particularly attractive in its notch-backed form, but Porsche fans will bewail the disappearance of the popular roadster. Successor to the Speedster and Convertible-D models, this was the sportiest Porsche and the cheapest by a fair margin. Production kinks are blamed for its demise; perhaps these will be corrected, but Porsche has no stated plans to resume the model.

Porsche has earned fanatical owner loyalty and huge prestige in North America with a design that has remained fundamentally unchanged for a decade, though in fact the car has been improved so much over the years that, part by part, it's almost totally different than ten years ago. Changes for 1962 largely ignore the mechanical side in favour of various detail refinments. Glass area is increased front and rear, the trunk redesigned with the gas filler cap put outside on the right front fender, a new fresh-air intake system introduced, and Carrera-like dual air intake grilles added to the rear deck.

TECHNICAL

The normal Porsche 1600 engine has a bore and stroke of 3.5 x 2.92 in. Displacement is 96.5 cu. in. and compression ratio 7.5:1 for a horsepower rating (SAE) of 70. Maximum torque is 81 ft. lbs. at 2800 r.p.m. Suspension (in case you didn't know) is independent all-round with torsion bars and telescopic shock absorbers. Optional equipment on all models except the Super-90, which has it fitted as standard equipment, is a compensating spring at the rear intended to reduce understeer and increase rear wheel traction. Heart of any Porsche is its all-synchro, four-speed gearbox. Drum brakes, Duplex in front and Simplex at the rear, provide 121 sq. in. of brake lining area.

While passing on technical matters, Porsche's driver manual is a lavish 114-page production that should win some sort of award for publications of its kind. With the aid of dozens of photos and charts, it really tells all.

STYLING

In appearance as well as mechanically, Porsches have been getting better all the time. The classic coupe gained a major improvement in looks with the 1960 model, which removed the drooping-snout look and cleaned up a few details such as bumpers. With larger window area, higher bumpers and generally cleaner lines the '62 version fits in well with today's styling trends while remaining a distinct personality and retaining its excellent aero-dynamic characteristics. Our test car was a hardtop coupe and not the prettiest Porsche ever made, but since this model was recently discontinued we won't quibble.

Finish and workmanship properly reflect the car's price tag and reputation. Inside or out, Porsches reveal honest, thorough and solid craftsmanship

rather than flashiness and the novice is inclined to wonder what all the shouting is about until he realizes that nothing is about to fall off, rattle or crack.

INTERIOR

Our test car's interior, finished in a drab grey, did little to show off the remarkable quality of its appointments but the impression of comfort is obvious. A pair of magnificent seats, covered in imitation leather and corduroy, have adjustable back rests which fold to a full reclining position and several stages between. These seats are softly cushioned, wide, and just about the most comfortable found in any sports car. Fore and aft adjustment on sliding rails allows generous footroom despite some intrusion of the front wheel wells. Two small folding seats in the rear might hold children on short trips, but considerable luggage space is gained by folding them down and forming a platform.

Instrumentation is logical and legible. Three large round dials behind the steering wheel incorporate fuel gauge, oil temperature gauge, tachometer, speedometer and lights for generator, oil pressure, high beam, parking lights and turn indicators. A clock sits in the centre of the dashboard below the ventilation and heater levers and above a plaque for radio installation and a pull-out ashtray. To its right is a locking glove compartment. Turn indicators and high-beam control are combined in a lever on the left side of the steering column. The dashboard top is well padded, and there are map pockets on the scuttle beneath the dash. Besides the fuel gauge, Porsches carry a reserve fuel supply of about two gallons brought into use by a lever under the dash. Choking is automatic but there is a hand throttle for warm-up or highway cruising.

Foot controls are well spaced, with the treadle-type accelerator pedal handily placed for heeling-and-toeing. The gearship lever has been considerably shortened and placed nearer the driver in recent years and is topped by a satisfyingly large plastic grip.

Driving position seemed higher than in other Porsches we've driven, perhaps due to firm new seats. Whatever the reason we liked the arrangement since it affords a commanding view ahead instead of that vague feeling of peering out of a hole. While we experienced no difficulty, a pair of taller drivers found considerable cramping between the lower rim of the steering wheel and the seat. The wheel itself feels small but is delightfully vertical with a sturdy thickness. Its three aluminum spokes look sporting, but the effect is blunted somewhat by having what are normally punched-out areas on bona fide racing wheels filled in with a patterned design.

Visibility in the hardtop is excellent ahead and behind, and with its enlarged rear window the coupe no doubt offers improvement in this department.

Headroom in the hardtop was found barely adequate for the six-foot occupant. Since the seats unquestionably tend to "give" with use, it may be expected to improve with age.

DRIVING

Starting during our test was instantaneous with a twist of the ignition key and a couple of stabs at the accelerator pedal. Warmup is quick and the engine responds briskly to throttle pressure. Remembering our own Porsche of some time back, we were impressed with the newest model's relative silence while idling. Hard revving, especially in the bottom two gears, still produces a healthy thrashing whine but noise appears to have been considerably muffled over older Porsches.

Clutch action on our test car was precise, and shifting gears as effortless and smooth as pushing a spoon through a bowl of pudding.

This Porsche gearbox encourages smooth driving; the most ham-handed driver can be flattered into thinking he's an expert by its flexibility and forgiveness. Gear ratios are ideally spaced for swift city-traffic acceleration. The red-line at 5500 r.p.m. is reached quickly in first and second, but third gear delivers a satisfyingly long pull to the limit and is useful from about 25 m.p.h. on up to 75. Top is plainly a cruising gear, yet puts out poke rapidly when needed.

The best of both worlds seems to be available with Porsches; fleetfooted performance in city traffic, yet high highway speeds that tax neither the engine nor the occupants' sensitivities. In fact, the faster our test car went the quieter and smoother it sounded.

Light but not oversensitive steering combined with the car's short wheelbase and low centre of gravity makes handling so precise, even at low speeds, that cornering is like being hauled around on rails. Other sports cars may get around as fast, but none do it with such agility and such complete lack of roll. So precise and obedient is this car that it takes some time to realize it will do exactly what the driver wants it to; once the exactitude of its handling qualities is realized the Porsche can be hurled about unreservedly.

Ride is phenomenally smooth — a word that keeps cropping up in any description of Porsches — and even the most miserable road surfaces are gobbled up by that supple suspension. On even pavement, under hard acceleration or during violent cornering, there is little tire-squeal and the car sticks tenaciously. Over the years the dreaded Porsche oversteer has been minimized to a point where even in extreme cornering situations the rear engine weight bias isn't felt ready to whip the rump around.

Brakes under normal usage responded quietly and effectively. With harsher stops some fade was noted but full effectiveness was quickly restored. Owners of older Porsches often complain about squealing brakes but our test car never revealed the slightest hint of this.

ECONOMY

Using premium fuel, our test car averaged 32 m.p.g. over a 350-mile workout including a heavy dose of city driving.

STORAGE

The redesigned trunk in '62 Porsches was a disappointment; while the Porsche-fitted luggage available at extra cost would fit into the new space, not much else could. It's too shallow. The best place for baggage is still behind the front seats and a surprising amount of room is available.

HEATING & VENTILATION

The familiar floor-level frame rail vents for warm air are aided by a dashboard control. An intake at the base of the windshield allows distribution of fresh air to the interior, and the dashboard lever controls its direction. A gasoline heater is optional.

LAST WORD

This is an impeccable piece of machinery and as such is beyond most criticisms we are usually moved to make of sports cars. Performance is not breathtaking but what there is can be used to the full; the Porsche cruises at very near its top speed, and does so at a highly satisfactory gasoline mileage rate. Comfort is worthy of some luxury sedans. Unfortunately for the many enthusiasts who would dearly love to step into a Porsche, price has steadily risen in recent years until the car now verges on the luxury class. With the demise of the roadster, prices start at $4,600 for the standard coupe and this is a heavy bite — even for a Porsche. Nevertheless, for those who can afford it the investment is worthwhile. Just ask any Porsche owner.

DATA AND SPECIFICATIONS — PORSCHE 356B

Engine: 4-cylinder horizontally opposed, air cooled.
Bore: 3.25 in.
Stroke: 2.92 in.
Displacement: 1582 cc.
Compression ratio: 7.5:1
Horsepower (SAE): 70 at 4500 rpm.
Maximum torque: 81 ft. lbs. at 2800 rpm.
Brakes: Hydraulic drums, 121 sq. in. lining area.
Front suspension: Dual trailing links attached to torsion bars.
Rear suspension: Diagonal trailing link, swing axle and trailing arm.
Steering: ZF single peg worm, divided tie rod with hydraulic damper.
Turning radius: 33.5 ft.
Wheelbase: 82.7 in.
Overall length: 158 in.
Overall width: 65.8 in.
Height: 51.8 in.
Gas Mileage: 32 mpg (premium fuel).
Fuel tank capacity: 12 gallons.
Weight: 2060 lbs. (dry).

Top Speed
98 mph

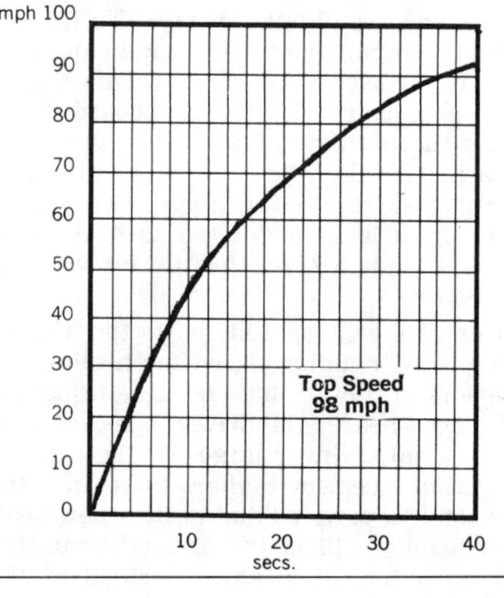

Porsche S

THE respect accorded the Porsche by motoring enthusiasts is truly remarkable, for this German firm of an Austrian founder has been producing cars for little more than a decade and the total production to date barely exceeds 50,000 units. Another significant ingredient of this Porsche success is the unflagging loyalty a Porsche owner will show his favoured marque. There would be more than a grain of truth in a slogan which went "once a Porsche owner, always a Porsche owner".

Having had but a few brief rides in Porsches of varying vintage over the past few years, the writer was always mystified by the remarkable popularity of the car, for it can be extremely expensive in some foreign countries, its passenger and luggage capacity is rather limited, and, as sports cars go, its performance on acceleration is nothing extraordinary. In January of this year the Porsche factory at Stuttgart was able to place a Porsche S at our disposal for a lengthy road test. The S (for Super) is the 1600 cc 75 DIN horsepower (88 SAE) version of the Type 356B, often referred to as the Super 75. The car we tested was the fixed head coupé, but, like the other two cars of the 356B range, the 1600 and the Super 90, it is also available as a convertible or in hardtop form.

The coupé has two Reutter front seats and two occasional seats at the rear, suitable for children or short adults. These rear seats have individual back rests which fold down to form a flat platform on which a good deal of luggage can be placed when only two people are travelling in the car. Good seats and Porsches are almost synonymous, and with any amount of fore and aft movement plus the invaluable adjustable backrest even the biggest drivers can assume a most comfortable and untiring driving position. The backrests are spring-loaded so are easily adjusted even when the car is moving, although we found the release catch which allows the seat to be folded forward to give access to the rear a little difficult to operate when the seat was set well back on its runners.

The coupé was fitted with an electrically controlled sliding roof and the surround rather lessened the headroom, so that although a tall driver had enough clearance in all normal circumstances a hump-back bridge or the like could occasionally cause him some discomfort.

Legroom is more than ample, and the pedals are well laid out, the organ type throttle pedal being suitably placed for "heel and toe" action. The gear lever is centrally placed and the right hand (the test car had left-hand drive) fell upon it instinctively. The box itself with the famous Porsche synchromesh system is delightful. Perhaps the best way to describe it to less fortunate

Top right: The low frontal area and good aerodynamic shape of the Porsche enhances the car's performance

Centre right: The attractive rear treatment with twin grilles on bonnet which distinguishes the latest models

Bottom right: The high side channel makes ingress a little difficult but the Porsche compares well with most sports cars in this respect

The flowing lines of the Porsche are seen in the side view on the opposite page while in the background is part of Count Carel Godin de Beaufort's Motel and Restaurant situated at Maarsbergen on the Utrecht—Arnhem Autoweg. Below are the rear seats with folding backs which can form the floor of a handy luggage space

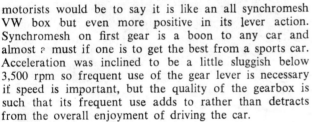

motorists would be to say it is like an all synchromesh VW box but even more positive in its lever action. Synchromesh on first gear is a boon to any car and almost a must if one is to get the best from a sports car. Acceleration was inclined to be a little sluggish below 3,500 rpm so frequent use of the gear lever is necessary if speed is important, but the quality of the gearbox is such that its frequent use adds to rather than detracts from the overall enjoyment of driving the car.

The instrument panel is well laid out, the rev counter being the middle of three large dials with the speedometer to the right and the oil temperature and fuel gauges to the left. The horizontal arrangement of the upper spokes of the steering wheel assured a clear view of all the instruments. The positioning of some of the switches left something to be desired, and the ignition starter switch, which is reached by groping the left hand around the steering wheel, proved most irksome.

One hears conflicting reports of Porsche roadholding; those who have long experience of the cars speak very highly of their roadability, while others with only brief experience can be quite alarmist. We suspect that part of the Porsche's popularity stems from the fact that it is not an easy car to drive round corners quickly, being of an unforgiving nature towards the unskilful. Swing axle rear suspension has its limitations and there are certain rules which must be adhered to rather strictly. For instance, you cannot "lift off" with safety in a corner if you go in a little too quickly. Nevertheless one soon gains confidence in the Porsche's handling, and after a while the driver gets considerable enjoyment from taking it through the corners quickly. The tendency is towards oversteer right through the speed range, although it is possible to get the car understeering through fast bends. The steering is inclined to be a little on the heavy side but quite direct and positive. The test car was fitted with German Dunlop SP tyres and these are truly among the best tyres we have ever experienced, their performance in cornering, braking, the wet or the dry being completely beyond reproach.

A truly fine feature of the Porsche is the manner in which it combines splendid handling qualities with ride comfort almost unique in the sports car field. The Porsche can be pushed across very rough Continental roads at extremely fast speeds without any discomfort whatsoever to the occupants. There is very little pitching or other side effects even when one realises that the suspension is working for all it is worth. Hump-backs and large undulations can set up some pitching, but only when they are taken very quickly. At high cornering forces the Porsche is inclined to roll a little, but the excellent shape of the seats keeps the occupants well located.

The straight line performance of the Porsche is most impressive for a 1600 cc car, and it is possible to exceed the maximum rpm (5500) in top gear, which represents a speed approaching 110 mph. 100 mph cruising is quite feasible, and at this speed the engine does not sound at all fussy and the wind noise is remarkably low. In fact the Porsche's excellent aerodynamic shape contributes a great deal towards the top end performance, for although the acceleration figure from 0-80 mph is not extraordinary by sports car standards, the car pulls steadily upwards to 100 mph in reasonably quick time. The brakes match the car's performance, the big drums doing their job quite efficiently although from really high speeds comparatively heavy pedal pressures seem necessary. Like all very good drum brakes, the Porsche's seemed always a little better than one expected, and when really required always managed to pull the car up shorter than was anticipated.

Night driving was quite untiring, the headlights giving excellent illumination, and the combined dip switch/flasher lever just behind the wheel was comfortably operated by one finger while the rest of the hand stayed on the steering wheel.

The overall impression of the Porsche is that it is an extremely fine grand touring car, and its effortless high speed performance combined with the high standard of ride comfort makes it an ideal car for two people travelling on the European continent. Docile enough to be driven by anybody, yet a driver who is prepared to handle it with care and skill can make the Porsche travel very quickly indeed on winding roads, even when these roads have surfaces so poor as to prevent the full use of most cars' performances. The distinctive shape, the rear-engine layout, and the comparatively limited production make the Porsche a rather individual car, and certainly one that any keen motorist should be proud to own. The Porsche owner gets a good deal for his money although the car remains rather expensive in Britain. We look forward to the day when Porsches are sold at a competitive price on our market.

The sliding roof is electrically operated and quickly converts the draught free coupe into an almost open car. You can't see the beefy Porsche engine but routine servicing is not difficult

SPECIFICATION :

ENGINE :

Flat four-cylinder, air-cooled, located at rear; bore 82·5 mm (3·25 in), stroke 74 mm (2·92 in). Cubic capacity, 1582 cc. Compression ratio, 8·5 to 1. Maximum bhp (net), 75 at 5,500 rpm. Maximum torque, 86 lb ft at 3,700 rpm. Inclined overhead valves, pushrod operated. Two Zenith 32 NDIX twin choke downdraught carburettors; mechanical fuel pump; tank capacity, 11½ gals. 6V 84 amp/hr battery.

TRANSMISSION :

Single dry plate clutch. Four-speed gearbox with synchromesh on all forward ratios. Overall gear ratios: 1st, 13·69; 2nd, 7·81; 3rd, 5·01; top, 3·61 to 1. Central, floor-mounted gear lever. Spiral bevel final drive.

CHASSIS :

Suspension: front, independent by transverse laminated torsion bars and trailing links; rear, independent by swing axles and transverse torsion bars. Telescopic shock absorbers front and rear. Hydraulic drum brakes front and rear. Worm and peg steering. Tyre size, 5·60-15 in.

DIMENSIONS :

	ft	in
Wheelbase	6	10¾
Track: front	4	2¾
Track: rear	4	2
Overall length	13	2
Overall width	5	5¼
Overall height	4	4¼
Ground clearance		6
Turning circle	33	0
Kerb weight	2060 lb	

PERFORMANCE :

Acceleration through gears :

kph		sec
0– 50	(31·07 mph)	4·8
0–100	(62·14 mph)	13·9
0–125	(77·67 mph)	21·3
0–150	(93·21 mph)	34·0

PORSCHE

CARRERA 2-LITER

STORY AND PHOTOS BY HANSJOERG BENDEL

LET'S LOOK BACK a few years: When the first Porsche appeared in 1948, it was little more than a hotted-up VW beautified by a streamlined coupe body—made of aluminum at that time—produced in very small numbers in very small workshops at Gmünd in Austria. The 1131-cc, air-cooled flat-4 engine had been talked into producing 40 bhp, the transmission incorporated that remarkably solid crash box good for a) delightfully professional, double-clutched changes, or b) changes without any use of the clutch, or c) the production of horrible noises without apparent ill effects, and the brakes used the original small VW drums. Top speed was around 87 mph, and the car soon got a reputation for "difficult" cornering because of a strong addiction to oversteer.

To the surprise of many, this modest theme—just like that of the VW itself—proved capable of fantastic development. After Porsche had returned to Stuttgart, large-scale production methods were adopted, and numerous improvements made later models faster, quieter, more refined and led to better handling and reliability.

The most obvious development concerned the pushrod engine. Enlargements first to 1300 and then to 1500 cc brought racing units which, when fed with alcoholic beverage, produced up to 98 bhp (DIN measurement, i.e., with all accessories and silencer) and propelled coupes and open 2-seaters at speeds exceeding 125 mph.

For some time these engines collected success after success, but in 1952 Ferry Porsche and his staff realized that, for serious racing, the days of the simple pushrod unit were numbered. A completely new, flat-4 engine of 1500 cc was built, air cooled again, but incorporating 4 overhead camshafts;

From the front, the 2-liter looks like any other Porsche.

the result was an initial power output of 115 bhp at 7500 rpm.

In an open 2-seater, driven by pre-war ace Hans Stuck, this engine had a few experimental sorties in 1953; entrusted to Hans Herrmann, it made its first successful bid for top racing honors in the 1954 Mille Miglia, where it delighted its creators by placing 6th overall and winning the 1500-cc class. Even today, the racing career of this design is anything but over, as the 1962 Porsche GP team started this season with a fuel-injected version credited with about 165 bhp—nearly 50% more than the original design target.

In the same year of 1954, this engine also commenced a second career which, as far as the private Porsche owner is concerned, is of even greater direct interest: It was installed in one of the Austrian-made aluminum coupes and appeared in the Liège-Rome-Liège, one of the toughest long-distance rallies ever; driven by Pølensky and Linge, it beat the entire competition and came first in general classification.

The winning potential of this combination was so convincing that series-production was decided; christened "Carrera" in honor of the Mexican Road Race and recognized as a "series-production GT car," it has since distinguished itself in countless events.

The Carrera, produced first with 1500, later with 1600 cc, was meant for the driver interested in serious high-speed motoring. Many Carreras never faced a starter's flag, and there was really not much point in preferring the more sophisticated engine and its exacting demands on maintenance unless the superior performance in the upper speed range could be exploited—the pushrod units were cheaper to buy and to run, less noisy and, in daily use, just as fast. One Carrera specialty merits recording: To this day, all pushrod engines have been cooled by virtually the original VW fan. This was not good enough for the 4 ohc engines, for which a powerful blower with twin rotors was evolved; at high revs, huge quantities of air were expelled underneath the engine, which on dry roads produced the most spectacular clouds of dust and a distinct "atmosphere of racing."

As the years went by, even the big touring cars got more power and began to trespass into performance regions hitherto considered private Porsche hunting grounds. To enable the air-cooled fraternity to keep in front, even in straight-line acceleration, something more powerful than even the Super 90 was desirable. The 2-liter "Carrera 2" was the answer.

This model was introduced at the Frankfurt Motor Show in the fall of 1961; its body has all the latest modifications mentioned in R&T's December 1961 issue (larger window area, modified front hood, fresh-air inlets ahead of windshield, external fuel filler cap, twin cooling air inlets on engine cover), while the chassis specification is identical to that

Twin ignition, 2 carburetors and 4 camshafts for the 2-liter.

of the Super 90, with its rear swing axle with transverse equalization leaf spring. In other words, body and running gear are modified in detail only; it follows that in comparison with the Super 90 and the 1600 (tested by R&T in March '60 and October '61), no radical departures are to be expected.

The only thing completely new is the engine. Porsche has often been named among those constructors who are wizards at achieving results which others (or theory) consider impossible; when it was decided to provide plenty of torque at low speeds—for real acceleration—and smooth, flexible running, even the fathers of the Carrera agreed that this could best be achieved by a little more displacement: When the 4-ohc engine was first laid down, it had already been decided that the design should permit a maximum size of 2 liters, and this then was the volume selected for the Carrera 2. With 92-mm bore and 74-mm stroke, it is decidedly oversquare; its peak power of 152 bhp (SAE rating) at 6200 rpm is definitely below the figure attainable by this unit in racing tune; maximum torque comes at 4600 rpm on a long, flat curve. In the interest of smoother running, longer life and easier maintenance, bearings are plain throughout, in contrast to the early models' roller bearings for the mains and connecting rods.

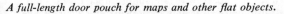

A full-length door pouch for maps and other flat objects.

Dust on the Solitude circuit is kicked up by the cooling fan.

Unlike standard model, the 2-liter has extra panel below bumper.

Unique air cleaners are used for the Solex-carbureted 2-liter.

PORSCHE CARRERA 2-LITER

Our test car was fitted with the "European" gearbox; for cars supplied to the U.S., standard ratios in 3rd (1.227) and 4th (0.885) are slightly "slower," in the interest of a little more pulling power.

As explained previously, we did not expect any surprises from the chassis; when we threw our test gear into the back of the car, we were prepared to find a well-known package in which only the new engine would merit special comment. In a way, we were right, because all the well-known features are there: the very comfortable Reutter seats, the quick gear-change, the familiar surroundings and, above all, the unmistakable feel of a quality car built for the connoisseur. But we did have a pleasant surprise. Apparently the "unchanged" chassis has again been subject to subtle detail development, which makes itself felt as soon as one takes the wheel. The steering is a little better—improved response with reduced vibration feedback—and there is unmistakable progress in the way the car keeps glued to the road at all times. There is better stability under fierce acceleration, at full speed and under heavy braking, and experiments like braking in a corner can result in a slightly ragged line but practically never bring real trouble.

It is likely that part of this improvement must be credited to the late-model "round shoulder" tires but, whatever the reason, the balance is perfect.

This is not useless luxury. The high torque promised on paper is certainly there, and when climbing winding mountain roads it is very easy to accelerate out of a corner with too much steam; under conditions such as this, the exceptional controllability is quickly appreciated.

The car's acceleration is truly exhilarating. The clutch takes quite a bit of throttle without protest, and when one finds that it is time for 2nd gear, down comes the stick in a flick, more acceleration, and other cars pass by as if in reverse. High up in the speed range, this is it—the effortless superiority of the true high-performance machine.

Performance figures are almost exactly as claimed by the manufacturer. Best recorded speed was 126 mph (Porsche says 124.5) and our acceleration times were just slightly slower than those given by a graph included in the specifications. Unfortunately, our test car was wanted "back as soon as possible," so we had no opportunity to check the fuel consumption. However, we have reason to believe that owners will find it easy to get better than the minimum 16.8-mpg figure indicated.

In the body department, the most notable innovation concerns the fresh-air intake, combined with electric fan and a separate heater which is situated in the front compartment, ahead of the battery. This combination is effective and (at last!) permits windshield defrosting without running the engine; it has the amusing peculiarity that, after switching the engine off, the burner continues with burbling noises until all the fuel previously aspirated is used up—which may lead to uninitiated parking lot attendants calling the fire squad when faced with a car obviously about to explode! At present, no figures are available concerning the additional fuel consumption of this heater but, anyhow, the extra comfort is worth something.

Points of criticism: When we first laid eyes (and ears) on the new engine, in the autumn of 1961, we were struck by a silkiness totally unusual for this kind of power unit. It was therefore with high expectations that we approached our test car. But these expectations were not entirely fulfilled: There was too much noise inside the car, and the engine appeared to have that certain roughness well remembered from older Carreras. In fairness, we must record that we tried a pre-production model, so we can only hope that this peculiarity will have disappeared on the cars supplied to customers. A second remark concerns the body as a whole. It is certain that Porsche has never tried to be "à la mode," and bless it for that—but after 14 years with an almost unchanged shape, even the accustomed eye begins to notice some signs of age. The instrument panel, for example, is higher up than is usual nowadays, and visibility could only benefit from a lower waistline.

Also, of course, the rear seating compartment remains impossible—at least for grown-ups—for distances over 5 miles. No doubt comparatively small production figures do not invite frequent body changes, even less so when the existing shape has many proven advantages and a solid following, but, in spite of this, we feel that Porsche should start to look ahead—if it hasn't already done so.

As a whole, the Carrera 2 is certainly one of the most desirable GT cars produced today; it is not cheap, and maintenance will not be quite as easy as on the simpler pushrod versions, but it should delight the owner looking for a car of high quality and exceptional roadworthiness.

Production is underway—in limited numbers—on both coupe and cabriolet models, and we understand that Porsche dealers are accepting orders. First deliveries are not to be until about September, however, so a certain amount of patience is required, along with the desire.

ROAD TEST

PORSCHE CARRERA 2-LITER

DIMENSIONS

Wheelbase, in	82.7
Tread, f and r	51.4/50.1
Over-all length, in	158
width	65.8
height	52.3
equivalent vol, cu ft	315
Frontal area, sq ft	19.1
Ground clearance, in	6.0
Steering ratio, o/a	16.0
turns, lock to lock	2.5
turning circle, ft	36
Hip room, front	2 x 21.0
Hip room, rear	
Pedal to seat back, max	42.0
Floor to ground	10.0

CALCULATED DATA

Lb/hp (test wt)	16.6
Cu ft/ton mile	84.4
Mph/1000 rpm (4th)	19.6
Engine revs/mile	3060
Piston travel, ft/mile	1485
Rpm @ 2500 ft/min	5150
equivalent mph	101
R&T wear index	45.4

SPECIFICATIONS

List price	$7595
Curb weight, lb	2220
Test weight	2520
distribution, %	43/57
Tire size	165-15
Brake swept area	149
Engine type	flat-4, ohv
Bore & stroke	3.62 x 2.91
Displacement, cc	1966
cu in	120
Compression ratio	9.5
Bhp @ rpm	152 @ 6200
equivalent mph	122
Torque, lb-ft	131 @ 4600
equivalent mph	90

GEAR RATIOS

4th (0.852)	3.78
3rd (1.130)	5.01
2nd (1.765)	7.83
1st (3.090)	13.7

SPEEDOMETER ERROR

30 mph	actual, 25.0
60 mph	54.0

PERFORMANCE

Top speed (4th), mph	122.7
best timed run	126.0
3rd (6800)	101
2nd (6850)	65
1st (6850)	37

FUEL CONSUMPTION

Normal range, mpg	16.8/23.5

ACCELERATION

0-30 mph, sec	3.3
0-40	5.3
0-50	6.9
0-60	9.2
0-70	12.4
0-80	15.8
0-100	27.2
Standing ¼ mile	16.9
speed at end	83

TAPLEY DATA

4th, lb/ton @ mph	131 @ 92
3rd	290 @ 70
2nd	575 @ 50
Total drag at 60 mph, lb	115

ENGINE SPEED IN GEARS

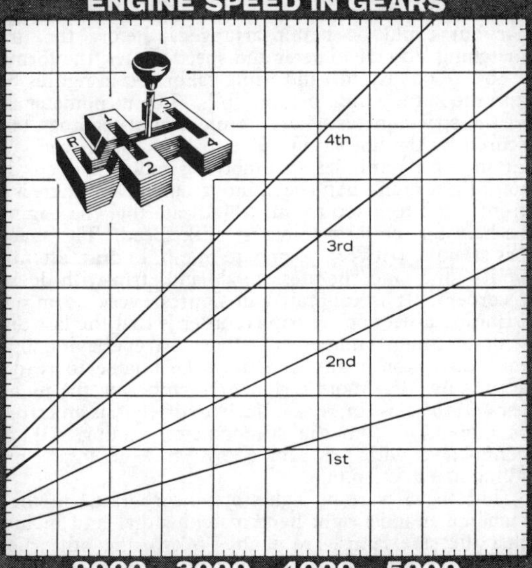

ACCELERATION & COASTING

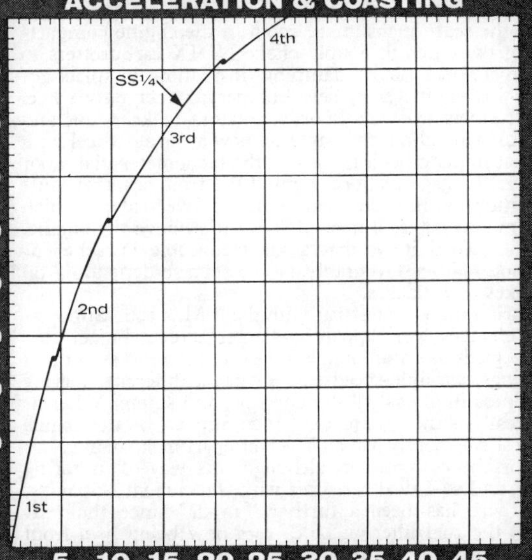

Analysis of the

Type 356B Porsche Super 75

Road Test Impressions of a Beautifully-made Completely-equipped 1,582 c.c. £2,348 German G.T. Car

A SHAPE NO ONE HAS COPIED.—This picture shows the clean aerodynamic lines of the Porsche coupé.

ALTHOUGH I am not privileged, like the Production Manager and Continental Correspondent of MOTOR SPORT, to have had regular experience of Porsche motoring, I was able recently to drive a Super 75 for over 1,000 miles on English roads, mostly fast miles, for this is a car that is not habitually driven slowly.

In many ways a Porsche is the modern equivalent of the pre-1939 Bugatti—expensive, but rewarding, a car for discerning owners, beautifully and individually made, and, like the famous French *marque* of pre-war times, somewhat temperamental, if experience of this test car, and the P.M.'s 1960 Super 75, is any criterion.

In coupé form the modern Porsche has not changed materially from the original conception of Dr. Ferdinand Porsche, dating back to 1949. Of the three body styles, coupé, hard-top and openable cabriolet, we are here concerned with the first-named, a low-drag, individually-styled car, with the Super 75 version of the rear-mounted flat-four air-cooled, push-rod inclined-o.h.v. engine that develops 75 b.h.p. (88 S.A.E.h.p.) at 5,000 r.p.m. on a compression ratio of 8.5 to 1.

The Porsche has undergone minor but significant changes down the years, for like VW, the little factory at Zuffenhausen-Stuttgart, controlled now by Ferry Porsche, believes in continual improvement of the basic car rather than model-changes at defined intervals of time. Compared to the quite early models you find a greater area of screen and rear window, less convenient adjustment of the seat squabs, more room in the engine compartment, enabling twin Zenith double-choke NDIX carburetters to be used, conventional sound-damping insulation in place of upholstery in this engine-boot, new bumpers, rather ugly wheel knave-plates, funnels over the floor ventilators to keep hot and cold air from blowing about the ankles, a new steering wheel with a horn-ring that impedes a clear view of the tachometer dial, door "keeps", a level luggage platform behind the front seats, exhaust pipes terminating within the rear bumper over-riders which discolours them and makes it more difficult to remove the engine, and many other small items that a knowledgeable Porsche enthusiast will note, either favourably or the reverse depending on his personal likes and dislikes.

Even comparing the 1962 test-car with the P.M.'s 1960 Super 75 a number of changes were apparent—larger screen, bigger rear window, twin grills on the engine boot, a different system of fresh-air ventings, variable-speed screenwipers, different steering wheel, a heaviness in almost all the controls, and so on. Whereas this 75 b.h.p. car has the type name "1600 Super" on the engine boot lid, the test car merely had an "S" after its make name.

I am no Porsche connoisseur, although this way of motoring appeals to me, and so I deal hereafter with the current Super 75. Incidentally, there has been a further "mod." since the test-car was made, the fuel filler on l.h.d. cars now being in a front wing instead of beneath the front bonnet, which, I understand, enables the tank to impinge to a smaller degree on luggage space and obviates petrol fumes being drawn from the filler cap and into the car *via* the fresh air ducts.

THE SUPER 75 IN DETAIL

It is general knowledge to MOTOR SPORT readers that a Porsche is splendidly constructed and finished. It is a very low car, so that you enter over a frame-sill, through doors which shut in a pleasingly positive manner of their own. The separate front seats have hard but comfortable cushions and the squabs have a big range of adjustment controlled by side levers against strong spring action, and they fall almost completely down to form rather lumpy beds. These seats are not nearly so convenient as those fitted to early Porsches, however, wherein the squab angle could be regained without operating the side levers. The doors have lockable quarter lights with the notable refinement of tiny knurled knobs that prevent the pip being depressed and thus serve to foil a thief who is not sufficiently enterprising to remove the back window. The windows lower completely with 4⅓-turns of the handles. Normal interior handles are used, which when lifted up lock the doors, even against the key, from within. The exterior push-buttons each have locks. The aforesaid interior handles are so contrived that it is impossible to be locked out of the car if the key is left within. The rear side windows open slightly, as ventilation panels, on well-made toggles and have a knob that locks them in position. Range of vision from the driving seat is quite good in spite of the low seating position, both front wings being in view, although the scuttle is now higher than before. There is stiff crash-padding above the facia in leatherette to match the interior trim, and soft vizors.

The instruments and minor controls reflect the quality of the car but could be better arranged. Before the driver are the matching Vdo tachometer and speedometer, the former reading to "60" (6,000 r.p.m.) and being calibrated in figures by thousands, and the latter going to 120 m.p.h. The tachometer is to the right of the speedometer where its more vital readings tend to be obscured by the horn-ring. The dial is straked from 3,000 to 5,000 r.p.m. as a reminder that nothing much happens in a Porsche until these crankshaft speeds are attained, and there is a red section from 5,000 to 5,500 r.p.m. to indicate that the engine should not be held for too long above its peak speed. The speedometer dial has straking between 30 and 40 m.p.h. to draw attention to speed-limits and incorporates total and trip-with-decimal mileage recorders. It is calibrated in figures every 20 m.p.h. A faintly irritating aspect of the trip recorder is that the last digit moves up with the decimal numerals, so that a driver obeying instructions of a rally navigator might sometimes be unable to read the mileage accurately. Far more serious, remembering the high price of the car and the class of person likely to drive it, is an error of optimism as high as 6% in the speedometer readings. The tachometer commences with "6," for 600 r.p.m., the engine of the test-car idling at 1,200 r.p.m.

The usual warning lights are incorporated in the dials of the tachometer and a right-hand matching dial, and include a warning that the side lamps are alight (green), the other lights covering dynamo-charge, high-beam (blue), oil pressure (green) and direction-flashers. The right-hand dial indicates oil temperature at the top and fuel contents at the bottom. Unfortunately, although the needle-sweep is considerable, there is no longer any calibration

THE EXTERNAL DIFFERENCES between the latest Porsche Super 75 and a 1960 model are here illustrated. Note the bigger screen and luggage-boot lid of 396 NMG and, in the right-hand picture, its bigger back window, and twin grilles.

of this thermometer. an indication that even at the Porsche factory the salesmen are taking over from the engineers! The fuel gauge is marked " 0," " $\frac{2}{4}$," " $\frac{4}{4}$."

Unlabelled neat black knobs are spaced rather haphazardly about the metal facia. That to the left of the steering wheel looks after the wipers, its knob turning to vary the blade speed from 40 to 80 strokes per minute. Next to it is the cigar lighter; it would be better were these two knobs reversed, because should the driver want to put the wipers on or off at the same moment as the passenger feels in need of nicotine, their hands must cross. Set up rather awkwardly behind the wheel is the lamps-control knob, bringing in first side lights, then headlights, and the rheostat instrument lighting by rotating it. A hand-throttle knob is set to the right of the lamps-knob, also behind the wheel; it pulls out against serrations to increase engine speed and turning the knob locks it in position.

A foot-operated screen washer, that squirts over the roof on too-vigorous pressure, is supplied from a plastic reservoir holding about 1½ qts. of water. Out of sight below the facia, but easily reached, is the useful reserve fuel tap, labelled " RES," " ZU," " AUF," that brings in rather more than a gallon of fuel. The petrol filter is located at the base of its operating-rod, but is out of the way of the driver's feet. A draw-type ash-tray is provided, also provision for a facia-mounted radio, above which is an *accurate* Vdo clock.

To the right of the 3-spoke steering wheel is a neat little stalk that controls the direction flashers, flashes the lamps if pulled up, and dips the headlamps of pushed down. Lamps flashing is on dipped beam if the sidelamps are alight, full beam in daylight, or, of course, from low-beam to high-beam. Some drivers will prefer a separate lamps' stalk, as it is possible to signal a turn inadvertently when operating the lamps in a hurry. A small-diameter horn-ring on the wheel sounds a loud horn but was rather stiff to use. The steering wheel is set sensibly low, although somewhat higher than on earlier models, to offer breathing space to German stomachs.

The heater controls are very neat—just a small quadrant with selection of off, ventilation to screen and ventilation to car, with a knob in front of the gear lever to bring in warm air. This knob calls for many turns and on the test car hot instead of cold air was directed on the feet even when it was screwed down. Markings on the quadrant are by International colour code. The chassis rails incorporate the air outlets with those neat sliding vent-hoods, now with funnels to direct the air forward. Another quadrant provides for a gasolene heater, if fitted.

On the extreme right of the metal facia is the ignition-key-cum-starter. Internal stowage in the Porsche is generous. Both doors and scuttle possess big pockets. There is a lined lockable cubby-hole, although it is too small to take a Rolleiflex camera. Its lid has elastic bands for holding pencil, route-card, etc. Twin non-swivelling anti-dazzle vizors are fitted, with a mirror for the lady passenger, and the rear-view mirror is of very effective anti-dazzle type. There is a neat VW-type Hella interior lamp on each side, each having its own switch which can be set for courtesy action. These lamps are usefully bright. Coat hooks are provided, also metal door " pulls " and a metal grabhandle on the facia.

The fuel tank and spare wheel occupy much of the space in the front boot, the lid of which has been enlarged recently, but there is useful stowage for soft bags, etc. A nice point of detail, typical of Porsche development, is that the bonnet-lifting handle is now rigid, to prevent it buckling when a heavy-handed pump attendant leans on it while closing the lid. Most of the luggage, of course, goes behind the main seats, two occasional seats, very nicely shaped and leather-upholstered, having backs that fold forward to make a flat, cloth-faced platform. On this sizeable suit-cases can be carried; lugs are provided for luggage straps but the straps themselves have to be bought by the owner. The front boot knob remains on the near-side in r.h.d. cars, which is rather casual in a car costing £2,400. The same applies to the engine-lid release knob. There is a rather " fumbly " safety-catch for the front boot lid and an emergency nylon rope for opening it should the main cable break—but this reduces the thiefproof effect. Both lids are self-propping; some people consider they should be separately lockable, to obviate locking the car doors.

The fuel tank has a commendable size filler orifice. A gear lever lock is provided at the base of the lever. Incidentally, a very clear and comprehensive driver's manual, on VW lines, is issued with the car. The test car was impeccably turned out, with spares kit, workshop manuals in English, a tin of oil, etc., but, as will be seen later, I would have been happier had the engine been developing its full power.

ON THE ROAD

The Porsche is essentially a low and small car and a driver unfamiliar with it has to get used to this and allow for the sensation that it is pivotting on the inside back wheel round acute corners. The driving position is very comfortable, although pedals offset to the left (the brake pedal is in line with the steering column) and the generous length of seat cushion may combine to cause leg strain.

This is essentially a car you "wear " rather than merely sit in—getting over a sill into the driving seat. Although so compact, only a very long-armed driver would be able to reach over to open or close the near-side rear vent-window from his seat, yet he has ample leg, elbow and head room in this compact G.T. coupé.

The rigid central gear lever is delightfully placed, its movements conventional, with reverse easy to find beyond bottom gear position. The pull-out handbrake is moderately accessible under the scuttle but stiff to release. The treadle accelerator enables " heel and toe " gear changing.

With memories of finding the VW's lightness of control handed on to the Porsches I drove some years ago, I was disappointed in the heaviness of the 1962 version. The steering calls for some effort and becomes heavier towards full-lock, all three pedals call for firm pressure, and although the gear-lever has much shorter movements than formerly, gone is the delightfully light " non-mechanical " swopping of ratios of the earlier Porsches.

The gear change is very quick, however, the change from 3rd to 2nd particularly rapid, and there is unbeatable synchro-mesh, gear changing calling for only a flick of the clutch pedal. But it is a heavier change than I had anticipated. As it is essential to keep engine speed above 3,000 r.p.m. if any sort of performance is to be obtained, the gear lever has to be operated continually. In this

THE PORSCHE TYPE 356B COUPE WITH SUPER 75 ENGINE

Engine: Flat-four cylinder, 82.5×74 mm. (1,582 c.c.). Inclined overhead valves operated by push-rods. 8.5 to 1 compression ratio. 75 b.h.p. (88 S.A.E. h.p.) at 5,000 r.p.m.
Gear ratios: First, 13.69 to 1; second, 7.81 to 1; third, 5.01 to 1; top 3.61 to 1.
Tyres: 165×15 Dunlop S.P., on bolt-on steel disc wheels.
Weight: Not weighed. Maker's figure: 18 cwt., 1 qr., 16 lb. (kerb weight, D.I.N.).
Steering ratio: Just under 2½ turns, lock-to-lock.
Fuel capacity: 11½ gallons (including 1.1 gallons in reserve). Total range approx. 316 miles.
Wheelbase: 6 ft. 11¼ in.
Track: Front, 4 ft. 4 in.; rear, 4 ft. 2¾ in.
Dimensions: 13 ft. 1¼ in.×5 ft. 5½ in.×4 ft. 3½ in. (high).
Price: £1,707 (£2,348 2s. 9d. inclusive of purchase tax and import duty.) As tested: £2,366 17s. 3d.
Makers: Porsche K.-G., Porschestrasse 85, Stuttgart-Zuffenhausen, Germany.
Concessionaires: A.F.N. Ltd., Falcon Works, London Road, Isleworth, Middlesex.

PORSCHE POINTS

[The general specification of the Porsche is given in the data table; below we publish a few additional facts that will be of interest to the technically minded.—Ed.]

The Super 75 engine gives 86 ft. lb. torque at 3,700 r.p.m. and develops 47.4 h.p. per litre (D.I.N.).

* * *

The 3-piece crankcase is of light alloy, the cylinders of cast iron, with light alloy heads. The forged crankshaft runs in four main bearings.

* * *

The cooling fan is driven by a V-belt through the dynamo, which runs at approx. 1.8 times crankshaft speed. The fan feeds air over the cylinder barrels at a rate of 290 cub. ft. a second at 2,000 r.p.m. and at 580 cub. ft. per sec. at 4,000 r.p.m.

* * *

There is full pressure lubrication with a full-flow oil cooler and by-pass Fram filter. The sump holds approx. 3 quarts of lubricant, the complete engine approx. 5 quarts.

* * *

The ignition setting at full advance is 5° b.t.d.c. and the test car was using Bosch W225 plugs.

* * *

Valve timing is:—inlet opens 17° b.t.d.c., closes 53° a.b.d.c.; exhaust opens 50° b.t.d.c., closes 14° a.t.d.c. Tappet setting=0.040 in.

* * *

The electrical system is 6 volt, with an 84 amp./hr. battery and 200 watt current and voltage regulator. There are 12 fuses, under the facia in the driving compartment.

respect the Porsche again recalls the pre-war Bugatti; you may remember how astonished was the wife of motoring journalist, the late Edgar Duffield, when she was driven from Aldgate to "The Bear" at Esher in top gear in a Type 44 Bugatti, because her husband's 8-valve and 16-valve Brescia Bugattis never got out of 2nd and 3rd speed until they were well out of London. With its 3.61 to 1 top gear the modern Porsche resembles the Brescia Bugatti; of vintage days . . .

If the excellent gearbox is properly employed, extremely useful acceleration all along the speed-range is available, together with maxima of 28, 51 and 78 m.p.h. in the three lower ratios without exceeding 5,500 r.p.m., to which the engine goes without any indication of distress. Top speed is 109 m.p.h., again at 5,500 r.p.m. but 95 m.p.h. was about the best I could get on English roads. This must be qualified by stating that carburation appeared to be suspect on the test-car, which was seriously down on power compared to the P.M.s 1960 Super 75, the engine "hanging" badly at 4,000 r.p.m. For this reason there was no point in taking acceleration figures. The engine is sensitive to different fuels—it refused to look at Shell, went better on Esso Golden and better still on BP Super Plus.

But it never went properly for very long and on account of this erratic running I had a rather trying run down from Oulton Park to Hampshire, although, a Porsche being a Porsche, the average speed was still impressive. This is largely due to the great ability to pick up speed very quickly indeed from 30 to 50 m.p.h., together with a very high degree of controllability. The steering, geared just under 2½ turns lock-to-lock, exhibits no free-play and is essentially accurate, and the Super 75 corners with no roll, its short wheelbase enabling it to "tuck-in" in traffic most effectively. It must *look* safe, too, because fellow users of the highway at far lower speeds never hoot or shake firsts at it. It is, indeed, a very safe car, possessing cornering powers and acceleration that keep it out of trouble.

The steering tendency is initial understeer, even on the test-car, which lacked the extra stabiliser leaf spring for the torsion-bar swing-axle i.r.s. This persists round fast bends but changes to oversteer on sharper corners. The Dunlop SP tyres (which cost extra) cling on very impressively indeed, especially in the wet, at the expense of a harsher ride than normal and rather sudden breakaway when the limit of adhesion is reached. Some die-hard Porsche enthusiasts prefer the old handling characteristics of considerable but consistent oversteer.

The ride is inclined to be lively, in a corner to corner choppiness that is typically Porsche, but only on very rough surfaces does this affect road-holding and even then steering precision is scarcely jeopardised. On unmade roads the Koni-damped suspension functions well. The steering has strong but slow self-centring action which, with the SP tyres, made it tiring on long runs. A rocking action, rather than kick-back, is set up by surface changes through the torsion-bar trailing-link i.f.s. and hydraulically-damped, worm-and-peg mechanism. Tyre squeal is virtually impossible to produce.

The brakes call for firm, even considerable pressure, no doubt due to hard linings, and they are then fully effective for all save really savage stops from near-maximum speed, when disc brakes might be just that much more reassuring. There was considerable squeal from the anti-fade linings as the car came to rest but the brakes did not pull off-course and had no vices.

The main point of Porsche motoring is effortless fast travel in luxury surroundings. Although the characteristic exhaust note of the flat-four engine intrudes considerably under acceleration, throttled back it becomes a pleasantly quiet power unit, functioning well within its limits. Cruising at 80 m.p.h., it is turning over at less than 4,000 r.p.m., the oil thermometer well over to the safe side of its scale.

With the windows open buffeting occurs but normally a Porsche owner contrives sufficient ventilation by adjusting quarter-lights and rear vents. Unfortunately with o/s quarterlight shut an irritating air whistle intruded; there is also some transmission hum on the over-run, although the gears are silent.

Petrol consumption of 100-octane fuel varied for 30 m.p.g. driving very gently (we were tailing a recently-collected Siddeley Special at the time) to 25½ m.p.g. crossing London. A fast drive to Oulton Park and back showed 27.5 m.p.g. The reserve supply suffices for a useful 38-39 miles and the total range is some 300 miles. In a mileage of 1,220 a pint of Valvoline oil sufficed to restore the sump level. The dip-stick is extremely accessible, and changing plugs with the good-quality tools provided, in an attempt (unsuccessful) to cure the hesitant acceleration, did not occupy too much time.

The engine starts instantly without choke and does not "pink" or run-on. At night the Bosch headlamps provide excellent illumination. The brake lights and flashers are incorporated in single units, incidentally, and the reflectors have been stuck on as an afterthought.

To sum up, my impressions of the Porsche Super 75 are that it is a genuine G.T. car in miniature, with accommodation for four people in fair comfort, two in extreme comfort and luxury. The care with which this highly individual car is constructed is reflected in the fine-paint finish of the beautifully-shaped Reutter body, and in the high grade leatherette and corduroy upholstery and the complete equipment provided, as well as by such effective items of detail as grease nipples on the door-hinges and thermostatically-controlled hot air supply to the carburetter intakes.

Granted that the car is expensive—as tested it is priced at a total of nearly £2,367—and that to a large extent Porsche ownership is an acquired taste, the Super 75 provides high performance from a small engine allied to the comfort and luxury expected of far larger cars and, above all, it is one of the most individualistic cars—possessed of real " character "—that it is possible to buy. I drove it for ten days only but another factor that contributes to enthusiasm for this Porsche is its durability over big mileages, about which I have asked the P.M. to enlarge in the following paragraphs.—W. B.

A PORSCHE SUPER 75 OVER 30,000 MILES

My own Porsche Super is very similar to the car tested and a fairly accurate log has been kept of mileage, fuel and troubles.

With 104 miles on the clock, the car was collected, and run-in at the recommended speed. At the 500-mile service the speedometer was changed as the original one was 10 m.p.h. out at 50 m.p.h. The new speedometer started at 13 miles and when it was showing 1,000 miles-plus, and the car was loosening up, the pronounced understeer became annoying, so the Michelin " X " pressures were put up until a reasonably neutral effect had been reached, e.g. 25 lb. front and 27 back.

During the 1,500-mile service several minor troubles were sorted out but the complained-of poor brakes were still as bad as ever, as I was to find out 3,000 miles later when in a damp lane they snatched, locking the front wheels however light the pedal pressure was, and the side of the car was " graunched " on another car.

At 6,600 miles, during service, a vibration of the gear lever was rectified, but the brakes were still terrible. I suggested different linings as there seemed no cure for the snatching, but it was two and a half thousand miles of " dodgy " motoring before Ferodo A.M.4s were fitted. This sorted out the snatching on wet roads, but appreciable fade developed when slowing from the region of 80 and 90 m.p.h. A short time later, a trip to Stuttgart was organised and arrangements were made for the car to be checked at Zuffenhausen and the brakes to be sorted out.

On the run from Ostend to Stuttgart I checked the fuel consumption very carefully and found it to be 32.2 m.p.g. with an overall average of over 70 m.p.h. Before leaving the car I checked the 0-60 time, so as to have a guide at any re-tune. This came out at 14 sec. before tuning and on the way home it took 12.4 sec. to reach 60 m.p.h. The brakes were changed back to German linings and for the first time worked very well, making the run home a real pleasure. This service at the works took place at 11,700 miles. At 13,100 miles the speedometer cable broke, and at 14,300 miles the car went in for a new cable. Unfortunately the British Concessionares detected a knock in the engine and on stripping down, they found excessive cylinder and piston wear, which necessitated a re-build. During the short period during which the engine was overhauled I was loaned a hack engine which propelled the car for 2,500 miles.

I ran the engine in again carefully, with a 1,500-mile service in Stuttgart, and the car was as good as ever. At this service the brakes were good and working perfectly, and O.Kd. by the factory, but 1,500 normal miles later the shoes and drums were changed in England, badly cracked, since when they have snatched and pulled badly.

During last winter the screen cracked and the wipers were strained by snow, but these were repaired and as the carburation was now very " ragged " the car was tuned by the Porsche agents in Liége, with highly satisfactory results.

In the 30,500 miles to date, 1,110 gallons of petrol have been consumed, giving an overall consumption of 27.5 m.p.g. Oil consumption is about 750 miles per pint, and although the car has been driven moderately fast, the Michelin " X " tyres are still the originals.

When a Porsche is going well, there is no more pleasant and comfortable car for getting quickly between two points.—M. J. T.

CONTINUED FROM PAGE 9

me say, straight away, that the car is considerably quieter than the Volkswagen from which it was derived. There is very little of the mechanical clatter which one used to expect from any air-cooled engine, and conversation is easy, even at the higher speeds. There is a "throbbing" sound during acceleration, which one has met with in other "flat-four" engines, but one could most certainly not call this a noisy car by any normal standards.

To anybody who is even slightly conversant with chassis design problems, it must be obvious that, in choosing to use a plain swing-axle rear suspension with a tail-heavy car, the designer has accepted an over-steering characteristic. The question that the tester has to settle is not whether the machine over-steers, because from first principles it obviously does, but whether that over-steering is, in fact, a serious disadvantage.

In practice, the Porsche does over-steer in quite a big way, but the experienced driver, having entered a corner at speed, allows the steering to unwind as the turn is negotiated, which can be a smooth and effortless operation. Many of us have owned the old chain-gang Frazer-Nashes, and there is a startling similarity between the handling characteristics of both these cars. The illusion is heightened by the power-weight ratio, which is of the same order. The resemblance ends, however, when one considers the comfort side of the equation, for the Porsche is a well-sprung coupé, and the 'Nash was an almost springless open one-and-a-half seater. Let me sum up by saying that the Porsche is very controllable and can be cornered fast, but that a driver who attempted advanced techniques on slippery roads, without first becoming fully conversant with the car, would probably finish up facing the way he had come.

On its high top gear, this little flyer covers the miles with effortless ease. At anything up to about 80 m.p.h., the comfort is remarkable for so small and light a vehicle. Above that speed, on certain types of surface, one can feel the swing-axles working. The sensation is due to track variation, and one soon ignores it; it might be better to have a slightly harder damper setting for sustained high speeds.

The body has very pleasing lines, and one cannot but admire the neat appearance, which is delightfully free of flashy ornamentation. This is a most comfortable car, regarded strictly as a two-seater, for the occasional seats are very much of the emergency variety, and are best used as additional luggage space. Point is lent to this remark by the "official" luggage compartment which, as is common among rear-engined cars, is almost filled by the spare wheel. The interior furnishing of the vehicle supplied for test was somewhat plain, having regard to the fairly high price.

Well, there you have the Porsche. With its short-stroke engine and high gearing, allied with an efficient aerodynamic body, it can easily maintain cruising speeds that are more in keeping with cars of at least double its cubic capacity. When one comes to fill the petrol tank, though, that efficient little engine pays dividends, and its thirst is moderate even for a 1½-litre. These are only brief impressions, after a short test, but I hope that they answer the queries which readers have been raising.

THE PORSCHE SUPER 75

For well over 10 years I have been testing Porsches. Other cars have come and gone, but the latest Porsche Super 75, of 1,582 c.c., bears a remarkable external resemblance to the first 1,300 c.c. machine which I drove. However, improvement has been continuous, and the 1962 model differs in almost every important respect from the earlier cars.

The first Porsches were very "dicey", having a pronounced oversteering characteristic. Nowadays, the oversteer has been tamed, and with much firmer suspension and extremely efficient steering the machine is particularly controllable. The voice of the air-cooled rear engine has been muted too, and though it is still audible on acceleration, fast cruising takes place in a remarkably quiet and restful manner. All the old features are there—the splendid gear change, the comfortable seats, the long-wearing qualities, and the perfection of finish. Above all, the Porsche hasn't grown and is still the right size for rapid negotiation of winding or crowded roads.

The immensely rigid body-chassis structure is a two-seater streamlined coupé with small occasional rear seats. In front, the wheels rise and fall on twin trailing arms controlled by laminated torsion bars, an anti-roll bar uniting the two stub axles. Behind, plain swing axles operate against transverse torsion bars, the rear wheels normally showing a small degree of negative camber.

The air-cooled engine is considerably over-square, and has inclined valves operated by pushrods. Two twin-choke Zenith carburetters provide one choke per cylinder, an arrangement which allows a wide torque range to be allied with notable fuel economy. Naturally, the all-indirect gearbox has the famous Porsche synchromesh for all four speeds.

To drive the Porsche is to realize how lacking in torsional rigidity most other cars are! On bad roads, there is a wonderful feeling that the car is utterly solid and all in one piece, which is truly satisfying. Although the suspension is strongly damped and the travel of the wheels is not great, the complete absence of pitching gives a comfortable ride on all reasonable surfaces.

As the rear wheels carry more weight than the front, and they are independently sprung, the traction is naturally very good. Wheelspin is never experienced, even on quite slippery roads, and it pays to use a lot of "engine" when cornering fast. The cornering power is high, and bumps do not cause the car to run wide. Fast curves may be taken without a sign of sliding at speeds which would cause considerable drifting in more orthodox cars. If the limit is passed, the rear end breaks away, but this may be quickly corrected with a flick of the steering wheel.

At speeds above 100 m.p.h., the machine can be deflected by gusts of wind. With a little experience one ignores this, driving with a light touch on the wheel and making no attempt to correct very slight swerves—the car will run straight again at once. The handling has all the "brilliance" which a slight oversteer can give, so one accepts the sensitive response to the steering at maximum speed.

The acceleration is very satisfying indeed. The gear ratios are so right, and the change is crash-proof and as fast as the hand can move. The carburation is particularly good, the engine having immense "punch" in the middle ranges. It pulls well from 2,000 r.p.m. upwards, and in the range from 3,000 to 5,000 r.p.m. it runs like a dynamo. It is usual to run up to 80 m.p.h. in third gear, and when top is engaged the acceleration continues, thanks to the excellence of the aerodynamic body shape. As the gears are all silent and the change is a sheer sensual pleasure, the top gear flexibility is not often tested, but it is quite satisfactory.

The running of the Super 75 gives the impression that a very large engine is pulling a very small car. The unit never feels as though it is at all highly stressed, and the efficient sound damping avoids that "air-cooled" clatter that the cheaper cars without water-jackets sometimes demonstrate. The seats can

m.p.g., and 35 m.p.g. can be recorded if one keeps below three-figure speeds.

The Porsche is a superb engineering job, built almost regardless of cost. For a small car, it is quite costly, but it gives a very special kind of motoring enjoyment that cannot be bought for less. Small enough to be really agile, it yet gives a great sense of ease and space to its two lucky occupants. The basic design has been developed over the years, resulting in a very refined car which is fun for short journeys, patient in London traffic, but at its best when hundreds of miles must be covered in the minimum time.

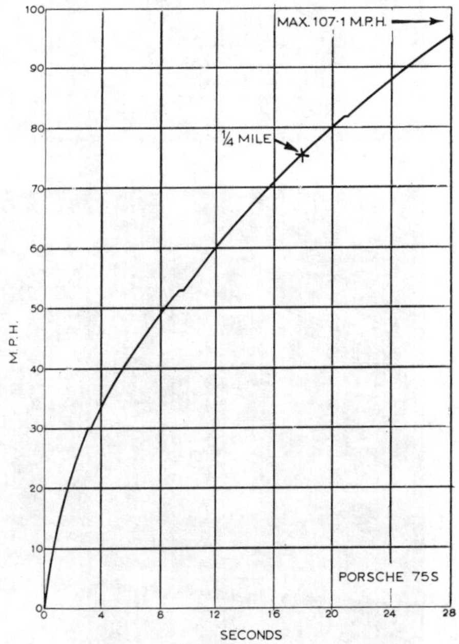

ACCELERATION GRAPH

★

be adjusted for people of any stature, and of course the angle may be vertical, reclining, or anything in between. The small of the back is well supported, which avoids fatigue, and the all-round visibility is greatly improved compared with earlier models.

At low speeds and light pedal pressures, the brakes sometimes make a slight scraping noise. Although they are of drum type, they have been developed over many years, and are both powerful and progressive. By violent misuse, some signs of fading can be provoked, but even a hard driver will not normally experience any signs of this.

The car is well equipped, the instruments being of very high quality. The absence of any decoration is an important feature, for the man who buys a car of this quality would be sickened by juke-box styling. The heater is adequate for temperate climates, but an extra petrol-burning device may be fitted for cold countries. The forward-mounted fuel tank, which occupies much of the front luggage locker, has a reserve tap, but it is possible to forget that the reserve has been turned on, and a red light in addition would be appreciated.

On long runs, a speed as high as 100 m.p.h. may be held indefinitely. 110 m.p.h. may be exceeded under slightly favourable conditions and the engine remains smooth and quiet. The oil temperature gauge proves that the unit never gets hot and bothered, either on long, straight roads or when revving hard on the gears. The windows must not be opened too far or a most unpleasant throbbing effect attacks the ear drums—Porsches have always behaved in this manner.

Unlike most cars, the Porsche does not become thirsty at high speeds. Even the really hard driver will approach 30

SPECIFICATION AND PERFORMANCE DATA

Car Tested: Porsche Super 75 coupé, price £2,348 2*s.* 9*d.* including P.T.

Dimensions: Wheelbase 6 ft. 11¼ ins. Track (front) 4 ft. 4 ins., (rear) 4 ft. 2¾ ins. Overall length 13 ft. 1¾ ins. Width 5 ft. 5¼ ins. Turning circle 31 ft. Weight 17½ cwt.

Transmission: Single dry plate clutch. Four-speed all-synchromesh gearbox with central remote control, ratios 3.61, 5.01, 7.81, and 13.69 to 1. Spiral bevel final drive and swing axles.

Chassis: Combined steel body and punt-type chassis. Independent front suspension by trailing arms and laminated torsion bars, with anti-roll bar. ZF worm and peg steering box. Independent rear suspension by swing axles and torsion bars. Koni telescopic dampers all round. 11 ins. hydraulic drum-type brakes. Bolt-on disc wheels fitted 5.60 x 15 ins. tyres.

Engine: Four cylinders 82.5 mm. x 74 mm. (1,582 c.c.). Air-cooled, horizontally opposed with pushrod-operated overhead valves. Compression ratio 8.5 to 1. 75 b.h.p. at 5,000 r.p.m. Twin Zenith double-choke downdraught carburetters. Bosch coil and distributor.

Equipment: 6-volt lighting and starting. Speedometer. Rev. counter. Oil, temperature and fuel gauges. Electric clock. Cigar lighter. Heating and demisting. Variable speed windscreen wipers and washers. Flashing indicators. Reversing light.

Performance: Maximum speed 107.1 m.p.h. Speeds in gears: 3rd 82 m.p.h., 2nd 53 m.p.h., 1st 30 m.p.h. Standard quarter-mile 17.8 secs. Acceleration: 0-30 m.p.h. 3.2 secs., 0-50 m.p.h. 8.2 secs., 0-60 m.p.h. 11.9 secs., 0-80 m.p.h. 20 secs.

Fuel Consumption: 26 to 35 m.p.g.

Porsche Super 90 1,582 c.c.

SOME people judge the true worth of a car by its size and carrying capacity, by its refinement of running and riding comfort, by the soft luxury or otherwise of its interior. Others are not much bothered by such considerations, looking for mechanical and constructional attributes which cannot always be allied with them. At £2,876 the Porsche Super 90 cabriolet under review may seem a very costly way of providing all-weather motoring for two at speeds which are now within the abilities of quite a few family saloons. But the Porsche has special attractions of design and behaviour on the road which combine to make it unique.

There is a choice between three mechanical installations in the Porsche 1600 (1,582 c.c.) range; first the standard 1600 with a net output of 60 b.h.p.; then the 75 b.h.p. Super 75, and finally the Super 90, for which 90 b.h.p. is claimed. The super-fast Carrera, with twin-overhead-camshaft valve gear, is now enlarged to 2 litres and 130 net b.h.p., so that the Super 90 has really taken the latter's place among the 1600s.

Since the primary interest in the Super 90 for some readers will undoubtedly be in its performance, to see how it compares with the Super 75 we tested in April of 1960, this report must commence with a puzzling enigma. It is that there is remarkably little difference between their figures, and indeed many of those recorded with the 75 were superior. For instance, the 75 covered the standing-start quarter-mile 0·2sec quicker, its acceleration times from rest were better up to 70 m.p.h., and even beyond this point the Super 90's extra power at high revs allowed it to gain only 1·6sec from zero to 100 m.p.h.

It was to be expected that the 90 cabriolet would not reach the top speed of 115 m.p.h. claimed for the equivalent, more aerodynamically clean 90 coupé, yet its 111·3 m.p.h. mean maximum is only 2·5 m.p.h. faster than that of the earlier 75 coupé. Although the 90 just tested had not covered many miles since new and in due time would almost certainly perform more vigorously, our acceleration figures are still considerably better than those shown on a performance graph for this model published in current advertising literature from the Porsche factory. For instance, the

PRICES

Cabriolet		£2,091		
Purchase tax		£785	2s	9d
	Total (in G.B.)	£2,876	2s	9d

Extras

Chromium-plated wheels	£28 10s

Make · PORSCHE Type · Super 90 Cabriolet

Manufacturer: Dr.-Ing. h.c. F. Porsche K.-G., Stuttgart-Zuffenhausen, W. Germany.
U.K. Concessionaires: A.F.N. Ltd., Falcon Works, London Road, Isleworth, Middlesex

Test Conditions
Weather .... Dry, with 5–15 m.p.h. wind
Temperature .... 61 deg. F. (16 deg. C.)
Barometer .... 29·5 in. Hg.
Dry concrete and tarmacadam surfaces.

Weight
Kerb weight (with oil, water and half-full fuel tank) 17·3 cwt (1,939 lb–880 kg)
Front-rear distribution, per cent F. 43·0; R. 57·0
Laden as tested ... 20·3 cwt (2,275 lb—1,032 kg)

Turning Circles
Between kerbs ......L. 34ft 3in.; R. 33ft. 10in.
Between walls ... L. 35ft 11in.; R. 35ft 6in.
Turns of steering wheel lock to lock............2·3

Performance Data
Top gear m.p.h. per 1,000 r.p.m...............19·8
Mean piston speed at max. power......2,667 ft/min.
Engine revs. at mean max. speed......5,620 r.p.m.
B.h.p. per ton laden.................................88·7

MAXIMUM SPEEDS AND ACCELERATION (mean) TIMES

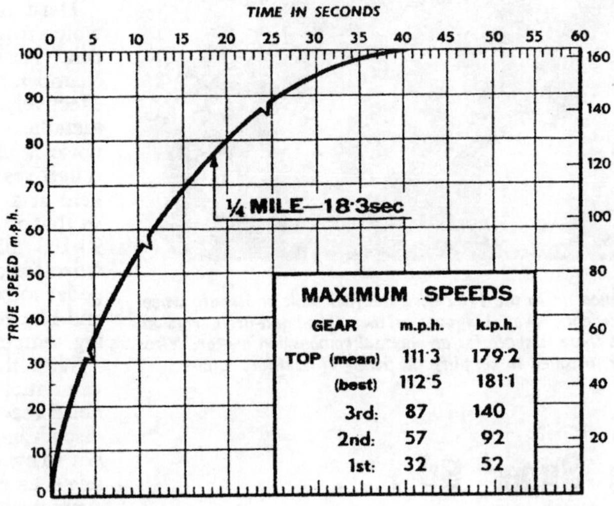

MAXIMUM SPEEDS

GEAR	m.p.h.	k.p.h.
TOP (mean)	111·3	179·2
(best)	112·5	181·1
3rd:	87	140
2nd:	57	92
1st:	32	52

TIME IN SECONDS		3·8	5·9	8·2	11·5	15·7	20·1	26·0	40·1	
TRUE SPEED m.p.h.	0	30	40	50	60	70	80	90	100	110
CAR SPEEDOMETER		30	39	49	59	69	79	89	100	110

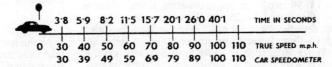

Speed time and range in seconds

m.p.h.	Top	Third	Second	First
10—30	—	—	5·3	3·1
20—40	—	8·0	4·9	—
30—50	11·2	8·0	4·9	—
40—60	12·0	7·7	—	—
50—70	13·4	8·4	—	—
60—80	14·5	9·5	—	—
70—90	16·4	—	—	—
80—100	23·0	—	—	—

FUEL AND OIL CONSUMPTION

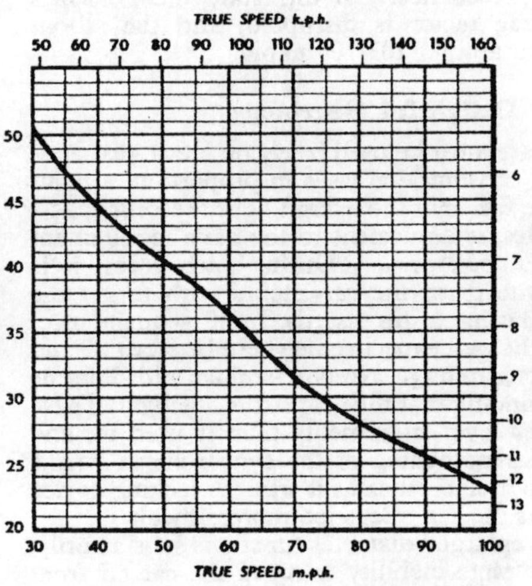

Fuel ....Super Premium Grade (101 octane RM)
Test Distance .... 921 miles
Overall Consumption .... 24·4 m.p.g. (11·6 litres/100 km.)
Normal Range...................22–30 m.p.g. (12·8–9·4 litres/100 km.)
OIL: HD S.A.E.20; Consumption: 2,500 m.p.g.

BRAKES (from 30 m.p.h. in neutral)	Pedal Load	Retardation	Equiv. distance
	25lb	0·15g	202ft
	50lb	0·78g	39ft
	60lb	0·92g	32·8ft
	Handbrake	0·40g	75ft

CLUTCH Pedal load and travel—35lb and 6·5in.

HILL CLIMBING AT STEADY SPEEDS

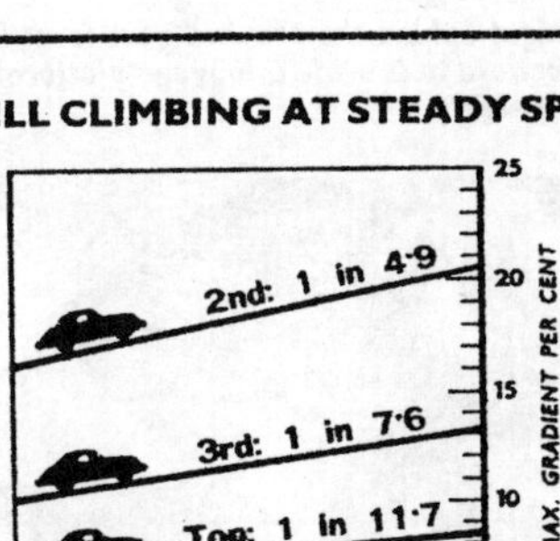

GEAR	Top	3rd	2nd
PULL (lb per ton)	190	290	450
Speed range (m.p.h.)	60–65	55–60	35–38

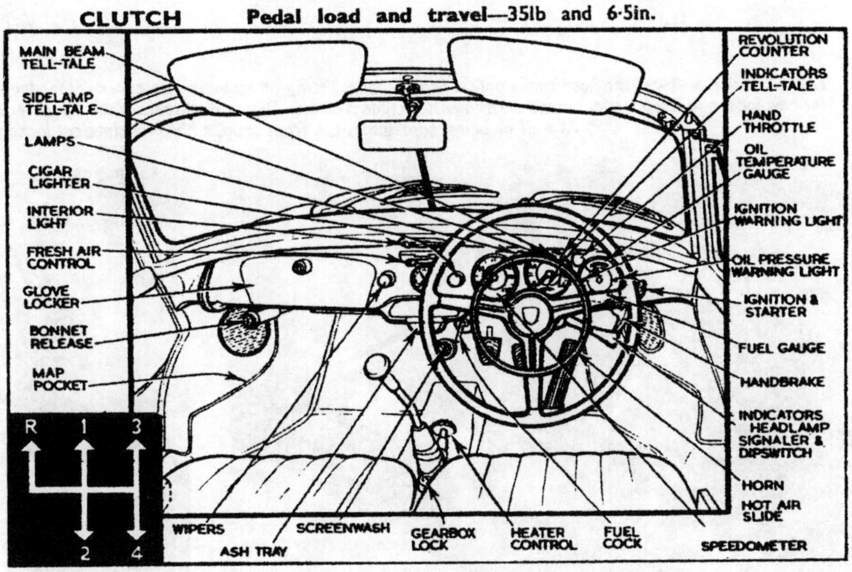

Under the widened lid in the 1962 nose the fuel tank and spare wheel still take precedence over luggage in the right-hand-drive version. Below the spare there is space for an optional combustion heater. Wires are ready installed to simplify the fitting of auxiliary lamps

Porsche Super 90 . . .

graph shows 0-90 m.p.h. in approximately 32sec, whereas we reached this speed in 26sec. From the foregoing it would seem that the 1960 Super 75 was particularly super.

Although its three lower ratios are common to the other 1600s, the Super 90 is slightly lower geared in top, since it develops maximum power at higher engine revolutions—5,500 r.p.m., as compared with the Super 75's peak at 5,000 r.p.m. One is advised not to exceed 5,800 r.p.m., and the top speeds quoted in the performance table for first, second and third gears (32, 57 and 87 m.p.h. respectively) correspond approximately to that engine speed. In fact one has to keep a close watch on the tachometer to avoid going above the limit, for it is not preceded by any sudden mechanical fuss or fall-off in power delivery. Incidentally, a speedometer that was accurate at some speeds and erred only on the pessimistic side was noteworthy.

While the air-cooled flat-four Porsche engine develops its maximum torque at 4,300 r.p.m., it is nonetheless a tractable unit which will pull smoothly, if not strongly, down to about 25 m.p.h. in top, and there are no sporting tantrums to be suffered. Yet it is a waste of such a car not to drive it hard, and the very nature of its design and handling qualities encourage this. It is wonderfully well suited to the varied road conditions in this country, particularly on tortuous and hilly country routes where its small overall dimensions, quick steering responses, leech-like adhesion and ready power render it almost unbeatable. On motorways and fast twin-track arteries it can be cruised with equanimity at any speed almost up to the limit, the all-important oil temperature gauge needle rarely creeping more than half-way along its dial (about 100 deg. C.) and never approaching the "red."

Hard driving is accompanied by noise inside the car, which troubles some people more than others during a long run. An air-cooled four, having no sound-absorbing water chambers cast around its cylinders, is difficult to silence effectively, and the noise it makes is rather harsh and metallic. One of the staff put it more colourfully: Porsche noise is untidy, like a badly trimmed paddle steamer in a rough sea. Most of this dies away when the car is being held at a semi-constant speed on a small throttle opening, so that it becomes quite restful and easy-going at a steady 90-100 m.p.h. Although no rich-mixture device is provided for cold-starting, a few jabs on the accelerator throttle pedal to squirt the accelerator pumps quickly get it going, and like all air-cooled engines it reaches a reasonable working temperature very quickly.

With the rear window unzipped and opened for added ventilation, while the folding hood remains closed, engine noise reaching the occupants becomes so oppressive as to discourage the practice. With the hood lowered one is not so aware of it because wind gusting and eddying around one's ears takes precedence. In this state the Porsche's customary low drag factor is disrupted, and the all-out maximum drops to around 103-104 m.p.h.

Delightful Gearbox

As the lower gears must be used freely on a fast give-and-take run, the fuel consumption rises in proportion, a point emphasized by the fact that the overall figure recorded, 24·4 m.p.g. for 921 miles, is equivalent to the car's requirement at a constant 95 m.p.h. or so. During such a test it is natural that all who drive the car should wish to get the most out of it during a necessarily brief acquaintance; actual owners might well expect somewhere between 25 and 30 m.p.g. over a long mileage. No one familiar with Porsche cars will need reminding that the gearbox is a delight. These days it has shorter lever movements than it used to, and following recent strengthening of the synchromesh baulks it is not quite so light and quick as it was. A locking device for the lever makes the car-thief's job more difficult.

A new clutch of enlarged diameter functions satisfactorily, apart from its complete inability to move the car off from rest on a 1-in-3 gradient; on 1-in-4 it was able to manage this. During standing-start acceleration tests it had to be fed in progressively to avoid bringing the engine revs too far down the power curve.

Wearing the remarkable SP tyres made by the Dunlop company's German factory, the Super 90 has extremely

Left: To raise or lower the hood takes only a few seconds, fitting or removing its cover rather longer. Out of sight behind the cranked gear lever is its new lock, and the practical round instruments include a clock. Right: Backrests of the token rear seats fold forward to provide a luggage platform. As well as being adjustable, the front squabs have mechanical locks for reasons of safety

Snugly fitting and padded to hold a smooth shape, the Porsche folding top is a minor masterpiece. Its back window is zipped for extra ventilation. The twin intake grilles above the engine incorporate threaded sockets for attaching a luggage rack

tenacious cornering powers which are affected much less than usual by a rainstorm. With all its wheels sprung independently and a single-leaf transverse compensating spring at the back to carry some of the cornering load back to the inner wheel, it holds its footing at each corner, even over bumpy surfaces. Porsche handling characteristics have changed progressively over the years, and this Super 90 has practically lost the oversteer, tricky in unfamiliar hands, of most of its predecessors. No special technique is now needed, although naturally it calls for an experienced and confident driver to make full use of its abilities. With the throttle kept open through a corner, the car's back end fairly "digs in," and when the tail does ultimately begin to slide, the action is progressively and easily controlled, generating no tingles of apprehension up and down the spine.

Very light and precise, the steering at first seems oversensitive to those accustomed to nose-heavy cars. Having a wheelbase of only 6ft 10·7in., the Porsche reacts very

Porsche engines and transmissions, when needing major attention, can be removed by experts within a few minutes. The installation is neat and keeps remarkably clean

quickly, darting about if the wheel is gripped too firmly and decisively. It answers best to a gentle touch, and calls for little physical effort except to hold it through a corner at high speed. In gusting cross-winds it is less affected than earlier types, although still requiring some concentration.

In one important respect Porsche have trailed behind most other European builders of fast touring or sports cars —brakes. Despite having elaborate drums encased in ribbed light alloy castings, they cannot match the overall efficiency and self-effacing smoothness of a first-class disc system. From low speeds they are particularly light to operate and provide powerful deceleration without wheel skidding up to a value around 0·92 g. From higher speeds they become cobbly and rough to such a degree that even the passenger is always aware of them. They can take a lot of punishment before fading seriously, and are only affected by water picked up in a deep ford, not by rainwater splashing up from a wet road. The handbrake, operated by a rather clumsy T-handle, can lock the rear wheels when the car is moving at 30 m.p.h., and it held securely on the 1-in-3 test hill.

While the suspension is necessarily fairly firm, as speed increases so does the ride comfort, but on the test car bumps were aggravated rather than damped by the seat springs. However, it is practically free from roll and, considering the brevity of the wheelbase, pitch is cleverly controlled. With the hood erect there are no creaks or rattles and very little wind roar, but with it lowered the doors can be felt moving slightly in their frames. Apart from this the body-chassis structure seems very much of-a-piece, as well as picking up extraordinarily little road noise.

Improved Outlook

It has been said already that this car's seats were bouncy; yet they were also rather hard and unyielding, as well as lacking the local support one has come to expect of Reutter seats. They might settle and improve with use. The angles through which the backrests can be adjusted are rather widely spaced, so that the alternative to a rather upright position may be to lean back more than one wishes. In this car one sat higher than is remembered of previous Porsches, and was less conscious of the height of the scuttle. Moreover, the screen is slightly deeper than it used to be; in wet weather it is very effectively cleared by wipers having three times their previous pressure and a motor whose rate is variable over a wide range.

The interior trim generally is rather Spartan, with numerous self-tapping screws to hold it in place. The rubber mats are admittedly practical, and the drab woven trim covering the rest of the floor area and scuttle sides is doubtless hard-wearing. But the folding hood deserves high praise for its neat internal trim concealing the frame, and for its fit and finish generally. It admits no rain or draughts when closed. The three over-centre catches securing it to the screen frame look aggressive in these days of acute safety consciousness. Its sides create rather large blind

Porsche Super 90 . . .

areas, but the rear window of flexible plastic is wide and deep.

Because of a long clutch pedal travel, a driver of average height may have to sit a little closer to the wheel than he would wish, but the Porsche does provide enough seat adjustment to put the tallest or shortest driver at ease. The pedals are nicely spaced, and deliberate simultaneous operation of the brake and accelerator by the right foot (the phrase heel-and-toe has become a misnomer these days) is easily managed. An outstanding hand control is the substantial lever behind the steering wheel which combines the functions of indicating turns, dipping and signal-flashing the headlamps. A practical feature is a three-way fuel tap under the facia—on, off and reserve. A positive reserve adds much to one's peace of mind during long night drives when open filling stations are none too frequent.

Bosch headlamps provide powerful lighting on full beam, with more concentration on range than spread, and very adequate asymmetrical dipped beams. Supplementing the familiar interior heating and demisting arrangements supplied from the engine cooling system, there is now a grille in front of the screen, through which fresh air enters via the luggage boot on its way to the passengers. The air does not pick up petrol fumes provided that the big tank is not filled to the brim, but the supply is not very plentiful at moderate speeds.

Having parked the Porsche and made use of all its thief-discouraging provisions, one can be reasonably sure that it will still be there when one returns. The door window vents have ingenious locks, there are separate keys for the ignition, doors, fuel filler cap and gear lever lock, and the nose lid release lever in the car also can be locked. Thoughtful Porsche features are the radio aerial mountings in the right-hand door hinges, built-in wiring for auxiliary lamps, a socket under the dash for a battery charging line or inspection lamp, a cavity beyond the passenger's toeboard for a non-transistor radio power pack, and a fuse box easily reached under the left of the facia including two spares for extra auxiliaries. Numerous listed options include a choice from 11 radio sets, fitted suitcases, a combustion heater, headrests and a variety of safety harnesses.

Porsche motoring is incomparable. No other car makes quite the same noise or has the same feel, very few are as well engineered and durable. The Super 90 can go like the wind on the straight, and hurry safely along minor roads where more clumsy cars have to take it easy. Apart from the very limited luggage space, it is a highly civilized conveyance for those who have to cover long journeys when time means money and prefer active to passive motoring.

Specification

ENGINE (rear-mounted)	
Cylinders ...	... 4, aluminium with sprayed molybdenum steel bores horizontally opposed, air-cooled
Bore ...	... 82·5mm (3·25in.)
Stroke ...	... 74mm (2·91in.)
Displacement	... 1,582 c.c. (96·5 cu. in.)
Valve gear	... Overhead, opposed valves, push-rods and rockers
Compression ratio	9 to 1
Carburettor	... Two Solex 40PJJ-4 twin-choke downdraught
Fuel pump	... Solex mechanical, diaphragm type
Oil filter ...	... Fram by-pass
Max. power	... 90 b.h.p. (net) at 5,500 r.p.m.
Max. torque	... 89 lb. ft. at 4,300 r.p.m.
TRANSMISSION	
Clutch ...	... Haussermann s.d.p., 8in. dia.
Gearbox ...	... Four-speed, all synchromesh
Overall ratios	... Top 3·78, 3rd 5·01, 2nd 7·82, 1st 13·69, reverse 15·77
Final drive	... Spiral bevel, 4·43 to 1
CHASSIS	
Construction	... Integral with steel body shell
SUSPENSION	
Front ...	... Parallel trailing arms with transverse laminated torsion bars, Koni telescopic dampers and anti-roll bar
Rear ...	... Independent swing axles located by single trailing torque arms, transverse round-section torsion bars, transverse leaf compensating spring, Koni telescopic dampers
Steering ...	... ZF worm-and-peg with hydraulic damper. Wheel dia 16·5in.
BRAKES	
Type ...	... Porsche drums, hydraulic operation
Dimensions	... F and R, 11in. dia., 1·58in. wide shoes
Total swept area...	218 sq. in. (215 sq. in. per ton laden)
WHEELS	
Type ...	... Slotted steel disc, 5 studs; 4·5in. wide rim
Tyres ...	... German Dunlop SP tubed, 5·90-15in. (165-15)
EQUIPMENT	
Battery ...	... 6-volt 84-amp. hr.
Headlamps	... Bosch, 45-40 watt
Reversing lamp	... One, standard
Electric fuses	... 12
Screen wipers	... Variable speed electric, self-parking
Screen washer	... Standard, foot plunger
Interior heater	... Standard. Hot air ducted from engine cooling system. Independent fresh air intakes
Safety belts	... Anchorages provided
Interior trim	... Leather seat trim standard
Floor covering	... Moulded rubber mats
Starting handle	... None
Jack ...	... Quick-lift cam-and-lever type
Jacking points	... One each side, under body sill
Other bodies	... Fixed-head coupé, detachable hardtop
MAINTENANCE	
Fuel tank	... 11·5 Imp. gallons (inc. 1 gal. reserve)
Engine sump	... 10 pints HD SAE30 (summer), SAE20 (winter). Change oil every 3,000 miles. Change filter element every 6,000 miles
Gearbox and final drive ...	... 6 pints SAE 90 hypoid. Change oil every 6,000 miles
Grease ...	... 4 points every 1,500 miles. 12 points every 3,000 miles
Tyre pressures	... F, 23; R, 26 p.s.i. (normal driving). F, 26; R, 28 p.s.i. (fast driving).

Scale: 0·3in. to 1ft.

Cushions uncompressed.

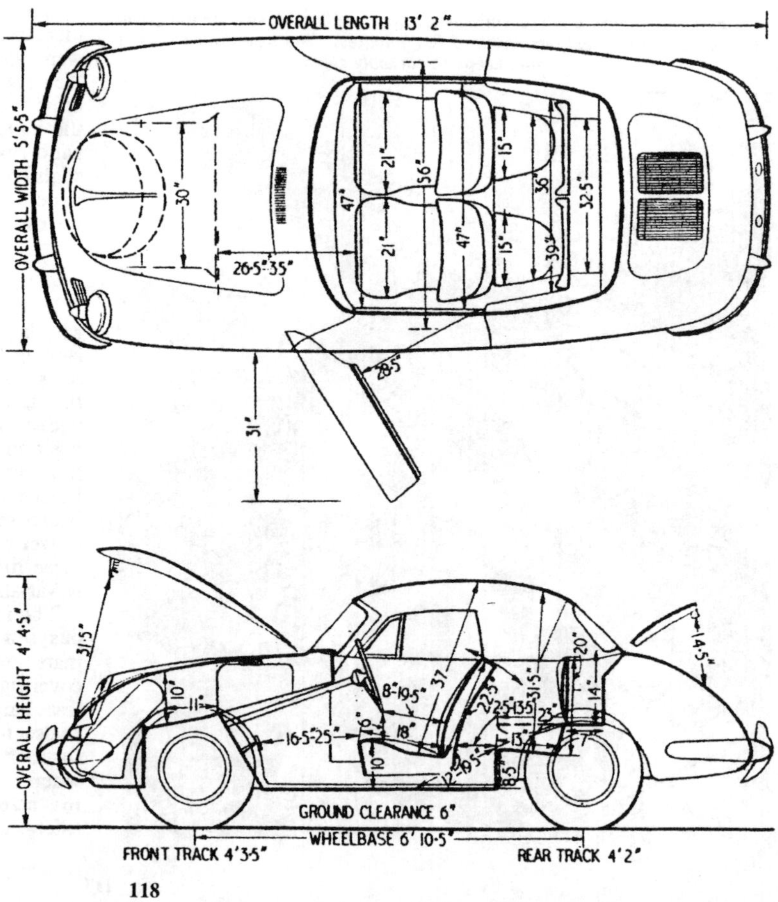

2 PORSCHE 1600 S

YOU DON'T HAVE TO BE IN THIS game long to realise that when it comes to Porsche's public image, Somebody Cares. The people over there in the press department at Stuttgart-Zuffenhausen have eyes like their own quality-control inspectors. Some well-meaning, God-fearing pressman on the Outer Woop-Woop Fortnightly Gazette has only to misquote the thread diameter of a Porsche rocker-box stud (help: it doesn't have one!) and along comes a letter in perfect Slav or Mongolian or whatever from Huschke von Hanstein pointing out in the politest possible way that such inaccuracy simply will not do. And if any of us regulars ever dares step out of line intentionally—wham-o! there's his name crossed off the Christmas-list for ever.

Now if Porsches were bad cars that Christmas list would long ago have shrunk to inconsiderable proportions (at least we hope it would) and there wouldn't be a single thing old Huschke could do about it. But the list is long Porsches are good, very good. Driving one you get the feeling that, just as somebody cares *chez-*Porsche about what we writers say, owners' complaints and constructive comments get equal attention.

This somebody-cares message hits you smack between the eyes as you contemplate a Porsche—and remember that in countries without Britain's scandalous import clip Stuttgart's products are selling around TR4 level. The fact that someone has actually stood over it and satisfied himself, as a thinking human being, that this particular

OVER ►

automobile is properly made shows up in six-foot neon letters when you get down to examining such things as detail finish, metal quality and the fit of panel on panel.

The car we chose was a cardinal-red 1600 S from Porsche's own test fleet, complete with left-hand steering and the extra front luggage space that goes with it. Other goodies included a Blaupunkt radio (which we rated distinctly more punk than its reputation suggests), a natty Golde sun-hatch with dashboard control, a pair of yellow-lens fog lamps (wired-out because they are illegal in Germany), a set of chrome-plated wheels with special crested hubcaps, a suit of German Dunlop SP high-speed tyres, a fire extinguisher and such miscellaneous odds and ends as fitted coconut floor mats and a chrome horn ring. Even the paint job was non-standard in the sense that it wouldn't have been on the car unless someone had asked for it, but then that's the way the Porsche system works. You order a basic automobile and then set about personalising it to taste from a 28-page illustrated equipment catalogue. The man who buys his Porsche unadorned is an odd fish indeed.

We drove our car about 2500 km in just six days, which is really driving. The session included two stints of more than 14 hours, with the same driver all the way and an alpine crossing or two thrown in. After that we felt we knew the Porsche S pretty well.

We know, for example, that anyone who complains about the coupe model's seats is talking through his soft-peak cap. Certainly they may feel a bit unyielding and rather too shallow around the thighs, but an aching human body certainly appreciates every hour of Stuttgart University's research as the daily mileage quota creeps up around the 500 mark. Actually our car had the cheapest seats of all, with corduroy instead of plastic or leather facings, and we found them the most comfortable Porsche seats yet.

Another thing we know is that the latest Porsche cockpit is one of the most livable in the business. Most of the vertical surfaces, including the carpet-covered ones beside the footwells, have really useful pockets built in. The optional armrests on our car made anarchisms of the map slots in the doors, but all the oddments we wanted for a week of Continental business fitted fine elsewhere.

Our experience also made nonsense of recent uppish claims that the Porsche's provision for heavy luggage is mean. In the left-drive test car anyway, we found we could get a small suitcase and a soft leather bag under the bonnet and two much bigger cases on the platform over the individual kid-seats in the back; a typewriter went in the space between one occasional perch and the underside of its folded backrest, two suits lay flat on top of the cases, a big basket and another soft bag filled in the gaps and still there was room for up to four bottles of wine and the odd personal what-not. As an extra the factory offers a baggage rack to go on the engine hatch at the back, which should keep any couple quiet.

An ideally positioned black-rim alloy wheel (almost vertical, slightly dished, with non-reflecting stippled spokes) helps to put a serious driver at his ease. So does a chunky central shift lever, although the ratchet-action handbrake handle under the dash takes putting-up with until you realise it works.

The pedals are offset far less than in many rear-engined cars, since the Porsche's occupants sit almost in the middle of the wheelbase. All are chunky and carefully sited, like most things on the car.

The same applies to the dashboard, which acts like a good valet and comes up unfailingly with the right button every time. Its nattier gadgets include a cigar lighter, an adjustable pull-out map light (neatest we've seen) and a godsend of a multi-speed wiper switch that will send the special high-pressure blades zipping across the screen so fast you can hardly see them. Instruments range from perfectly adequate speedometer and tachometer dials through an oil thermometer and a fuel gauge to a surprisingly accurate clock. All are well placed and well lit via a variable rheostat.

Willing is hardly the word for the 1600 S engine. It starts promptly with hardly any choke, and from there on the problem is to keep it out of the red on the tachometer dial—usable, according to the 100-page spiral-bound handbook, for brief periods only. The unit's outstanding characteristic is the evenness of its power and torque delivery all the way from minimum revs to the peak at 5500. Actually the high-

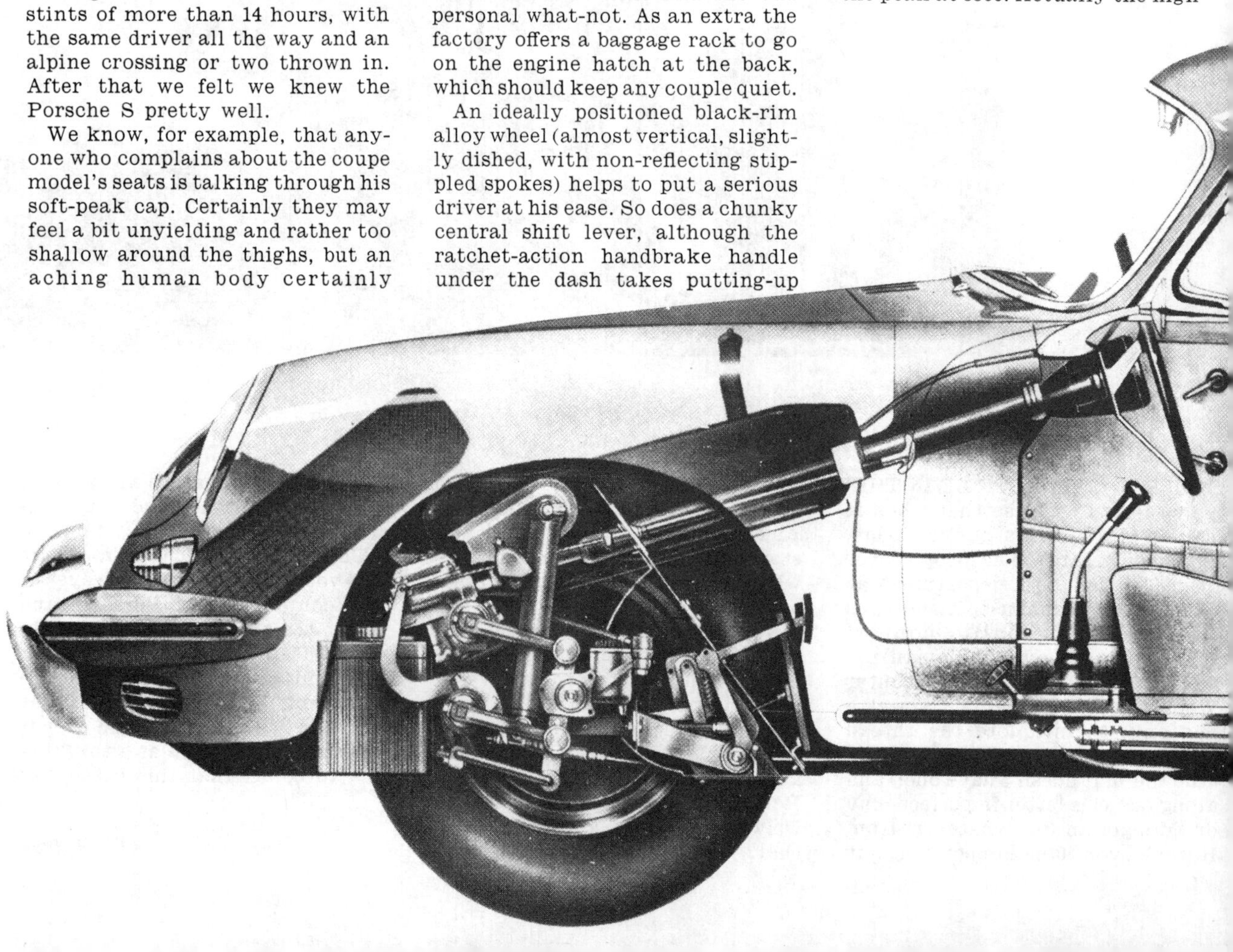

point in the torque curve is well up towards peak revs, and for that reason it's as well to keep the needle in the green-shaded operating zone (viz, above 3000).

One of the riders to this extreme engine smoothness is that you can't play a Porsche by ear. Another is that it seems natural always to drive the car as hard as it will go, making full use of every gear and giving the unit its head. The sound volume hardly swells from its normal muffled beat wherever the telltale may be.

Choosing gear ratios must be an even bigger responsibility than usual with a torque curve like this. Porsche engineers have done their best and compromised with peaking speeds of 30, 50, and 80 mph in the indirects; in most conditions full use of the incomparable all-synchromesh box produces smooth, undramatic, aircraft-style acceleration with only the slightest pause at every shifting point. A really competent driver setting out with the express aim of playing Beethoven on the box will find himself wishing for more revs on occasion, particularly in second gear. On some of the more entertaining alpine passes we found it possible to hold the needle almost permanently between 4500 and 5000 rpm while we put in some really vigorous accompaniment with right arm and right foot; then alone we had trouble keeping those rocketing revs in check on the lowest cogs.

You will have gathered that the gearshift itself is a delight. It is, it really is. First may be hard to get on occasion from rest, but make no mistake. That old magic has survived a recent strengthening of the synchro cones on top of 1960's cut-down on lever travel: all you have to do is remember to throw the clutch *right* to the floor and it's all wide open, boy.

Porsche steering is not quite up to the gearbox's standard, saying which is tantamount to calling it marvellous with no italics. We felt we could do with just a little less insulation, yet it certainly was relaxing to sense ourselves just one step removed from the more disagreeable sorts of road surface. Probably the neatest way out is to describe the mechanism as non-mechanical in the nicest possible way. Gearing, for the record, is just 2½ turns lock to 30-ft lock, yet because of the car's weight distribution the setup is far from heavy.

We don't feel justified, either, in spending our very best superlatives on the brakes. Certainly they stopped the car absolutely faultlessly in every aspect of normal daily use – but, and we draw breath

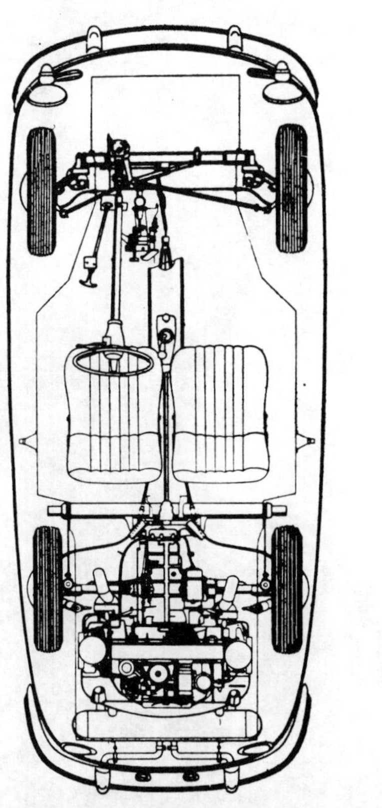

FACTS PORSCHE 1600 S

How much? £2348 (including tax)
How fast? 108 mph.
Acceleration: 0–30 4.2 sec, 0–40 6.5 sec, 0–50 8.9 sec, 0–60 13.2 sec, 0–70 18.3 sec, 0–80 22.8 sec, 0–90 32.6 sec, 0–100 49.0 sec
How thirsty? 28 miles per gallon (premium)
How big? 13 ft 1¾ in long, 5 ft 5¼ in wide, 4 ft 3½ in high
How heavy? 1965 lb
Mechanical details: Four-cyl horizontal opposed light alloy ohv air-cooled engine at rear, 1582 cc developing 88 bhp; drum brakes; all-independent suspension by transverse torsion bars and trailing arms
Greasing: 12 points every 1500
Oil change: Every 3000 miles
Body: Two-four seat two-door closed coupe; folding rear baggage platform; front boot

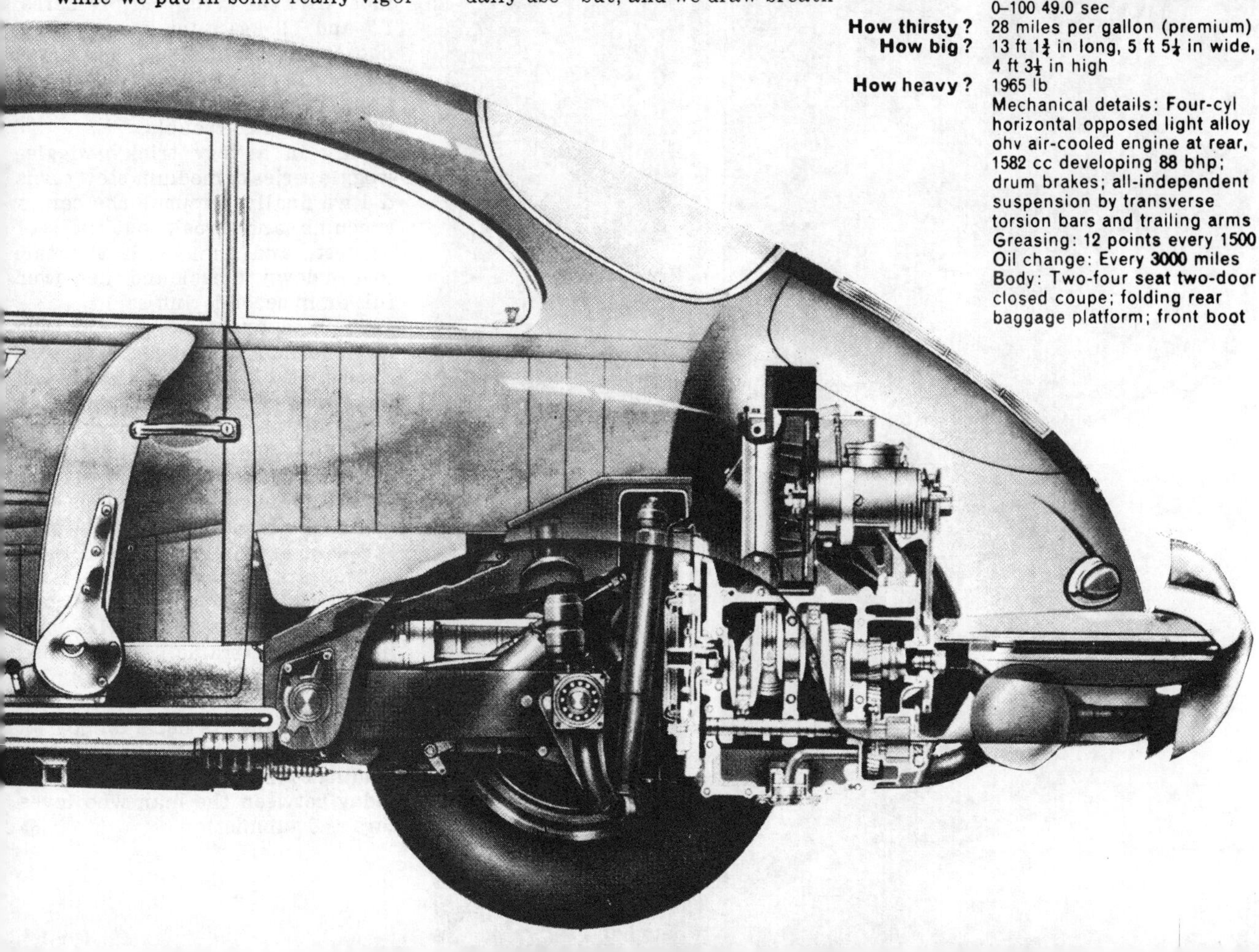

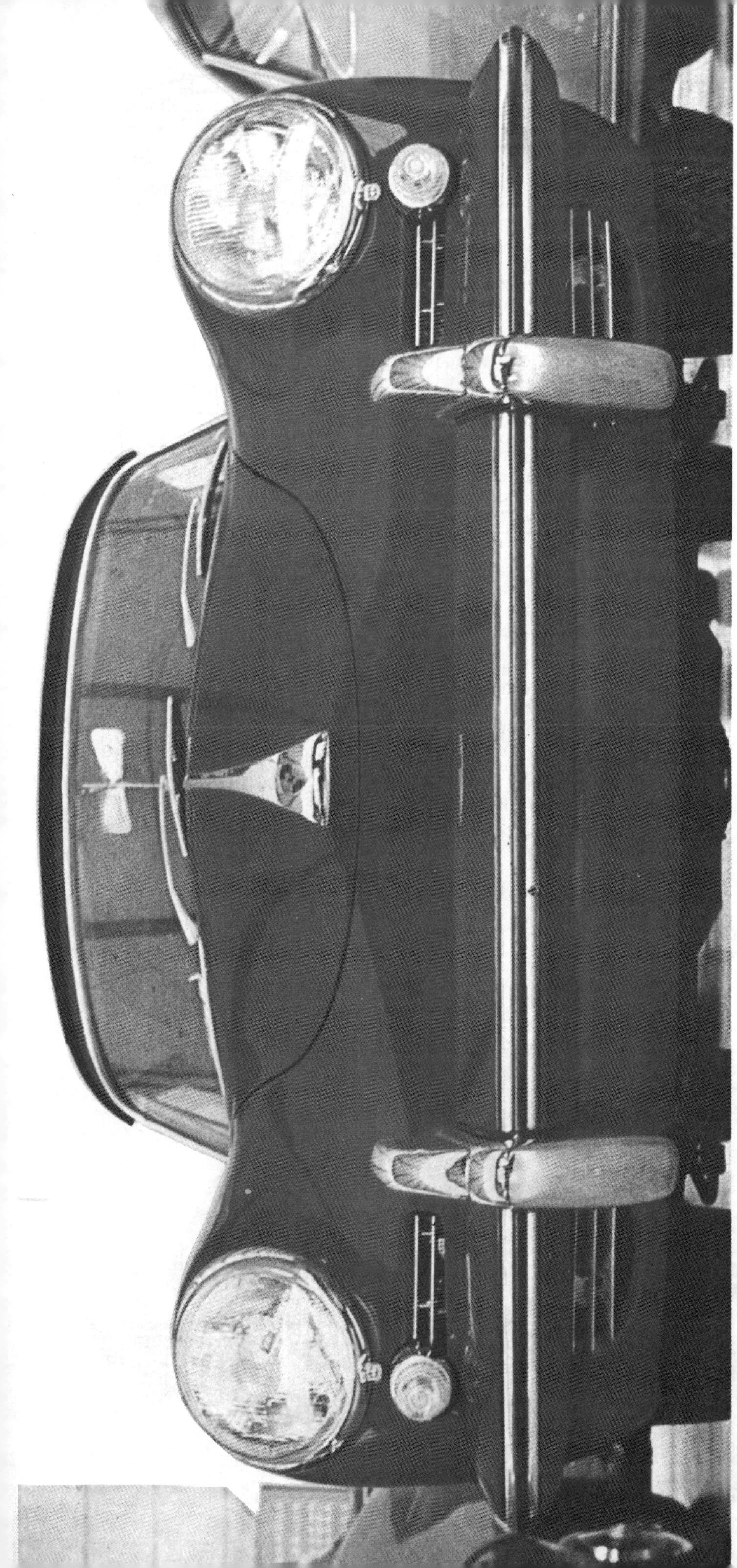

to say it, they did fade quite noticeably on two distinct mountain passes. Never once did we feel we weren't going to be able to stop, even when the cockpit was ripe with fried Ferodo (or its German equivalent); it was just the brakes weren't 100 per cent with us for quite 100 per cent of the time.

For that reason alone we recommend that Porsche gets a move-on with installing its rather complex but no doubt highly efficient disc brakes throughout the range (at present they're confined to the back wheels of the Carrera 2). Even if they do mean higher pedal pressures and less satisfactory low-speed stopping performance. . . .

Roadholding used to be a sore point with Porsche fans. Not any more. Today this is one of the best-handling of all medium-price sports cars, and certainly the most drivable rear-engined road car in the world. The predominant characteristic is still oversteer, but of such a refined kind that many an owner could live with it for years without knowing anything about it.

Body lean is negligible. There is no nose dive, no fore-and-aft pitch in even the harshest turns. The car's behaviour is dignified enough all the way for a driver to be able to sit back calmly at the wheel and think it out. For the most part the tyres (our pressures, 1.7 and 1.9 kg) cling fiercely to a chosen line right through; a fierce jab of throttle will send the tail away momentarily, but it is just playing and no trouble.

Only in a very tricky wiggle-woggle series of medium-slow turns did we finally persuade the car to succumb and break out in real earnest, and that with the tail loaded down to heck and the power full on in second. Nuff said.

Summed up as a road car, the Porsche has two distinct personalities. It can be very much the mannerly grand-tourer, floating along with barely a sound at near-maximum speed, converting bumps and corrugations into mere hints (that torsion bar suspension is still super, no matter what you may think of Issigonis) and generally setting its driver very much at peace with the world. Or it can curl back its lips and snarl, demolishing the traffic on crowded trunk routes, spitting contemptuously at brick-paved mountain bends, kicking its heels for joy on those winding, climbing, swooping, binding back-roads that stand alone today between the man who loves cars and submission. ●

Tired of this view of the Porsche?

Try this one.

Only from the driver's seat of a Porsche can you really understand why so many who are knowledgeable about cars believe that there is no more desirable automobile on the world market at any price.

Porsche was a great car in 1948 when Dr. Ferdinand Porsche created it with the wisdom gained in half a century of automobile designing. It is an even greater car today because of his refinements and those contributed by his son, Ferry Porsche, and the other gifted engineers to whom the Porsche legend has been entrusted. For fifteen years these talented men have been refining this one model!

The Porsche is virtually hand-built. That alone doesn't make it great. But performance does—and performance is a measure of how well a car does what a car is supposed to do.

We invite you to experience Porsche performance from the driver's seat. Discover a new kind of steering—sensitive, responsive, and easy. Shift gears and understand why this fast, smooth transmission is built under license from Porsche into racing cars many times the price of a Porsche.

Feel the smooth, certain stopping power of Porsche's race-tested disc brakes.

Try Porsche on a turn, and over a rough road. Try to remember another car that hangs on like that, no slide, no squeal, no sway. Test the acceleration of the hand-assembled aluminum-alloy engine tucked away in the rear.

For name of nearest Porsche dealer, write Porsche of America Corp., 107 Wren Ave., Teaneck, New Jersey.

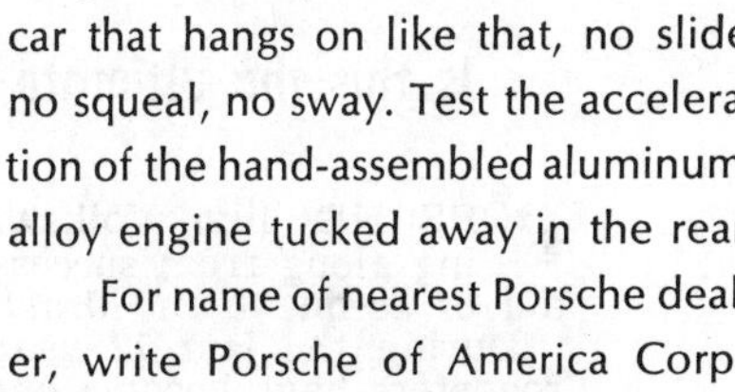

PORSCHE

New Porsches have larger rear window and two piece air vent on the engine compartment lid. There are other body improvements.

PORSCHE WITH BIG CAPACITY PUNCH

Is this the ultimate touring Porsche?

PORSCHE, like Volkswagen, just keeps rolling along from success to success without the aid of frequent and drastic model changes.

During the last 12 years, Porsche coupes and roadsters have become one of the most respected marques in both touring and competition.

Although the first Porsches used certain parts and features borrowed from Volkswagen (both were designed by the same man), there has never been anything humble about their conception. Nothing has been able to sway them from performance and quality.

The first Porsche car was built in 1949 and by the end of 1950, there were 298 Porsches on the road. In 10 years, the number of people working at the factory in Stuttgart had increased 10 times, to 1000 and the annual output of cars was 7700.

When Dr Ferdinand Porsche died in 1951, his son Ferry took over and continued to make both cars and the firm progress steadily and surely.

Today, Porsche employs 1250 men, but only about 350 of them are actually engaged in assembling the cars — and one out of every five is an inspector who makes sure that the quality for which these cars are renowned is maintained. Production is about 45 vehicles a day.

Every Porsche car made has followed a basic design concept. In every case the engine has been mounted in the rear and has been a flat four, air cooled. Cubic capacities have varied considerably — some have been only 1100 cc, others 1300 and so on, right up to the newest high speed touring car which is a full two-litres.

This car — the Carrera Two — incorporates everything that Ferry Porsche and his team of engineers consider best in design and refinement. For some years now the firm has endeavored to have at least one model that bridges the almost indefinable gap between pure touring and competition machines.

The first serious attempt to do this brought about the 1500 cc Carrera. This car was basically the Type 356A, the main difference being behind the rear axles. A de-tuned version of the renowned RS overhead cam sports/racing engine was fitted. The de Luxe model developed 100 bhp, while the Grand Tourismo was raised by 110 bhp.

This venture was not altogether successful and the 1600 cc Super 90 series was eventually introduced as a successor to the Carrera. The one and a half litre overhead camshaft engine remained optional on special order however, for enthusiasts intent on extremely rapid touring or competition. All Porsches have flat four engines, of course.

The Super 90's prime function was to give Carrera-like performance at considerably less cost. Another point in favor of the pushrod engine was that service was less of a problem than with the cammy motor. This was important, for about 68 percent of all Porsche production is exported.

There was a slight drop in performance, but this was not unexpected for the Super 90 engine developed about 15 bhp less than its more refined cousin, and the car to which it was fitted was heavier than the Carrera model. Even so, the 90 had a maximum speed of 115 mph and would go from 0 to 60 mph in 12 seconds and 0-100 mph in 36 seconds.

Externally there is little difference between 2-litre car and ones of other size. Streamlining is good.

In the latter part of 1961, however, Porsche pulled an unexpected rabbit from the hat — a two litre overhead camshaft engine with two dual-throat downdraft Solex carburettors and an output of 145 bhp.

When coupled with this engine the one ton (dry) coupe has a maximum speed of 125 mph. Surely the ultimate road Porsche.

The two litre engine has bigger bores than the 90, but both units have the same 74 mm stroke. This gives capacities of 1966 cc and 1582 cc. The most notable difference between the two motors (apart from size) lies in the method of valve actuation. Both the Carrera's cylinder heads have two overhead camshafts driven by bevel-geared shafts. The engine also features dry sump lubrication in place of the conventional oil system used on other production models.

Despite the fact that maximum power is obtained very high in the rev range (at 6200 rpm) the torque (119 ft/lb) is such that the car is entirely tractable in congested traffic. Porsche is most emphatic on this point, being justifiably proud of its ability to tame what is basically a racing thoroughbred. ●

Two-litre Carrera engine is development of the older 1.6-litre models and, of course, the highly successful racing models.

Make and model	Porsche Carrera Two
ENGINE:	
Cylinders	four, opposed
Cubic capacity	1966 cc
Valve arrangement	double overhead cams
Maximum power	145 bhp at 6200 rpm
GENERAL:	
Brake type	drum
Transmission type	four speed
Wheelbase	6 ft 10¾ in
Weight (approx.)	16¾ cwt
PERFORMANCE:	
Top speed	127 mph
Speeds in gears:	
I	42 mph
II	64 mph
III	104 mph
IV	127 mph
V	NA
Standing quarter mile	17.2 secs
0 to 30 mph	3.7 secs
0 to 50 mph	7.7 secs
0 to 70 mph	11.1 secs
0 to 100 mph	21 secs
0 to 120 mph	NA

JOY FOR TWO

12,000 miles in a Porsche Super 75

by

Ian Meiklejohn

HAVING launched the "Peoples' Car", Dr Ferdinand Porsche sought in vain for blessing to design a sporting version. This was not then approved and it was not until the Geneva Motor Salon of 1949 that the Porsche car made its appearance, developed under the impetus of his son, Ferry Porsche.

Since then the car has been progressively developed and improved, retaining the same basic design. Whilst engine output has more than doubled, the physical dimensions of the car have hardly changed. We are told that a larger multi-seat car as a mere means of transport could never come into being from the house of Porsche. From the original concept of a sporting version, the intention has been changed into that of providing "driving in its finest form". This is explained as providing performance in a cultured way—with comfort. And *I* would add "and with quality to the point of excellence".

Such a concept must be costly, so that the car will not be ordered without a close examination and a demonstration run. My impression from the outset was that the car required no salesman. The satisfying sound of the closing doors, the ease of entering, the comfort of the seats, with generous fore and aft and rake adjustments; the functional lay-out of the instruments and controls; lighting control without moving the hand from the wheel; control of instrument lighting level; two jet washers; foot-operated and variable speed windscreen wipers.

Depressing the throttle primes the carburettors for starting; the two-step starter switch engages the starter pinion and then applies current to the starter motor, to give an unfailing and crashless first time start followed by a tick-over at 600 rpm. Accepting the makers' performance figures—105 mph maximum speed and acceleration from 0-80 mph in 23 seconds, I was at this stage a buyer. My wife was impressed by the quality, comfort, ease of handling and beauty of line.

It is surprising the amount of space which is available for luggage, but you must accept that this is a car for two people. Pushed to the limit for space, we prefer to put the spare wheel on a small grid over the engine hatch, making room for an extra suitcase in the nose.

The makers say, in their house magazine, that the new-profile Dunlop SP tyres are unreservedly recommended for use under all conditions. Road holding in dry is very good; under bad conditions it is remarkable. In snow, the approach to our house is a severe test, with a sharp turn off a narrow road, across a cattle grid at the start of a one-in-seven gradient. The Porsche may require more weight added over the rear wheels but one is spared the cold and messy job of fitting chains.

Running-in proved to be a period which, as a mature motorist, I can only describe as one of absorbing motoring culture. With a prescribed maximum speed of 75 to 80 mph this is by no means dull. In fact, it was not until we had reached 5,000 miles that the transmission became as smooth as silk. Why bother about automatics?

Cat-like, the car keeps herself very clean; such dirt and traffic film as manages to stick to the dynamic shape is quickly removed without catching the hand on any protuberances. The absence of unnecessary chrome in no way detracts from the appearance of the car.

Any misgivings on the high initial cost are outweighed by the joy of driving a thoroughbred and the surprisingly low petrol consumption. A very careful check gives a figure of 33 mpg, some on motorway and on 'A' class roads and some on country roads on which one never gets out of third. This is because drag and rolling resistance have been reduced to a very low figure; lower than that of any other production car. Tyre wear is also very low.

The figures for cost of the first 12,000 miles were:—

Road tax	£15.0.0	
Insurance	£18.0.0	(50 per cent NCB)
Petrol, 362 gals	£90.0.0	
Oil, 12 pints	£ 1.4.0	
Service charges	£23.0.0	Includes changes of oil, 4 plugs, CB points
Tyres	£24.0.0	Estimated on probable replacement at 25,000 miles
	£171.4.0	

Living, as we do, well off the beaten track, I had some misgivings about servicing which have proved unfounded. Greasing is required every 1,500; it takes 10 minutes and is a good opportunity to have a good look underneath and to check brake hoses and mechanism. When the car is on the garage hoist, I have the transmission oil changed or checked; this has to be done from underneath. The car has had two routine inspections by appointed service stations, the rest of the servicing I now do myself.

Having neither pit nor hoist, I lift the car on the jack and put two wood blocks under the jacking points; it can then be rocked to give reasonable room to work under either front or rear end. Having seen the results of a jack folding when a man was working underneath, I obtained these blocks from a timber yard.

The Porsche is a rugged, reliable car. The only replacements have been a set of plugs and contact breaker points, required recently. It is the only post-war car, regardless of price, which I have not had to return to the dealer, very early in its life, to have some annoying fault rectified which was inexcusably overlooked by both the dealer and delivery driver.

Although in Britain the Porsche has no myth or legend, one is entitled to be severely critical of an expensive car. The handbrake is the most effective which I have met; but to release it fully is not simple. Control of the output from the heater is by turning a knob many times; a lever would be easier. (This is now fitted). Drum brakes are often criticised; but my only emergency stop was accomplished within a distance which appeared far too short. Without driving the car near to its limit, I find the rev counter coming close to the red at 5,000 rpm very often in second. Now that three-speed gear boxes are out, we will surely advance from four to five speed boxes. (This will be fitted to the Type 901). The knob under the scuttle which releases the catch of the front bonnet requires too much effort; compared to the rest of the car, this device is crude. The car is neither noisy nor silent; doubtless the air cooling is responsible for some of the engine noise escaping but this noise is all behind you. Gear noise is very low. The normal heating and ventilating system is completely satisfactory in the coldest weather experienced in this country. Because the car is air cooled, warm air is noticeable after only two miles' running from a cold start.

Because so many owners require a car which will carry four adults, the Porsche cannot be everybody's car. The yearly output of only 8,000 rigorously inspected cars from the factory, of which more than half are exported, is hallmarked with quality.

After running 12,000 miles, I find that the car is still a joy to drive under all conditions and I also find that ownership of a Porsche results in a permanent loss of interest in other motor cars.

Flat-four engine design makes possible a low and compact unit with ancillaries mounted in accessible places.
Below: the author with his car; the luggage carrier makes an excellent mounting for the spare wheel

Carrera Olé!

RETIRED COMPETITION PORSCHE GIVEN A LONG STRIDE

PERHAPS we ought to explain at the outset that this Porsche was offered to us for a Used Car Test; but those are strictly for cars "picked with a pin" from the smalls ads in the back of the journal. In other words, we ask for them rather than wait for them to be offered. Moreover, this particular Porsche, a 1600 Carrera, is one with something of a history, and it seemed to deserve a little different treatment.

There are few production cars that one can buy off the shelf, so to speak, and put straight on the race track, but the Carrera (named after the Carrera Panamericana road race in Mexico) is one of them. This particular example was bought by Dick Stoop in 1960, and raced pretty regularly, on the Continent as well as in this country, until he bought his 2-litre version to replace it in July, 1963; a Porsche addict, he now has a 904 GTS as well.

Although a Carrera looks identical to the standard Porsche, sharing the same steel body shell, its engine is fundamentally different in having twin overhead camshafts for each pair of cylinders, and dry sump lubrication. The latter enables a much larger quantity of oil to be kept in circulation as well as increasing ground clearance beneath the crankcase. Incidentally, the Carrera engine is behind the transmission, as in the standard car.

Changes in the body in this case include light alloy doors, with plastic windows, and rather spartan competition seats trimmed in sombre corduroy and leathercloth. For some reason Mr. Stoop had supplemented the normal rev. counter by fitting another one beneath it, both giving very similar readings. Perhaps he had had repeated trouble with the one provided, or for some reason doubted its accuracy.

As supplied from Stuttgart-Zuffenhausen, the 1600 Carrera engine developed 128 b.h.p. net at 6,700 r.p.m., and compared with the standard products it was geared down to enable it to attain its high peak revs in top gear; in other words about 125 m.p.h. at 7,000 r.p.m. Now this particular car has been fitted with the higher final drive giving 20

Corduroy and leather seats to Dickie Stoop's taste and fit and an extra rev. counter are the only modifications to the interior

Acceleration Times: *Speed range and time in seconds:*

m.p.h.	**Top**	**3rd**	**2nd**	**1st**
10–30	—	—	—	2·6
20–40	—	—	4·7	2·6
30–50	—	8·7	4·2	—
40–60	14·8	8·0	4·3	—
50–70	14·9	8·5	4·6	—
60–80	16·8	8·5	—	—
70–90	18·2	8·8	—	—
80–100	21·1	10·4	—	—
90–110	27·2	—	—	—

Standing quarter-mile: 16·2 sec.

Approximate overall fuel consumption: **19·0 m.p.g.**

Price: £2,000
Price new: £4,250

From rest through gears to:

30 m.p.h.	**3·0 sec.**
40 „	**4·4 „**
50 „	**6·7 „**
60 „	**9·0 „**
70 „	**11·6 „**
80 „	**16·2 „**
90 „	**20·5 „**
100 „	**26·6 „**

Maximum speeds in gears:

Top (mean)	**117·5**
(best)	**120·0**
3rd	**100**
2nd	**72**
1st	**43**

m.p.h. per 1,000 r.p.m. in top, the object being to cut down mechanical fuss and to give it effortless 100 m.p.h. cruising for motorways at only 5,000 r.p.m. This has killed top gear acceleration, of course, but the indirect gears have a considerably increased range to compensate for this. In third it can now reach 100 m.p.h. at 7,000 r.p.m. and over 40 and 70 in first and second respectively.

With a long run we just reached 120 m.p.h. on our electric speedometer in one direction, but only 115 in the other, engine revs at 120 being just 6,000. Despite the relatively high first gear, which made it tricky to get off the mark really smartly without abusing the clutch, the standing-start quarter-mile figure of 16·2sec is quite impressive. This and the other acceleration from rest figures could be bettered if one were to take liberties, but we preferred not to overstress a retired warrior, remembering that the next owner would not thank us for it. Even so, zero to 90 in 20·5sec is good going, and should see off the Super 90s.

Although the strongest bite takes hold at around 4,000 r.p.m., the Carrera's teeth are not exactly blunt below this, as witness the second gear figures over 20 m.p.h. ranges, of which the four quoted vary by no more than half a second.

For our testing the engine was fitted with fairly hard plugs which are inclined to soot up if one has a lot of 30 m.p.h. pottering in heavy week-end traffic to contend with. However, every time this happened they were cleaned quite quickly as soon as a stretch of clear road enabled one to put in a few bursts at high revs—a good thing, as it's apparently quite a labour to change them.

To increase the car's cornering power for racing, Stoop had its rear swing-axle suspension set down to give the wheels a very pronounced negative camber (that is, they lean inwards at the top), which may look a bit odd but certainly pays dividends. We never dared to try for the limit, and were content to discover that this lay rather beyond what one would hazard on a public road.

This almost phenomenal grip, to which the German Dunlop SP tyres contribute very considerably, combined with the car's light control and quick responses, makes it potentially very fast indeed on give-and-take roads as well as being tremendous fun. The only sacrifices, compared with a standard Porsche, are an excess of phons from engine and exhaust and rather stiff suspension damping combined with those form-fitting but unresilient seats. But it would be simple enough to convert back to production seating, to add some thick felt between cabin and engine and perhaps to improve on the exhaust silencing without losing too much power.

One characteristic phenomenon on Carreras of this era is some strange gurgling when the engine oil is cold, apparently a hydraulic resonance in the pipeline returning the lubricant from reservoir to engine. Presumably some cavitation is responsible. We were told we might detect another strange noise due to flutter of a thermo-valve in the line with the oil hot, but this one escaped us. It goes without saying for a Porsche that, although this car had travelled far and fast (the speedometer recorded just under 37,000 miles), there was not a creak, rattle or any sign of movement in the body structure.

Gentlemen, you are offered this very desirable two-seater sporting carriage, late property of famous racing motorist, for the sum of £2,000.

R.B.

THE PORSCHE AND ME

Henry Manney III tries Porche's latest getaway coupe

PORSCHES ARE A DIFFERENT breed of cat. There are others, like the VW, with roughly the same mechanical specification. There are others with rear engines. There are others with air cooling, even others with Porsche-type synchromesh. But none of 'em command exactly the blind and unquestioning loyalty found among Porsche owners. Why? As in all kinky addictions there are certain aspects of the car which are worn as an albatross around the neck. Examples should include the lack of occasional passenger space (seats are provided but not head- or leg-room for them), mechanical noise, lack of baggage area, rearward weight bias and a somewhat dated shape. In spite of all this it's comparatively rare for Porsche owners, faced with the problem of replacement, to settle for anything different. Let it be our purpose here to enquire the reason for their consistent lack of inclination to look elsewhere.

Do they miss the agonised flinch as wobbly moped approaches those bulging sides? Do they miss the exhilarating feeling of zooming backwards down the Hog's Back? Do they miss the cheerfully supplied crank, rods, pistons, and rings when all they wanted was new roller bearings? Do they miss the sudden-death quality of the tachometer's red line? Do they miss the glorious fresh breeze while the heater reluctantly warms up? Do they miss dislocating an elbow while they're changing plugs? Is all this a throwback, craftily calculated by our German cousins, to the happy days when high performance cars were a bit delicate and the manufacturers had you over a barrel? Are we becoming as masochistic as schoolboys? Is this another symptom of the rising wave of flagellation and . . .

We are getting off the subject. To go into a bit of history, the first Porsches were nothing but hot-rodded VWs—rather a comedown after the monstrous P-Wagens of Auto-Union, but after the war one had to take what was availalbe. As their performance at first was only minimally better than that of the parent vehicle (and that due to lower frontal area) Porsche encouraged its customers to race with the result that soon pushrod coupes and the famed 550 Spyder were cleaning up in that Italian province, the Mille Miglia. A car which won't finish the Mille Miglia is no perishing good. A car which will win its class *is* good.

As engine outputs rose with the aid of long-throw cranks, big barrels, twin-choke carbs and doppelknockers it became painfully apparent to Porsche that its trailing link front and swing axle rear suspension was not everyone's glass of Steinhager. People like the lamented Trips, Linge, Edy Barth and S Mooss learned to live with it

Porsche's new braking system uses Ate discs made under UK Dunlop license with special handbrake drums

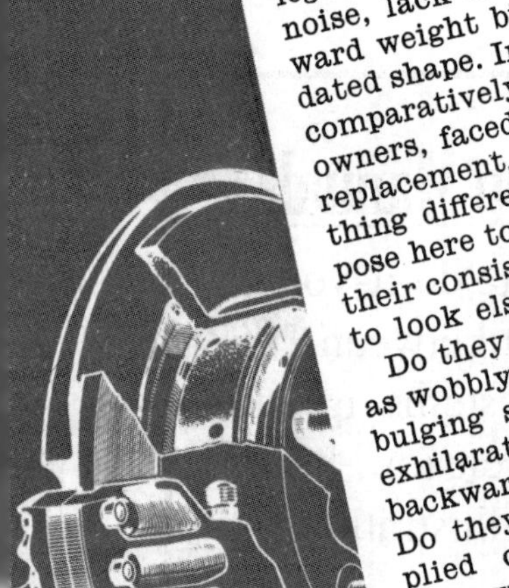

PORSC

SC engine is second-hottest in normal Porsche range, has twin dual-throat carburettors

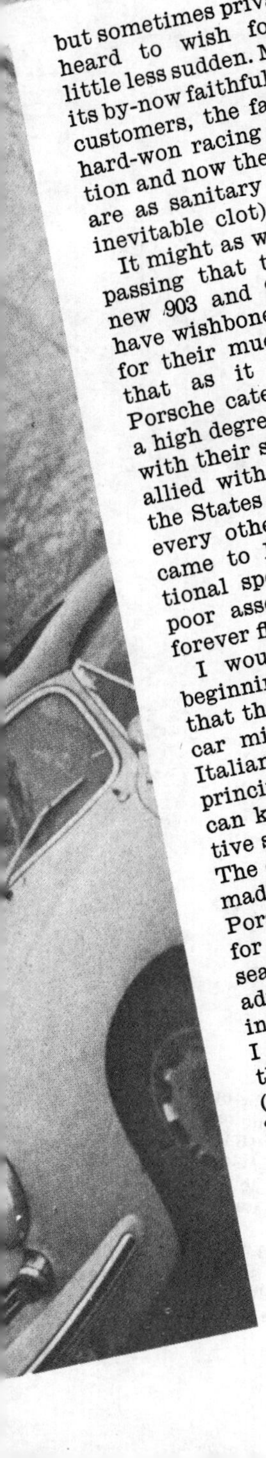

but sometimes private owners were heard to wish for something a little less sudden. Mostly to protect its by-now faithful stream of return customers, the factory applied its hard-won racing lore to the question and now the cooking Porsches are as sanitary (one excludes the inevitable clot) as can be.

It might as well be mentioned in passing that the F1 car and the new 903 and 904 GT racers both have wishbone suspension to cater for their much higher speeds. Be that as it may, the everyday Porsche caters for those who like a high degree of finish and comfort with their sports performance—all allied with sound engineering. In the States at any rate, practically every other doctor owns one and came to Porsche from a conventional sports car with hard ride, poor assembly and side curtains forever flapping.

I would like to state at the beginning (is this the beginning?) that the greater part of my sports car mileage has been covered in Italian cars, mostly Alfas, on the principle that any designer who can keep the Italians from collective suicide is good enough for me. The question of Porsche had never made much impression, since Porsches for me looked too small for self and family and besides even seasoned Porsche hands would admit that they needed watching in the wet. Watching is something I may not have time to do when the road is streaming with rain (pavé, of course), that inevitable 2 cv van lurches out across my bows and the gaggle of Dauphines coming the other way commence to get all sideways. Consequently it was with some trepidation that I picked up racing director Von Hanstein's personal hardtop (they all tell us that) from the Stuttgart works late the other evening. All the nig nogs going home were going home, the temperature was hovering around freezing, the road to chez Sloniger wound in Welsh rally-like country, and . . . well . . . you sort of hate to look an absolute clot phoning up 20 minutes afterward and squeaking 'Do you mind very much coming out here and getting me?'

Actually I shouldn't have worried. The Porsche is one of those cars that settles into familiarity right away. The well-known Reutter seats are both supporting and comfortable, controls demand arms only of normal length, steering is both accurate and precise, the SPs impart a feeling of reassurance and a veritable forest of little dials makes available such information as is required. There was some delay before I figured out the correct combination on the heater (now boasting a floor handle instead of that miserable wheel): cold air seemed to come out no matter what I did until eventually some spare BTUs became available in the back and measures had to be taken to turn it down. There was fitted, on this particular wagen, a super petrol heater activated by another control but I thought that I might as well see how the poor lived first.

Eventually there was more time to look about and wonder what a certain little red light was doing illuminated. Trying all the available switches resulted in a multitude of unforeseen effects—like the bonnet popping open, the petrol filler cover in the wing following suit, the roof suddenly yawning above me, wipers, squirts, and whirring noises. The parking brake turned out to have its own light, as do the headlamps. The oil pressure and temperature were both in

order, the fanbelt was in situ, and if the rods sounded as if they were coming out . . . well, all Porsches seem to sound like that. Eventually close inspection revealed that two little hands allied with the red light followed temperature-marked scales and that one said 0 deg C. Ha! Open windows caused the other to descend from 25 to 15 deg C and the penny dropped; an inside-outside thermometer and the light was simply an ice warning. Very practical. Must have one.

The next few days' drive encompassed a blast across to Paris via Nancy, German autobahn and heavy Paris traffic, then a run back to Stuttgart with melting verglas and slush the order of the day. Aside from the disconcerting discovery that wheelspin could be obtained with rather too much ease, the Porsche proved itself to be a magnificent road car. While I won't say that the bumpy French roads ironed themselves out to glasslike smoothness, equally one's stomach muscles didn't become sore from the car floating up and down. I personally prefer a somewhat firmer ride for this reason and was very pleased with the seats as well. They feel initially somewhat hard but, being closely damped, leave one free of stiffness or queasiness at the end of a long journey.

Much work has been done on the Ate disc brakes, which work as well as one could hope, and on the subsidiary transverse spring at the back which holds the dreaded side-slip in thrall. On tight uphill hair-pins, I found the back could be kicked out (giving rise to some rear-wheel hop) in enthusiastic Manney-was-appreciably-faster fashion but on the long sweepers or sharper curves the Porsche under-steered if anything. This effect was also a great help on long humpy straights or at 100 mph on the autobahn, where there was no need constantly to correct wandering . . . Swing Axle Walk seemed mostly to be absent and the driver could relax at his work.

As far as roadholding goes, there seemed to be no tendency to fly madly off and in fact during the passage of some extremely slippery bits we kept going without qualm (although at fairly reduced speed, naturally) while many around us were sliding quietly off into the ditch. As I am about the most cowardly driver that ever lived, this steadiness was entirely due to the Porsche.

In town the car proved itself to be equally at home. There was no sign of fluffiness or loading-up in the traffic blocks. When a hole presented itself the race-bred acceleration enabled one to make the best use of it, agility and short overall length being an appreciated corollary. The only criticism that might come to mind, besides the swelling unprotected sides, was that there was a definite flat spot down low where the engine would bog down. Of course one *is* expected always to be in the proper gear, but sometimes it can be tiresome to whine along in bottom when second or even third would be more relaxing. For one used to the Alfa and its multiples of rpm, the Porsche seemed rather short-geared and cammy.

The SC is, of course, the successor to the Super 90 and develops around 95 hp. To get this satisfactorily, Porsche has arranged the cams and induction tract to provide a fairly narrow power band compared with some other cars. Engineers with Tapley meters will undoubtedly shoot me down, but that's how it felt to me. The performance in general was certainly sparkling even if the engine wasn't terribly flexible. And it would be an ungrateful client who couldn't learn to adapt himself to such modest requirements.

Briefly, then, here's a first-class businessman's express with sporting overtones. It embodies the two qualities most needed on the road today—fierce acceleration and good brakes—plus an extra gift in th way of excellent behaviour. I addition, the Porsche owner ca find in his car that which seems be out of fashion these da quality finish and assembly. wonder the factory still has waiting list,

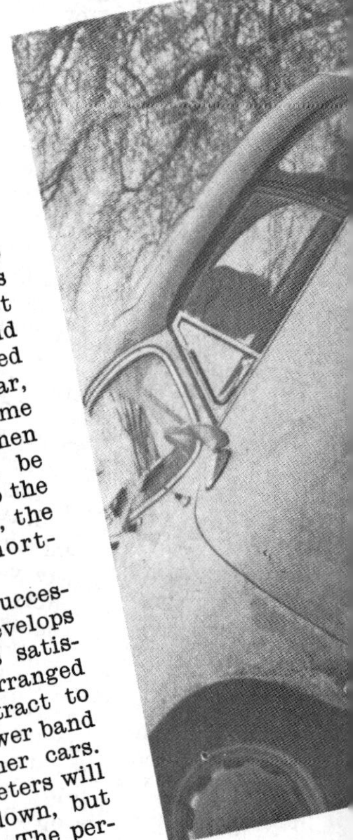

FACTS PORSCHE SC HARDTOP

How much?	£2277t
How fast?	115 mph Acceleration 0-30 3.5 sec, 0-40 5.2 sec, 0-50 7.7 sec, 0-60 10.6 sec, 0-70 14.8 sec, 0-80 19.1 sec
How thirsty?	23.7 mpg
How big?	158 in long, 65.5 in wide, 53 in high
How heavy?	1940 lb
How hairy?	Four-cylinder air-cooled horizontally-opposed cast alloy pushrod engine at rear driving rear wheels; 1582 cc developing 107 bhp SAE (95 DIN) at 5800 rpm; disc brakes on all wheels; suspension by transverse laminated torsion bars and double trailing arms (front) and transverse torsion bars, single compensating spring and swing axles
How often?	Greasing at 4 points every 1500 miles, oil change every 3000 miles
How roomy?	two/three-seat, two-door hardtop with optional cloth hood, front boot, rear parcels tray

SLONIGER REPORTS:

TO MONTE CARLO BY PORSCHE

Umpteen suitcases, a female companion, camera equipment and a one dog act all make for a crowded Monte Carlo tour

THEY have been building Porches now for a decade and a half, with so little relative change in appearance that most laymen still have difficulty telling the original 1100 coupe from the current 356C or SC. Yet the SC we tried for these lines has more than twice the power of the first Porsche and about as much in common with it as Cassius Clay has with my maternal grandmother.

That first Porsche introduced in Geneva in 1949 carried the family number of 356, the latest variations produced at the end of 1964 go under the names of 356C and SC. To sort them out — Porsche dropped the old 60 bhp normal when the C arrived and made the old 75 bhp Super the new plain C. The former Super 90 became the SC with a 5 bhp boost with an SAE rating 107. In other words, larger German sedans were beginning to pass Porsche normals on the autobahn and the embarrrassment was too great.

A natural corollary of this repeated Porsche habit (dropping the small and/or cheap member of the line) is that the cars become ever more expensive. It's personal opinion, granted, but I feel they have priced themselves right out of the GT market and into the starlet and noveau riche prestige category, where cars are purchased for their known price, not their road qualities.

In Porsche's case, this is a particular shame because the product continues to be a fine-handling automobile, of impeccable assembly and trim, with large built-in safety margins — (perhaps a good thing considering the types who buy them in Germany), and great touring appeal.

It was thoughts of super-safe motoring, inherent speed and driver comfort that prompted me to arrange for a 356 SC to cover the Monte Carlo Rally earlier this year. For the same reasons I asked for, and Porsche kindly supplied, tungsten-studded Dunlop belted SP tyres. They prevented top speed and acceleration runs, but doubtless saved our skin and the factory's sheet metal on more than one occasion when a dry but fog-bound midnight hairpin suddenly became full of glaring ice at speed. The drawbacks were a top limit of 85-90 mph on dry autobahns and a hula motion when the car was flung into bends. Both were gladly accepted for the safety margin.

These tyres naturally influence my reactions to the handling since you had to have ice or snow

Okay, so have you ever lived with a pooch for three days, and liked it. Lock him in the boot.

to play with the tail. For the SC line Porsche has softened the rear torsion bars, stiffened the front anti-roll bar, and discarded the camber compensator in the rear. All these changes doubtless make for a softer ride — though you aren't likely to notice it without a 356B to compare directly. The minimal difference in curve behavior is less than different tyres, or even different tyre pressures, would make. The tail does come around a touch more quickly, perhaps — but this may be my imagination, because I like the camber compensator or single-leaf transverse spring for any swing-axle car and was sad to see it go.

The other major change arriving with the new line was four-wheel disc brakes made by Ate, under Dunlop licence. Porsche drums were already outstanding. The new discs are merely a trifle more durable in the mountains. A Porsche design contribution was vestigial drums in the rear discs to house a two-shoe handbrake, thus eliminating a major woe with most disc setups. Always thinking, those Zuffenhausen elves.

Other changes in the SC included better-flowed cylinder heads, largely responsible for the extra five ponies in conjunction with the larger carburettors, and various interior changes. The already-excellent seats were even further fitted to the human anatomy, arm rests appeared for the doors, the various knobs were re-sited for easier action, and the car discarded that idiotic heater knob in favor of a lever much like the newer Volkswagen's.

Considering the new engine first, I couldn't help thinking of a Super 90 tested some time ago, which was particularly impressive for its elasticity and indifference to slow running, despite the relatively high state of tune for a pushrod 1600. The extra 5 hp seem to make considerable difference — allowing for the fact that one of each model doesn't make a production run.

The SC is simply not happy under 3000 rpm, and tends to get all choked up if you let it lug around town. It never lets you down, understand, but obviously isn't happy with its job, nor putting out much power. At the other end, Porsche is quite strict about staying under 6000 rpm, although you would have to go over that figure to post their rated top speed of 115 mph. Holding the red line is good for nearly 110, of course, and you don't get many chances to go faster than that anyway.

The point is, the SC engine is so beautifully put together it takes constant attention to stay under 6000 in the gears. The engine never complains, there is no danger of valve damage and it is still putting out power with the tach in the red.

They seem to be victims of their own precision assembly here. The penalty for exceeding 6000 — and I'd bet a Porsche every SC driver *will* sooner or later, both knowingly and unwittingly — is simply new bearings at 15 or 20 thousand miles. Under that mark you can run the SC like the 75C as far as repairs are concerned. Incidentally, almost every continental report of summer tests with a Porsche SC has returned better acceleration figures than the factory gives. Ours seemed peppier than old Porsches, too, so those five bhp are not an illusion.

Another area where the Porsche outdid its makers' claims was in oil consumption. Any highly tuned engine uses oil, and Porsche indicates more than the two quarts per 1000 miles. Also, if used gently, you will get away with far less. Taxi service around Monaco or a gentle run into the mountains with the electric sliding roof open to let the constant companion enjoy the view, used zero oil. The consumption only comes when you thrash along at 6000 rpm in II and III through the Maritime Alps, trying to catch a rally.

That same treatment naturally returned the worst mileage of the 2000 mile jaunt at 16.4 mpg. On the other hand the best figure was nine mpg over that and the average a very decent 21.4, using the car extremely hard. Remember, too, that studded tyres are good for 2-4 mpg on the bad side and the consumption is really something to boast of. An eleven gallon fuel tank was great comfort too, at three in the am, bashing through the uninhabited Alps.

The total test of 2000 miles doesn't really tell the story of living with a Porsche. About 1500 of those were shoved into two virtually non-stop stretches, and you certainly come to love or hate an automobile after 14 hours at the wheel with less than a quarter-hour outside, divided among three panic-speed fuel stops. Right off-hand I don't know another automobile which would have served as well on the comfort front.

First a qualification. The accumulation of spare cameras, typewriters, flash guns, portable film labs and (naturally) clothing two people need for climates varying from sea-bathing to deep snow fills considerable space. Throw in a 25 pound mutt poodle who somehow knows when the southland is mentioned and oozes into the car unbidden and a Porsche begins to get a little crowded.

We quickly discovered the reason for those motor-lid luggage racks fully 60 percent of the German Porsches carry. Ours didn't. Precisely one spare fuel can (unused), a bag of tyre chains, two pairs of winter boots, an overcoat and a

The redoubtable old flat four produces 107 bhp, but still looks like a twin carburettor VW.

small brief case filled the front boot until the lid was hard to close.

Nine further pieces — not counting self, constant companion and hound — had to get under the roof. The only way for two adults (by birth certificate, if not intelligence) and a dog to share the car with that much baggage is by pushing those wonderful seats right up until the steering wheel wore a groove in my navel. This is hardly ideal for long-distance driving, but at least possible.

The point is that we still arrived at various stops unkinked, if somewhat woeful. Other runs with the seats back proved how wonderful those reclining roosts can be, but they are more than adequate at their worst, and that's considerable solace. I wouldn't recommend those marginal rear seats for people, however, even around town.

On other fronts, Porsche has certainly made various improvements in the interior, though the general level of Porsche excellence tends to set one desiring the moon — in other words, I still have reservations.

The knobs are better placed now, but a few labels would help not only first-comers, but even forgetful owners who probably have another car (sedan) as well, if they aren't in the wealthy bachelor or rich man's darling class. Also, I continually barked my knuckles on the ash tray shifting into I or III in a hurry, proving that drivers shouldn't smoke. The handbrake may be a dream among disc-braked cars but the umbrella release is out of keeping. Also the horn ring blocks the tachometer. The heater lever is an improvement on the silly knob, but too far to reach — and you need many changes to suit engine revs.

It boils down to an obvious fact of life — cars like the Porsche SC are meant for precision drivers, yet more than reasonably forgiving of the most of us. On a give-and-take mountain road, for crossing Europe at speed with overwhelming safety, or simply to recall how much fun driving really is, the Porsche SC is hard to beat. This is the sort of automobile which develops your unprintable vocabulary when traffic thickens and turns drivers with a love of the open road into midnight-to-dawn travellers.

It's always hard to imagine a better Porsche but apparently the Zuffenhausen engineers can — and do. #

Facia alters little. Speedo often sees 115 mph and tacho ends at 6000, so does the engine.

"One of the most solid, one-piece cars ever made . . . for the connoisseur who pays and expects quite a lot."

Number 27
MOTOR
TESTED
1877 MILES

PRICE
£1,884 plus £393 1s. 3d.
equals £2,277 1s. 3d.

PORSCHE 1600 SC

How they run . . .

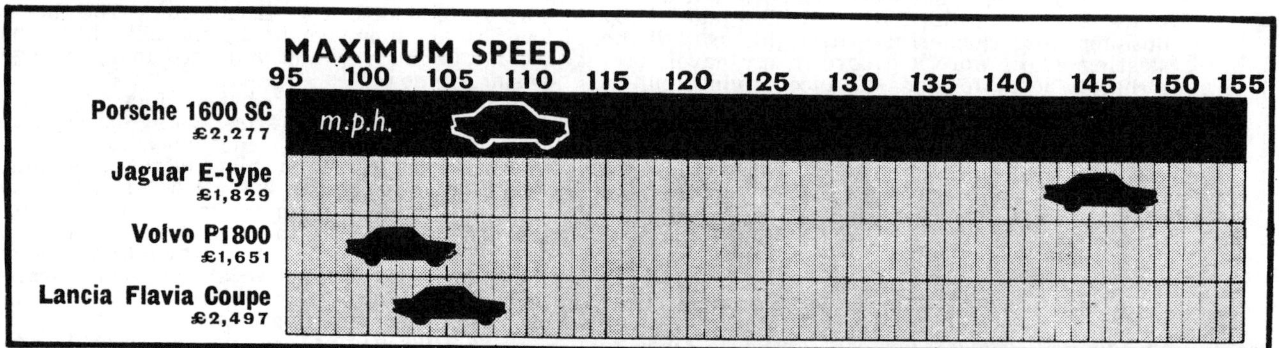

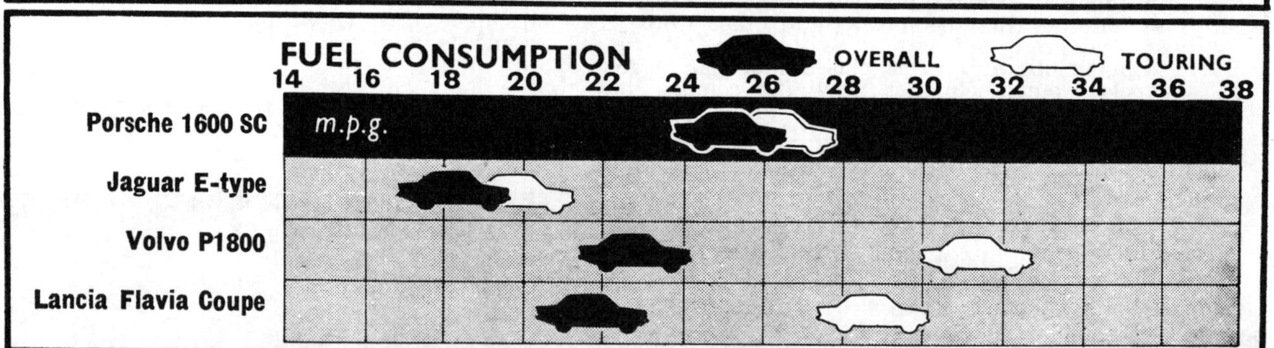

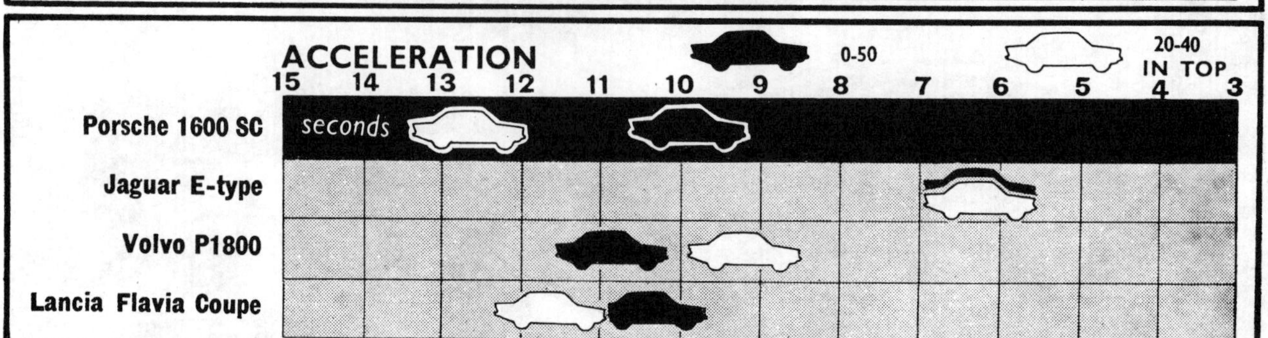

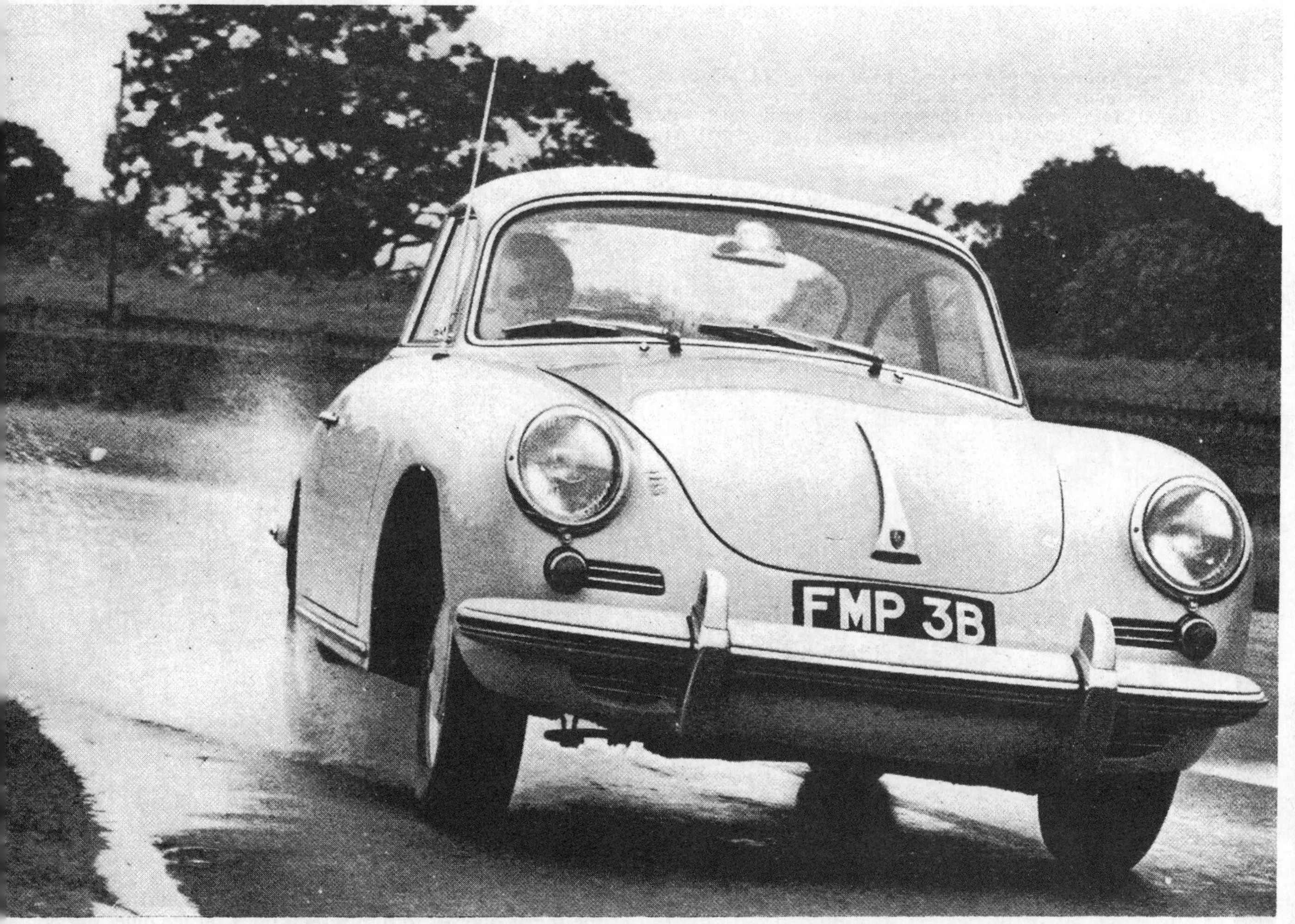

We tried it at Goodwood; "... the response to the steering is very quick; a slide can be corrected instantaneously."

THE Porsche is still a leader in its field and as a small, fast, long-distance tourer it has very few rivals. It can be driven really hard with a feeling of security and an absence of fatigue, even on very long journeys indeed, and yet it needs just that degree of skill to get the best out of it which the first-class driver finds rewarding. By repute it has a long life expectancy, a high resistance to wear and the sort of durability which comes from years of racing development.

As with most designs which remain basically unchanged for many years, progress has caught up with the Porsche in some ways. The highly tuned 95 b.h.p. engine is rather noisy under full throttle conditions and suspension which gives a firm comfortable ride on normal roads feels rather bouncy on bad surfaces. But it still feels one of the most solid, one-piece cars ever made and its reserves of structural stiffness are matched by an engine which seems just as unstrained and unruffled at the rev limit as it does at half the speed.

Produced just after the War along much the same lines as it follows today, the Porsche was the only production car ever to bear its famous designer's name. Its relationship to the Volkswagen in the late 'forties was obvious. An air-cooled, horizontally-opposed engine at the back; independent suspension to each wheel by trailing arms at the front and swing axles at the back; unit construction based on a stout, welded-up floor were all derived not just from the same author, but even the same factory. The main difference lay in the very low, ultra (for the time) stream-lined body and higher performance. It was, it is said, the car Dr. Porsche wanted to build—the Volkswagen was the one he was told to.

Now, the Volkswagen ancestry is, if not obscure, at least not so apparent. The layout is still the same, but development has refined it to a peak which has made it a car for the selective; for the connoisseur who pays and expects quite a lot. There are other cars at the same price, or cheaper, which are faster, quieter or have more luggage room but the Porsche has an all round balance of virtues which is most unusual.

Porsche drivers are carefully catered for. The driving position, the steering, gearbox and the instruments are all designed for the enthusiast. The car is made to be enjoyed by drivers; although passengers are comfortable and luggage is accommodated, they are of secondary importance. It is for long, fast touring, and if you want to take someone else and a few suitcases well and good; if you don't, you're not going to carry around a lot of unfilled air space.

The 1600 Porsche Type 356 comes in two versions, the C and the SC, and is offered with Coupe or Cabriolet bodywork The car we tested, the Coupe 1600 SC, has a 1,582 c.c. engine like the C, but produces 95 b.h.p. instead of 75. It has a 9 : 1 compression, light alloy instead of cast iron cylinders and the carburetters are Solex 40 PJJ-4 instead of Zenith 32 NDIX. The specification is otherwise substantially the same.

Performance

IF YOU think speed should be in proportion to cost, the Porsche is not a good buy: there are cars that cost less and go faster. Whether or not they would all go as fast for as far as the Porsche is outside the scope of this report, but our guess is that the Porsche would outlast a number of its quicker competitors.

The acceleration is not the sort that jerks your head back.

The very comfortable front seats have contoured squabs for lateral support and generous adjustment for reach and rake. They tip forward to reach the sparse rear seat which folds down to form an alternative luggage platform.

PORSCHE 1600 SC

It is more the progressive kind that goes on a long time very uniformly in every gear without the car feeling much faster or even getting much noisier. The engine idles with a little flutter from the back; when the throttle is opened there is an intake roar from the two downdraught twin-choke Solex carburetters (one per bank of cylinders) which does not increase much with speed. Fan whine does, however, and this is a car which one normally drives with the windows shut keeping out most of the noise.

Figures show the acceleration to be deceptively quick and the top speed of just over 112 m.p.h. is reached at 5,800 r.p.m. in the high top gear. No cold-starting device is fitted but this proved very easy in fairly mild weather provided the obligatory two dabs were taken at the accelerator to operate the pumps. Starting when warm was sometimes chancy unless the accelerator was held one-third open and the engine allowed to turn several times on the quiet starter before firing.

The low-drag body shape and high gearing of the Porsche result in a fuel consumption of over 26 m.p.g. when driven really hard. Owners who do not use the full potential on motorways will probably reach the touring figure of nearly 28 m.p.g. quite easily and many people will do better than this. A penalty of high gearing and poor low speed torque was an inability to restart on a 1 in 4 gradient. Fuel of 100 Octane was used throughout the test and there was no roughness or tendency to run-on. Under hard acceleration there is a certain throb, but most of this is noise, not vibration. Recommended tachometer readings are up to 5,500 r.p.m. for normal use, up to 5,800 r.p.m. (" dotted " red on the tachometer) occasionally, and above 5,800 r.p.m. (full red)

Performance

Conditions: Weather: Warm, dry, no wind. (Temperature 60°-75° F, Barometer 29·6 in. Hg.). Surface: Dry concrete and tarmacadam. Fuel: Super premium (101 octane).

ACCELERATION TIMES

0-30 m.p.h.	4·6 sec.	
0-40	6·7	
0-50	9·2	
0-60	13·2	
0-70	16·7	
0-80	21·2	
0-90	31·4	
0-100	43·2	
Standing quarter mile	18·7	
	Top sec.	3rd sec.
20-40 m.p.h.	11·9	7·6
30-50	11·1	7·4
40-60	11·7	7·5
50-70	12·4	7·8
60-80	13·2	8·9
70-90	14·7	—
80-100	19·6	—

MAXIMUM SPEEDS

Mean maximum speed	112·5 m.p.h.
Best one way ¼-mile	113·1
3rd gear at 5,800 r.p.m.	85
2nd gear at 5,800 r.p.m.	54
1st gear at 5,800 r.p.m.	31

" Maximile " Speed: (Timed quarter mile after 1 mile accelerating from rest)

Mean	107·1
Best	108·5

HILL CLIMBING

At steady speed		lb./ton
Top	1 in 10·9	(Tapley 205)
3rd	1 in 7·1	(Tapley 310)
2nd	1 in 4·2	(Tapley 520)

FUEL CONSUMPTION

Touring (consumption mid-way between 30 m.p.h. and maximum less 5% allowance for acceleration) .. 27·9 m.p.g.
Overall .. 26·6
Total test distance .. 1,877 miles
26·6 m.p.g.=10·7 litres/100 km.
Fuel tank capacity (maker's figure) 11 galls.

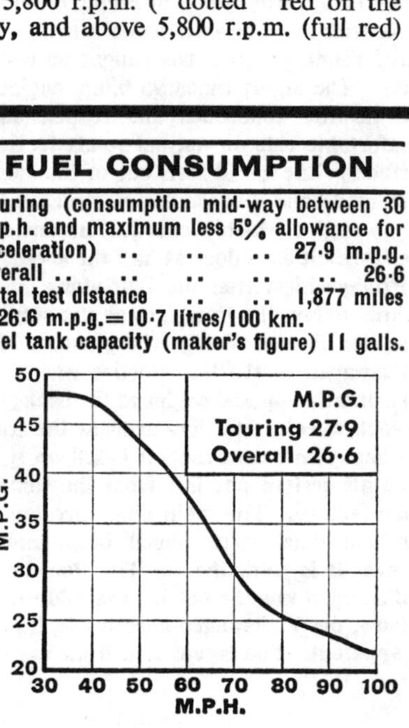

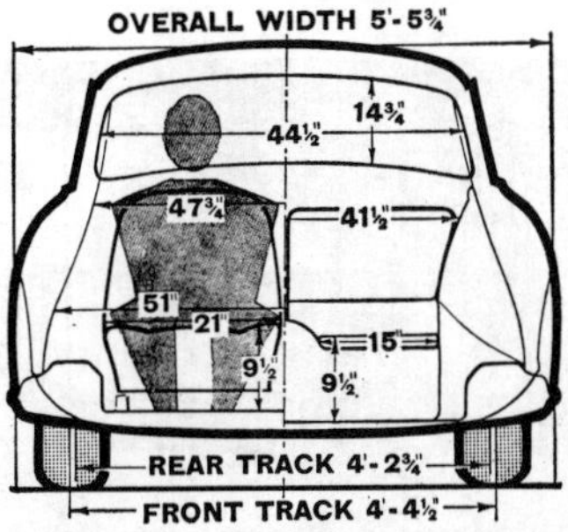

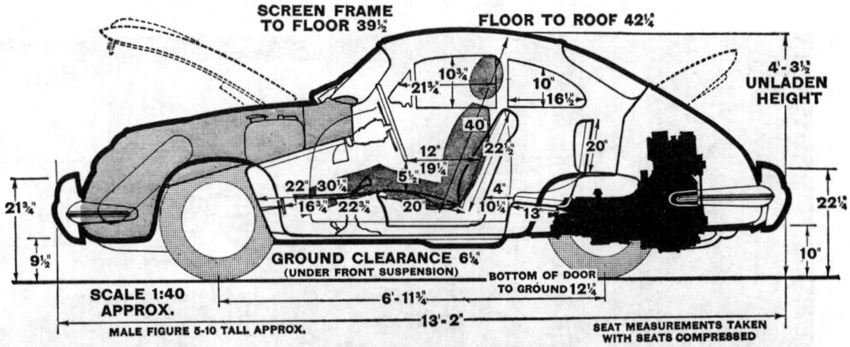

never. There is no audible limit and no sense of increasing strain at high r.p.m., so close attention should be paid to the tachometer.

Transmission

THE NAME Porsche is famous for baulk-ring synchromesh, so it is entirely appropriate that a car bearing the famous label should have an outstanding gearbox. The change is by a short lever on the small central tunnel between the seats. Lever travel is quite long and the linkage has some free play but the movement is very smooth, and engagement quick, quiet, and positive. Clutch travel is also rather longer than average, but the drive is taken up firmly and pedal pressure (there is a diaphragm spring) is moderately light.

All the four gears are indirect, and all are provided with synchromesh. The gear ratios are well chosen apart from rather a wide gap between second and third, so that the engine goes briskly into the " dotted " red in first and second then has to struggle momentarily in third to reach the higher revs where it gives its best. Third and top are close, a useful feature when third is used so much; all the gears are very quiet indeed.

Handling

THERE WAS once a bogy about Porsches. Early examples had massive oversteer, making the tail treacherous in the wet and skittish in the dry. It was a highly skilled job driving them fast on twisty roads, but now the ghost has finally been

Paddock Porsche—natural habitat for a car that is equally at home on road or track.

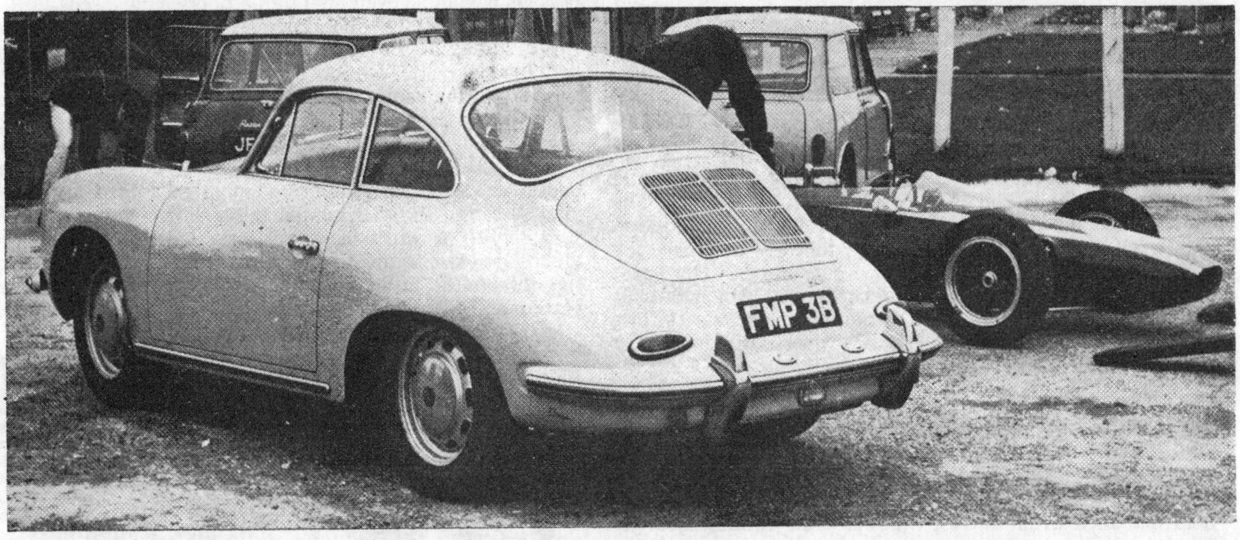

BRAKES

Pedal pressure, deceleration and equivalent stopping distance from 30 m.p.h.

lb.	g	ft.
25	0·20	150
50	0·48	62½
75	0·74	40½
100	0·92	32½
120	0·96	31¼
Handbrake	0·38	79

FADE

TEST 1. 20 stops at ½g deceleration at 1 min. intervals from a speed midway between 30 m.p.h. and max. speed (=71 m.p.h.)

	lb.
Pedal force at beginning	65
Pedal force at 10th stop	80
Pedal force at 20th	80

WATERPROOFING

Increase in brake pedal force for ½g stop from 30 m.p.h. after two runs through shallow watersplash at 30 m.p.h.=5 lb.

OVERTAKING

Starting at 40 m.p.h. in direct top gear, distance required to gain 100 ft. on another car travelling at a steady 40 m.p.h. =570 ft.

STEERING

	ft.
Turning circle between kerbs:	
Left	33
Right	31
Turns of steering wheel from lock to lock	2½
Steering wheel deflection for 50 ft. diameter circle	²/₃ turn
Steering force (at rim of wheel) to move front wheels at rest	22 lb.
Steering force to hold car on 100 ft. diameter circle at 15 m.p.h. (=0·3g approx.)	12 lb.

CLUTCH

Free pedal movement	⅞ in.
Additional movement to disengage clutch completely	5 in.
Maximum pedal load	35 lb.

WEIGHT

	cwt.
Kerb weight (unladen with fuel for approximately 50 miles)	17¾
Front/rear distribution	42/58
Weight laden as tested	21½

SPEEDOMETER

30 m.p.h.	3% slow
60	3% fast
90	7% fast
Distance recorder	2% fast

PORSCHE 1600 SC

Visibility: 180° from the driving seat. Shaded areas show one-eye visibility.

laid. Porsche tackled it in several ways and in the latest models they offer a transverse compensating rear spring to help keep the back in place on corners by reducing weight transfer at the rear. Skill is still needed, but the behaviour is now predictable.

Slow corners produce some understeer. As the speed is built up this alters gradually and progressively to a neutral condition, then oversteer, culminating in the back gently breaking away. Few people will drive fast enough on the road to reach this condition. The response to the steering is very quick; a slide can be corrected instantaneously. One learns to feel the changes in attitude due to the camber angles of the back wheels altering and the understeer/oversteer transition is gradual and undramatic. To cope with the change when travelling fast, however, takes some skill on the part of the driver.

The handling inspires confidence with familiarity—at first one finds a tendency to take a rather irregular line round corners—and body roll is almost completely absent. The car stays flat and even in the wet approaching loss of adhesion can be felt in time for something to be done about it. Steering is high-geared and fairly light at moderate speeds. The worm and peg mechanism has a hydraulic damper which fails to eliminate completely kick-back on bumpy roads. Very strong castor action makes it rather heavy when cornering really hard on sharp bends.

Brakes

A MAJOR innovation on Porsches of the last few years has been the adoption of disc brakes. Until recently, the firm held that their drum brakes, with elaborate cooling arrangements, were as good as any disc. Now they have adopted discs for all four wheels, the rear discs incorporating small diameter drums for the handbrake. For high-speed stopping, the discs are a success. Pedal forces are rather heavy but, as our prolonged twenty-minute test shows, even the hardest use failed to raise them by more than a few pounds and recovery was quick. There was never any deviation from a straight line and the brakes remained quiet throughout.

Some early all-disc systems had notoriously weak handbrakes. Most manufacturers have now overcome the problem, but Porsche, with typical thoroughness, took no chances and attached special auxiliary drums to the rear discs. Worked through a mechanical linkage from the twist-and-pull handbrake beneath the facia, these small drums are surprisingly powerful and will easily lock the rear wheels or hold the car on a 1 in 3 slope.

Comfort and Control

CONSISTENT with the motorway character of the car the springing is firm, giving a level ride on smooth roads, but pitching on rough ones. Uneven surfaces produce quick, vertical movements although the smoother sorts of pavé can be taken at speed with less discomfort. There is no body drumming, very little road or suspension noise and wind-noise is negligible even at 100 m.p.h. cruising speeds.

The seats are well-shaped and the driving position good. Big cushions do not give much lateral support on corners but this is made up for by curved backrests which give support all the way up to the shoulders of drivers of average height. One sits very low, with lots of headroom in the high-waisted body and with the unfashionably large steering wheel a little close. Seat adjustment is generous and the rake of the backrests can be altered or they can be folded forward to give access to the rear compartment. The pedals are offset very slightly towards the centre of the car (the front wheel arches are close to the driver's feet, but make little inroad into the toe-board) and the brake and accelerator are ideally placed for heel-and-toe gearchanges. The handbrake is a

Although the flat-four engine is practically shrouded by cooling ducts, most of the ancillaries are easy to reach. 1. carburetter 2. coil 3. petrol pump 4. distributor 5. oil filter 6. dip stick 7. oil filler 8. carburetter air cleaner. The sparking plugs look inaccessible, but are not as difficult to remove as it might appear from the picture.

long reach twist-and-pull handle under the facia. For drivers who sit well back the gear lever demands a long arm in the first and third positions.

With air cooling, the obvious way to run the interior heating system is to bring the engine cooling fan and air into play. This has certain advantages but also the serious shortcoming that it is dependent on engine speed. To ensure warmth constant adjustment of the controls is necessary to meet the changing conditions of fast cruising and town speeds. Certainly when the engine is turning quickly the installation is very effective indeed, but even in cool spring weather there were times in traffic when the occupants felt the need for a more consistent supply. Adjustment of the quantity of heat is by a lever just ahead of the gear lever, and direction of the warm air stream to windscreen or interior is by means of a facia switch and shutters just below the leading edge of the doors.

Forward visibility is good for drivers of above average height, but the facia is rather high for short people on account of the low driving position. The view aft is not very good because of the high window demanded by the tall engine cooling fan, but the rear-view mirror takes full advantage of what space there is. The lights give a good wide beam for night driving with a sharp cut-off when dipped.

Fittings and Furniture

THE INSIDE of the Porsche looks rather barely furnished for a £2,277 car. The facia is painted metal and the floor rubber covered, but all the fittings are well made and look durable. Quarter-light catches for example have a precise action to hold them in place. The effect is one of practicality rather than ornament. The instruments are comprehensive, but obscured by the steering wheel and have rather small lettering. Switchgear is an unlabelled, irreducible minimum, convenient and uncomplicated with useful features like a headlamp flasher/dipswitch/direction indicator all incorporated in one stalk on the steering column. There is a splendid, foot-operated screen washer, and a reserve petrol tap under the facia.

The rear compartment is really a luggage space (the petrol tank takes up most of the space under the bonnet not occupied by the spare wheel) but the carpeted floor conceals two seats suitable for children. There is a lockable compartment in the facia, but the front is not well provided with space for small objects, or parcels. The screen wipers have a variable speed adjustment and except when operating at their maximum speed they remain quiet.

Boot without boxes. All 6·2 cu. ft. of our test luggage went inside behind the seats. Not even the smallest box would fit the boot which is strictly for compact, flexible bags. The lid must be opened to refuel the large tank which shares most of the front with the spare wheel.

The facia layout is clean and simple. 1. clock 2. heater 3. lights 4. speedometer 5. mileage recorder 6. rev counter 7. parking light tell-tale 8. main beam warning light 9. oil pressure warning light 10. oil thermometer 11. spare warning light 12. and 14. radio controls 13. cigar lighter 15. wipers 16. fuel filter with main and reserve tap 17. horn ring 18. ignition warning light 19. flasher, dip and indicator stalk 20. fuel gauge 21. handbrake 22. handbrake on (and low fluid) warning light.

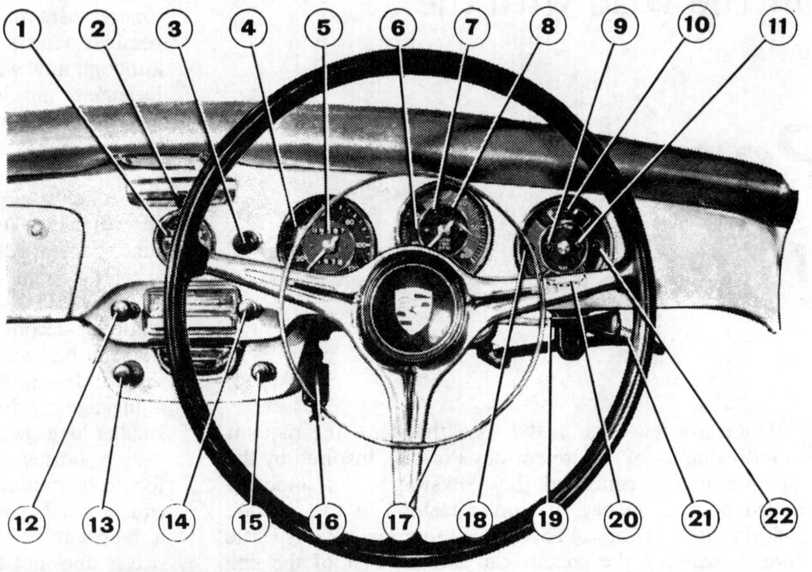

MAKE Porsche • MODEL 1600SC • CONCESSIONAIRES A.F.N. Ltd., Falcon Works, London Road, Isleworth, Middx.

ENGINE

Cylinders	4, horizontally opposed
Bore and stroke	82·5 mm. × 74 mm.
Cubic capacity	1,582 c.c.
Valves	Pushrod o.h.v.
Compression ratio	9 : 1
Carburetters	Two twin-choke down draught Solex 40 PJJ-4
Fuel pump	Mechanical
Oil filter	By-pass
Max. power (net)	95 b.h.p. at 5,800 r.p.m.
Max. torque (net)	91 lb. ft. at 4,200 r.p.m.

TRANSMISSION

Clutch	S.d.p. diaphragm spring
Top gear (s/m)	0·85
3rd gear (s/m)	1·13
2nd gear (s/m)	1·765
1st gear (s/m)	3·09
Reverse	3·06
Final drive	4·428
M.p.h. at 1,000 r.p.m. in:—	
Top gear	19·4
3rd gear	14·6
2nd gear	9·4
1st gear	5·3

CHASSIS

Construction	Welded, unitary

BRAKES

Type	Disc front and rear
Dimensions	8·9 in. dia. front discs 9·6 in. dia. rear
Friction areas	29·5 sq. in. lining

SUSPENSION AND STEERING

Front	Independent by dual trailing links and laminated torsion bars
Rear	Swing axle and diagonal trailing link, with torsion bar and optional compensating spring
Shock absorbers: Front } Rear	Telescopic
Steering gear	ZF worm and peg with hydraulic damper
Tyres	165—15 braced tread

COACHWORK AND EQUIPMENT

Starting handle	None
Jack	Mechanical pillar
Jacking points	Under body each side
Battery	Under spare wheel—front compartment
No. of electrical fuses	Twelve
Indicators	Self-cancelling flasher
Screen wipers	Self-parking, variable speed
Screen washers	Foot-operated pump
Sun visors	Two
Locks:	
With ignition key	Both doors
With other keys	Glove compartment and gear lever
Interior heater	Fresh-air, standard
Upholstery	Plastic
Floor covering	Rubber
Alternative body types	Convertible

MAINTENANCE

Sump	10 pints Quality HD
Transmission	6 pints S.A.E. 90
Steering gear	S.A.E. 90
Cooling system	Air cooled
Chassis lubrication	Every 3,000 miles to 14 points
Ignition timing	3° b.t.d.c.
Contact breaker gap	·016 in.
Sparking plug type	Bosch, Champion or Berv
Sparking plug gap	Depending on type
Tappet clearances (cold)	Inlet ·006 in., Exhaust ·004 in.
Front wheel toe-in	1/32 in. to 3/32 in.
Castor angle	5°
Tyre pressures	23 front, 26 rear; 26 front, 28 rear for fast driving

Wind-cheater par excellence: the front of the Porsche has very obvious aerodynamic qualities. It also offers a good forward view and limits under-bonnet carrying space

On the road with the

Porsche 1600SC

THERE are few cars on the road that have the piquant individuality of the present-day Porsche. Inspired by the same thinking as conceived the Volkswagen, its smoothly rounded body form has, in similar fashion to the 'beetle', stood the test of time. There is really ramarkably little difference between the present car and the first of the line some seventeen years ago. What is true externally is in large measure true internally also.

During its decade and a half of steady refinement, the Porsche has changed from a crude but effective road-going competition car to a well-behaved, docile grand tourer in the real sense of the word. The basic ingredients remain exactly the same. An aerodynamically efficient, all-steel body shell has a flat-four light alloy engine stowed behind the back wheels, driving them. Unusually in European practice, torsion bars provide the springing medium and the independent rear suspension remains of the swing-axle type, although now with the low pivot point pioneered by Porsche. Despite origins in the late '40s, the Porsche is still a low car by any standards and still draws many looks from passers-by because of its smooth purposefulness.

Good aerodynamic shape and low overall size have some immediately apparent disadvantages. The front luggage compartment, for instance, is virtually non-existent. By the time spare-wheel, fuel tank and front wheel arches have been accommodated nothing is left except a shallow depression which will take a large briefcase and no more. However, the engine is accommodated in such a compact manner that the Porsche has more than the usual area of space behind the seats and is equipped either with two small occasional seats or a luggage platform, or even as one occasional seat and a smaller luggage platform. Individual backrests fold down, are fully upholstered and leave a perfectly flat area when down for accommodating luggage. Moreover, good-sized suitcases can be fitted in without obscuring the rear view. Legroom for a rear-seat passenger is strictly limited but providing the driver does not need his seat at its full rearward adjustment, a moderate-sized adult can travel thus without too much discomfort. For children, the seats are excellent. Even when the rear seats are occupied, there remains a small luggage area behind.

The rounded contours of the Porsche convey a chummy appeal not altogether in keeping with its sharp performance

It is obvious even so that the Porsche has been designed mainly for a driver and one passenger. The door opens sufficiently widely to give easy access even if the lowness of the seats does not exactly make the operation elegant for a lady. Space inside is surprisingly good: there is plenty of elbow room and a long leg-tunnel allows even six-footer-pluses to be accommodated in comfort. The view is not perhaps as panoramic as one generally expects from a present-day car, mainly due to the rather high scuttle in the forward direction and the shallowness of the rear window when viewed through the mirror from the horizontal. The steeply sloping bonnet gives an early view of the road even if rounded contours do not make for the most easy judgement of width until one is used to the car.

There is nothing flashy about the instrumentation, but all is sensibly laid out and the controls are precisely what one would expect from a driver's car. In front of the driver is speedometer and revolution counter, both in circular dials with clear lettering. Another circular dial contains ancillary instruments: oil temperature, fuel level and warning lights for oil pressure, ignition, handbrake and low hydraulic fluid. A stalk sprouting from the steering column has a threefold function: turn indicators, dip and main beam for headlights and headlight flasher for day or night. In the centre of the board there is a heater control, a clock and switches for lights and wipers, the latter having a rheostat to enable them to be set at precisely the speed desired by the driver. The sturdy gear lever comes directly to the left hand and the handbrake is of umbrella-handle design under the fascia on the right-hand side.

Interior refinements

The finish of the Porsche's interior is a trifle strange by British standards. Although superficially on the stark side, with rubber mats on the floor and a painted metal fascia, the actual workmanship is of the highest possible class. Everything that is done is done to perfection. There are no rough edges, hanging wires or other examples of hasty assembly. Attention to detail is meticulous and if some of the design appears a trifle spartan, where it matters most—such as the seats—exactly the contrary is the case. The Porsche's seats are among the finest we have ever used. They are firm where they should be firm and soft where they should be soft; but, above all, the length of the seat cushion is such that adequate support is given beneath the knees. To the Porsche driver, a journey of 200 miles is no more fatiguing in respect of seating comfort than a journey round the block in most cars. Other items of utility and comfort in the Porsche's equipment are worth mentioning. The heater, for instance, is not only immensely powerful, it has simple controls and it starts to work within a few minutes of starting the engine. A control by the foot of the gear lever regulates the amount of air despatched from the engine compartment and a slide on both the driver's and the passenger's side regulates how much of this is required per person. Another control regulates how much is needed for feet and how much for the windscreen. In addition there are vents to the rear window which keep it clear of mist all the time. The only disadvantage of the system that we could discover was that in the absence of a passenger, the driver would have to stop the car to close off the nearside duct. There is also a fuel tap in the driving compartment which allows the fuel to be turned off completely and reserve capacity to be selected without getting out of the car. This is, of course, a useful anti-theft device but there is also a gearbox lock to make doubly sure. Both luggage and engine compartment lid are openable only from the interior of the car and the windscreen washers, which are foot-operated, are the most efficient that we have had the pleasure of using, directing twin jets of water in generous quantity to both sides of the screen.

It would not be true to suggest that the Porsche is the easiest car on the market to drive quickly but it is child's play to drive at moderate speeds. Clutch, accelerator, brakes and steering wheel are all light to the touch and have no vices.

One seat down and one seat up in the rear. The depth of the rear allows large pieces of baggage to be stowed without impingeing on backward visibility, and the occasional seats are nicely upholstered

The gearbox is a perfect delight, even in these days of much-improved boxes on the British market. The Porsche box has immensely powerful synchromesh with a freedom of movement and feeling of mechanical solidity rarely found in the one unit. The engine, which requires no choke to start from cold, merely a couple of dabs on the accelerator before switching on, remains sweet even with its 95 bhp in SC form. It is very flexible and if the driver wishes, the revolutions can be kept right down with the car behaving in the most docile fashion. As soon as the rev counter is taken over the 3000 mark, the

The somewhat spartan interior is offset by those magnificent seats, which are even more comfortable than they look

The small underbonnet space is given scale by the car, which stands on the magnificently comprehensive workshop manual

performance becomes really dynamic, but there is also a very considerable increase in mechanical noise.

At low speeds, the springing is a little on the choppy side, but as speed mounts, the bumps are ironed out in exemplary fashion and the car feels increasingly more at home. Indeed, if you don't mind a little bit of bumping around, the Porsche is immensely satisfactory on rough surfaces, the feeling of unity and solidity imparted by the unitary construction taking the credit for this. For high speed work along twisting roads, it is a pure delight to handle. The lightness and quick response of the steering allows the car to be placed accurately and the lack of roll allows the minimum amount of road to be used and causes no upset to passengers. Only when the car is pushed to the limit of wheel adhesion should it be necessary to use above average skill. The inherent oversteering characteristics of the car are partially responsible for the quickness of the steering and the unwary driver could be trapped by a sudden increase of oversteer in some circumstances. But as we have remarked before, for normal road use there are advantages in an oversteering car because it allows the driver to take a consistently tight line, and in this respect the Porsche excels. The competent owner will soon learn to assess accurately the car's and his own limitations. The weakness which is a function of the oversteering characteristic lies in lack of directional stability. At high speeds the Porsche is unduly affected by cross winds and by bumps in the road, and in some of the gale force winds which we encountered while driving the car on motorways, the vehicle would move literally feet to one side before the driver could correct. It is acknowledged, of course, that these circumstances were rather unusual.

As did their near neighbours at Stuttgart, Porsche held out for a long time against the use of disc brakes. The SC 1600 now has Porsche's own disc brakes fitted to all four wheels

Power-pack extraordinary. Even in this, its 95 bhp form, the engine is smooth at low speeds, if a little raucous at high revolutions

and superbly well they operate. The combination of a light car and generous disc sizes (surprisingly, larger at the rear than at the front) allows the Porsche to be pulled up repeatedly from high speeds without sign of pulling or fading and response is also good from snap stops at low speeds. Although the handbrake operation is a trifle clumsy, the brake itself is powerful when applied.

The Porsche has always been a fiercely individualistic motor car and even after all these years it remains so. Smoother, quieter and more sophisticated than it used to be, it still remains very much a driver's car with that indefinable ability to respond to the judgement and skill of the man at the wheel. It has its shortcomings, but it is a remarkable tribute to the original design of the car that so much of it is still so good. Our test was a short one, but our affection for the car grew with every hour that we drove it, and it became more and more easy to understand the burning devotion of Porsche owners to their cars and to the marque.

SPECIFICATIONS

ENGINE	**PORSCHE 1600 SC**
No. of cylinders	4
Bore	82.5 mm (3.25 in)
Stroke	74.0 mm (2.92 in)
Cubic capacity	1,582 cc
Compression ratio	9.5:1
Max power (net)	95 bhp at 5,800 rpm
Max torque (net)	91 lb ft at 4,200 rpm
Carburettor	2 twin-choke downdraught Solex 40 PJJ-4
Valves	Overhead, pushrods and rockers
Fuel pump	Mechanical
Tank capacity	11.0 galls
Water capacity	(air cooled)
Sump capacity	10 pints
Battery	6v 84 amp/hr
TRANSMISSION	
Clutch	sdp diaphragm
Gearbox	4-speed all synchromesh
Overall gear ratios	1st, 3.09; 2nd, 1.765; 3rd, 1.13; 4th, 0.852
Gearing	19.4 mph per 1,000 rpm in top
CHASSIS	
Suspension, front	Independent by dual trailing links and laminated torsion bars
Suspension, rear	Swing axle and diagonal trailing link, with torsion bar and optional compensating spring
Brakes	Disc brakes on all wheels
Steering	ZF worm and peg with hydraulic damper
Wheels	Pressed steel disc
Tyres	165-15 in braced tread
DIMENSIONS	ft in
Wheelbase	6 10.7
Track, front	4 3.4
Track, rear	4 2.1
Overall length	13 2.0
Overall width	5 5.8
Overall height	4 3.8
Ground clearance	6.25
Turning circle	33 6.0
Kerb weight	19 cwt
PERFORMANCE	secs
0 - 30 mph	3.6
0 - 40 mph	4.8
0 - 50 mph	7.9
0 - 60 mph	11.1
0 - 70 mph	14.4
0 - 80 mph	19.0
0 - 90 mph	28.6
0 - 100 mph	34.8
MAXIMUM SPEED IN GEARS	mph
1st	33
2nd	57
3rd	88
Top	114
Overall Fuel Consumption	26.2
Price	£2,278

USED CARS ON THE ROAD

No. 238 1960 PORSCHE SUPER 75 CABRIOLET

PRICE: Secondhand £945; New—Basic £1,620, with tax £2,299

Petrol consumption	*28-32 m.p.g.*	*Date first registered 29 January 1960*	
Oil consumption	*negligible*	*Mileometer reading*	*31,491*

MUCH the same sort of "make allegiance" infects Porsche enthusiasts as it does owners of Rovers, for example, but for different reasons. Re-acquaintance with the 1600 for this used car test recalls some of the characteristics which so easily can turn one into a Porsche fanatic. In congested traffic or tight parking spaces it may seem cumbersome and its bulbous sides are an embarrassment, but once on the open road it really streaks along in effortless fashion, covering the ground at high speed yet still returning around 30 m.p.g. on the cheapest grade of petrol available. It is also a long-life car, as this five-year-old example illustrates.

Signs of mechanical wear are very few indeed, and while it seems obvious that a lot of well-deserved care has been lavished on the car it has certainly lasted extremely well; the finish, both inside and out, shows little evidence of age. The only blemish in the appearance is the exterior brightwork, which has quite a lot of rust pock marks and places where the chromium has been polished away. It is in marked contrast to the very clean and unspoilt interior, and the sound and rust-free paintwork. The finish is in off-white or cream, not the original colour.

When new, the extra cost of the cabriolet model was £300, and its scarcity probably influences the rather high asking price. The hood is in good shape, though the interior lining is a little soiled, and is quick and easy to put up or down. An unusual feature of this particular car is that it has a bench front seat with individual reclining backrests. If the front seat is moved well forward, the occasional seats in the rear are quite practical for two adults in reasonable comfort, especially when the hood is out of the way, giving unlimited headroom.

An automatic choke looks after immediate cold starting and the air-cooled engine is ready for full power at once, without a moment's pause for warming up. It is a rear-mounted, horizontally opposed 4-cylinder, of course, like the Volkswagen's, but its capacity is 1,582 c.c. and there are twin Zenith carburettors. There is a lot of fan noise and general commotion at speeds below about 50 m.p.h., but the car is relatively quiet, both mechanically and in respect of wind noise, when settled down to its 80-90 m.p.h. cruising pace.

The clutch take-up is smooth, and the gear lever can be whisked from one gear to the next extremely quickly; even in bottom the synchromesh is still thoroughly efficient, but slight play has developed, accentuating the vagueness of the gear lever action.

Just as the engine seems happier and less fussy at speed, so does the suspension settle down; the ride is then transformed from low-speed harshness with much firm vertical movement, to even and well-damped springing at high speeds. The steering has developed slight free play, noticed most when driving fast in a strong side wind, but adjustment is easy. Very high cornering speeds are possible, and the car remains easy to handle, with little or none of the severe oversteer of earlier Porsches. The car is on Michelin X tyres, which all appear less than half worn, and the spare is unused. Also in its place in the diminutive front luggage locker is the very comprehensive toolkit, still practically complete, and the handbook is in the glove locker.

Original equipment included a vigorous heater, using air piped from the cooling system. Fortunately the weather was warm enough for it not to be needed, as even after a fuel leak from one of the carburettors had been cured, it continually introduced a smell of petrol into the car unless turned right off.

The only serious need for attention on the Porsche, especially for a driver who will make full use of the available performance, is to the brakes, which although fully effective are rough when applied hard at speed. Many would also want to improve the weak (6-volt) headlamps, which limit its night driving speed. The pull-out handbrake under the facia is in good adjustment, and dependable for parking on a severe gradient.

Like the Volkswagen, Porsches will accept a lot of hard work and neglect without suffering too badly, but when well cared for, as this has been, the years seem to pass harmlessly. Anyone buying secondhand has a good chance of finding one like this, with the promise of long trouble-free service ahead.

As well as the unusual feature of a bench seat with individual reclining backrests, the car comes with an old but still very good Motorola radio, a Cibié spotlamp, a clock and a wing mirror. Original equipment included a windscreen washer, which is the only item of equipment not working, and a cigarette lighter

PERFORMANCE CHECK

(Figures in brackets are those of the original fixed head Road Test, 15 April 1960)

0 to 30 m.p.h.	4·5 sec (3·2)	Standing quarter-mile	**18·3** sec (**18·6**)
0 to 40 m.p.h.	6·6 sec (5·6)		
0 to 50 m.p.h.	9·4 sec (7·8)	20 to 40 m.p.h. (top gear)	**13·2** sec (–)
0 to 60 m.p.h.	12·5 sec (11·4)		
0 to 70 m.p.h.	16·1 sec (15·6)	30 to 50 m.p.h. (top gear)	**10·9** sec
0 to 80 m.p.h.	21·3 sec (20·6)		
0 to 90 m.p.h.	28·8 sec (28·8)		
0 to 100 m.p.h.	40·6 sec (41·7)		

Car for sale at: Mead of Maidenhead, Market Street, Maidenhead, Berkshire. Telephone: Maidenhead 25371.

PORSCHE

FRANK COGGINS
EDITOR

Now we are going to talk about a car! You'll find our conversation larded with a lot of seemingly extraneous facts from here on but we think this will give you an idea of the rabid, total enthusiasm that owners have for this automobile.

We found, for example, that few Porsche owners let anyone else, family or not, drive their car. One girl we know shopped around in New York until she found a garage that would let her park the car herself and lock it. In Manhattan this is not easy! Porsche ownership is almost like a cult and before we say anything about the model we roadtested we freely admit to a strong susceptibility to this automobile. We could very easily be one of those "Keep your cotton-picking hands off my Porsche!" owners and will not swear that we may not own one yet. We don't have accurate figures on this, but we've found that many of our VW owner/friends are also Porsche owners and that many Volka owners buy up to Porsche. VW dealers consider dualing with Porsche (handling both cars in the same agency) a real natural.

In any event whenever we get our hands on one for a long weekend we just figure in advance that we're in for a lot of sheer joy of driving good, exotic machinery and the 356 C/1600 SC was no exception.

First of all, the minute you just sit in the car you feel that you are ready to go places. The seats are among the most comfortable obtainable in any automobile. Adjustable to fully reclining with loads of forward and backward movement, it's almost impossible not to get a good driving position. The gear shift falls right to your hand and has that solid feel through the gears that has become legend with Porsche owners.

Our test car had the 107 horsepower engine and frankly this package would seem to be the ultimate particularly with the new 911 just around the corner. Surprisingly, we got some great kicks out of the car, of all places, right in the midst of Manhattan traffic on Third Avenue during the rush hours. Here, the lovely, quick steering and that fabulous acceleration took so much of the bore out of working our way uptown that it was about the best thing a salesman could do to push the car to a prospective customer.

We are not going to go into the history of Porsche too deeply this time around—we're saving this for our story on the 911. You get bits of it in our VW stories every month in any event. The name Porsche keeps cropping up whenever talk about cars-at-speed occur.

Now, one of the things that really bothered us somewhat, and we mention this in connection wtih our MGB story, was the dashboard. The top of it is padded, which is great but why the painted metal in an expensive automobile such as this? Your gauges, of course, are well placed and can be read with no effort through the steering wheel (three spokes). The grab handle is worked

in nicely but I can't help admitting disappointment about this one facet. The upholstery is excellent and you can't beat the Porsche top for construction (we drove the Cabriolet, too).

The four speeds forward are all synchronized which helped immensely in that mad, mad New York traffic. On the turnpikes, of course, the Porsche comes into its own aided and abetted by by those powerful discs on all four wheels.

You can power your Porsche with either an 88 or 107 horsepower engine. In normal use, one of the men at Porsche of America felt that the average owner could tell not the difference and, further, that the "C" (88 hp) could outdrag the "SC" (107 hp) for a couple of car lengths. Then, we hasten to add, the SC leaves the C and takes off for parts unknown. Now this may be heresy to some of the Porsche purists but we mention it just to keep people from settling for the 88 horsepower engine and then wishing they had gone for the 107 horsepower mill.

Accessories for the Porsche include luggage racks, exhaust extensions, radios, mirrors, safety belts, floor-mats and of all things, an electric sunroof. Prices start about $4200 East Coast POE. If you feel that this report sort of teased you—that you want to know more about the Porsche we highly recommend that you get over to your nearest dealer and have a demonstration drive. You may find yourself deliberating about whether or not you want the detachable hardtop for the Cabriolet you've ordered.

The name, incidentally, is pronounced like the girl's name: Por-tia and, readers, we dig the Porsche—it sure does sort of get under your skin! ●

PORSCHE OWNERS REPORT
By Trudi Dembi

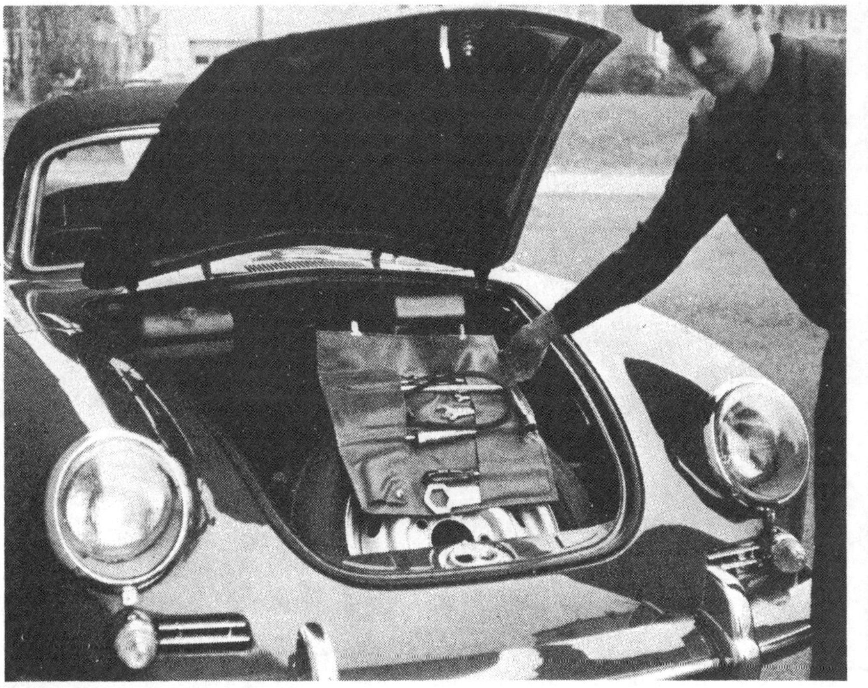

When our Porsche was about six months old, we went on a business trip to Washington, D. C. and my husband drove downtown to his appointment; double parked; hopped out and blithely said: "Call for me here at four o'clock", disappearing before I could protest. In that unfamiliar city, with my heart quaking, I strapped myself into the driver's seat. By this time, I had years of VW driving experience, so that I was not helpless, but I never expected that within five minutes I would be kicking myself for not having tried the Porsche sooner. I can still remember how quick and how pleasant my adaptation was. The only thing I had to restrain was my right foot, which had become heavy on the throttle pedal from pushing VWs through the gears but otherwise I felt immediately as though the Porsche was my friend.

According to the market research wiseacres, such phenomena as three-tone automobiles and similar vulgarities result from the fact that women in the United States have an ever-increasing influence on the selection of automobiles. These "M.R." guys have never met my husband. I have never been given a chance to express an opinion as to the timing, or the selection of make or model of the family car either in the days when there was one, or now that we have more than one at a time, and one is for my use.

The first car we ever owned was a 1948 Prefect, then a 1950 Plymouth with manual gearshift, on which I learned to drive, then an MG-TD; thereafter two Morgan Plus 4-TR-2 four-seaters, with a second-hand VW acquired for and assigned to me.

Torn between his undiminished love for the Morgan and his desire, on occasion at least, to have his family ride with him, Husband was brainwashed, and after a couple of mistakes, acquired a 356B Porsche convertible, which pleased all of us more or less. Husband concedes that it is more comfortable than his lamented Morgan, but grumbles that it doesn't corner as flat. Besides, he keeps reminding me, the rough ride in the Morgan was an exaggerated complaint and disappeared at speeds of 80 and over, which is possibly true. The kids are bigger, and their legs are much longer, and they drive their own cars now, but they are very happy to borrow the Porsche on the rare occasions when husband will trust them with it.

Like a burnt child wary of fire, I had avoided driving the Porsche when it was new because of my remembered dread of the hairy Morgans. Nor was I put at ease by being growled at during the maiden voyage to keep my dirty hands off the pure white headliner inside the convertible top. I was more than content as a passenger and probably would never have taken over the controls voluntarily.

I was already familiar with the luxurious little touches which distinguish this marque from all other cars from the passenger's standpoint. I can rhapsodize about the seats, for example. The passenger seat can be moved backward and forward and the angle of the backrest can be anything from straight up to sleeping

position without interfering with the driver. The seat is also deep enough so that with the top down and window raised my hairdo survives more or less. Visibility is ideal, even for a 4′ 11½″ Brunhilde like me. The heater controls are flexible, like a dual control blanket, so that husband can direct most of the flow from him, who always wants less, to me, who never has quite enough in any other car.

I remember being stunned by the all-of-a-sudden recognition of the pleasure of driving the Porsche. It turns at a thought. Shifting up or down is effortless and one finds oneself playing with the gearbox for the fun of it. My confidence in driving in traffic, on the highway, yes, and in parking, too all overwhelmed me within the space of the first few minutes that beautiful day.

Since then I have had occasion to wonder if it was wise for me to declare flatly that I was perfectly content to drive VWs and leave the sportscars to The Man. When I figure my way out of that cul-de-sac, the next thing I will have to work on is a deeply seated prejudice of husband's. Whenever I say to him, "The next time we rally, you navigate and I'll drive," he always says: "No! If you funk out while navigating, all we lose is a few points, or at most, the rally, but if you're driving, we could lose the car." How do I convince him that even in the excitement of a rally, I couldn't get rattled driving the Porsche? Cheetahs never stumble. ●

TIME was when all the Super Porsches had roller-bearing engines and clattered merrily. Since those days, however, the noisy sports car has gone out of fashion and the Porsche has become much more refined. The latest SC is mechanically quiet, the valve gear now being inaudible, which is remarkable for an air-cooled engine. Perhaps the machine is a little heavier, but this refined, plain-bearing model seems just about as fast as the old Super was.

Dr. Porsche designed the Volkswagen, and the sports car, to which he gave his name, is recognizably the product of the same brain. The combined steel body and chassis is suspended in the front by trailing arms coupled to transverse laminated torsion bars. Behind, there are swing axles with flexible radius arms and round-section torsion bars, this model having an auxiliary transverse spring with a centre pivot to lower the rear roll resistance. The disc brakes are built under Dunlop licence and have small auxiliary drums at the rear for the hand brake.

The over-square flat-four engine is air-cooled, of course, but the SC has aluminium cylinder barrels as well as heads. The bores have a chromium-plated surface to resist wear and there are two twin-choke downdraught Solex carburetters. The unit is mounted behind the rear hub line where its short length is advantageous to avoid excessive tail-heaviness. Naturally, the so-famous Porsche synchromesh is employed on all four speeds of the gearbox.

This is a very compact car, and the body is most luxurious for the driver and passenger. Two tiny occasional seats are hidden in the luggage compartment, for use over short distances by very small passengers. When they are covered over, there is some useful luggage space, though there is considerable effort involved in manhandling a heavy suitcase in through the door and over the front seats. The front boot is just about full of spare wheel and petrol tank.

On the road, the Porsche is unusually flexible for a car with one carburetter choke per cylinder. It is a remarkably effortless machine, having no favourite cruising speed and never appearing to hurry. There is a small red mark on the rev. counter dial at 6,000 r.p.m., but I went fractionally over this to attain 60 m.p.h. in second gear. Third is good for 85 m.p.h., and on winding roads one may use this gear with advantage for considerable distances.

During normal fast driving all the controls work smoothly, and the gear change gives much pleasure. A really rapid start, however, produces some juddering in the transmission, which detracts slightly from the initial acceleration. The average owner will not be making racing getaways, however, so the point is perhaps unimportant.

The test car was fitted with German Dunlop SP tyres, with lots of little holes pierced in the tread. They hang on very well, giving good cornering power, the car understeering a little at first, becoming neutral for most driving, then over-steering when really pressed. Some tyre noise is produced during spirited cornering. At high speeds, the Porsche is somewhat susceptible to the effects of gusts of wind, and I prefer

JOHN BOLSTER road tests the

PORSCHE 356 SC

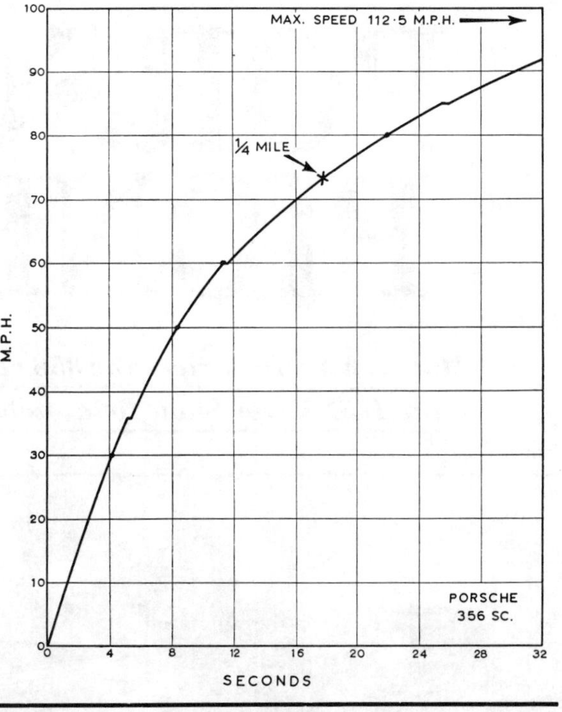

not to drive at more than 100 m.p.h. when strong side winds may suddenly be encountered. Unfortunately, the weather tended to be windy throughout my test, and that may be why I did not quite attain the claimed 115 m.p.h.

With disc brakes all round, stopping is no problem. It is relatively easy to slow down so small a projectile, and the braking system copes with the greatest of ease with the most determined driving. Warm praise must be given to the hand brake, for with shoes which are self-wrapping in both directions, the small central drums give safe parking on any gradient. I am at present waging a battle against inefficient hand brakes with badly placed levers. The Porsche therefore gets full marks here, though the discs are sometimes inclined to whistle.

Another very good point is the reserve petrol tap. When I was a boy, almost every car had a reserve tap, and jolly useful they were, too. As it happens, a miscalculation did cause me to exhaust the main supply, and the reserve tap saved me a walk in the rain. It is usual to expect heavy fuel consumption with multiple twin-choke carburetters. The SC is quite reasonable, giving a useful 23 m.p.g. when pressed and an economical 27 m.p.g. during gentle driving.

Most cars nowadays are nose-heavy, a weight distribution that is advantageous when one is after a boulevard ride. The Porsche at first feels rather choppy, largely because its tail-heavy distribution is so unusual. Once one becomes used to its manner of going, though, the ride is entirely acceptable.

Perhaps few cars have more passionate devotees than the Porsche. That there are other drivers who are not attracted in the same way is no criticism of the car, for a machine with so much personality will never appeal to everybody. Your typical Porsche fanatic will never buy anything else, and so the future of the *marque* is assured. The man who is not yet familiar with the car may think it costs an awful lot of money for a rather small package. The only answer is to take an extended trial run, but if the magic works on you, you'll have to have one!

SPECIFICATION AND PERFORMANCE DATA

Car Tested: Porsche 356 SC fixed-head coupé, price £2,278 1*s*. 3*d*. including P.T.

Engine: Four-cylinders, air-cooled, horizontally opposed. 82.5 mm. x 74 mm. (1,582 c.c.). Pushrod-operated overhead valves with light-alloy heads and cylinder barrels. Compression ratio 9.5 to 1. 95 b.h.p. (net) 107 b.h.p. (gross) at 5,800 r.p.m. Two Solex twin-choke downdraught carburetters. Bosch coil and distributor.

Transmission: Single dry plate diaphragm clutch. Four-speed all-synchromesh gearbox with central lever, ratios 3.77, 5.0, 7.82, and 13.68 to 1. Spiral bevel final drive, ratio 4.428 to 1.

Chassis: Combined steel body and chassis. Independent front suspension by trailing arms and transverse laminated torsion bars. Anti-roll torsion bar. Worm and roller steering gear with hydraulic damper. Independent rear suspension by swing axles and flexible radius arms with transverse round-section torsion bars. Auxiliary transverse spring with centre pivot. Telescopic dampers all round. Disc brakes on all four wheels with auxiliary rear drums for hand brake. Bolt-on ventilated disc wheels fitted 165-15 ins. braced-tread tyres.

Equipment: Six-volt lighting and starting. Speedometer. Rev. counter. Oil, temperature and fuel gauges. Clock. Cigar lighter. Heating, demisting, and ventilation system. Windscreen wipers and washers. Flashing direction indicators.

Dimensions: Wheelbase, 6 ft. 10¾ ins.; track (front), 4 ft. 3½ ins.; (rear), 4 ft. 2⅛ ins.; overall length, 13 ft. 2 ins.; width, 5 ft. 5¾ ins. Weight, 17 cwt. 3 qtrs.

Performance: Maximum speed, 112.5 m.p.h. **Speeds in gears:** third, 85 m.p.h.; second, 60 m.p.h.; first, 36 m.p.h. Standing quarter-mile, 18 secs. Acceleration: 0-30 m.p.h., 4.2 secs.; 0-50 m.p.h., 8.4 secs.; 0-60 m.p.h., 11.22 secs.; 0-80 m.p.h., 21.8 secs.

Fuel Consumption: 23 to 27 m.p.g.

PORSCHE PIONEER

Malcolm McKay drives the 356 cabriolet, imported for the 1951 Motor Show to launch Porsche in Britain

Above, the first 356 cabriolet in Britain, on the Connaught stand at the Earl's Court Motor Show in 1951. Who bought it?

Right, the same car in 1987 when David Mills found it: complete and largely original

AFTER the War, Porsche found itself in an old sawmill at Gmund, Austria, with a workforce in excess of 200 making an assortment of agricultural machinery. Professor Ferdinand Porsche was in prison, but his son Ferry and daughter Louise continued his work and managed to arrange his freedom during 1947. Meanwhile, racing car designs had been undertaken for Cisitalia of Italy, but plans for a sports car for Cisitalia came to nothing.

To Porsche's surprise, the Volkswagen plant at Fallersleben, far from being dismantled after the war, had ground back into production with British encouragement, producing over 10,000 cars in 1946 and 9,000 in 1947; a Porsche design, it was the obvious choice of base for the sports car Ferry was keen to produce.

The project began officially on June 11, 1947, designated Type 356. This first design – only one car was built to it – shows what Porsche would really have liked the 356 to be: it was mid-engined. A lightweight spaceframe chassis was used, carrying the Volkswagen 1131cc flat four engine *in front* of the rear wheels. In fact, the complete VW engine, gearbox and suspension assembly was used in reverse, with the trailing arms acting as leading arms!

By early 1948 the chassis was out on test; soon after, it was fitted with a lightweight aluminium two-seater open sports body, designed by Erwin Komenda, who had joined Porsche in 1931 from Daimler-Benz. Its simple, uncluttered and remarkably aerodynamic lines were a revelation.

Quite why this car, the 356/1, did not go on to production is not entirely clear. Certainly the mid-engined layout restricted cabin and storage space; inevitably it would have cost more to build than the conventional system; it has been suggested too that the reversed suspension was not entirely satisfactory, but journalists who tested the car at Bern in June gave no hint of this.

Developed alongside it was the 356/2, with conventional Volkswagen engine location, and this very similar but coupé design was to be the 356 as we know it today. Shorter and narrower than 356/1, it had far more space inside. Suspension was independent by torsion bars with trailing radius arms attached to the ends; one at the back, using swing axles, and two at the front.

The 356/2 was built, not on a spaceframe, but on a welded-up steel platform floorpan which provided all the strength required while also forming part of the bodywork and enabling lower and narrower sills to give more interior space. Completed in 1948, the frame was thoroughly road-tested before receiving its hand-beaten aluminium coupé bodywork. Orders from Switzerland undertook to provide not just the cash needed to launch the 356 into production, but many of the raw materials too.

As production got under way, Porsche turned to the engine, fitting twin carburettors and developing a new cylinder head design to accept larger valves and better porting; the result, from 1131cc or 1086cc, was a commendable 40bhp on the very low octane fuels available. These engines were painstakingly assembled by individual craftsmen and stamped with their initials.

The first 356 cabriolet was bodied by Swiss coachbuilder Beutler and appeared with a coupé at the Geneva Motor Show in March 1949. Reaction was good, though the high price, especially compared with its pedestrian base car, raised eyebrows. By the end of the year Porsche had built two cabriolets itself but, with acute shortage of materials, production was desperately slow. Porsche was to produce less than 60 cars at Gmund: its interests were being diverted.

From late 1948 Porsche had

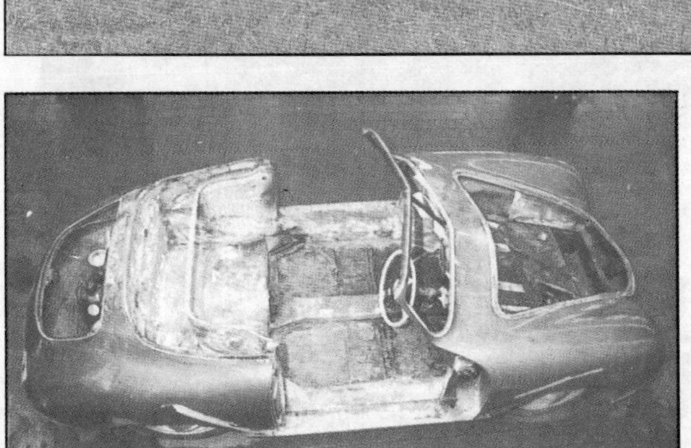

Left, the cabriolet at Porsche headquarters in Germany, part way through stripping it for restoration

Above, perfection: the car as it is today, returned to the original cream which was so striking in 1951

renewed its design contract with Volkswagen, which was now growing fast. This link proved far more profitable than building cars and for a while it looked as if the Porsche car might die. Fortunately, however, the car programme proved just the enterprise needed to set Porsche up again in Stuttgart and set against the Volkswagen profits! Better still, the move meant Porsche could draw on local coachbuilders to produce its bodies, saving the time and cost of hand-beating them itself. In November 1949, Reutter of Stuttgart received an

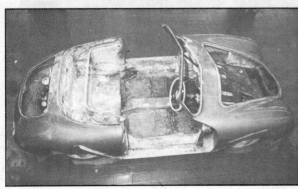

Photography: Simon Childs

order for 500 bodyshells; with Porsche's original works still occupied by the American forces, Reutter was to provide Porsche with factory space to assemble them, too.

The first German Porsche was on the road in the spring of 1950, and by the end of the year 300 had been built: production was taking off at last. Erwin Komenda had incorporated several changes to the body design, smoothing the lines, with a wider screen and higher front boot line. It was all-steel, too, welded to the platform chassis. Hydraulic brakes had now replaced the original cable variety and tubular shock absorbers replaced the lever arms by 1951. Also launched in 1951 was a new engine, of 1,286cc and using finned aluminium cylinder barrels with chrome-plated bores. 44bhp at 4,200rpm was available on basic 78 octane petrol – compare that with today's 97 octane four star! – and it was made quieter than the rorty 1100.

By the end of August, over 1,000 cars had been built in Germany and a sole coupé had won its class at Le Mans, finishing 20th overall. The Paris salon had launched the car in France in 1950 and an agent was soon appointed. Three cars also went to the United States in that year, followed by 32 in 1951; by 1954 agent Max Hoffman was selling 11 a week.

Britain was next: Charles Meisl, then Sales Manager at Connaught Engineering and casting around for something to sell, imported a left-hand drive Porsche coupé at the end of March. *The Autocar* leapt at the chance of a brief drive. Their conclusion? "It is not a car for everyone's taste, but it offers a unique combination of comfort, performance and economy, for which some people will pay a very good price." The low build, comfort, quietness and performance – especially above 50mph – were liked, but the gearbox, tendency to oversteer and instability in crosswinds were not. At least there was "headroom enough for the average man to wear a hat . . ."!

A further coupé and a cabriolet – the very car now owned by David Mills – were imported for the Earl's Court Motor Show in October, where they shared the stand with three French Salmsons. John Bolster described it in *The Autocar* as "one of the prettiest coupés I have ever seen". It was the first German car to be shown in England after the war – but the massive import duties levied at the time made its price of £2,300 absurdly high; an XK120 was £1,678 and an MG TD £732!

Connaught was not interested in the Porsche agency, however, and Meisl took it with him to John Colborne-Baber's Volkswagen garage nearby, through which two coupés and a cabriolet were sold in 1953, all left-hand drive. By this time, the Aldington brothers of AFN, whose

" . . . it offers a unique combination . . ."

costly Frazer Nash cars were attracting fewer customers than ever, had decided to follow up an initial interest sparked off at the Geneva Show in 1950. With excellent contacts in Germany from the days of the Frazer Nash-BMWs, they made an impressive pitch to Porsche; the conclusion was for Meisl to join AFN as Sales Manager for Porsche, at the end of 1953.

The first car to arrive at AFN was the second right-hand drive cabriolet, used as a demonstration car. By May 1954 only two coupés had been sold; fortunately AFN had numerous other interests, from tractors through motorcycles and sidecars, Invictas and DKWs to muck-spreaders! However, slowly but surely Porsche sales built up and by 1958 the last Frazer Nash car had been built.

Meanwhile, changes to the 356 had continued thick and fast. By the end of 1952, a 1,488cc engine with 60bhp was available; that winter a one-piece windscreen, perforated wheels and higher-set bumpers were phased in with revised instruments and

Above, with all the trim out it was clear that, though not badly holed, the floor would have to be replaced: the body was inverted, below. Outer body panels required local repair, left

Left, the engine received new barrels, pistons and crankshaft while most of the ancillaries were rebuilt. It was possible to run it up on Porsche's engine test rig before refitting

Below, simple shape: yet almost every detail part proved hard to find

switchgear. This makes David Mills' car, which predates those changes, exceptionally rare, but it is not quite the only survivor from those days: the Earl's Court coupé from 1951 also survives and is undergoing a lengthy restoration by John Atkinson.

David Mills had not owned any old car before he bought this Porsche. However, being a keen motorist, he had joined the Porsche Club; an advert in *Porsche Post*, winter 1987, caught his eye. A small garage in Sussex had found, stored in a barn, an original and very early right-hand drive cabriolet. David's mind went back to 1960, when he had bought a 1953 left-

hand drive 356 coupé: memories flooding back, he went to see the cabriolet and, impressed by its originality – it had covered only 56,000 miles – he bought it.

Without time to restore the car himself, David sought the assistance of Porsche. The Porsche factory itself was delighted to take on the restoration and the car was transported across in early 1988 for an estimate. That estimate cost £2,000, for which the car, engine and all, was completely stripped! David gave the go-ahead in June, and the car was restored under the guidance of Eric Brett, the Service Manager, who had worked at Zuffenhausen when it was built; the restoration became his final project.

The shell was stripped out and inverted on a jig before the rusted floor panels were cut out and replaced. The upper body panels, however, were sound enough to be locally repaired; in the case of the front wings, a two-inch wide strip was taken out at the back of the wing, from sill level almost up to the windscreen, and new steel let in. The body was then zinc sprayed to protect it from future rust, before painting.

"... Porsche was delighted to take on the restoration ..."

When purchased, the car had been painted blue, and this was the colour shown on the 1959 log book, but David was able to establish that the original colour was the cream in which it is now painted – a dramatic colour in 1951 when most of its Motor Show contemporaries were in sober, dark colours.

The engine was found to be the original and received a full rebuild on the original crankcase with new cylinders, crankshaft and pistons. Meanwhile, David was researching various components that were proving difficult to find. During reassembly, the windscreen became cracked; replacements for the early split screen were not available, but David managed to track down the original manufacturer and had one made. The glass rear window in the hood was even more difficult, being of a double curvature, so very expensive to have made; after extensive searching, a Spitfire windscreen was found to be a perfect match when cut down to size.

Most difficult of all were the rear light lenses; in the end they had to be specially made – Porsche had ceased using this type in 1953 and none could be found anywhere. The correct 16 inch wheels are very hard to find now and the car actually has the 1952 wheels at present. The bumper insert strip was another unobtainable part; David managed to track down a British company that could make a die and produce it, so he had enough made for 30 cars while he was at it.

Finally the car was completed and David went to Zuffenhausen to collect it; Ferry Porsche himself was waiting for him and asked to take it for a drive. No sooner had he climbed in than he looked at the sunvisors and said: "Those should be rivets, not screws"! He also asked the weight; the car was duly taken to a weighbridge, where it weighed in at 830kg. Concours had not been his aim, but David decided to enter it for the Porsche Club's two concours in 1990 and 1991; though it narrowly missed an overall win, it took the visitors' choice award at one and the Judges' favourite at the other. David made a point of driving the car to both events, and in future intends to keep it to use, rather than show, whenever he can.

The 356 is delightful to drive: there is a delicacy about it that reflects the quality of build and would have gone some way towards vindicating the purchaser for spending the cost of three MGs on a 1300cc foreign car ... The ride and the steering are most impressive: the ride because it is smooth, supple and combined with a remarkably stiff floorpan giving no trace of scuttle shake; the steering because it is amazingly light and direct at a time when many of its rivals had heavy imprecise steering requiring much spinning of the wheel to turn.

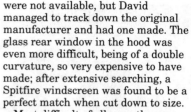

Left, red trim and red-painted dashboard set off the cream exterior and components: the radio was standard
Right, the pristine engine bay; note the lid hinges, drilled for lightness
Below, the bodyshell was zinc sprayed throughout before painting to protect it against rust in future

Left, Eric Brett, left, and David Mills, right, look through RPB 742's restoration file with Ferry Porsche, who took a great interest in the car

The gearchange seems incongruous, however: it is a crash box, requiring careful double-declutching whether changing up or down and, until the driver becomes fully accustomed, it can be quite obstructive. It marks the car's basic origins, being a Volkswagen component that was not so easy to disguise as the rest! By late 1952 this handicap had been overcome with the introduction of an all-synchromesh four-speed gearbox using Porsche patented synchro rings. By this stage the 1.3 convertible had a claimed maximum speed of 90mph and fuel consumption of 33-37mpg; *The Autocar* was obviously unaware of Charles Meisl's sales efforts, as it stated: "Not available in Great Britain"!

Above, the first Porsche 356/2 takes shape in the old sawmill at Gmund, Austria in 1948: the alloy body was hand-beaten

Above, the first 356 cabriolet, bodied by Beutler in Switzerland, awaits its launch at the 1949 Geneva Motor Show

Above, imported in 1957, ULD 23 was David Mills' first Porsche; does it survive?

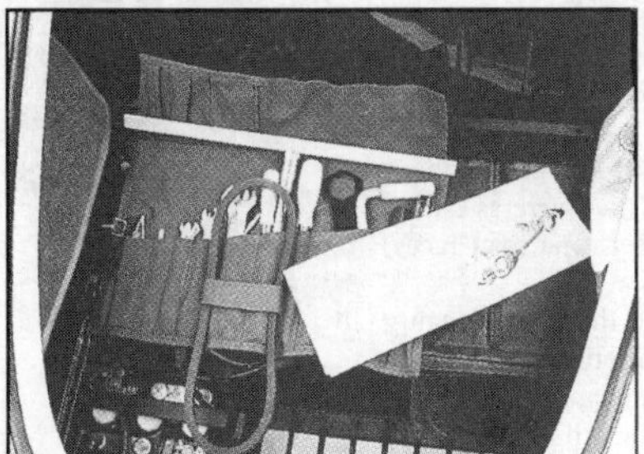

Above, original features under the bonnet of RPB 742. The wooden dipstick was supplied instead of a fuel gauge! Right, the first ever right-hand drive 356 cabriolet went to Australia for the Melbourne Show in 1951; where is it now?

PORSCHE 356

The classic Porsche shape was evident right from the start

Eventually there were more than two dozen engine types, from 1100 to 1600cc ■

Engine:	Horizontally-opposed, four-cylinder, air-cooled, ohv
Capacity:	1086cc
Max power:	40bhp at 4200rpm
Max torque:	52lb ft at 3000rpm
Transmission:	Four-speed manual
Suspension:	Independent front, torsion bars, trailing arms. Independent rear, torsion bars, swing-axles.
Brakes:	Drums front and rear
Weight:	1850lb
Max speed:	88mph
0-60mph:	14.1sec

If anyone ever made a silk purse out of a sow's ear it was Porsche, for the humble Volkswagen was surely an unlikely basis for a sports car – not a cheap-and-cheerful sports car in the British MG Midget or Frogeye Sprite genre, but a handcrafted vehicle that was high-priced (grossly over-priced, said the uninitiated) and destined to become the darling of the very rich. As long ago as 1950, the award-winning Porsches in the Rally to the Midnight Sun were driven by two German princes, navigated by two German counts, and the ladies' prize went to a Swedish countess . . .

Early Porsche owners were as loyal to their cars as Bugatti fans had been to the idiosyncratic Molsheim make in its heyday in the 1930s – and as blind to their built-in faults. In the Porsche 356 these included a nerve-shattering oversteer which, ironically, did not exist in the car as Ferry Porsche designed it. What the world knows as Type 356 is strictly 356/2, for the *original* prototype was a one-off roadster in which the VW engine, gearbox and rear suspension was turned around, making it mid-engined. But in the 356/2 prototype, the first coupé version, the back end reverted to the VW rear-engined configuration to allow more luggage space. Bad enough in a Beetle, the oversteer was much more pronounced in a short-wheelbase sports coupé, and in retaining this set-up for the 1948-9 production models Porsche gave themselves a 16-year headache. The really fast competition Porsches were mid-engined, not rear-engined.

With sleek light-alloy bodies, the first 50 or 60 cars, built in Austria in the small Porsche workshop in Gmund, scaled only 1425lb and went well on a modest 40bhp. More power was obviously needed when production moved to Zuffenhausen in 1950, the all-steel cars weighing 400lb more, and the following two years brought the first 1300 and 1500cc engines. Eventually there were more than two dozen engine types, from 1100 to 1600cc, and some small-capacity units out-performed some bigger ones because in Germany the road tax was by capacity, the insurance by horsepower.

In pushrod-overhead valve units anything up to 95bhp was catalogued, this giving about 115mph from a 1600, but the more specialised four-cam Carrera units (the Carreras taking their name from Porsche's early racing successes in the Carrera Panamericana road races) offered up to 130bhp.

Coupé, cabriolet or roadster, the little Porsches were soon renowned for their build quality and the continual improvements that were made. The 356A for 1956 not only had a 1600cc engine but also a diaphragm clutch, smaller wheels, a lower floorpan and a one-piece windscreen. It was altogether a smoother and more controllable car, though it looked the same as before. Four years later came the 356B, which looked much different with its bigger, raised bumpers and higher front, while it also had better brakes, better synchromesh, and a compensating spring to reduce rear roll stiffness.

After a further four-year interval came the last of the series, the 356C. Vastly improved in detail, it too was little changed in appearance, but it handled better, was a lot more comfortable, and at last had disc brakes all round. Porsche, who originally thought they might build 500 cars, had sold almost 78,000 – and gained a reputation for producing the sort of vehicle almost every discerning driver wanted to own. ■

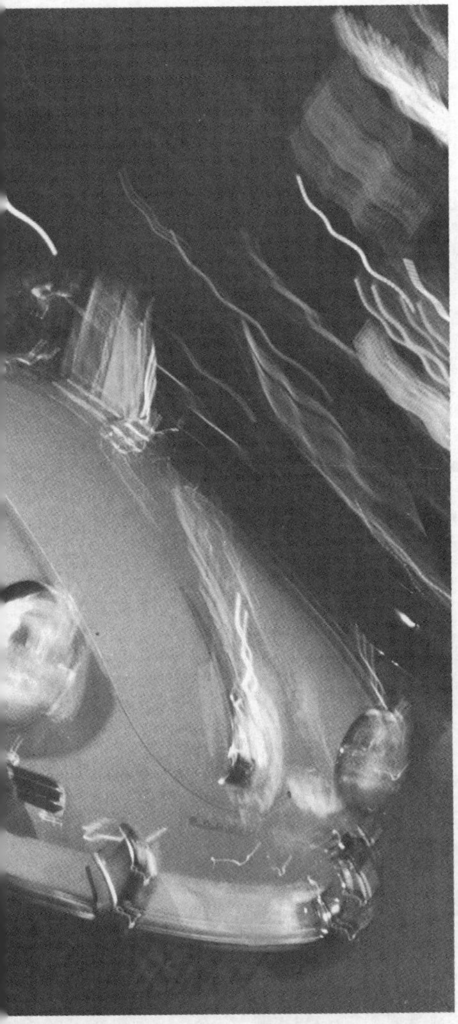

BEST BUY: Porsche 356

It's a safe bet that for each Porsche addict whose inclinations lean to the 356, there are a hundred more who would prefer a 911. Despite its undoubted engineering quality and dynamic finesse, the 356, in British minds at least, has always been a poor relation to its revered successor. Yet in many ways, it makes a far more attractive classic choice than any 911.

For a start, 356s make more sense financially. Although these cars are no longer the bargains they were 10 years ago, they will always have a spectacular advantage over any 911 in maintenance costs – provided you pick a good one. All 356s, from the pre-A to the C models, have a delightful blend of period charm, quality engineering and tactile precision that is beguiling the first time you drive one. A 911, dare I say it, can feel heavy and ham-fisted alongside the 356's exquisite lightness of touch.

Porsche has developed a speciality for quick-fire specification changes which make its long-running model ranges bewildering to unravel – the 356 is no exception. It has two major design eras, several convertible body styles, engine permutations ranging from 40bhp to 95bhp, and a multitude of small running changes. From all these possibilities it's tricky to pick out an all-round Best Buy, but here are a few pointers.

The pre-A and A models, built up to 1959, best suit the more committed 356 enthusiast, for they are relatively thin on the ground and not quite so rewarding to drive – but Porsche's original body shape might clinch the argument for some. The Cs – with disc brakes, slightly more powerful engines and good ventilation – are nicest to live with, and by a slender margin offer the most car for the money. But the Bs, only a whisker behind in driveability, have a significant advantage – they are the easiest to find because nearly twice as many were built.

To find out about the 356's intricacies we spoke to two of Britain's leading specialists. Despite only four years' involvement with old Porsches, Devon-based Roger Bray is the country's leading bodyshell restorer – he has seen all the traps into which unwary buyers can fall. The 1959 356B Roadster illustrated here is his own concours-winning car. On the mechanical side, few people can match the expertise of Bob Garretson, who is Porsche Club GB's technical advisor. An American who now runs a restoration shop in Lancashire, he has been active in 356 circles since he bought his first Porsche in 1957. He is also an accomplished racing driver: his victory in the 1981 Daytona 24 Hours, sharing a Porsche 935-K3 with Bobby Rahal and Brian Redman, helping him to the World Endurance Drivers' Championship title.

UK or US?

If you set out on the trail towards 356 ownership, the chances are that most of the cars you look at will be left-hand drive US imports. Buy with the utmost care and you can find excellent Coupés which come close to the mythical ideal of the rust-free Californian car. But be on your guard: most US cars are nowhere near as good as this.

Depressingly, the typical US car these days seems to have been tarted up, sometimes using the most unscrupulous methods, for sale to a European buyer. It will look pretty, with a shiny new coat of paint, gleaming chrome and not a pinprick of rust in sight. You may fall for it and enjoy a 12-month honeymoon with the car, but gradually the ravages of use and the British climate will go to work and tarnish your affair. The filler will sink and crack, sub-surface rust will erupt through paint and underseal.

356 PRICES

£4500-£8000 Rusty Coupés which may run, but probably won't have MoT – and will need total body restoration. Good engine spec, right-hand drive and lots of originality carry a premium.

£8000-£11,000 Useable but poor cars – they will inevitably need substantial body restoration. Little price difference between A/B/C, but rare pre-As worth more.

£11,000-£14,000 A car to jump in and drive, but will need cosmetic work. Major structural expense probably necessary one day – but a car you can enjoy for a few years. Convertibles for restoration.

£14,000-£17,000 This is where the real bargains are. Bodily sound cars which should never demand major expense if you keep on top of them. A basket-case Speedster might just be on.

£17,000-£22,000 Properly restored cars, but not the exceptional ones; really original low-mileage specimens should be around this mark. Worthwhile Convertibles start here.

£22,000-£30,000 Restored Coupés of rare quality and perfect authenticity – top concours standard towards the top of the scale. Good Convertibles.

Over £30,000 Good restored Convertible territory, with perfect examples in the £40,000-£45,000 bracket. Blue-chip Speedsters and Carreras go higher still.

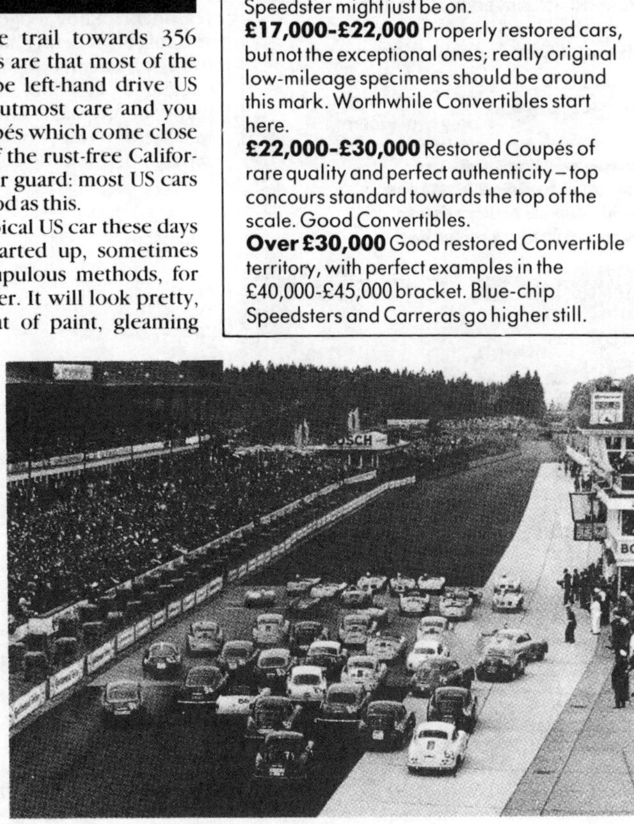

Late-fifties sports car race at the Nurburgring, supporting German GP: 356 Speedsters, Roadsters and Coupes start behind Porsche Spyders and beside Alfas

WHICH MODEL?

356 Model years 1950-55. The aficionado's choice: colloquially known as 'pre-A'. Original jelly-mould shape with two-piece or 'bent' screen. Narrow wheels, tail-happy handling, modest power from 1100/1300/1500 engines, lever-arm dampers and crash 'box – the least driving appeal but very valuable.

356A Model years 1956-59. The nostalgic's choice: this one's nicer to drive but the shape hasn't changed. Curved screen and new dashboard are only visual differences, but engines are now mainly 1600s with 60bhp or 75bhp – plus a few 1300s.

356B Model years 1960-63. The enthusiast's choice: prettier body with higher bumpers, raised headlamps, quarterlight windows and larger rear screen. Same 60bhp/75bhp engines as before, plus desirable Super 90 model with 90bhp and 115mph top speed.

356C Model years 1964-65. The driver's choice: all-round disc brakes and more powr for this short-lived 356 swansong. New badging and slightly different wheels are only external clues. 1600SC, with 95bhp, is the most powerful 356 (barring exotic four-cam Carreras).

Coupés Practical all-weather cars with reasonable room inside – these have two-plus-two rear seats. Much cheaper to buy at between one-third and half the price of a soft-top.

Convertibles Several styles through 356 evolution were labelled Cabriolet, Speedster, Convertible D and Roadster. Lightweight and low-line Speedster tops desirability list, but any of these are top money. Convertible D and Roadster styles are only two-seaters.

Early flat-four air-cooled engine derived from and very similar to Beetles: non-original parts from that car may have been used

On plenty of cars, simple running repairs have been done out of financial necessity, whether in Europe or the US. Ten or 15 years ago, a well-used 356 was worth only a few hundred pounds, so welding had to be cheap to keep the car on the road. It's preferable, of course, to find an original car that has not been messed around, rather than a bodged example on which old repair work will have to be undone – but the difference is not always easy to spot.

Roger Bray has bought 356s on many trips to the US, and even he, with experience of looking at over 400 cars in the past few years, occasionally finds it difficult to sort the wheat from the chaff. Armed with all the guidance you can gather, you could go to the US and search for a 356 yourself – or buy one from a dealer here after having it inspected by a 356 specialist. What you must *not* do is purchase from the US on the strength of a photographic portfolio, for pictures will tell you nothing about a 356's structural condition.

One British Porsche enthusiast with reasonable knowledge and a collection of several cars recently bought a Speedster from the US. It seemed a good specimen, with an excellent paint job, good mechanicals and plenty of original features. Expecting to have to spend money on only minor running repairs, he took the car to his local Porsche dealer for an MoT once it arrived in the country. It failed, so Bray was called in to advise – and ended up with the Speedster in his workshop. Only with the car on a ram were the horrors revealed: beneath disguising layers of bitumen, the underside was patched up with lengths of angle iron and

Engine and transaxle are robust: rebuilds £3000 and £600. Watch heater ducts (bottom) are not detached

STUDIO PHOTOGRAPHY BY PHIL TULK

Line-up of 356 Coupés outside Roger Bray's premises, Okehampton: these are the cheapest cars

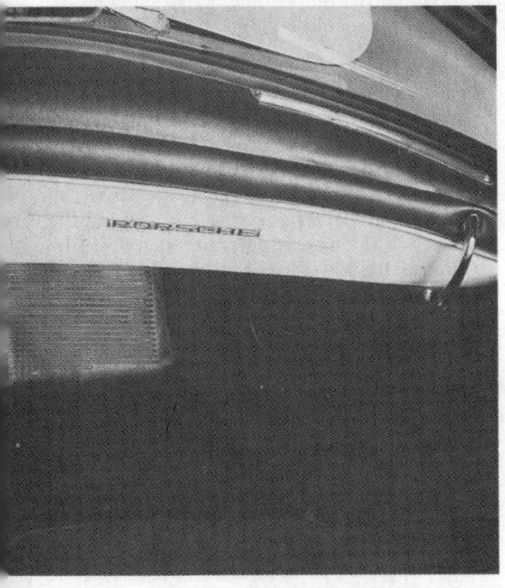

Roadster interior left, is unique: grab handle on right purely cosmetic, pulls off

steel plates welded and bolted in place to hold the corroding structure together. The car needs a £15,000 bodyshell restoration.

This is an extreme example, but 356s that have been bodged for a quick sale are commonplace. The conclusion for a prospective purchaser is simple: above all else, you must buy a car with a sound bodyshell. If you want a restoration project, this almost inevitably means buying an honest US car that has not had a cosmetic going-over. If you want a mid-priced useable car, check it out *very* carefully. If you want a restored car, buy a first-class job with a photographic record of restoration work carried out by a recognised specialist.

As with any other classic car, try to think long-term when you buy. In an ideal world, it's best to spend bottom money on a basket-case or top money on an excellent car. Buying in the mid-range, around £8000-£12,000 for a 356 Coupé, will invariably mean major expenditure a few years down the road – to the point where you would have been better off buying a cheaper car in the first place.

If you reach the point where you are satisfied with a potential purchase, don't rely on your own judgement unless you really have become a 356 expert. Spend £100-£200 on a professional inspection and written report: Porsche Club GB or many of the specialists listed at the end of this feature can advise. This modest investment could be repaid many times over.

ROGER BRAY ON RESTORING 356s

Roger Bray has been restoring cars for 20 years and produces some of the UK's best rebuilt Porsche 356s – even though he has only been working on them for about five years: "It began when I was restoring a customer car, and at first I was taking the mick – putting on VW badges and so on – but as the restoration progressed I fell in love with it – they are so beautifully engineered."

Now Bray employs five full-time mechanics at his Okehampton base, restoring mainly 356s: "Before I discovered these cars, I didn't care whether I did an Escort or an Aston – but for me they all have to be finished to the same high standards." Proof is his own beautiful white 356A Roadster pictured on these pages; restored 3½ years ago, it is now for sale.

Immaculate underside, below: bodging is easier to detect here than in the body, but check sills, battery box (top)

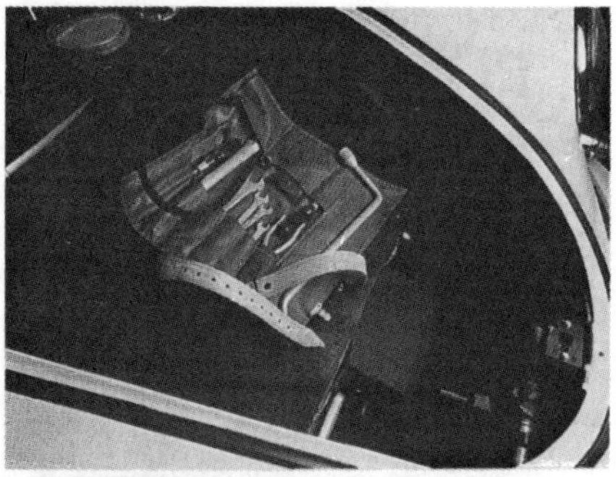

Original 356 tool kit looks like this. While you are at the front of the car, check the tyre well and battery box for rust

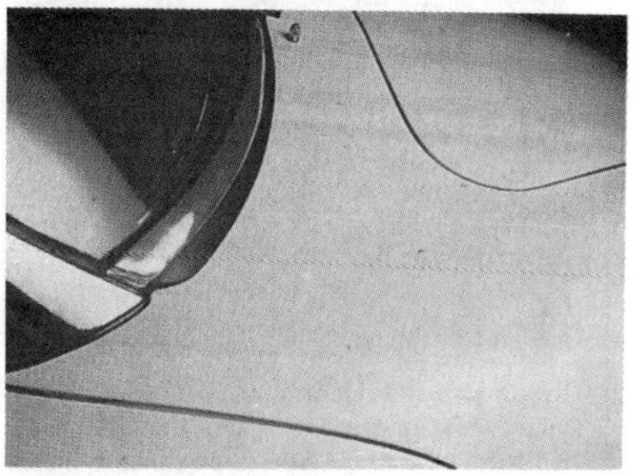

Sight across this pillar/ scuttle/front wing joint for ripples: it's leaded, hard to fix. Uneven shuts spell trouble

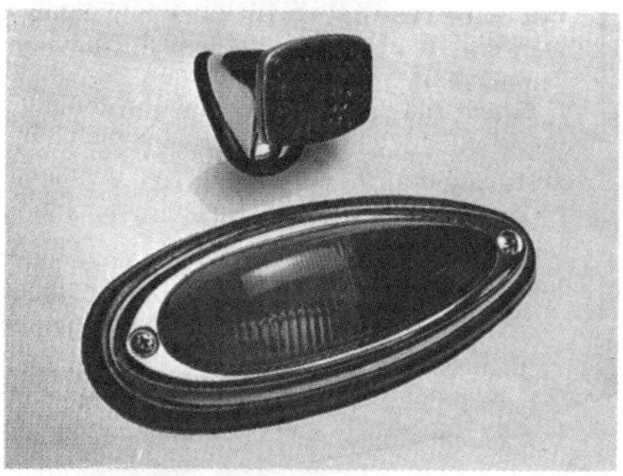

Repro parts such as light fittings are generally available: check the list of specialists on page 53

DETAIL PHOTOGRAPHY: PAUL HARMER

TEN THINGS YOU DIDN'T

● The first prototype 356, created in 1947, was very different from the production cars which followed. It featured three-abreast seating, a spaceframe chassis, an open body and mid-engined configuration – the power unit sat ahead of the rear axle. It was the *second* prototype which established the 356 mechanical layout.

● Few people can have covered as many Porsche 356 miles as Denis Jenkinson, 'DSJ' of *Motor Sport*. Over a period of 10 years he clocked up nearly half a million miles throughout Europe – 350,000 of them were in his own 356A.

● The most numerous model in this family ws the 356B. Production figures break down like this: 356, 7627; 356A, 21,045; 356B, 30,963; 356C, 16,668.

● The first Porsche 356 manufactured in Stuttgart (early cars were built at Gmünd in Austria) was unfortunately written off, after 156,000 development miles, in a high-speed *autobahn* accident while being driven by engine specialist Rolf Wütherich. Several years later Wütherich was lucky to survive an even more serious accident – he was James Dean's passenger when the film idol crashed his Porsche Spyder.

● The great Pete Coltrin, doyen of car photographers, lived in Modena and absorbed himself in Ferrari and Maserati circles. But his own transport for several years must have seemed provocative to Italy's automotive elite – it was an immaculate 356B.

Bodyshell tell-tales

Although Porsche's engineering has always been in a special league, the rust-resisting properties of the 356's unitary steel bodyshell were no better than any other mass-produced monocoque car of the 1950s. Only the most cosseted fair-weather examples have escaped severe corrosion during their lifetimes.

With any 356, you need to start by generally sizing up the bodyshell, looking for obvious areas of external rust, eyeing the line and smoothness of panels, and assessing whether any filler has been used, possibly over unrepaired steel. Poor filler work will reveal itself through uneven surfaces, badly shaped edges and cracks in the paint, but a magnet is useful to detect where the skilled bodger has been operating.

Examine the door, bonnet and engine cover gaps. Athough not quite perfect, Porsche gapping is so good that you should expect neat shut-lines close to the correct 3½mm width. Hidden structural corrosion can cause gaps to open or close up, especially on a soft-top, so it's worth lifting the car at each corner to see if any gaps change.

The way the doors are mounted on shimmed hinges mean that it should always be possible to obtain an accurate fit for them, although inept repairs fore and aft of the doors can be surprisingly well-disguised by bringing the door striker outwards to restore some semblance of the original flank line. The doors themselves tend to corrode badly when the drain holes become blocked, so check along the lower areas. It is also worth peering at the flat floor of the deep recess into which the front of each door pivots.

The nature of a 356's construction means that the bodyshell is riddled with mud traps and moisture. Behind many areas of the car, such as the door shut-faces or where inner and outer wings join; there are cavities where steel panels are separated by half an inch or so. Paint often didn't penetrate this far and in some places underseal closed off these narrow gaps, allowing a natural habitat for condensation to work away at the steel. Since the rust eats away from within, any visible corrosion (or filler repairs) means serious sub-surface problems – key places to check are the

New headlamps can still be bought from the factory in Germany: only pre-A series panels are difficult to final

ABOUT THE PORSCHE 356

● Jim Clark won his first big race in a 356A 1600 Super, at Charterhall in 1957. Clark's mentor, Ian Scott Watson, was so impressed by his early performances in a DKW that he bought a secondhand 356A – from band-leader Billy Cotton – to set the future World Champion on his way.

● The least powerful 356 was the 40bhp 1100 version produced between 1950-54 – it was also by far the most numerous of the 'pre-A' models. The most powerful mainstream model was the 95bhp 365C in 1600SC form, but competition versions of the Carrera pushed out as much as 155bhp from their 2-litre four-cam engines. You're unlikely to find one of these; they're very rare and very specialised.

● Porsche 356s were quite expensive in Britain. In 1963, for example, the 1600 Super 90 (£2277) was pitched against these rivals: AC Ace Bristol (£1873), Alfa Romeo Giulia 1600 Sprint (£1597), Austin-Healey 3000 MkII (£1045), Jaguar E-type roadster (£1828), Lotus Elan (£1317), MGB (£834), Triumph TR4 (£949) and TVR (£1040).

● Porsche enjoyed instant racing success with the 356. One of the Gmünd-built aluminium Coupés was used in 1951 for the company's international race debut at Le Mans, where the French crew of Veuillet (Porsche's distributor in Paris) and Mouche succeeded in winning the 1100cc class.

● All 356s built up to 1955 used fuel tanks without an electrical float for a fuel gauge: a calibrated wooden dipstick was supplied.

Roadster dash, above: less basic than Speedster. Steering wheels almost impossible to find

vertical edges of the wings adjacent to the doors. On a restored car there's nothing to worry about, if all damaged metal has been cut away properly and replaced.

Bonnet surrounds tend to rust more than their counterparts at the back. If no rust is showing, check the fit of both lids – they can sit well but commonly don't – and the profile of the edges of the surrounding steelwork. The correct original appearance for these is a clean edge with a more or less right-angled shape, but if filler has been applied over rusted steel a more rounded and variable profile is likely – and most often found around the rear corners and curved front of the bonnet. On the bonnet itself, look for distortion near the hinges: someone may have tried to force the bonnet down against a sticking ratchet on the prop.

The bonnet's shape means that water tends to drain into the front of the car. This is where the spare wheel lives, so make sure you remove it and examine the battery box below. This is such a vulnerable area on cars which have stood unused in the open that the floor of the battery box is often badly corroded from the combined onslaught of battery acid and pools of water. The slender gaps between the joins of inner and outer front wings – more moisture traps – also add to the problems in this area.

Cabriolets, Roadsters and Speedsters invariably suffer more corrosion than Coupés because the weather gets in. With today's rarified Speedster values, it's often forgotten that this lightweight model for the US was the cheap one: since a Speedster hood is really only storm-proof, these cars can rust badly if they haven't lived in a dry climate.

So many of these tell-tales are points of tiny detail requiring an experienced eye. There's no substitute for thoroughly familiarising yourself with the appearance of a good original or restored car – best done at a club gathering – so that you can spot the duds.

Traps on the underside

The underseal that was applied to these cars at the factory has been a mixed blessing over the years, and many short-cut restorers have compounded the problems by plastering on extra bitumen over shoddy repairs. While the flat areas of the floorpan should have been

Outer skin only visible here, but a good indicator of overall body condition. Crawl underneath to reach sills

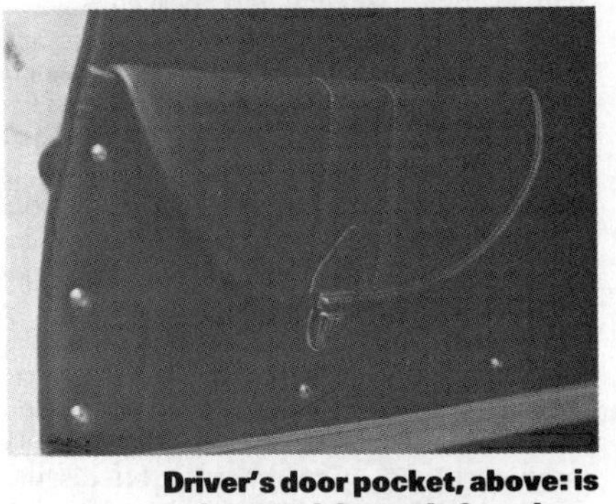

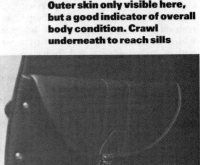

Driver's door pocket, above: is a nice touch but only found on Roadster, whose interior is different to other cars

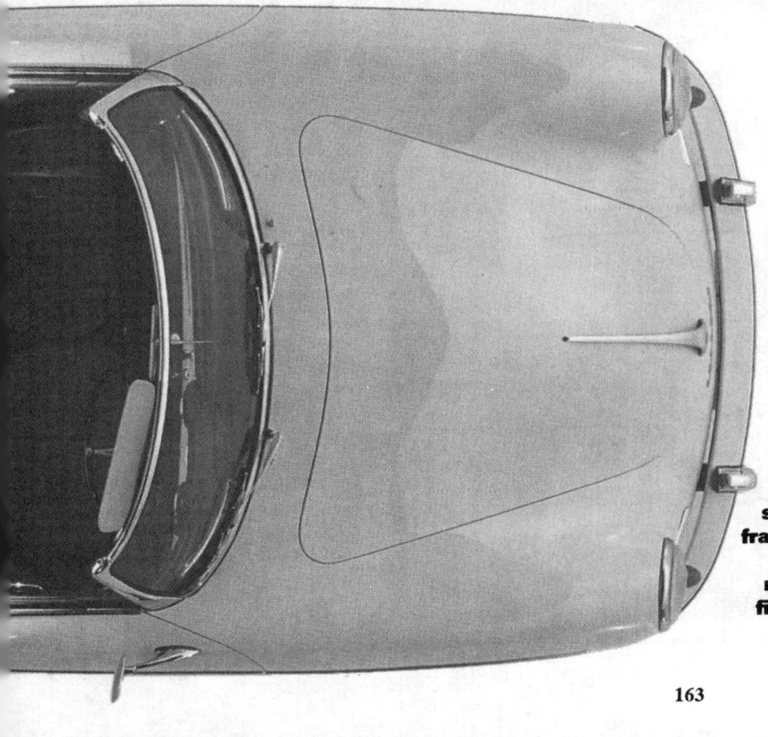

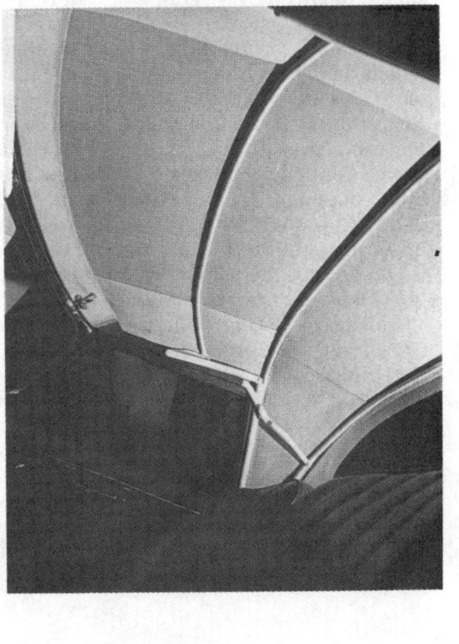

Unlined hood is simple as is hood frame, right, which is not available new, but you can find reproduction parts

THE CLUB

Porsche Club GB, a highly professional operation with a full-time office and over 10,000 members, has a growing 356 division which organises its own activities. Although the main aim of this group is to hold social events, it can offer plenty of practical assistance – such as last March's AFN evening with lectures from Eric Studer and Barry Curtis about the complexities of 356 suspension and brakes. Top event on the calendar is the international 356 meeting, which this year drew 200 cars to Harrogate from all over Europe – next year's fixture will be at Wurzburg, Germany. *Porsche Post* is a polished quarterly which always contains news of 356 affairs. Details of membership from Roy Gillham, Ayton House, West End, Northleach, Glos GL54 3HG (tel 0451 60792; fax 0451 60011).

reasonably well protected by underseal, this layer tends to harbour rust traps in seams and cavities. One of the time-consuming tasks of restoration is removing all the underseal, which can take 100 hours of laborious work with a scraper, solvents and a heat gun.

An expert can recognise where underseal has swollen over corroded areas or where fresh bitumen stands unusually proud over a suspect repair. But a novice has little chance unless the surface is actually splitting up, or he has intimate knowledge of the shape of a 356's underside. One example of camouflaged repair should illustrate that there is frankly no substitute for specialist guidance.

Distorted underseal is commonly found at the rear part of the front wheelarches, where internal corrosion can break through from the longitudinal members within. It's no problem to spot on an honest car, but disguise is simple. All a quick-sale merchant has to do is weld on a covering plate and slap on lots of underseal to create a flat surface. A professional ought to recognise the signs, but would you?

Corrosion in the longitudinal channels which run up each side of the centre section of a 356 is the root of this particular problem. Heater tubes carrying hot air to the front of the cabin pass through these members and attract condensation, particularly if the flexible couplings to the engine have been detached – as is often the case with cars from hotter parts of the US. But cars of European origin are equally vulnerable from mud and water which can be trapped underneath.

Collapsed jacking points are an obvious sign of expensive problems here, but examine this entire 'sill' area carefully, as advanced corrosion seriously weakens the whole car. Once again, US cars from good climates are not necessarily sound: one Arizona-sourced 356 currently undergoing restoration in Roger Bray's workshop is peppered with rust in the longitudinal members because sand has penetrated through the jacking points and acted like a sponge.

Some restoration notes

Although a competent amateur can cope with most mechanical aspects of a 356 restoration, specialist skills are almost inevitably needed for the bodyshell – and it can be very expensive. Select a restoration project carefully and you may get away with little more than the cost of painting, but poor specimens can swallow as much as £15,000.

The good news, though, is that reproduction panel availability is excellent, despite the huge number of complex pressings that make up a 356 body. Purists favour the high quality parts from Porsche itself, but good pattern parts are available from the US, primarily from Stoddards and PB Tweeks. Everything for an A, B or C bodyshell can be obtained, but some pre-A panels have not been remanufactured. Compared with other sports cars of similar scarcity in Britain, the parts supply position for 356s is exceptional, thanks to the model's popularity in the US.

Imported cars usually remain left-hand drive. Besides the fact that 356 enthusiasts tend to like total originality, there's a parts dificulty – pedal boxes can only be obtained from broken right-hand drive cars.

Strong mechanicals

If the foregoing has made you gloomy about the prospect of 356 ownership, take heart. All mainstream 356s, from early 40bhp 1100s to late 95bhp 1600SCs, are strong and relatively inexpensive on the mechanical side. Check over a possible purchase carefully, of course, but avoid letting mechanical health dominate your decision-making.

The VW-derived air-cooled flat-four engine will happily run beyond 100,000 miles between overhauls provided it has been treated to regular oil and filter changes. The cost of major work is not astronomic: Bob

356A Coupé shell undergoes restoration: jig

Rot below rear trailing arm mounting

Same, underneath. Underseal hides sins

ALAN FOWLER ON TACKLING

The conventional way to buy a 356 might be from a dealer, but Alan Fowler's came from a garden centre. Seven years ago, when his Porsche interest revolved around a modern 944, he went to the opening day of a local garden centre in Yorkshire and spotted a 356A Coupé languishing in an outbuilding under a pile of hay.

Alan had never restored a car before, but the discovery sparked an ambition. He wanted to buy this particular 1957 356A (it was built in the year he was born), rebuild it and go motor racing. Four years and one house move went by before the owner finally gave in to Alan's persuasion, selling the car to him in September 1988 for £3000. Complete but slightly damaged, it was a very original 32,000-mile specimen that had done some racing in its time.

"I wasn't completely sure what

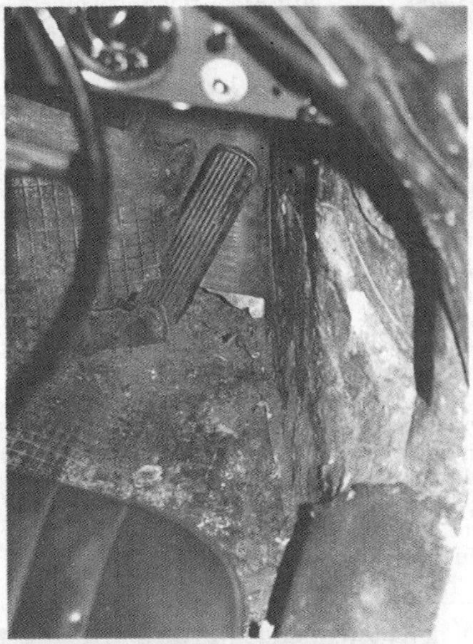

Lift carpets to check for floorpan horrors

Garretson's estimate for a top-end overhaul is £600,, while complete rebuilds are unlikely to exceed £3000. Engines in need of serious attention seem to deteriorate worst at the bottom end: cars with non-counterbalanced crankshafts tend to suffer, like VW Beetles, from a whip effect which can crack the crank and pound out the centre main bearing.

Check for oil leaks, as these engines are prone to throwing oil around, particularly from the rocker box gaskets and the oil cooler. An engine that has just been cleaned should make you suspicious. The condition and level of the oil are essential clues to maitnenance, but listening to the engine with the lid up at standstill should reveal any major problems.

A good engine will crank over evenly on all four cylinders, idle smoothly and quietly, and emit no odd noises – from big ends, main bearings or piston slap – when you back off the throttle. Idling on older cars is commonly affected by air bleeding into the mixture past worn carburettor butterfly shafts, which are costly to rebuild.

Although VW parts became virtually non-existent on 356s after 1958, a car that has been maintained cheaply will probably have been fitted with plenty of Beetle components – items like the coil, distributor, filters, fan belt and dynamo. These might be a pointer to a car's background, for a purist would insist on proper Porsche parts.

Gearboxes are so robust that they last almost indefinitely in careful hands, but they can suffer from abuse. As with the engine, gearbox overhaul never involves frightening expense, £600 being the ballpark figure for a typical job on a tired unit. You need a good drive in a 356 to assess the gearbox by running up and down through all the gears, feeling for the baulking and crunches which indicate worn synchromesh, and listening for continuous growling from the bearings.

One of the delights of driving a good 356 is the gearchange, which is unusually exact and silky despite the length of the linkage. Any noise or sloppiness from the lever indicates that plastic bushings in the linkage are worn. A useful clue to gearbox bearing condition is to press the clutch while in neutral and see whether the noise level drops significantly. Any additional noise when the clutch is pressed means a worn clutch release bearing.

As far as the rest of the running gear is concerned, the picture is one of good durability with a few known trouble spots. Two in particular can be checked with the front of the car jacked up. Any movement or clunking when you rock the wheels at top and bottom indicates either that the link pins are out of adjustment, or that they're so badly worn they can no longer be adjusted. Then grip the wheels fore and aft to check for play in the worm and peg steering, but make sure you do this with the wheels pointing straight ahead, as the

BEST BOOK

It's not exactly light reading, but the most thorough survey of these cars is *The 356 Porsche: A Restorer's Guide to Authenticity* by Dr Brett Johnson. Published in the US by Beeman Jorgensen Inc, it costs £14.95. Those who appreciate arcane detail will love the way it guides the reader through the complexities of 356 genealogy. The accurate text is supported by several hundred close-up photographs in rather fuzzy black and white.

HIS FIRST RESTORATION

I was buying," says Alan, "but it turned out to be a pretty good example. Minor frontal damage and creased wings made me wonder whether the car had been distorted in an accident, but I took a chance. The windscreen was cracked, the engine seized and the carpets mouldy, but all the parts were there. It wasn't long before I decided it would be sacrilege to race it, so my wife, Josephine, and I restored."

After photocopying a workshop manual borrowed from Porsche Club GB, they dismantled the car, carefully labelling and storing all the parts. Despite being novices, they planned to do all the work themselves except where specialist help was essential. They made mistakes along the way, such as the occasion when Alan lifted the engine onto the kitchen table. He was certain that he had drained the oil, but found himself and the floor dripping in six pints of it.

The fact that the previous owner had stripped the underseal to lighten the car for racing was a blessing. Since this layer normally tends to retain moisture and promote corrosion, the underside of Alan's car was in unusually good condition. Apart from the damaged nose, there were typical areas of rust where the wings meet the doors and along the door bottoms, but nothing too serious. After a Porsche dealer's unsatisfactory attempt at structural work, Alan sent the car to 356 specialist Roger Bray for repairs.

The only other significant area of specialist work was the interior. Alan and Josephine taught themselves basic upholstery skills, but their efforts were wasted because the old leather was too brittle to retain – they were forced to use a professional trimmer. Replacing the 356A's curved perspex sun visors, which had warped in the sun, might have been a problem, but a signmaker was able to replicate them. Apart from having engine valve guides and bearings replaced by Holbay Engineering, Alan rebuilt all the mechanicals himself.

For a total outlay of £18,000 on parts and labour, Alan and Josephine now have a useable car which looks respectable in concours company. Its first outing, to the international 356 meeting at Harrogate in the spring, saw it finish second in its class. Alan found himself parked that day next to a car renovated by Porsche for a reputed £68,000 – he reckons few people could have told the difference.

This spares Coupé is a bodged restoration, beyond repair

TONY SOWERBY ON RUNNING A 356 ON A SHOESTRING

Denis Jenkinson, who wrote in *Motor Sport* about criss-crossing Europe in a 356, is solely responsible for Tony Sowerby becoming a Porsche owner. Tony had never even seen a 356 at the time 'Jenks' was raving about the little German car, but he knew he had to have one.

In 1969, he finally tracked down a five-year-old 356C coupé on 52,000 miles and paid £850 for it. He remembers the previous owner as an "absolute gent" who released the car for £500 and trusted Tony to return with the remaining £350 once his MG Midget was sold. Tony's subsequent 22 years with this car are a marvellous tale of 356 motoring on the cheap.

The disc-braked 356C had seen some hard use, but it was an honest example which gave Tony and his wife, Chris, reliable daily service until 1974. At that point, Tony felt the car was "getting a bit jaded" and gave it a break with the mileage on 85,000. He planned to titivate it and get motoring again – but the car was laid-up for nine years.

"It was very tired bodily but not too bad mechanically," says Tony. "The early signs of body corrosion appeared soon after I bought it, for a jacking point gave way the first time I serviced it. My approach is total DIY maintenance, so I removed both jacking points, plated over the holes and made a horrendous framework of angle iron underneath the back of the floorpan. Needless to say, I still get a few comments about this!"

When Tony finally got round to renovating the 356C, the bodyshell needed considerable work: the front of the car had rotted badly, the wheelarches were ringed with rust and the doors were in a terrible state. His home-made solutions would offend purists, but they made the body presentable for little cost.

Curved panels were beaten to shape with a hammer and a block of wood, and fitted up with an electric welder. New 2in sections of steel were attached round the wheelarches, but Tony didn't bother to match the original wired edges because he thought his flanged finish looked adequate. He did all the painting himself with 'Bessie', a piece of home-built equipment assembled from an old fridge compressor, an army motor and a vacuum bottle from a lorry's air-braking system.

Interior and exterior trim pieces he improvised himself, using real low-budget ingenuity. Most brightwork parts, especially those made of Mazak, were so badly pitted that they could not be rescued, so he had two useful friends at work cast new pieces in brass, which was then plated. His 356C's brightwork should outlast the rest of the car!

The engine had to be removed to fit a new clutch, but otherwise it wasn't touched – the heads have never come off. Now on 120,000 miles, it still runs fairly well thanks to oil changes every 3000 miles. On the suspension side, front link pins and king pins have been replaced and new Koni dampers fitted, while the braking system has been completely overhauled.

"None of the car's really correct, but that doesn't bother me," says Tony. "The important thing is that I still enjoy it, even though it's in bits again for another major rebuild. You don't have to spend a lot of money on these cars. Parts I've had to buy – like rubber seals, a door mirror and a plastic washer bottle – have cost only £500 or so."

There's never been a shortage of Porsche 356 models. The tradition continues with a wide range of 356 diecasts, precision models and plastic kits currently available. Clockwise from top are two superb 1:24 kits from Fujumi complete with engine detail right down to crank and pistons (£13.50); outstanding white Coupé from Burago (£12.95); Brumm's Carrera racer (£8.20), red and white Speedsters from Corgi (£8.50), and Brumm's blue Cabriolet (£8.20)

steering box has provision for some movement on lock.

Make sure the hydraulic hoses are free of cracks and do not 'balloon' under pressure. If they are sound, any brake problems are usually caused by leaks from the gearbox or wheel cylinders, so check for signs of stickiness around the wheels. Apply the brakes reasonably hard to make sure the car pulls up straight, as brake shoes – or pads on a disc-braked C – can become contaminated with brake fluid. If a drum-braked car has been left standing, a corrosive reaction can occur between the drum's steel liner and alloy outer; severe banging through the pedal can be due to the steel liner breaking up. Brake shoes seem to be indestructible.

Interior and electrics

Apart from satisfying yourself about the general condition of the interior, there is little to worry about because parts availability is comprehensive on all but the pre-A cars. Make sure that you have a complete and authentic interior, for there are restored cars, particularly from the US, that have been re-upholstered with complete disregard for originality.

A few detail points are worth checking. One trouble spot with the front seats, especially on the driver's side, occurs where the backrest bolts into the reclining mechanism. There are three screws on each side that can work loose, causing the metal inside to flex and break – at which point the seat falls apart. The interior light can be a niggling problem: nobody makes the original 6W bulbs so 10W bulbs are often fitted, and these can melt the housing and destroy the switch if a door is left open. Run the windows up and down, as the mechanisms can bind up with rust.

On the electrical side, check whether the system is 6-volt or 12-volt – 6-volt is original but plenty of owners have upgraded to 12-volt in the interests of reliability and decent headlamps. A 6-volt car can be difficult to

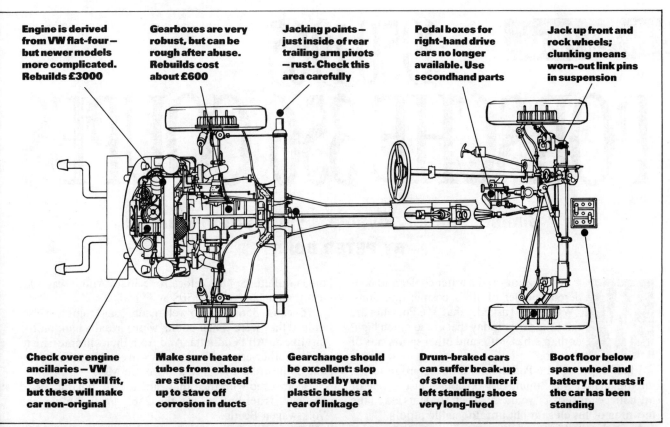

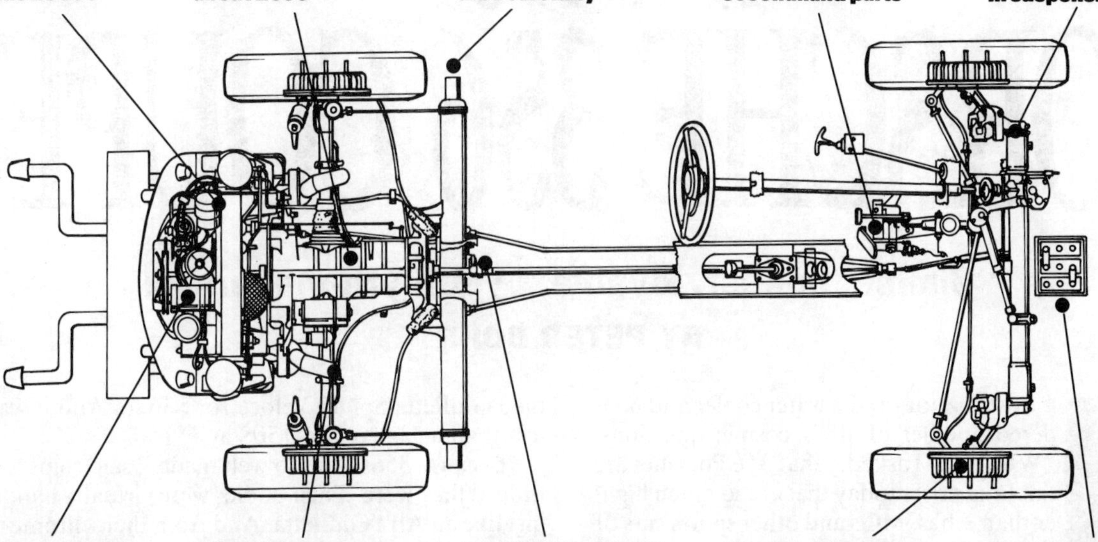

Engine is derived from VW flat-four – but newer models more complicated. Rebuilds £3000
Gearboxes are very robust, but can be rough after abuse. Rebuilds cost about £600
Jacking points – just inside of rear trailing arm pivots – rust. Check this area carefully
Pedal boxes for right-hand drive cars no longer available. Use secondhand parts
Jack up front and rock wheels; clunking means worn-out link pins in suspension
Check over engine ancillaries – VW Beetle parts will fit, but these will make car non-original
Make sure heater tubes from exhaust are still connected up to stave off corrosion in ducts
Gearchange should be excellent: slop is caused by worn plastic bushes at rear of linkage
Drum-braked cars can suffer break-up of steel drum liner if left standing; shoes very long-lived
Boot floor below spare wheel and battery box rusts if the car has been standing

start if the timing is incorrect and the plugs and points are tired. Have a look at the fusebox, sited in the luggage or glovebox areas depending on the age of the car. Except for the first four fuses with large red wires, all of them should be 8amp – larger fuses are likely to be a sign of electrical problems in those functions.

A point to consider on a US car is whether you want to adapt the lighting to UK-specification indicators. Apparently, some MoT stations wrongly fail US imports for their original combined turn signals and brake lights, but pre-1967 cars are in fact exempt from UK requirements. Altering the lights is a pain to deal with, says Bob Garretson, but it's a sensible safety precaution.

Later cars have twin rear grilles

Conclusion

Thanks to their excellent road manners and precision engineering, Porsche 356s appeal to a particularly discerning breed of enthusiast. None of the mainstream models are out-and-out road-burners, but these cars make up for their modest performance by handling with real flair and agility. It's hard not to be captivated when you drive one.

Do all your research and you can secure an excellent 356, but never forget that bodyshell restoration is expensive. There are plenty of people out there who have paid too much money for poor cars or worse, rotten, cars – be on your guard.

R&T Used Car Classic

1950-1965 PORSCHE 356 COUPES

"Simple, honest, lovable," yet myth-makers all

BY PETER BOHR

WE STOOD AROUND the water cooler and pondered another of life's cosmic questions. "Why is it," I asked, "that 356 Porsches are fetching prices today that are so much higher than Alfas, MGs and other sports cars of that era?"

I half expected the Porschephiles in the group to tell me the answer was "intuitively obvious," just as one of my college professors would say when students asked the meaning of his elegant but unfathomable proofs.

Instead, somebody said, "Because Porsches were more expensive than other sports cars when they were new."

Hmm . . . is that so? I quoted some prices straight off the data panels in *Road & Track's 1959 Road Test Annual.* The *Annual* listed a Porsche Super Speedster for $3928, which was toward the upper end of the sports-car price spectrum in an era when a new Austin-Healey Sprite was $1795 and a Triumph TR3 cost $2835. But some of the more performance-oriented cars then were close to the Porsche's price: an Austin-Healey Mille Miglia went for $3395, an MGA Twin Cam for $3345 and an Alfa Romeo Giulietta Spider Veloce for $3686. And it was a lot less than a Jaguar XK-150S at $5150.

"Because 356s were so well made," said someone else. Indeed they were. Their bodies were virtually handbuilt—just like an Alfa Giulietta. And from their chrome trim to their leather-covered seats, they were beautifully detailed—just like a Healey, a Jag or an MG.

"Compared with the other cars, they're reliable," said another. True, but so was the 356's lowly sibling, the Volkswagen Beetle.

The confab ended. Nobody had mentioned the 356's handling because we all knew about *that*—oversteer that's quick to land the car on its roof if the driver is over-exuberant and under-experienced.

It still wasn't intuitively obvious to me why 356SC Cabriolets can be worth $50,000, Speedsters up to $85,000 and Carreras as much as $200,000.

Then the answer came: These funny overturned bathtubs, these inverted soap dishes, these simple and honest vehicles are downright lovable. And we all know folks do crazy things for love. To be lovable is, in fact, the reason

PHOTO BY JOE RUSZ

old British and Italian sports cars exist; they're not good for much else. German cars are rarely objects to love. Respect and admire—yes. But love? Nah.

But the 356 is lovable, and as my colleagues pointed out, well-made and reliable, too. It was also the foundation for the mystique the Porsche marque enjoys today. Altogether, that's a potent formula for a high-priced collectible car. Yet not all 356s command insane sums of money. While the exotic 4-cam Carreras and the open cars have mostly become too valuable to drive, cooking-version 356 coupes still abound in the $5000 to $15,000 price range. Which means they can still be used as their creators intended. Which also means the Porsche 356 coupes are perfect subjects for our Used Car Classic series.

The ABCs of 356s

THE HOUSE OF Porsche was in disarray at the end of World War II. Dr. Ferdinand Porsche was doing time after the French arrested him for designing such famous Nazi-backed machines as the Volkswagen and the Tiger tank. His freelance design firm, Porsche Konstruktionen GmbH, was being run by his son Ferry in the Austrian hamlet of Gmünd.

In 1947, Ferry dusted off an old plan for a Porsche sports car. All things Porsche, from engines to automobiles, were always assigned a project number dating back to the firm's founding before the war. The sports car's number was, of course, 356.

Ferry knew his sports car had to be based on components from an existing car, and his father's design, the VW, was the obvious choice. The first Porsche had an aluminum body covering a VW suspension and a modified VW engine. It was a roadster, but it had the unmistakable lines of the 356 coupe that immediately followed.

The layout of the 356 coupe was a la VW, with a rear-mounted engine. The car held two in comfort and, from 1952 on, had a rear kiddie seat as well. The chassis consisted of a boxed, pressed-steel assembly with an integrated floorpan. Beginning with the 1950 models, the brakes were hydraulically operated drums. The car had independent suspension on all four wheels, albeit primitive swing axles in the rear, which was still pretty exotic stuff for a sports car in those days.

The engine was a VW-inspired air-cooled boxer 4-banger. The earliest ones were 1.1-liter units, but in 1951 Porsche developed 1.3- and 1.5-liter configurations as well. From 1952 fully synchronized 4-speed transmissions with Porsche-patented, split-ring synchromesh were standard.

The factory completed fewer than 60 cars in Austria before moving to Zuffenhausen, near Stuttgart, in early 1950. The ailing Ferdinand Porsche, now released from prison, lived just long enough to see 298 cars carrying his name leave the factory by the end of that year.

By 1954 U.S. Porsche importer Max Hoffman was selling 11 of what he called "the German automotive jewel" each week in the States, all with the 1.5-liter engine. Hoffman pressured Porsche to build some relatively inexpensive models so he could more easily compete with British sports cars in our market. In 1955 the Hoffman-conceived Speedster, a stripper model with an attractive $2995 price tag, made its debut. And alongside the Speedster came another Hoffman package, the 1500 Continental at $3590, a nicely appointed coupe with a 1.5-liter engine. However, Ford Motor Co. wasn't amused when these odd little foreign cars appeared with the name of its big Lincoln gunboat on their flanks, so Porsche dropped the Continental moniker the following year.

The first of the 356s designated as "A" models came for 1956. The 356A had a new windshield and dash, new wheels, a revised transmission and a softer suspension. But most significantly, there was a bigger 1.6-liter engine with increased power and torque. Like the 1.5-liter, the new engine came in two power configurations, what Porschephiles call the "Normal" version and the "S" or "Super" version.

The 356B was introduced in September 1959, as a 1960 model. Despite the new "B" designation, changes weren't all that profound. But the 356 did take on a new look with raised bumpers and headlights. More important, Porsche announced a third, more powerful variant of the pushrod 1600 engine. Logically enough, it was called the Super 90 because it developed 90 bhp DIN.

In 1961 Karmann began production of a controversial new body style, the hardtop coupe or notchback. It was essentially a cabriolet body with a fixed top, and it proved to be something of a sales flop.

For 1962 twin air-intake grilles replaced the single grille on the rear lid, and the coupe got a larger rear window. The cars also received a new outside gasoline filler (the old one was in the trunk) and a revised front trunklid.

The 356 reached the height of its development with the "C" model, which entered production in July 1963. Except for new wheels and hubcaps, the 356C looked just like the 1962 356B. But there was an important change under the skin: 4-wheel disc brakes.

PHOTO BY RALPH POOLE

■ Hot-rodded 1600 Super is preferable to Normal engine.

Porsche 356C buyers had the choice of two engines (besides the Carrera): the 1600C, derived from the 356B's 1600S engine, and the 1600SC, derived from the 356B's Super 90 engine. The Normal engine was discontinued.

Production of the 356C officially stopped in September 1965. And with the end of the "C" model came the end of the Type 356, which made way for the 911. After a decade and a half of production, Porsche had built 76,303 356s. Of that total, 7627 were 356s, 21,045 were "As," 30,963 were "Bs" and 16,668 were "Cs."

Picking favorites

TO HELP YOU choose among the alphabet soup of 356 models and engines, I asked several prominent members of American Porschedom for their thoughts.

Roger Bursch, the creator of the Bursch exhaust system for Porsches, prepared many of the successful racing Porsches driven by Alan Johnson during the Sixties. Today he operates Scientific Auto, a Porsche repair shop in Pasadena, California.

At the tender age of 16, Gary Emory began selling Porsche parts in a Porsche dealership. Now 45, he owns Porsche Parts Obsolete, a sizable facility in Costa Mesa, California that specializes in selling parts for 356s.

John Hoke is an Oklahoma City vintage-collectible-classic car dealer who also publishes the monthly *Porsche Market Letter.*

Harry Pellow, who bills himself as "The Maestro," is a prolific writer and producer of books and videotapes on the 356 and 912 Porsches. He also owns HCP Research in Cupertino, California, a facility that specializes in rebuilding 356 engines and transmissions.

Gene Tomazin grew up in his father's body shop in Riverside, California. Now fortysomething, Gene runs the shop, where he specializes in repairing, painting and restoring imported car bodies, especially early Porsches.

The experts are split between those who favor the "C" and those who prefer the "A." The "B" seems to be the neglected child of the family.

Those who find the 356A most appealing—Type A personalities?—like the early cars for their funkiness. "They're more 'bubbly'-looking, less Americanized," says Emory. Critics of the 356A dislike their more fragile engines and transmissions.

Those who favor the "Cs" appreciate them because they're more refined, more civilized. "I'd buy a 356C for its disc brakes alone," says Bursch. Critics of the 356C say they somehow feel heavier and more lethargic than the earlier cars, though objective test data might not show it.

With the "Bs," it's important to distinguish between the 1960–1961 356B—what the factory designated the "T-5" body—and the 1962–1963 "T-6" 356B. Pellow: "I hate the look of the T-5 coupe. The small rear window with the later bumpers makes it look hunchbacked." On the other hand, Pellow is quite fond of the later "B," the one with the "C's" good looks.

As for the early 356s, those made before 1955, Pellow says, "These are such strange and rare cars that driving

PHOTO BY STUDIO WÖRNER

■ Raised bumper and headlights, among other differences, distinguish 356A (left) from 356B.

■ Early and late 356Bs: the 1960 T-5 (left) and the 1962 T-6 bodies.

■ Hooded instruments, 3-spoke wheel typify 356B, which got dual grilles in 1962.

PHOTO BY STUDIO WÖRNER

■ **Unusual but unloved, 1961 hardtop cabriolet by Karmann.**

them on the street daily is neither fun nor wise."

Finally, there's that oddball, the Karmann notchback 356B. Emory and Tomazin say they're sleepers, that their rarity will make them valuable some day. "People have been saying that for 20 years," retorts Pellow. "It looks like a cabriolet? In the way a T-Bird with a vinyl roof looks like a convertible."

When it comes to engines, generally speaking, the later the engine the better. Pellow especially likes the Super 90 and SC engines. But Bursch finds them a bit too temperamental for everyday use. However, Bursch does prefer the midrange or "S" version of most years to the Normal engines because, he says, they're stronger.

The inspection

THE FACT IS, you'll be damned lucky to find *any* 356 coupe, "A," "B" or "C," Normal or Super, in good, original shape that hasn't undergone a costly restoration—especially if you live outside California or the Southwest. And it's far more important to buy a coupe that's in good condition than to buy any particular model.

Rust is the bane of the 356s. Even those 356s that have led pampered lives in California's sunny clime usually have a little corrosion somewhere. "Nearly 100 percent of the cars will at least need their battery boxes (in the front of the trunk) replaced," says Tomazin. At around $250, that's not a major undertaking.

A proper 356 inspection begins in the nether regions of the car's underbelly. Look behind each wheel, wherever the suspension mounts to the body. If you find a lot of corrosion at these mounting points, run—don't walk—away from the car. "You'll face a lifetime of repair projects," says Tomazin.

Find the jack receivers; if they're not there, or if they're not much more than iron oxide, that's a bad sign. The jack receivers are welded onto the "longitudinals," the thick structures that run along the floorpan on either side of the car and provide much of its strength. And can you stick your fingers through the floorpan? Floorpan rust is extraordinarily common. Repairing the longitudinals and replacing the floorpan are expensive to do right, about $3000, according to Tomazin.

It's a rare 356 that doesn't have some rust in the bottom of the doors. Redoing a door costs $400–$500. Grab the door; if you can lift it up and down, the hinge pillars are rotting away—a more serious proposition.

Until the T-6 356B, the gasoline filler was inside the trunk. Chances are, some gasoline-station jockey tried to shut the hood without releasing the safeties, which bent the hood. Or the hood might have flown open at speed and put a crinkle in the cowl. Tomazin says it can take a day and a half to repair such damage.

"It's a very tedious job to restore a 356 properly," says Tomazin. "The doors, the hood and the rear lid were each hand-fitted and leaded to a particular car." The typical 356 body with some rust here and there (but not in critical areas like the suspension mounting points) will cost around $8000 to restore to a decent, though not necessarily concours, standard. Interior restoration—dash, steering wheel, upholstery, headliner—could easily add another $1500–$2000 to the tab.

"If you're looking at a 356 that's supposedly been restored, check the carpet carefully," says Emory. "If it's an original-type German carpet and not an American weave, that's a good clue the seller didn't cut corners in the restoration."

Let's assume body rot hasn't frightened you off your prospect. Now comes more fun: determining which engine resides under the rear decklid. Be warned there are a lot of 356s running around with the wrong engines. To make matters worse, an engine may be a conglomeration of pieces from different engines.

But make a stab at identifying the engine anyway. The Maestro directs: "Read the number on the case just below where the generator stand attaches. If it's a 5-digit number beginning with 6 or 7, it's an 'A' Normal. A 5-digit number beginning with 8 means it's a 1958–1961 Super. If it's a 6-digit number beginning with 6, the engine is a 1960–1963 Normal, and a 6-digit number beginning with 7 means it's a 1961–1963 Super. A 6-digit beginning with 7 and above 710,000 means it's a 'C' engine. A 6-digit number beginning with an 8 means it's a Super 90 or SC." There are many other checks you can make, as Pellow outlines in his book, *Secrets of the Inner Circle.*

Okay, so the prospective purchase isn't a rustbucket with a VW engine. Now you can go through the usual buying-an-old-clunker routine—compression check, test drive, etc. Should a 356 transmission need rebuilding, expect to spend $1500–$2500. Rebuilding an engine will run $2500–$5000, depending upon how far you go with balancing, blueprinting, powder-painting and so forth. By the way, that's about half the price of a 911 engine

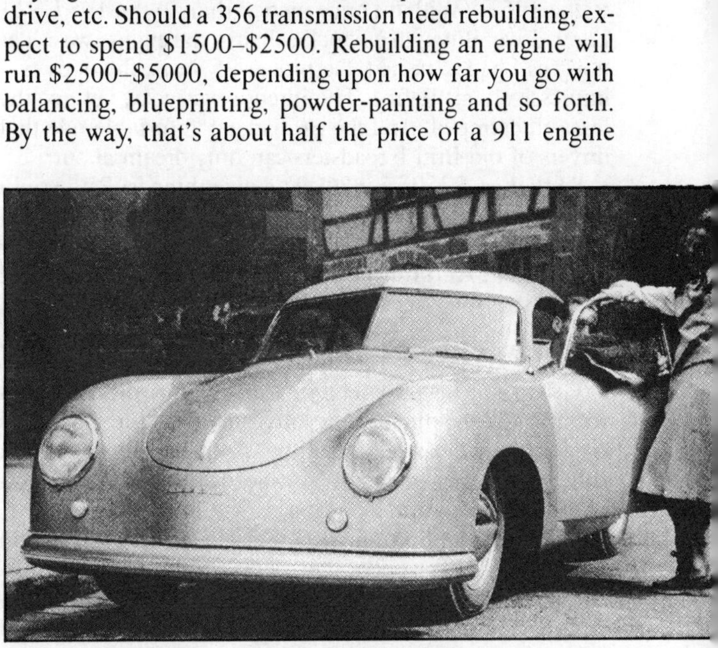

■ **Rare, desirable, pricey, early split-windshield 356.**

rebuild—yet another reason the 356 is so lovable.

And finally, *meine Damen und Herren,* a pop quiz:

True or false? Porsche 356s are nothing more than fancy Beetles, so you can substitute VW—read "cheaper"—parts on the cars. False! After about 1954, only a handful of parts are interchangeable between the two cars.

True or False? Parts for these old Porsches are difficult to get. False again. One of the joys of owning a Porsche 356 is the good supply of body panels and mechanical parts. New-old-stock, reproduction and used parts are all available.

True or False? If you can tune-up a Beetle or a Campmobile, you can tune-up a 356. True. According to Bursch, anyone who can synchronize carburetors and has a good manual can perform most of the service on a 356.

Try a little TLC

FOR $7500 THESE days, you could buy a street-pretty Triumph TR3, a decent Alfa Giulietta convertible, or even a pair of really nice early MGB roadsters. Or you could buy Paul Tomazin's Porsche 356SC Coupe—if it were for sale (it's not).

And here's what you'd get with Paul's 356: Paint that glistens in the sunshine like a piece of chalk. Fine leather upholstery, aged into strips of beef jerky. An engine that, at the touch of the key, wheezes to life. And brakes that pull to the right with more vigor than delegates at a GOP convention.

Yes, Paul's Porsche needs a little work. Or as the ads say, "a little TLC."

But, hey, Paul didn't just fall off the knockwurst truck. Like his brother Gene, he grew up in his dad's body shop and can recognize a concours car in the rough when he sees one. That chalky paint is the *original* paint. The only rust is a small patch under the driver's right foot, nowhere near the critical longitudinal. And the car is all there, from the correct SC engine to the owner's manual.

I won't pretend that I explored the limits of the car's handling (those brakes!). In fact, I said a "Hail Mary" and drove only around the block. The car felt more akin to the 1957 VW that I once owned than to the 1967 911 I now drive. But with its stock exhaust, the engine wasn't as noisy as I had expected. Despite its 25 years, the body was impressively rattle-free. The interior was cozy, yet not the least bit cramped. And the car had a comfortable ride that drivers of old British roadsters can only dream about.

So that's a $7500 356SC. The nice thing is, Paul could put the requisite $10,000 or $12,000 into his Porsche, and the market being what it is, it would be worth the investment. And for the price of a modest new car, he'd have a stunning yet thoroughly practical classic.

Investment potential

UNFORTUNATELY, YOU CAN'T talk about old Porsches without talking about their "investment value." Monied speculators who wouldn't know a roller bearing from a roller skate are snapping up Speedsters and Cabriolets like pork-belly futures.

"The market is dominated by speculators," says John Hoke. "Prices for open 356s doubled and tripled in just the last two years," he says. "The Japanese are a heavy influence, but they only want open cars, and spectacular examples of them."

If the prospect of rich foreigners driving up the prices of neat old Porsches makes you slightly nauseous, John has some soothing news. "Everyone says that where the open cars go, the coupes are sure to follow. I don't see it. There are just too many around. They won't fall in value, but if investment is your main concern, don't buy a coupe."

It's only fair to mention that back in a 1984 Used Car Classic on Ferrari V-12 2+2s, much the same was said of those cars. At the time they were selling for less than $25,000. Today they sell for more than $100,000.

SPECIFICATIONS

	1957 356A Normal	1961 356B Normal	1964 356C
Curb weight, lb	1930	1980	1970
Wheelbase, in.	82.7	82.7	82.7
Track, f/r	51.4/50.1	51.4/50.1	51.4/50.0
Length, in.	155.5	157.9	157.9
Width, in.	65.7	65.7	65.7
Height, in.	51.6	52.4	51.7
Engine type	flat-4	flat-4	flat-4
Bore x stroke, mm	82.5 x 74.0	82.5 x 74.0	82.5 x 74.0
Displacement, cc	1582	1582	1582
Bhp @ rpm	70 @ 4500	70 @ 4500	88 @ 5200
Torque, lb-ft @ rpm	81 @ 2800	81 @ 2800	90 @ 3600
Transmission	4-sp M	4-sp M	4-sp M
Suspension, f/r	ind/ind	ind/ind	ind/ind
Brakes, f/r	drum/drum	drum/drum	disc/disc
Steering type	worm & nut	worm & peg w/hydraulic damper	worm & peg w/hydraulic damper

PERFORMANCE DATA

	1957 356A Normal	1961 356B Normal	1964 356C
0–60 mph, sec	14.4	14.4	13.5
Standing ¼ mile, sec	19.3	19.4	18.9
Avg fuel use, mpg	30.0	29.5	26.0
Road test date	8-57	10-61	2-64

TYPICAL ASKING PRICES[1]

356 & 356A	$4000–$15,000
356B T-5	$3000–$14,000
356B T-6	$4000–$15,000
356C	$5000–$16,000
356SC	$6000–$20,000

[1]All prices are for coupes. Lowest prices are for complete cars with minor rust and in need of restoration. Highest prices are for excellent, though not concours, cars. Add $500–$2000 to 356B prices for Super or Super 90 engine. Add $1000–$2500 for factory sunroof. Prices compiled with assistance of John Hoke.

Recommended reading

The following books and publications are especially recommended: *Porsche: Excellence Was Expected,* by Karl Ludvigsen, Automobile Quarterly Library Series, available from Classic Motorbooks, P.O. Box 1, Osceola, Wis. 54020, $64.95; *Illustrated Porsche Buyer's Guide,* by Dean Batchelor, Motorbooks International, P.O. Box 2, Osceola, Wis. 54020, $15.95; *Secrets of the Inner Circle,* by Harry Pellow, The Maestro c/o HCP Research, 20655 Sunrise Dr., Cupertino, Calif. 95014, $26.95; *Porsche Market Letter,* P.O. Box 60328, Oklahoma City, Okla. 73146, $40.00 per year.